# Memory, Imprinting, and the Brain

# OXFORD PSYCHOLOGY SERIES

EDITORS
DONALD E. BROADBENT
JAMES L. MCGAUGH
NICHOLAS J. MACKINTOSH
MICHAEL I. POSNER
ENDEL TULVING
LAWRENCE WEISKRANTZ

# Memory, Imprinting, and the Brain

An Inquiry into Mechanisms

GABRIEL HORN

*Professor of Zoology,*
*University of Cambridge*

OXFORD PSYCHOLOGY SERIES No. 10

CLARENDON PRESS · OXFORD
1985

Oxford University Press, Walton Street, Oxford OX2 6DP
Oxford New York Toronto
Delhi Bombay Calcutta Madras Karachi
Kuala Lumpur Singapore Hong Kong Tokyo
Nairobi Dar es Salaam Cape Town
Melbourne Auckland
and associated companies in
Beirut Berlin Ibadan Nicosia

Oxford is a trade mark of Oxford University Press

Published in the United States
by Oxford University Press, New York

British Library Cataloguing in Publication Data
Horn, Gabriel.
Memory, imprinting, and the brain: an inquiry
into mechanisms.
1. Learning—Physiological aspects 2. Memory
transfer 3. Learning in animals
I. Title
591.1'88    QP408
ISBN 0-19-852157-X
ISBN 0-19-852156-1 Pbk

Library of Congress Cataloging in Publication Data
Horn, Gabriel.
Memory, imprinting, and the brain.
Includes bibliographies and index.
1. Memory—Physiological aspects. 2. Imprinting
(Psychology) 3. Learning—Physiological aspects.
I. Title.
QP406.H67 1985    153.1'2    85-13644
ISBN 0-19-852157-X
ISBN 0-19-852156-1 (pbk)

Set by Cotswold Typesetting, Cheltenham
Printed in Great Britain by
St Edmundsbury Press,
Bury St Edmunds, Suffolk

To my family

# Preface

Learning is a complex set of processes involving the acquisition, storage, and retrieval of information. Acquisition is studied in various guises and includes the encoding, transmission, and processing of sensory information, behavioural arousal, and attention. This list of subprocesses is far from complete. Recent advances in several of these fields have been little short of spectacular. In contrast, little is known of the physiological basis of the retrieval process, and advances in our understanding of the mechanisms by which information is stored in the brain are recent and have been made on a limited front. The purpose of writing this book is to say something about these advances. The book is not, nor is it intended to be, a general review of this field, but gives an account of work in which I have been involved, over the past two decades or so, on habituation and imprinting. During that time modest success has been achieved in analysing habituation—a common change of behaviour, but a rather special form of learning. Some of this work, particularly as it impinges on the nature of information storage in nervous systems, is described in the first chapter. But the bulk of the book is devoted to imprinting. If the small amount of space allotted by some textbooks of psychology is used as a guide, then imprinting too is a rather special form of learning. I hope this book will clarify what is special about imprinting, and what it shares in common with other kinds of learning.

The problem of the neural bases of memory has taken a long time to yield; one of the reasons is that the problem lies at the boundary between the brain sciences and the behavioural sciences. I consider that the intellectual and technical resources of scientists from both fields need to be pooled to maximize the chances of resolving the problem. In so far as this hope has been realized in this study of imprinting, it is because such skills have been deployed. The study began in 1966. At that time, while I was working on habituation, I met Pat Bateson. His background was in the behavioural sciences, mine in the neurosciences. After discovering our common interest in learning in general, and in imprinting in particular, we began to collaborate in experimental work. It proved to be a very fruitful collaboration.

The experiments on imprinting which are described in this book employed many different techniques. It is inevitable, therefore, that the ground covered is wide, ranging from molecular biology through neurophysiology, neuroanatomy, and endocrinology to behaviour. The range is further extended because of the need to refer to work on humans and other primates. I have attempted throughout to define the technical terms used so that anyone who has attended undergraduate courses in some of these subjects should have little difficulty in following the arguments. There is extensive cross-referencing in the text, but this is unlikely to meet all requirements and I hope that the reader will make full use of the index when the cross-references fail to meet a particular need. Because relatively few people have easy familiarity with the structure of the avian brain an appendix has been written to provide an outline of the major features of this part of the central nervous system.

The analysis of the neural mechanisms of memory, and it almost goes without saying of imprinting, cannot be achieved by a single, 'critical' experiment. Once a change in the nervous system associated with training has been identified, it becomes necessary to determine to what aspect of behaviour that change relates. This determination is critical. The degree of confidence the experimenter has that, say, a biochemical change in the brain is related to learning, depends on the confidence he or she can place in the specificity of this relationship. Only if confidence is strong is it worth taking the analysis to a deeper level. This is how my colleagues and I have proceeded. And this book tells that story. I have not hesitated to speculate when attempting to interpret or to synthesize the results of the experimental analyses. I take the view that further advance in science depends critically on this synthetic operation. It is, however, essential to distinguish hard experimental evidence from speculation. I have made this distinction explicit in some chapters by including a separate section for discussion. This arrangement could not be adopted in all chapters, but I hope that I have made clear to the reader the points at which I have departed from the hard base of experimental evidence.

I am deeply indebted to my colleagues for their stimulating collaboration. It has been a pleasure to work with them. Besides Pat Bateson and Brian McCabe these include in alphabetical order Johan Bolhuis, Philip Bradley, Malcolm Brown, José Cipolla-Neto, Ceri Davies, Gordon Edge, Dick Hill, Ann Horn, Mark Johnson, Stephen Jones, Alex Milne, Jeremy Payne, Steven Rose, Hugh Rowell, Gerry Stechler, Zsuzsanna Wiesenfeld, and Mick Wright. The work benefited greatly from the skilled technical assistance of Barrie Fuller, Kevin Chapman, and Wendy Nix. I have received generous financial support from the Science and Engineering Research Council, the Medical Research Council, the Leverhulme Trust, the Wellcome Trust, the Nuffield Foundation, and the National Institutes of Health of the US Public Health Service, to all of whom I express my thanks.

I wish to acknowledge my indebtedness to those colleagues who read various parts of the typescript, Michael Berridge, Malcolm Brown, Malcolm Burrows, Ceri Davies, Nick Davies, Felicia Huppert, Mark Johnson, Brian McCabe, Jeremy Payne, Jean Thomas, Larry Weiskrantz, and Oliver Zangwill. Their critical comments have improved the book, but its shortcomings are mine alone. John Rodford drew most of the illustrations and I am grateful to him. I also greatly appreciate the photographic work of Neal Maskell and Frances Pang.

I owe an especial debt of gratitude to Chris Percival who typed the whole of the manuscript and worked under difficult circumstances with dedication and good humour; to Robert Hinde who read all of the chapters, commented on them in detail and was a constant source of encouragement; and to my wife Priscilla Barrett who critically read all the chapters, drew the illustrations of the jungle-fowl and the cover design, and who for several years has had to put up with conversation which rarely ranged beyond memory, imprinting, and the brain.

*January 1985* G. H.
*Cambridge*

# Contents

# 1

# Approaches to the analysis of the neural bases of memory

There is a long history of interest in the mechanisms by which information is stored in the brain. The explanations that have been offered have varied down the centuries, but with few exceptions they share a common theme. A particular experience or event leads to the formation or strengthening of particular pathways in the brain. Once formed or strengthened in this way the pathway is viewed as a 'trace' which 'represents' the particular experience or event. This trace may be linked to other traces so that the two representations become associated. If one trace becomes activated in some way, the other is likely to be activated as well. When this happens the events or experiences which the traces represent are 'brought to mind', or recalled. These ideas, although not stated in quite this form, can be traced to Descartes (1649; see Descartes 1961) and Locke (1690).

Whilst it was recognized that the retention of information over relatively short periods of time might be achieved by transitory activity, long-lasting memories were thought to involve strucural changes in the brain. Descartes (1649; see Descartes 1961) foreshadowed the idea of morphological change when he wrote that the traces were '... pores of the brain ... [which had] acquired a greater facility than the rest to be opened again ...' (Article 42). Freud (1895; see Freud 1966) envisaged the existence of barriers between neurones of a certain class. He suggested that the activation of these neurones led to an irreversible decline in the resistance of the barriers, and hence to the formation of a memory trace. For Cajal (1911) the critical change was the development of new connections, for Tanzi (1893) and for Hebb (1949) it was the strengthening of pre-existing connections. A number of more recent formulations are variants on these basic themes (see, for example, Milner 1957; Griffith 1966; Brindley 1967; Marr 1969).

Of course there has been some shift of ground and change of emphasis throughout this long period of speculation. For some writers the enduring trace was a dynamic one involving, for example, reverberating activity in chains of neurones. But for many the trace was structural. These 'structural' theories have included not only those referred to above, but also the following: changes in the 'supporting' cells of the brain, in the molecular organization of ribonucleic acid (RNA) in neurones, and in specific lipopeptide patterns in nerve-cell membranes. This list is far from exhaustive.

1

Despite their diversity these views have two things in common: the neural changes were inferred from behaviour, and direct experimental evidence for these changes was at best tenuous and at worst non-existent (see, for example, Lashley 1950). The mismatch between the plethora of theories and the dearth of experimental evidence is not, however, remarkable. The great interest in the neural processes that underlie 'higher mental functions' inevitably generated speculation as to what these processes might be; and in so far as these speculations related to the real nervous system, they were necessarily constrained by the state of knowledge at the time that the views were expressed. If the deep understanding that derives from experimental evidence seems unduly to have lagged behind speculation, it is salutory to reflect that less than a hundred years have past since Waldeyer, drawing on the work of the great neuroanatomists of the nineteenth century, enunciated the 'neurone theory', that the terminal swellings of axons were first clearly described in 1897 by Held, and that, in the same year, the term 'synapse' was coined by Sherrington to refer to the junctions that these swellings make with the cell body (Foster 1897). At that time the most effective strategy for advancing knowledge of the actions of the nervous system in behaviour was to investigate physiological processes which are relatively stable over a wide range of experimental conditions. Certain spinal reflexes have some of these characteristics and by 1906 Sherrington, in a masterly analysis, had laid bare the basic mechanisms by which these reflexes are integrated within the spinal cord. Learned patterns of behaviour do not have these characteristics in any simple way. Behaviour is modified during the course of learning and so too, it may be inferred, is the state of the nervous system. Before any viable attempt could be made to understand the nature of this change of state, it was essential to know a great deal about the fundamental organizations of the system, and much of the work on the nervous system conducted in the present century was directed to this end. Viewed in this light, the discrepancy between the scarcity of experimental evidence and the abundance of theories about the neural mechanisms of learning and information storage becomes more comprehensible.

Certain benefits have accrued from the delay in investigating the neural bases of learning and memory. On the one hand, a multitude of powerful, highly sophisticated techniques have recently become available, and the application of these techniques to the study of the nervous system has radically changed our understanding of its structural and functional organization. On the other hand, there have been major advances in the ways in which behaviour is described, analysed, and modelled. All of these advances have conspired to deepen and refine understanding of behavioural processes. Here and there the interests of the behavioural scientist and the neuroscientist have converged. One result of this convergence has been that speculation about the ways that information is stored in the brain is now being informed by experimental evidence. The first step in providing that evidence came from the study of habituation.

## 1.1 Memory and habituation

### *1.1.1 Some behavioural characteristics of habituation*

Humphrey (1930, 1933) showed that the snail, *Helix albolabris,* retracted its antennae when the platform on which it was moving was vibrated once every few seconds. Gradually the withdrawal response diminished and ultimately the snail no longer appeared to be affected by the vibrations. This gradual waning of a response is a component of a behavioural change known as habituation, a phenomenon which is widespread in the animal kingdom (Humphrey 1933; Thorpe 1956). The properties of habituation have been investigated extensively in the laboratory by studying the 'orientation response' (Pavlov 1927; Sokolov 1960, 1963). This response is elicited by a novel stimulus and gradually wanes if the stimulus is delivered repeatedly. For example, if a sound is suddenly presented to a cat, it may direct its gaze to the source of the sound. If the sound is repeated a few times it gradually ceases to elicit a response from the cat. Habituation is, within limits, stimulus-specific, so that when the response to one stimulus has waned the same response may be elicited by a different stimulus. The response to the repeated stimulus may be restored if this stimulus is withheld for a time before being reapplied.

Habituation is a learning process which confers some obvious benefits. An animal ceases to respond to a repeated stimulus which is, and may continue to be, of no consequence to it (Humphrey 1933; Thorpe 1956). But the animal is still able to detect and respond to a novel stimulus which may signify danger, or food, or perhaps a mate. The memory that is implied by habituation is a curious one. It is a memory not to respond; if an habituated response returns the animal may, in some sense, be said to have 'forgotten'. The neural analysis of this memory would greatly be facilitated if changes in some aspect of neural function occurred which paralleled the behavioural changes of habituation. The first evidence for such neural changes came from an unlikely source, a series of studies of an animal with an incomplete nervous system.

### *1.1.2 Physiological analysis*

If the skin of the back behind the shoulder of a 'spinal' dog is rubbed or tickled or tapped, a series of rhythmic scratching movements is evoked in which a foot is brought towards the site of stimulation. Sherrington (1906) found that when the mechanical stimulus to the skin was maintained, the individual beats of the 'scratch-reflex' usually became slower and their amplitude smaller. The scratch-reflex recovered if the stimulus was withdrawn for a few seconds, though recovery was not always complete with such a short remission time. Within certain limits the response decrement was specific to the area of skin stimulated: when the reflex had waned it could easily be elicited by stimulating the skin a few centimetres away. The waning of the scratch-reflex has some features of habituation: the response decrement is relatively specific to the site at which the stimulus is applied, the decrement is not attributable to fatigue of the muscle and probably not attributable to a change in the receptors in the skin and the response recovers following a lapse of time.

Sherrington's experiments involved stimulating the skin or sensory nerves, and recording the movements of a hind-limb. Events taking place within the spinal cord were inferred, but not directly measured. Recordings of neural activity during habituation came some years later; and the activity first studied was of the brain, not of the spinal cord. One of the first approaches was to examine the changes which occur in the rhythms of the electroencephalogram when a novel stimulus is repeatedly applied. These investigations were first conducted on humans (Berger 1930; Knott and Henry 1941; Sokolov 1960), unanaesthetized rabbits (Ectors 1936), and cats (Rheinberger and Jasper 1937). The changes were studied in detail by Sharpless and Jasper (1956). In their experiments, unanaesthetized cats were allowed to fall asleep, as indicated by both behavioural and electro-encephalographic criteria. A 500 hertz tone was used to awaken the cat. When this happened the slow-waves, which characterized the electroen-cephalogram during sleep, were replaced by runs of low-voltage fast activity; that is, the electroencephalogram was 'activated' (Fig. 1.1(a)). As soon as the cat fell asleep and the electroencephalographic sleep pattern had returned, the tone was sounded again. In the course of twenty or thirty presentations of the tone, the stimuli were progressively less effective in waking the cat and in activating the electroencephalogram (Fig. 1.1(b)). When the animal had ceased to be aroused by the repeated 500 hertz tone, another tone with a frequency of 100 hertz (Fig. 1.1(c)) or of 1000 hertz (Fig. 1.1(e)) was presented. The novel tones awakened the animal and activated the electroencephalogram. Once this cortical activation response had become habituated to a repeated tone, it was often possible to elicit the response again, with the same tone, provided that 15 minutes or more were allowed to pass before presenting the stimulus again. The duration of this pause depended, in part, on the number of times the stimulus had previously been presented. In some cases it was necessary to interpose several days of rest between successive recordings for a response to be elicited once more by the repeated tone.

Although the changes in the electroencephalogram possessed many of the characteristics of stimulus-specific habituation, Sharpless and Jasper were of the view that these studies shed little light on the ultimate nature of the habituation process. Nevertheless, the work was important in at least two

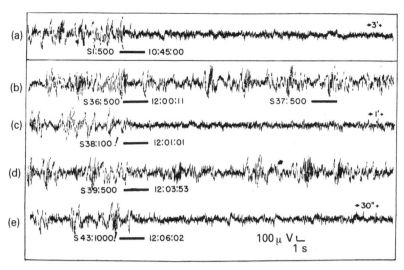

**Fig. 1.1.** Cortical electrograms from the suprasylvian gyrus of a normal cat showing typical habituation of the arousal reaction to a 500 Hz tone after about thirty trials. In the first tracing (a) the response to the first presentation of the 500 Hz tone is shown (S1: 500). The solid bar shows the duration of the stimulus followed by the time at which it was delivered, given in hours, minutes, and seconds (10:45:00). When the sound was presented the electroencephalogram was 'activated'. In the second tracing (b) are shown the thirty-sixth and thirty-seventh trials (S36 and S37). (c) A novel tone (!) of 100 Hz is presented in the thirty-eighth trial (S38: 100!) followed (d) by a repetition of the habituating tone (S39: 500) and then (e) another novel tone (S43: 1000!). The figures at the right above the electroencephalogram traces indicate the duration of the electroencephalographic activation in each trial. (After Sharpless and Jasper 1956).

respects. It established a link between a change in a physiological measure and a change in behaviour, and it drew attention to the process of habituation at a time when techniques were becoming available which would allow the process to be analysed at the cellular level with microelectrodes.

One such analysis involved recording the activity of single neurones, or units within the optic tectum (Horn and Hill 1964, 1966; Horn 1965; Masland *et al.* 1971; Cynader and Berman 1972), an important visual area in all vertebrates. In mammals the output neurones of the retina, the ganglion cells, send axons to the lateral geniculate body, or nucleus. Cells in this nucleus project to the visual cortex. Another target of ganglion cells is the optic tectum. The optic tectum contains two elevations, the superior colliculi. Single neurones in the optic tectum respond to visual stimuli if an image of the stimulus is focused on the appropriate part of the retina. This region of the retina is referred to as the receptive field of the tectal neurone. Some cells in the superior colliculus respond only to visual stimuli. Contrary, however, to the expectations of function implied by its name, the optic tectum receives also input from other sensory pathways (Horn and Hill 1964, 1966; Jassik-Gershenfeld 1966; Gordon 1973; Dräger and Hubel 1975).

The response of some neurones recorded in the optic tectum of the anaesthetized rabbit wane when a stimulus is repeatedly presented (see Fig. 1.2). The unit whose responses are plotted in this figure discharged 'spontaneously', in the absence of any deliberate sensory stimulation, and responded with a burst of impulses, or 'spikes' when a puff of air was delivered to the shoulder. When this stimulus was repeated once every few seconds the response was stable for the first half-dozen or so presentations, and thereafter began to decline. After approximately twenty presentations, the stimulus failed to evoke a discharge that could be distinguished from the spontaneous background activity. For many such units the response recovered if the stimulus was withdrawn for some time before being pre-

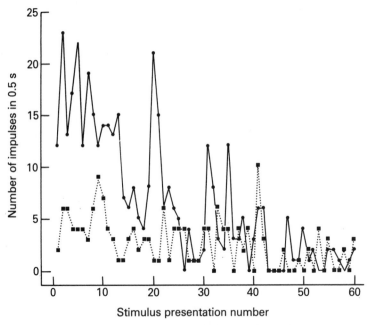

**Fig. 1.2.** Responses of a unit in the optic tectum of an anaesthetized rabbit. The unit responded to a puff of air blown on to the right shoulder. The puff of air had a duration of 2 s and was presented at 3-s intervals. The number of spontaneous impulses or spikes (squares) present in the 0.5 s before each stimulus was delivered, together with the number of evoked impulses (circles) in the first 0.5 s following application of the stimulus were plotted against stimulus presentation number (abscissa). The response gradually became less brisk as stimulation proceeded. After the twenty-third presentation, the number of impulses present during the time the stimulus was being applied was not consistently different from the number present during the prestimulus period. (After Horn and Hill 1966.)

sented again. The magnitude of the recovery often, but not invariably, depended on the duration of the period of remission: within limits the longer the period, the greater the response. A lapse of a minute or so was often sufficient to re-establish the response, depending on the number of previous stimulus presentations.

The response decrement was, but only to some extent, stimulus specific; the lack of precision implied that there was some 'stimulus generalization'. The two effects are illustrated by the activity of a tectal unit which responded to an auditory stimulus (Fig. 1.3). After a period of several

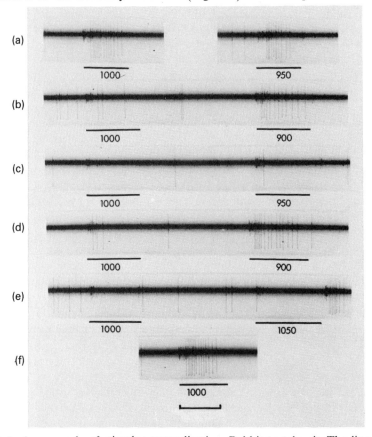

**Fig. 1.3.** An example of stimulus generalization. Rabbit tectal unit. The line below each record shows the time at which the stated tone was presented. The unit initially responded briskly to a 1000 Hz and to a 950 Hz tone (a). When the response to the 1000 Hz tone had waned the unit responded to a 900 Hz tone (b) and (d) and gave an 'off' response to a 1050 Hz tone (e). The unit failed to respond to 950 Hz tone (c). All these traces are continuous. Several minutes after this sequence had been completed the unit responded again to the 1000 Hz tone (f). Note that a small unit is present in each record; its response showed no sign of waning. Scale 0.5 s. (After Horn 1969.)

minutes during which all deliberate sensory stimulation was avoided, a 1000 hertz tone was presented. The unit responded briskly to this tone and also responded briskly to a 950 hertz tone (Fig. 1.3(a)). After the response of the unit had been tested in this way, the 1000 hertz tone was presented repeatedly at 2-second intervals. After the response had waned, alternate 1000 hertz tones were omitted and tones of other frequencies presented instead. Although the response to the 1000 hertz tone was weak or absent the unit responded to a 900 hertz tone (Fig. 1.3(b), (d)) and gave a burst of spikes after a 1050 hertz tone had been delivered (Fig. 1.3(e)). The response decrement was therefore quite specific to the 1000 hertz stimulus. But the specificity was less than perfect. Although the unit originally responded to the 950 hertz tone, it ceased to do so after the 1000 hertz tone had repeatedly been presented (Fig. 1.3(c)). There had, in other words, been some stimulus generalization. After a rest of several minutes the unit responded again to the iterated tone (Fig. 1.3(f)).

When a behavioural response has waned it sometimes reappears spontaneously. An operationally similar effect was occasionally observed after the response of a tectal unit had waned (Fig. 1.4). For no obvious reason, this unit abruptly began to respond vigorously to the repeated stimulus and just as abruptly ceased to do so. At the behavioural level it is sometimes possible actively to re-establish the response to the repeated stimulus by presenting an extraneous, intercurrent stimulus (Humphrey 1933; Lehner 1941). This effect is most dramatic if the intercurrent stimulus is presented in between successive presentations of the repeated stimulus. Recovery of responsiveness brought about in this way was not observed when recording from tectal cells in the anaesthetized rabbit. Such recovery was, however, observed whilst recording from a neurone in the brain of the locust *Schistocerca gregaria* Forskål (Horn and Rowell 1968; Rowell and Horn 1968). The neurone was recorded from the tritocerebral lobe of the brain. A characteristic of this neurone was that the response to a black disk moved across the field of vision declined rapidly when the stimulus was repeated a few times (Fig. 1.5). The brain of the locust is linked to the ventral nerve cord by two bundles of nerve fibres known as the neck connectives. When the response to the moving disk was weak the contralateral neck connective was briefly stimulated by a train of electrical shocks. The responsiveness to the repeated visual stimulus was greatly increased by this procedure (Fig. 1.5). Stimulation of the ipsilateral connective, that is the connective on the same side as the recording electrode, was without effect on the response of the tritocerebral unit to the visual stimulus. The potentiating effect of intercurrent stimulation of the contralateral connective waned (Fig. 1.5, curves 4 and 5). Similar changes are observed when behavioural responses are repeatedly dishabituated by intercurrent stimulation (Lehner 1941).

Once the response of the tritocerebral unit had been quenched by repeated movements of the black disk, the response could usually be re-

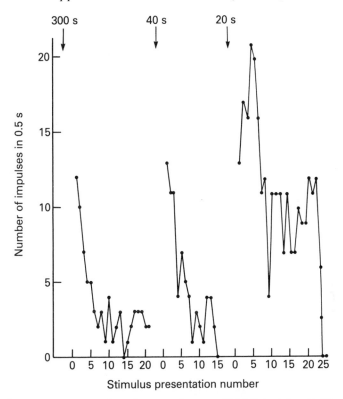

**Fig. 1.4.** Spontaneous recovery of responsiveness. Rabbit tectal unit. The stimulus was a brief (0.5 s) tone of 1000 Hz delivered once every 2 s. The first set of stimuli, presented after a pause of 300 s, evoked responses which are plotted in the first curve (reading from left to right). Brisk responses (middle curve) were elicited by the first few stimuli of the next series, presented after a pause of 40 s, but again the response rapidly declined with successive presentations. Following a 20-s interval the unit repeatedly responded vigorously to twenty stimuli before the response declined (third curve). (After Horn 1970*a*).

established if the disk was withheld for some time. This recovery was not, however, invariably observed. For example, the unit whose responses are plotted in Fig. 1.6 responded to a black disk moving upwards across its receptive field at intervals of 10 seconds. Following a 23 minute period of stimulus remission the unit responded briskly to the disk and the response waned. There was little recovery of response after 5 hours had elapsed between the end of the first sequence of movements and the beginning of the second set of movements (Fig. 1.6, curves 1 and 2 respectively). Obviously it was necessary to consider whether such a prolonged depression resulted from a general deterioration of the experimental animal. This was unlikely because the cell responded to a forward movement of the disk (Fig.

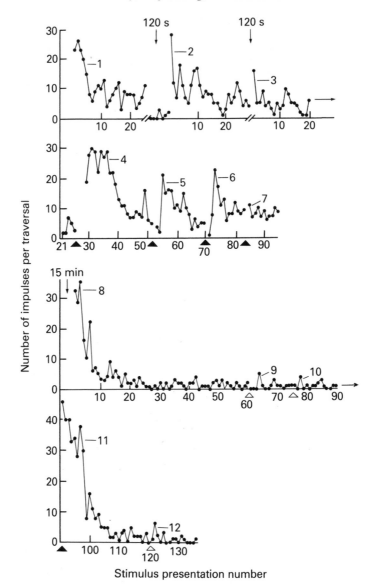

**Fig. 1.5.** Response decrement to a repeated stimulus and recovery following stimulation of the contralateral neck connective, but not following stimulation of the ipsilateral neck connective. The visual stimulus was a disk moved through an angle of 40° in 1.4 s. The interval between successive movements was 10 s. The large filled and open triangles below an abscissa indicate that a train of shocks was applied to the contralateral and ipsilateral connectives respectively between successive presentations of the disk. The numbers above the arrows indicate the interval of time

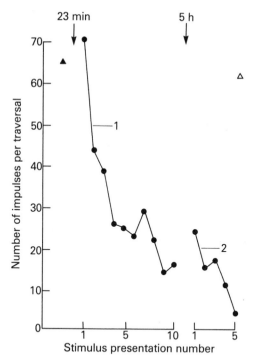

**Fig. 1.6.** Long-lasting stimulus-specific decrement. Each solid circle represents the number of impulses elicited by an upward movement of the disk, presented once every 10 s. The first sequence of movements (responses plotted in curve 1) was preceded by a period of 23 min during which no stimulus was presented. An interval of 5 h elapsed between the first and second sequences of movements. The initial stimulus of curve 2 evoked only a relatively weak discharge (twenty-five spikes) compared with the initial discharge in curve 1 of seventy-one spikes. Movement in a forward direction, immediately after the second group of upward movements, evoked almost as many spikes (open triangle) as were evoked before the first set of upward movements was presented (solid triangle). (After Rowell and Horn 1968.)

1.6, open triangle) presented immediately after the second set of upward movements almost as vigorously as it had been done before the first set of upward movements had been delivered (Fig. 1.6, solid triangle).

During the 1960s the characteristics of response decrement in single neurones was investigated in detail in various areas of the vertebrate brain, including the hippocampus (Vinogradova 1970), the brainstem (Lettvin *et al.* 1961; Grüsser-Cornehls *et al.* 1963; Bell *et al.* 1964), and the spinal cord

---

elapsing between successive groups of stimuli. The arrow parallel to the abscissa indicates that stimulation was continued without a break in the sequence of movements. The curve between curves 1 and 2 is a control, giving dummy counts in the absence of stimulation. (After Rowell and Horn 1968.)

(Buchwald 1965; Spencer *et al.* 1966*a,b,c*). Detailed investigations were also being undertaken of neurones in the brain of some invertebrates (Holmgren and Frenk 1961; Roberts 1962; Hughes and Tauc 1963; Horridge *et al.* 1965; Bruner and Tauc 1966; Krasne and Roberts 1967). Although there were considerable variations at the neuronal level, as there are at the behavioural level (Hinde 1970), in the time-courses of response decrement and recovery, in the degree of specificity, and in the extent and characteristics of the recovery brought about by intercurrent stimulation, a general pattern was emerging across a wide range of animals. Furthermore, the pattern of neuronal changes was similar in a number of ways to that of behavioural habituation. Before considering whether the neuronal and behavioural events may be related in any causal way it is useful to consider the cellular mechanisms of the neuronal changes.

### 1.1.3 Cellular mechanisms

Sherrington (1906) provided good evidence that the waning of the scratch-reflex was not referable to the muscles subserving the reflex. When the motor nerve to one of these muscles was directly stimulated the muscle contracted well, although the reflex had waned. Sherrington considered that the motor neurones which innervate the muscles are relatively indefatigable. He suggested, instead, that the command over these motor neurones exercised by the receptors and afferent path becomes less strong; under prolonged excitation their hold upon these neurones becomes loosened. The site of the fatigue he suggested was within the spinal cord, where the cell bodies of the motor neurones lie, rather than in the skin or in the sensory nerves connecting the skin to the cord. He considered that the place of incidence of the fatigue lay at the synapse.

Sherrington (1898) had observed that the amplitude of the flexor reflex also declined when the eliciting stimulus was repeatedly applied. This change in the strength of the reflex was later studied in detail by Prosser and Hunter (1936). The reflex is elicited by stimulating the skin or the appropriate sensory nerve fibres (Fig. 1.7). Such stimulation evokes a contraction in certain flexor muscles of the limb. These contractions are directly controlled by motor neurones in the spinal cord. Spencer and his collaborators (1966*a,b*) and Wickelgren (1967*a*) studied the way in which the amplitude of this reflex in the cat declined when the stimulus was repeatedly applied. They found a change in the extent to which the afferent input invaded the spinal cord, but the change was not adequate to account for the decrement in response of the motor neurones. Sherrington's view that the control over these motor neurones became less strong, but that these neurones, the final common paths, were relatively indefatigable, was vindicated by the experiments of Spencer and his collaborators (1966*c*). These workers introduced microelectrodes directly into motor neurones in the spinal cord. They found that response decrement was associated with a reduction in the excitation

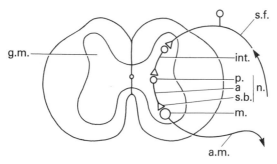

**Fig. 1.7.** Diagram of cross-section of mammalian spinal cord to show some components of a multisynaptic reflex arc. Afferent impulses, initiated by stimulating the skin, are carried to the spinal cord by sensory nerve fibres of which one is shown (s.f.). Some of the terminals of these fibres make synaptic contact with interneurones (int.). These neurones, which lie in the grey matter (g.m.) of the spinal cord ultimately transmit the evoked impulse activity to the motor neurone (m.). The axon of this cell (a.m.) passes out of the spinal cord to innervate a flexor muscle. The major parts of a vertebrate neurone (n.) are the cell body, variously known as the soma or perikaryon (p.) an axon (a.) and a variable number of synaptic boutons, or knobs, of which one is represented diagrammatically (s.b.). The dendrites of this neurone are not shown. Dendrites are cytoplasmic processes which often branch extensively and typically arise, in vertebrates, from the soma. The diagram is not drawn to scale: the diameters of the perikarya vary from approximately 10 to 70 μm whereas the spinal cord has a mean diameter which is in the millimetre range, the actual size varying widely between species.

falling on the neurone; the decrement was not attributable to any change in the ability of the motor neurone to respond to the input. Transmission failure must therefore develop somewhere between the afferent input to the cord and the motor output from it (Wicklegren 1967*b*; Wall 1970).

The depression of transmission could occur in a number of ways. One possibility is that it is brought about by inhibitory processes. For example, as each burst of action potentials traverses a chain of neurones there is a progressive build-up of activity in an inhibitory side-arm of the chain. This build-up of inhibition might act back on, and finally block, transmission in the chain. Whilst such a mechanism is inherently plausible and may operate in some systems, it is unlikely to operate in all. A particularly important set of experiments in this context is that of Bruner and Tauc (1966). They made intracellular recordings from a giant neurone in the left pleural ganglion of the sea hare, *Aplysia*, a marine mollusc. When a drop of water was allowed to fall on a restricted area of the head, one or both tentacles were withdrawn. When the drops of water were applied at intervals of 10 seconds or so the tentacular response progressively declined. It recovered to some extent, depending on various factors, if the stimulus was withdrawn for some time. The response could also be reinstated, without rest, by scratching the animal's head or by stimulating a nerve. When the drops of water evoked a tentacular contraction, a large excitatory postsynaptic potential (EPSP) could be recorded in the giant cell (Fig. 1.8(a)). The changes in amplitude of the EPSP followed the same pattern as the changes in amplitude of the tentacular contraction. The EPSP was a compound one, and was probably composed of a number of unitary EPSPs from several presynaptic neurones. However, the pattern of response decrement of unitary EPSPs (FIg. 1.8(b)) closely resembled that of compound EPSPs. The unitary EPSPs were probably recorded from a monosynaptic junction. If this was so, then the unitary potential reflected the discharge of a single impulse in the presynaptic nerve fibre. Bruner and Tauc provided good evidence that the reduction of this EPSP was not due to changes in the postsynaptic cell; the evidence pointed to a presynaptic mechanism for the breakdown in synaptic transmission.

When a nerve impulse travels along an axon it usually invades the terminals of that axon. At 'chemical' synapses, this invasion is followed by the liberation of a transmitter substance which may increase or decrease the excitablity of the postsynaptic cell. Evidence of an excitatory effect is that the membrane of the postsynaptic cell is depolarized. The depolarization is detected as the EPSP. If this is of sufficient amplitude then an action potential may be generated in and sweep along the axon of the postsynaptic neurone. Inhibition is expressed as a shift in the membrane potential of the postsynaptic cell in the opposite direction. The potential is an inhibitory postsynaptic potential, an IPSP. The transmitter substance is liberated in multimolecular packets, probably wrapped up in small vesicles contained within the synapse (for reviews see Katz 1969; Kelly *et al.* 1979). Bruner and Tauc suggested that the response decrement which they had observed was due to synaptic depression brought about by a diminution of transmitter release. This diminution of transmitter output, they suggested, was probably caused by a depletion of the transmitter in the terminals and its slow mobilization. The resulting block of transmission across the synapse is an example of an activity-dependent, or self-generated depression of information transfer within the nervous system (Horn 1967); that is, the activity of the neurone depresses its own capacity to pass on signals.

Bruner and Tauc's hypothesis depended on the assumption that the changes in the unitary EPSPs, which they had observed, reflected changes in the presynaptic fibres alone, unaided, as it were, by side-chains of neurones. Bruner and Tauc were cautious, however, in their assumption that their records were from a monosynaptic junction. Such a junction, relatively massive in size, is contained within the stellate ganglion of the squid, *Loligo vulgaris* (Young 1939). The ganglion almost certainly contains no interneurones. A further advantage, is that, because the pre- and postsynaptic elements are very large the changes in potential associated with transmission are also large and can be detected with suitably placed extracellular

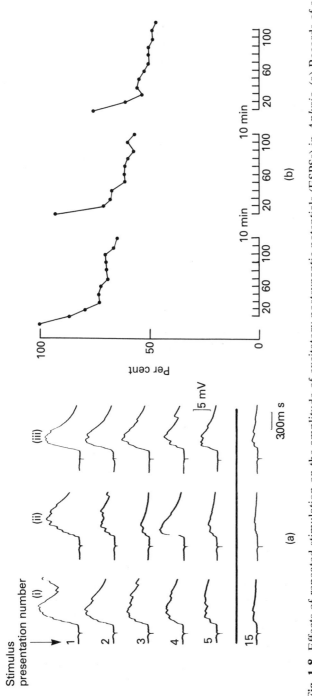

**Fig. 1.8.** Effects of repeated stimulation on the amplitude of excitatory postsynaptic potentials (ESPSs) in *Aplysia*. (a) Records of a compound EPSP. Drops of water were applied at 10-s intervals to the head near the left anterior tentacle. (i) First series of fifteen stimuli. (ii) Second series of stimuli showing restoration of the EPSP after a ten minute rest. (iii) Continuation of series (ii) without break in stimulation frequency, but following a 2-s period of repetitive stimulation (five per second) of the left posterior pedal nerve. Note the restoration of the amplitude of the EPSP. (b) Accumulation of the effects of stimulation on recovery processes observed in a unitary EPSP. The EPSP was evoked by stimulating at intervals of 10 s a bundle of nerve fibres, the left pleuro-visceral connective. Ordinate: percentage of amplitude of initial EPSP. Abscissa: time in seconds and minutes. (After Bruner and Tauc 1966.)

electrodes (Bullock 1948). Furthermore, transmission across this synapse has been studied extensively.

Does synaptic transmission across the giant synapse fail on repeated, intermittent stimulation of the presynaptic fibre? If so, is the pattern of response decrement and recovery similar to those patterns shown in Fig 1.5 (curves 1–3) and 1.8(b)? In order to answer these questions, the stellate ganglion was dissected out (Horn and Wright 1970). The prenerve, containing the presynaptic fibre, was stimulated with electrical shocks and the response of the giant postsynaptic axon in the postnerve recorded with extracellular electrodes. When the presynaptic nerve was stimulated by a short train of shocks every 10 seconds each shock in the train evoked a spike in the postsynaptic axon and transmission was maintained almost indefinitely. When the number of shocks in a train was increased to twenty delivered in half a second, each shock of the first train evoked a spike in the postsynaptic cell (Fig. 1.9, curve 1). The response declined and the fifth train of twenty shocks to the prenerve evoked only fourteen spikes in the postsynaptic fibre. If the stimulus was withdrawn, there was a variable degree of recovery. For a given number of trains the magnitude of the recovery depended on the length of the period of remission. With repeated trains there was an accumulation of the effects of stimulation (Fig. 1.9) which resembled that seen in *Aplysia* (Fig. 1.8(b)). The progressive failure of shocks to the prenerve of the stellate ganglion to generate spikes in the postsynaptic nerve fibre was associated with a progressive reduction in size of the EPSP.

Factors effecting this change in size of the EPSP recorded at the giant

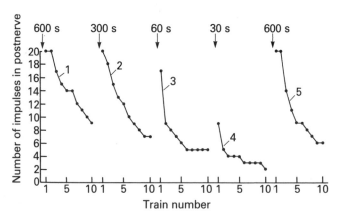

**Fig. 1.9.** Effects of varying the period of stimulus remission on transmission across the stellate ganglion. Each train of shocks contained twenty pulses delivered at a rate of forty per second for 0.5 s. The interval between successive trains was 10 s. Number above each arrow is the duration of the remission interval. (After Horn and Wright 1970.)

synapse have been investigated by a number of workers. Microelectrodes have been introduced into both pre- and postsynaptic elements of the junction and the prenerve repeatedly shocked. Under these conditions the amplitude of the postsynaptic response declines (Bullock and Hagiwara 1957; Bryant 1959); but action potentials continue to invade the presynaptic terminal. Thus, stimulus repetition brings about an uncoupling between the action potential present in the presynaptic terminal and the expression of transmitter release manifest as the EPSP. The well documented evidence for the dependence of this potential on the events in the presynaptic terminal in the giant synapse of the squid suggests strongly that the uncoupling takes place wholly or largely at this side of the junction (see Katz and Miledi 1969). A number of possible molecular mechanisms by which the uncoupling might take place were considered and several excluded (Horn and Wright 1970). It is known that when the synaptic terminal is invaded by an action potential there is an influx of calcium ions into the terminal. This influx is essential for the release of transmitter (Katz and Miledi 1967; Miledi 1973). Hence changes in the concentration, movement, or reactions of calcium ions were considered as likely candidates for the change in transmission which resulted from repeatedly stimulating the prenerve (Horn and Wright 1970; Horn 1970b).

Bruner and Tauc pointed out that the giant cell which they studied was not situated in the reflex arc of the tentacular response. However, the kinetics of the amplitude modifications of this response were similar to those of the EPSP. Because of this similarity they suggested that the synaptic changes might be one of the elements subserving behavioural habituation. The relationship between the synaptic changes and the behavioural changes would become clearer when it became possible to study transmission in a circuit which directly controlled the behavioural response.

The basic circuit controlling the flexor reflex response in mammals is known, and Wickelgren (1967a,b) and Wall (1970) provided evidence that the transmission failure associated with habituation of the reflex probably occurred at a particular locus in the reflex arc. The cellular mechanisms involved in this transmission failure are, however, difficult to study because of the sheer complexity of the neuronal networks in the spinal cord. Kupfermann and Kandel (1969) had meanwhile worked out the anatomy of the neuronal circuit involved in the gill-withdrawal reflex of *Aplysia*. When parts of the body surface, the mantle shelf or the syphon are touched, the gill, the mantle shelf, and the syphon contract. When the stimulus was repeatedly applied, the response waned. Recovery was actually observed if the stimulus was withdrawn for a time or if an intercurrent stimulus, for example an electrical shock to a part of the receptive field of the reflex, was applied (Pinsker *et al.* 1970). The waning of the withdrawal response was not associated with a change in the afferent discharge in the sensory neurones; and direct electrical stimulation of a gill motor neurone consistently evoked a vigorous response in a gill (Kupfermann *et al.* 1970). The breakdown in transmission was found to be at the junction between the sensory and motor neurones of the reflex. The decline in the behavioural response was associated with a decrease in the EPSP recorded in the motor neurone (Castellucci *et al.* 1970). Because the junction is probably mono-synaptic the decline in the EPSP was ascribed to a reduced output of transmitter from the terminals of the sensory neurone much as Bruner and Tauc (1966) had postulated.

Klein and his collaborators (1980) sought to examine the relationship between the release of transmitter and the ionic currents at the terminals of the sensory neurone. These currents were not directly measured; instead, the ionic currents of the cell body were studied. It was shown that the progressive decrease of the EPSP was accompanied by a decrease in the inward calcium current. Recovery of transmission with rest was associated with an increase in this current. If the changes in calcium current at the cell body accurately reflect changes taking place in the axon terminals, then these results support the views (p. 17) that had earlier been expressed, that the synaptic depression which is implicated in habituation, results from changes in the movement of calcium ions.

Many studies of behavioural habituation were concerned with short-lasting changes in responsiveness, with recovery occurring in minutes or hours. There are, however, numerous examples of habituation lasting days or weeks (see, for example, Hinde 1960; Glaser and Whittow 1957; Griffin and Pearson 1967). Is it possible that the neural mechanisms underlying short-term habituation, of the kinds that have been discussed above, are similar to those of long-term habituation? Stimulus-specific response decrement lasting for 5 hours was observed in the tritocerebral unit of the locust (Fig. 1.6) but much longer-term neuronal changes have been studies. Castellucci and his collaborators (1978) showed that the gill-withdrawal reflex of *Aplysia* may remain habituated for several weeks following appropriate stimulation. This consisted of repeatedly stimulating on five or more successive days a site in the receptive field of the reflex. Transmission at the sensory to motor neurone junction was found to remain depressed for up to 3 weeks after this procedure.

An intercurrent stimulus, usually intense or even painful, may restore an habituated behavioural response. The effect is known as dishabituation if only the attenuated response recovers. Commonly, however, the amplitude of other responses are also increased by the procedure. This more general facilitation of responsiveness is often referred to as 'sensitization' (see Thompson and Spencer 1966). If synaptic depression is the basis of some forms of behavioural habituation, how might the intercurrent stimulus restore transmission?

The amount of transmitter substance released at a synapse can be varied by manipulating the level of polarization of the presynaptic terminal. For example, the amplitude of the synaptic potential at the squid giant synapse wanes if the prenerve is continuously stimulated with brief electric shocks. The amplitude of the EPSP may be restored by increasing, or hyperpolarizing the resting potential of the presynaptic terminal (Hagiwara and Tasaki 1958; Takeuchi and Takeuchi 1962; Miledi and Slater 1966). The effect is thought to be brought about by increasing the amount of transmitter available for release. Using the data from the squid stellate ganglion as a model, it was suggested that the response recovery which follows the application of an inter-current stimulus might be achieved by hyperpolarization of the depressed presynaptic terminals (Horn 1967). An intense or painful stimulus is likely to activate a widely connected system of fibres known as the reticular system of the brainstem core (see Hobson and Scheibel 1980). This 'non-specific' system is probably present in all vertebrates; analagous systems may exist in some invertebrates (see Rowell 1970). If neurones of such systems hyperpolarize the depressed terminals, activation of the system by an intercurrent stimulus could restore transmission (Fig. 1.10). A sudden increase in the activity of the non-specific system, unprovoked by a sensory stimulus might have the same effect. When this happens there would be a 'spontaneous' recovery of the waned response to the repeated stimulus. Such recovery is found at the neuronal (Fig. 1.4) and at the behavioural levels. The connections made by the non-specific system need not involve direct neurone to neurone synapses. Some substances, known

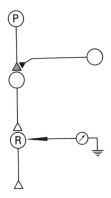

**Fig. 1.10.** A possible neuronal mechanism of dishabituation, or sensitization. A stimulus excites a burst of impulses in cell P. This response is transmitted to cell R. The activity of cell R is recorded through the microelectrode. Repeated applications of the stimulus are associated with a consistent discharge in cell P, but with a progressive reduction in the response of cell R. The block in transmission is assumed to result from synaptic depression in the terminals of cell P. An intense intercurrent stimulus re-establishes transmission. In the model, the effect is mediated by the inhibitory neurone activated by the reticular information of the brainstem core. Symbols: open triangles represent non-decremental excitatory synapses; hatched triangle represents a decremental excitatory synapse; and the closed triangle represents an inhibitory non-decremental synapse. (After Horn 1967.)

as neuromodulators, may not be secreted at specialized synaptic junctions, but may be released near to synapses and modify transmission in a number of them (see Shepherd 1979). The indoleamine serotonin was shown by Dudel (1965) to increase the release of transmitter substance at a crayfish neuromuscular junction. In *Aplysia* an appropriate intercurrent stimulus restores the behavioural response as well as restoring transmission at depressed synapses (Bruner and Tauc 1966; Pinsker *et al.* 1970). The facilitating effect of the sensitizing stimulus may be brought about through the action of a serotonin-like substance. Such substances may act by increasing the normal influx of calcium ions into the nerve terminal which occurs during an action potential (see Schwartz *et al.* 1983).

Synaptic depression is economical of neurones since no elaborate circuitry is required to block transmission. Only the synapses which have been activated by the stimulus are affected, though not all of them are. In the intact organism some synapses, when activated within the physiological range, have a high factor of safety and continue to transmit whenever the presynaptic fibre fires. Such synapses are commonly found in the primary sensory pathways, and are also found close to the motor outflow, for example the synapses of a monosynaptic reflex in the spinal cord (Sherrington 1906; Prosser and Hunter 1936; Spencer *et al.* 1966*c*) and the neuromuscular junction. Other synapses, some of which have been described above, have a low factor of safety, rapidly fail to transmit, and recover only slowly. There is thus a very wide range of safety factors in junctional transmission and also a wide range of recovery times. Indeed, if this were not so it is difficult to see how synaptic depression could be invoked to account for behavioural habituation which, from system to system and from animal to animal varies widely in its characteristics (Hinde 1970). Even so, it is much too soon in the experimental analysis of habituation to close the options by supposing that all examples of behavioural habituation, even in a given animal, use the same cellular mechanisms for bringing about response decrement and sensitization (Horn 1967; Sokolov *et al.* 1967; Wickelgren 1967*b*; Wall 1970; Weight and Erulkar 1976). In unicellular organisms, which exhibit behaviour resembling habituation, the underlying mechanisms can hardly by synaptic (Applewhite and Gardner 1971).

*1.1.4 Possible neuronal networks for habituation*

In the above discussions the neural basis of a behavioural change, habituation, was considered at progressively lower levels, from changes in the electroencephalogram to changes in the electrical activity of single neurones down to synaptic and then to molecular levels. It is not easy to proceed in the reverse direction because new properties may emerge at the higher level which could not have been predicted from the analysis at the lower level. It is, however, worth attempting to synthesize the results obtained at the different levels of analysis if only because, in doing so, further gaps in our knowledge may be revealed.

In the discussions which follow it is supposed that the activity of one of the neurones which directly control a behavioural or a physiological response is being recorded with a microelectrode. Suppose that such a neurone ceases to respond to a repeated stimulus but responds vigorously to another stimulus applied elsewhere, and that when the original stimulus is withdrawn for some time, and presented again, the cell responds once more. This behaviour would be expected if there were a self-generated depression in the pathways transmitting the signal evoked by the repeated stimulus (Fig. 1.11(a)). In this figure stimulus S1, say a light touch to the skin evokes activity in the recorded neurone R over the pathways represented by P–R. If the touch is applied repeatedly, transmission to R is blocked because of synaptic depression in the terminals of cell P. If another area of skin were touched and activity evoked in neurone R over a pathway represented by Q–R, then a brisk response would be evoked. So long as the synaptic depression persists, stimulus S1 would fail to evoke a response in cell R and accordingly fail to evoke a behavioural response; that is, the duration of the synaptic depression sets the limit of the memory not to respond. Thus the

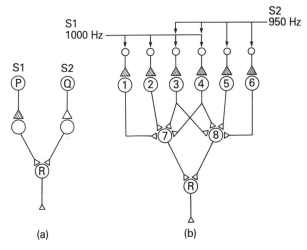

**Fig. 1.11.** Models of neuronal networks for behavioural habituation. (a) Simple network for stimulus-specific response decrement in a recorded neurone R. Stimulus S1 excites a set of neurones that excite cell R over a pathway represented by P–R. When stimulus S1 is repeatedly applied, the synapses of cell P with the next cell gradually fail to transmit so that cell R gradually ceases to respond to this stimulus. Cell R responds, however, to stimulus S2 which excites cell R over the pathway represented by Q–R. This pathway is anatomically independent of P–R. (b) A network exhibiting stimulus generalization. Symbols for synapses are the same as those used in Fig. 1.10. For further discussion see text. (After Horn 1967.)

of the original stimulus to elicit a response after a period of rest would depend on the rate at which the synaptic depression is dissipated. When this process is complete and the response fully restored the memory is lost. The way in which an intense intercurrent stimulus induces 'forgetting' by restoring transmission across a depressed junction has already been discussed (see Fig. 1.10).

The gradual failure of a response, and its recovery after a lapse of time can thus be accounted for by assuming that the activity evoked by the repeated stimulus and by the second stimulus reach the recorded cell over anatomically independent pathways. This is a reasonable assumption. There is good evidence in may animals that specific features of a stimulus excite activity in specific groups of neurones. For example, a line moving across the retina in one direction may excite different groups of neurones in the cerebral cortex from those excited by the same line moved in the opposite direction (see Hubel 1982). In the auditory system many neurones respond selectively to a sound having a particular frequency (see Whitfield 1967); a change in the frequency components of a sound would thus result in a shift in the array of neurones excited by the stimulus. Some neurones in the auditory system are only excited by sounds of particular frequency *and* intensity (Goldberg and Greenwood 1966). For these cells, a change of stimulus intensity alone would be sufficient to activate a different population of neurones.

A neuronal mechanism of habituation must be able to account for stimulus generalization, an example of which is illustrated in Fig. 1.3. The unit originally responded to a 1000 hertz tone and to a 950 hertz tone. When the response to the 1000 hertz tone had waned so too had the response to the 950 hertz. This effect could be accounted for by pathway overlap as illustrated in Fig. 1.11(b). In this network it is assumed that stimulus S1 is a 1000 hertz tone which excites neurones 1–4 and hence cell R. Stimulus S2 is a 950 hertz tone and also excites cell R, but over a pathway which includes cells 3–6. Stimuli S1 and S2 each elicit activity in cells 3 and 4. Cells 7 and 8 are considered to require activity in three or more of their input neurones in order to discharge. When the 1000 hertz tone is delivered repeatedly the responses of cells 1–4 decline due to synaptic depression at their inputs. The responses of cell 7 and R also decline. The 950 hertz tone is now presented. Cells 5 and 6 are excited but cells 3 and 4 are not since their input synapses are depressed. As a result, the conditions necessary to excite cell 8 are not met since the cell is not excited by the minimum number of inputs. Cell R will not therefore fire.

There is one set of results that cannot be accounted for solely in terms of a self-generated depression of transmission in sensory-motor pathways. Sokolov (1960), working with human subjects, found that after the orientation response to a regularly repeated stimulus had ceased, a response appeared when one of the stimuli in the sequence was omitted. Sokolov

(1965) also detected single cells in the rabbit hippocampus which gave a discharge when one of the stimuli in a sequence was omitted.

In order to account for this time-dependent pattern of neuronal activity— and also for that at the higher, behavioural, level of the orientation response—it seems necessary to introduce a process additional to self-generated depression of synaptic transmission. Such a process could require the operations of a difference-detecting system. The way in which this system might operate may be considered by referring to Fig. 1.12(a). Suppose that cells P and K are simultaneously activated by a sensory stimulus and each discharge $n$ spikes in a given unit of time. Cell J will be excited by $n$ spikes in K, but inhibited by $n$ spikes from P. The excitatory and inhibitory inputs exactly balance and cell J is silent. For similar reasons cell H is silent. Because cell G is not excited by cells J or H, it also is silent.

The difference-detecting circuit is incorporated into the diagram shown in Fig. 1.12(b). It contains cell K which is assumed to have the properties shown by a number of cells that have been recorded in the hippocampus and visual cortex of rabbits and cats (Horn 1962; Kopytova and Rabinovich 1967; Vinogradova 1970; Brown 1982). The discharge of these cells becomes entrained by a regularly repeated stimulus. The mechanism of entrainment is not know, but a consequence of the entrainment is that the cells give one or more extrapolatory discharges; that is, when the stimulus is withheld the cells fire at the time that next stimulus would be expected to occur.

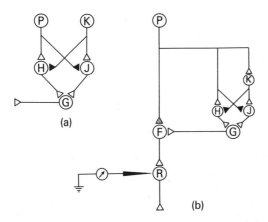

**Fig. 1.12.** A system in which an effector neurone may 'respond' to an omitted stimulus. (a) A difference-detecting circuit in which the activity of cell G is equal to the difference between the activities in cells P and K. (b) A neuronal system in which the effector cell R, which controls some response, exhibits time-dependent response properties, one of which is discussed in the text. Symbols for synapses are the same as those used in Fig. 1.10. (After Horn 1967.)

When a novel stimulus is presented cell P fires and cell R is excited over pathway PFR (Fig. 1.12(b)). Cell G is silent because the discharge in cell K is equal to that of cell P. The stimulus is now repeatedly presented and after the response of cell R has waned one stimulus of the series is omitted. Cell K now gives an extrapolatory discharge. Cell J also discharges because it is excited by cell K, but receives no inhibitory input from cell P, which is silent. Cell G will discharge and so also will cells F and R, which thus 'respond' to the omitted stimulus.

## 1.1.5 Comment

The neuronal mechanisms discussed above could account for many aspects of the behavioural changes that are consequent on the repeated presentation of a stimulus. The neural basis of the memory not to respond may be the self-generated depression of transmission in the pathway initially excited by the repeated stimulus; the inactivated pathway constitutes a neuronal model, or representation of that stimulus. But can such systems and mechanisms, together with those which need to be invoked to account for the time-dependent effects discussed above, adequately account for all aspects of the behavioural changes? Probably not. The difficulty becomes apparent when considering the results of Hinde's studies of the mobbing response given by chaffinchs (*Fringilla coelebs*) to certain predators. In the continued presence of the predator, a stuffed owl, the response ultimately waned. The owl was presented for a second time 24 hours later. The mobbing response was smaller than on the first presentation (Hinde 1954*a,b*). Whilst this change in behaviour could be understood in terms of self-generated depression of transmission in the pathways linking the sensory input to the neuronal systems controlling the mobbing response, an additional process is needed to account for Hinde's (1960) subsequent findings. In these experiments two stimuli were used, one of which, the owl, was more effective in eliciting the mobbing response than the other, a dog. Stimuli were presented on two occasions with an interval of 24 hours between presentations. The stimuli were used in all possible combinations, and the length of the initial presentation was varied. With most stimulus combinations recovery, as indicated by the strength of response on the second presentation, was smaller the longer the first presentation. When the strong stimulus was followed by the weak stimulus, however, the opposite was the case: the longer the initial presentation of the owl, the stronger the subsequent response to the dog. Thus, sometimes there was a long-term decremental effect of the first stimulus presentation on the second, sometimes there was an incremental effect. These two outcomes cannot both be understood in terms of a single decremental process; Hinde (1960, 1970) therefore suggested that two interacting process are involved, one decremental and one incremental. The physiological studies which have been described in this chapter have been concerned with the decremental process, habituation, and its control, not with the incremental process, even though both may be involved when an animal is repeatedly exposed to a stimulus.

The neural analysis of certain aspects of habituation has made substantial progress over the last two decades or so, and the tide of enthusiasm has been sufficiently compelling to encourage attempts to account for certain kinds of associative learning in terms of the mechanism of habituation and sensitization (Horn 1971*a*; Hawkins and Kandel 1984). Be that as it may, the success of this analysis of habituation is attributable to a number of factors. One factor is the development and availability of techniques which allowed the problem to be analysed in the first place. Another is the nature of the problem itself. Habituation is a change of behaviour which can be specified reasonably well, and can be observed over a wide range of conditions. Furthermore, the stimulus and the response are usually closely related to each other in time. Neuronal changes having close parametric similarities to the behavioural changes were observed in the nervous systems of many animals and even in parts of nervous systems. All of these factors conspired to bring the behaviour into the neurobiologist's laboratory. The selection of a behaviour that was likely to yield to analysis at the lower level of neuronal activity, was, however, crucial to the success of that analysis.

Some fifteen years ago the prospect of understanding the neural basis of information storage that accompanied other forms of learning was not encouraging. The reasons are not hard to come by. In many learning situations a stimulus may not initially elicit a specific response, but comes to do so in the course of training or exposure. In these situations, stimulus and response may not bear a close temporal relationship to each other; the responses may not be expressed at the time of training but only at some later occasion; reward or punishment often enters into the establishment of the new behaviour, which may be complex and involve movement of the whole animal; and the subject's past history may be of prime importance in determining the nature of the response. In the face of this bewildering array of variables it is not surprising that great difficulties were encountered in identifying changes in the brain that form the basis of information storage. These difficulties are compounded by the fact that the study of learning and memory poses problems which lie at the interface between the behavioural and brain sciences. Behavioural scientists have the skill to analyse behaviour but rarely the skill to analyse neural mechanisms; and neurobiologists have the skill to analyse mechanisms but rarely the skill to specify the conditions under which the behavioural change will occur, and to identify the behavioural change to which these mechanisms might refer. It may well be that for such reasons the high promise of success in the 1960s for biochemical studies of learning and memory was largely unfulfilled (see Horn 1971*b*).

Since that time exciting progress has been made in the analysis of the memory necessary for classical conditioning, in which a previously neutral stimulus, such as a light flash, comes to predict the occurrence of reward or punishment. These studies have been the subject of several excellent reviews and will not be discussed in any detail in this book (see Voronin 1976; Woody 1982; Thompson *et al.* 1983; Alkon 1984). However, another type of learning gave some promise of yielding to experimental analysis— imprinting in the domestic chick (*Gallus domesticus*). There are a number of reasons why this should be.

## 1.2 The characteristics of filial imprinting

Imprinting occurs in the young of many species which are capable of walking or running about within a few hours of birth. Such 'precocial' species differ from 'altrical' species which are almost helpless at birth and may remain so for days, weeks, or months. Although imprinting occurs in some mammals, including sheep, goats, guinea-pigs, and some antelopes, the behaviour has been studied most intensively in precocial birds (Spalding 1873; Heinroth 1910; Lorenz 1935, 1937; Hinde 1962; Bateson 1966; Sluckin 1972; Hess 1973;).

Soon after hatching young precocial birds follow their mother. This following response is not, however, elicited only by the natural mother. Young domestic chicks, for example, will approach a wide range of objects, especially moving objects. If the chicks continue to be exposed to a particular object they form a social attachment to it, comparable to the attachment they form to their natural mother. When the chicks are close to the familiar object they show signs of contentment: they emit soft calls, peck at small particles of food, and if the object moves about the chicks will follow it. What is more, instead of approaching other conspicuous objects, as in the native state they would have done, they may now actively avoid them, showing signs of fear or even panic. This pattern of behaviour suggests that the chicks learn the characteristics of the maternal object when they are exposed to it.

The time during which the chicks approach a wide range of objects is often referred to as the 'sensitive period'. Before this period, chicks appear to sleep a good deal and when awake their movements are poorly co-ordinated. The beginning of the sensitive period may thus be constrained by developmental factors, including locomotor immaturity and drowsiness, in the first hours that follow hatching. The end of the sensitive period is signalled by the chicks avoiding highly novel objects.

Filial imprinting is a process whereby young birds form an attachment to their mother, or some artificial substitute. Sexual imprinting which effects the choice of mate occurs later than filial imprinting (Schutz 1965; Vidal 1980). Sexual imprinting is affected by the young bird's experience of other birds, especially of its sibs, as well as of the mother. The consequences of sexual imprinting are not usually observed until later in life when the bird reaches sexual maturity, weeks or months later. In the intervening time the bird will be subject to many experiences, some of which are likely to make their mark on the nervous system. In contrast, during filial imprinting the young chick makes its response, approach or following, at the same time as it is being exposed to an object. The immediacy of the effects of training made filial imprinting attractive for analysing the neural mechanisms of this learning process.

In deciding what animal and what training conditions to use for this analysis a number of factors had to be taken into account. Evidence for the development in precocial mammals of attachments through exposure is relatively scanty (see Sluckin 1972). Where imprinting in mammals appears to be robust, olfactory stimuli may play an important role in the development of the preferences (Carter and Marr 1970; Porter and Etscorn 1974). Olfactory stimuli are difficult to control. For example, whereas an auditory stimulus may be switched on and off, olfactory stimuli tend to persist. In addition, young mammals are fed by their mother, so that the young are likely to form a filial attachment to her smell. These factors impose severe constraints on the experimental study of imprinting in precocial mammals. These animals were not, therefore, the first choice for the neural analysis of imprinting.

A number of precocial birds may be imprinted easily enough on auditory or visual stimuli. Auditory stimuli have certain drawbacks for the study of imprinting. For example, mallard duck embryos begin to vocalize before hatching (see Gottlieb 1971). As a result, it is difficult to control this bird's experience of sound. The domestic chick was finally selected as the experimental animal since its filial behaviour has been well studied, its brain is large enough for experimental manipulation, its yolk sac provides it with nourishment for many hours after hatching, and the birds are in plentiful supply. A major advantage of studying imprinting in the domestic chick is that under appropriate conditions the young birds learn the characteristics of the first conspicuous visual object that they see. By rearing chicks in darkness before exposing them to such an object the experimenter can be confident that no information derived from visual experience has been stored in the brain prior to training. The brain of a chick is not a *tabula rasa* on which experience makes its mark; but the chick's brain may be as good an approximation as many brains are and possibly better than some.

## 1.3 Summary

There is a long history of interest in the neural basis of information storage in the brain. In the last two decades or so some success has been achieved in analysing the storage processes associated with certain aspects of habituation. Habituation is a form of learning in which a behavioural or physiological response to a repeatedly applied stimulus wanes if the stimulus is not associated with reward or punishment. The 'memory' is a 'negative' one; its existence is inferred from the absence of a response to the stimulus. Habituation is found in animals of all evolutionary levels. Responses which are controlled by isolated parts of the nervous system may also habituate, though the parametric properties may differ from those of habituation occurring in animals with intact nervous systems. The evidence presented suggests that behavioural habituation is brought about by a self-generated depression of transmission occurring somewhere, especially at synapses, in the pathway linking the sensory receptors to the neurones controlling the response. Depressed transmission occurring in a particular set of neurones activated by a particular stimulus probably forms the basis of the memory not to respond to that stimulus.

Other forms of learning entail, for example, the elaboration of a new response, or the modification, but not merely the loss, of an old one. The neural bases of information storage in these forms of learning have posed problems that are less tractable than those posed by the 'decremental' behaviour of habituation. Reasons for this difference are given. Reasons are also given why the study of imprinting held promise for the neural analysis of memory. The characteristics of filial imprinting in the domestic chick are briefly described.

## References

Alkon, D. L. (1984). Calcium-inactivated potassium currents: a biophysical memory trace. *Science* **226**, 1037–45.

Applewhite, P. B. and Gardner, F. T. (1971). Theory of protozoan habituation. *Nature new Biol.* **230**, 285–7.

Bateson, P. P. G. (1966). The characteristics and context of imprinting. *Biol. Rev.* **41**, 177–220.

Bell, C., Sierra, G., Buendia, N., and Segundo, J. P. (1964). Sensory properties of neurones in the mesencephalic reticular formation. *J. Neurophysiol.* **27**, 961–87.

Berger, H. (1930). Uber das Electrenkephalogramm des Menschen. Zweite Mitteilung. *J. Psychol. Neurol.* **40**, 160–79. (English translation in *Electroencephal. clin. Neurophysiol.* 1969, Suppl. 28, 75–93.)

Brindley, G. S. (1967). The classification of modifiable synapses and their use in models for conditioning. *Proc. R. Soc. B* **168**, 361–76.

Brown, M. W. (1982). Evidence for a temporary memory in activity of cat hippocampal neurones. *J. Physiol., Lond.* **328**, 42–3P.

Bruner, J. and Tauc, L. (1966). Habituation at the synaptic level in *Aplysia. Nature, Lond.* **210**, 37–9.

Bryant, S. H. (1959). The function of the proximal synapse of the squid stellate ganglion. *J. gen. Physiol.* **42**, 609–16.

Buchwald, J. S., Halas, E. S., and Schramm, S. (1965). Progressive changes in efferent unit responses to repeated cutaneous stimulation. *J. Neurophysiol.* **28**, 200–16.

Bullock, T. H. (1948). Properties of a single synapse in the stellate ganglion of the squid. *J. Neurophysiol.* **11**, 343–64.

—— and Hagiwara, S. (1957). Intracellular recording from the giant synapse of the squid. *J. gen. Physiol.* **40**, 565–77.

Cajal, S. R. (1911). In *Histologie du système nerveux de l'homme et des vertébrés*, Vol. 2, pp. 886–90. Maloine, Paris. [Republished 1955, *Histologie du système nerveux*. Instituto Ramon y Cajal, Madrid.]

Carter, C. S. and Marr, J. N. (1970). Olfactory imprinting and age variables in the guinea-pig. *Anim. Behav.* **18**, 238–44.

Castellucci, V. F., Kupfermann, I., Pinsker, H., and Kandel, E. R. (1970). Neuronal mechanisms of habituation and dishabituation of the gill withdrawal reflex in *Aplysia. Science* **167**, 1445–8.

——, Carew, T. J., and Kandel, E. R. (1978). Cellular analysis of long-term habituation of the gill-withdrawal reflex of *Aplysia californica. Science* **202**, 1306–8.

Cynader, M. and Berman, N. (1972). Receptive-field organization of monkey superior colliculus. *J. Neurophysiol.* **35**, 187–201.

Descartes, R. (1961). In *Essential works of Descartes* (transl. L. Blair), Bantham Books, New York.

Dräger, U. C. and Hubel, D. H. (1975). Response to visual stimulation and relationship between visual, auditory and somatosensory inputs in mouse superior colliculus. *J. Neurophysiol.* **38**, 690–713.

Dudel, J. (1965). Facilitatory effects of 5-hydroxytryptamine on the crayfish neuromuscular junction. *Naunyn-Schmiedebergs Arch. exp. Path. Pharmak.* **249**, 515–28.

Ectors, L. (1936). Etude de l'activité électrique du cortex cérébral chez le Lapin non narcotisé ni curarisé. *Arch. int. Physiol.* **43**, 267–98.

Foster, M. (1897). *A textbook of physiology.* Macmillan, London.

Freud, S. (1966). Project for a scientific psychology 1895. In *The complete psychological works of Sigmund Freud* (ed. J. Strachey), Vol. 1. Hogarth Press, London.

Glaser, E. M. and Whittow, G. C. (1957). Retention of a warm environment of adaptation to localised cooling. *J. Physiol., Lond.* **136**, 98–111.

Goldberg, J. M. and Greenwood, D. D. (1966). Response of neurones of the dorsal and posteroventral cochlear nuclei of the cat to acoustic stimuli of long duration. *J. Neurophysiol.* **29**, 72–93.

Gordon, B. (1973). Receptive fields in deep layers of cat superior colliculus. *J. Neurophysiol.* **36**, 157–78.

Gottlieb, G. (1971). *Development of species identification in birds: an inquiry into the prenatal determinants of perception.* University of Chicago Press, Chicago.

Griffin, J. P. and Pearson, J. A. (1967). Habituation of the flexor reflex in the rat. *J. Physiol.,* **190**, 3–5P.

Griffith, J. S. (1966). A theory of the nature of memory. *Nature, Lond.* **211**, 1160–3.

Grüsser-Cornehls, U., Grüsser, O. J., and Bullock, T. H. (1963). Unit responses in the frog's tectum to moving and non-moving visual stimuli. *Science* **141**, 820–2.

Hagiwara, S. and Tasaki, I. (1958). A study on the mechanism of impulse transmission across the giant synapse of the squid. *J. Physiol., Lond.* **143**, 114–37.

Hawkins, R. D. and Kandel, E. R. (1984). Is there a cell-biological alphabet for simple forms of learning? *Psychol. Rev.* **91**, 375–91.

Hebb, D. O. (1949). *The organization of behavior.* John Wiley, New York.

Heinroth, O. (1910). Beitrage zur Biologie, namentlich Ethologie und Psychologie der Anatiden. *Verh. 5th int. Orn. Kongr.* **5**, 589–702.

Held, H. (1897). Beiträge zur Struktur der Nervenzellen und ihren Fortsätze. *Arch. Anat. Physiol. Lpz.* **204**, Suppl. 273.

Hess, E. H. (1973). *Imprinting: early experience and the developmental psychobiology of attachment.* Van Nostrand Rheinhold, New York.

Hinde, R. A. (1954a). Factors governing the changes in strength of a partially inborn response, as shown by the mobbing behaviour of the chaffinch (*Fringilla coelebs*). I. The nature of the response and an examination of its course. *Proc. R. Soc. B* **142**, 306–31.

—— (1954*b*). Factors governing the changes in strength of a partially inborn response, as shown by the mobbing behaviour of the chaffinch (*Fringilla coelebs*). II. The waning of the response. *Proc. R. Soc. B* **142**, 331–58.

—— (1960). Factors governing the changes in strength of a partially inborn response, as shown by the mobbing behaviour of the chaffinch (*Fringilla coelebs*). III. The interaction of short-term and long-term incremental and decremental effects. *Proc. R. Soc. B* **153**, 398–420.

—— (1962). Some aspects of the imprinting problem. *Symp. zool. Soc. Lond.* **8**, 129–38.

—— (1970). Behavioural habituation. In *Short-term changes in neural activity and behaviour* (eds G. Horn and R. A. Hinde), pp. 3–40. Cambridge University Press, Cambridge.

Hobson, J. A. and Scheibel, A. B. (eds) (1980). The brainstem core: sensorimotor integration and behavioural state control. *Neurosci. Res. Program Bull.* **18**, 1–173.

Holmgren, B. and Frenk, S. (1961). Inhibitory phenomena and 'habituation' at the neuronal level. *Nature, Lond.* **192**, 1294–5.

Horridge, G. A., Scholes, J. H., Shaw, S., and Tunstall, J. (1965). Extracellular recordings from single neurones in the optic lobe and brain of the locust. In *The physiology of the insect central nervous system* (eds J. E. Treherne and J. W. L. Beament). Academic Press, London.

Horn, G. (1962). Some neural correlates of perception. In *Viewpoints in biology* (eds J. D. Carthy and C. L. Duddington), Vol. 1, pp. 242–85. Butterworth, London.

—— (1965). Physiological and psychological aspects of selective perception. In *Advances in the study of behaviour* (eds D. Lehrman, R. A. Hinde, and E. Shaw), Vol. 1, pp. 155–215. Academic Press, New York.

—— (1967). Neuronal mechanisms of habituation. *Nature, Lond.* **215**, 707–11.

—— (1969). Novelty, attention and habituation. In *Attention as a concept in neurophysiology* (eds C. R. Evans and T. Mulholland), pp. 230–46. Butterworth, London.

—— (1970*a*). Behavioral and cellular responses to novel and repeated stimuli. In *The neural control of behavior* (eds R. E. Whalen, R. F. Thompson, M. Verzeano, and N. M. Weinberger), pp. 103–27. Academic Press, New York.

—— (1970*b*). Changes in neuronal activity and their relationship to behaviour. In *Short-term changes in neural activity and behaviour* (eds G. Horn and R. A. Hinde), pp. 567–606. Cambridge University Press, Cambridge.

—— (1971*a*). Habituation and memory. In *Biology of memory* (ed. G. Adám), pp. 267–84. Akadémiai kiadó, Budapest.

—— (1971*b*). Biochemical, morphological and functional changes in the central nervous system associated with experience. *Activitas nervosa superior* **13**, 119–30.

—— and Hill, R. M. (1964). Habituation of the response to sensory stimuli of neurons in the brain stem of rabbits. *Nature, Lond.* **202**, 296–98.

——, —— (1966). Responsiveness to sensory stimulation of units in the superior colliculus and subjacent tectotegmental regions of the rabbit. *Exp. Neurol.* **14**, 199–223.

—— and Rowell, C. H. F. (1968). Medium and long-term changes in the behaviour of visual neurones in the tritocerebrum of locusts. *J. exp. Biol.* **49**, 143–70.

—— and Wright, M. J. (1970). Characteristics of transmission failure in the squid stellate ganglion: a study of a simple habituating system. *J. exp. Biol.* **52**, 217–31.

Hubel, D. H. (1982). Exploration of the primary visual cortex, 1955–78. *Nature, Lond.* **299**, 515–24.

Hughes, G. M. and Tauc, L. (1963). An electrophysiological study of the anatomical relations of two giant nerve cells in *Aplysia depilans. J. exp. Biol.* **40**, 469–86.

Humphrey, G. (1930). Le Chatalier's rule and the problem of habituation and dehabituation in *Helix albolabris. Psychol. Forsch.* **13**, 113–27.

Humphrey, G. (1933). *The nature of learning in its relation to the living system.* Harcourt, New York.

Jassik-Gerschenfeld, D. (1966). Activity of somatic origin evoked in the superior colliculus of the cat. *Exp. Neurol.* **16**, 104–18.

Katz, B. (1969). *The release of neural transmitter substances.* Liverpool University Press, Liverpool.

—— and Miledi, R. (1967). The timing of calcium action during neuromuscular transmission. *J. Physiol., Lond.* **189**, 535–44.

——, —— (1969). Tetrodotoxin resistant activity in presynaptic terminals. *J. Physiol., Lond.* **203**, 459–87.

Kelly, R. B., Deutsch, J. W., Carlson, S. S. and Wagner, J. A. (1979). Biochemistry of neurotransmitter release. *A. Rev. Neurosci.* **2**, 399–446.

Klein, M., Shapiro, E. and Kandel, E. R. (1980). Synaptic plasticity of the modulation of $Ca^{2+}$ current. *J. exp. Biol.* **89**, 117–57.

Knott, J. R. and Henry, C. E. (1941). The conditioning of the blocking of the alpha rhythm of the human electroencephalogram. *J. exp. Psychol.* **28**, 134–44.

Kopytova, F. V. and Rabinovich, M. G. (1967). [Microelectrode study of the conditioned reflex to time.] *Pavlov. J. higher nerv. Activ.* **17** (6) (in Russian).

Krasne, F. B. and Roberts, A. (1967). Habituation of the crayfish escape response during release from inhibition induced by picrotoxin. *Nature, Lond.* **215**, 769–70.

Kupfermann, I. and Kandel, E. R. (1969). Neural controls of a behavioral response mediated by the abdominal ganglion of *Aplysia. Science,* **164**, 847–50.

——, Pinsker, H., Castellucci, V. and Kandel, E. R. (1970). Neuronal correlates of habituation and dishabituation of the gill withdrawal reflex in *Aplysia. Science* **167**, 1743–5.

Lashley, K. S. (1950). In search of the engram. *J. Symp. Soc. exp. Biol.* **4**, 454–82.

Lehner, G. F. J. (1941). A study of the extinction of unconditioned reflexes. *J. exp. Psychol.* **29**, 435–56.

Lettvin, J. Y., Maturana, H. R., Pitts, W. H., and McCulloch, W. S. (1961). Two remarks on the visual system of the frog. In *Sensory communication* (ed. W. A. Rosenblith), pp. 757–76. MIT Press, Boston, and John Wiley, New York.

Locke, J. (1690). *Essay concerning human understanding,* Book II, Chapter XXXIII, paragraph 6. London.

Lorenz, K. (1935). Der Kumpaan in der Umwelt des Vogels. *J. Orn., Lpz.* **83**, 137–213, 289–413.

Lorenz, K. (1937). The companion in the bird's world. *Auk* **54**, 245–73.

Marr, D. (1969). A theory of cerebellar cortex. *J. Physiol., Lond.* **202**, 437–70.

Masland, R. H., Chow, K. L., and Stewart, D. L. (1971). Receptive field characteristics of superior colliculus neurons in the rabbit. *J. Neurophysiol.* **34**, 148–56.

Miledi, R. (1973). Transmitter release induced by injection of calcium ions into nerve terminals. *Proc. R. Soc. B* **183**, 421–5.

—— and Slater, C. R. (1966). The action of calcium on neuronal synapses in the squid. *J. Physiol., Lond.* **184**, 473–98.

Milner, P. M. (1957). The cell assembly: Mark II. *Psychol. Rev.* **64**, 242–52.

Pavlov, I. P. (1927). *Lectures on conditioned reflexes.* International Publishers, New York.

Pinsker, H., Castellucci, V., Kupfermann, I., and Kandel, E. R. (1970). Habituation and dishabituation of the gill withdrawal reflex in *Aplysia. Science* **167**, 1740–2.

Porter, R. H. and Etscorn, F. (1974). Olfactory imprinting resulting from brief exposure in *Acomys cahirinus. Nature, Lond.* **250**, 732–3.

Prosser, C. and Hunter, W. S. (1936). The extinction of startle responses and spinal reflexes in the white rat. *Am. J. Physiol.* **117**, 609–18.

Rheinberger, M. and Jasper, H. H. (1937). Electrical activity of the cerebral cortex in the unanesthetized cat. *Am. J. Physiol.* **119**, 186–96.

Roberts, M. V. B. (1962). The giant fibre reflex of the earthworm *Lumbricus terrestris* L. II. Fatigue. *J. exp. Biol.* **39**, 229–37.

Rowell, C. H. F. (1970). Incremental and decremental processes in the insect central nervous system. In *Short-term changes in neural activity and behaviour* (eds G. Horn and R. A. Hinde), pp. 237–80. Cambridge University Press, Cambridge.

—— and Horn, G. (1968). Dishabituation and arousal in the response of single nerve cells in an insect brain. *J. exp. Biol.* **49**, 171–83.

Sharpless, S. and Jasper, H. (1956). Habituation of the arousal reaction. *Brain* **79**, 655–80.

Shepherd, G. M. (1979). *The synaptic organization of the brain* (2nd edn). Oxford University Press, Oxford.

Sherrington, C. S. (1898). Experiments in examination of the peripheral distribution of the fibres of the posterior roots of some spinal nerves. *Phil. Trans. R. Soc.* **190**, 45–186.

—— (1906). *The integrative action of the nervous system.* Constable, London.

Schutz, D. P. (1965). *Sensory restriction.* Academic Press, New York.

Schwarz, J. H., Bernier, L., Castelluci, V. F., Palazzolo, M., Saitoh, T., Stapleton, A., and Kandel, E. R. (1983). What molecular steps determine the time course of the memory for short-term sensitization in *Aplysia*? *Cold Spring Harb. Symp. quant. Biol.* **48**, 811–9.

Sluckin, W. (1972). *Imprinting and early learning.* Methuen, London.

Sokolov, E. N. (1960). Neuronal models and the orienting reflex. In *The central nervous system and behavior* (ed. M. A. B. Brazier), pp. 187–276. Josiah Macy Jr Foundation, New York.

—— (1963). *Perception and the conditioned reflex.* Pergamon Press, London.

—— (1965). Inhibitory conditioned reflex at a single unit level. *Proc. XXIII int. Congr. Physiol.* **4**, 340–3.

——, Arakelov, G. G., and Levinson, L. B. (1967). [Habituation of the neurones lacking spontaneous activity to repeated electrical stimulation in the mollusc *Limnaea stagnalis*.] *J. evol. Biochem. Physiol.* **3**, 147–53 (in Russian).

Spencer, W. A., Thompson, R. F., and Neilson, D. R., Jr (1966*a*). Response decrement of the flexion reflex in the acute spinal cat and transient restoration by strong stimuli. *J. Neurophysiol.* **29**, 221–39.

——, ——, —— (1966*b*). Alterations in responsiveness of ascending and reflex pathways activated by iterated cutaneous afferent volleys. *J. Neurophysiol.* **29**, 240–52.

——, ——, —— (1966*c*). Decrement of ventral root electrotonus and intracellularly recorded PSPs produced by iterated cutaneous afferent volleys. *J. Neurophysiol.* **29**, 253–274.

Spalding, D. A. (1873). Instinct, with original observations on young animals. *Macmillan's Mag.* **27**, 282–93. [Reprinted in 1954 in *Br. J. Anim. Behav.* **2**, 2–11.]

Takeuchi, A. and Takeuchi, N. (1962). Electrical changes in pre- and post-synaptic axons of the giant synapse of *Loligo. J. gen. Physiol.* **45**, 1181–93.

Tanzi, E. (1893). I fatti e le induzioni nell' odierna istologia del sistema nervoso. *Riv. sper. Freniat. Med. leg. Alien. ment.* **19**, 419–72.

Thompson, R. F. and Spencer, W. A. (1966). Habituation: a model phenomenon for the study of neuronal substrates of behavior. *Psychol. Rev.* **173**, 16–43.

——, Berger, T. W., and Madden, J., IV (1983). Cellular processes of learning and memory in the mammalian CNS. *A. Rev. Neurosci.* **6**, 447–91.

Thorpe, W. H. (1956). *Learning and instinct in animals.* Methuen, London.

Vidal, J. M. (1980). The relations between filial and sexual imprinting in the domestic fowl: effects of age and social experience. *Anim. Behav.* **28**, 880–91.

Vinogradova, O. (1970). Registration of information and the limbic sysem. In *Short-term changes in neural activity and behaviour* (eds G. Horn and R. A. Hinde), pp. 95–140. Cambridge University Press, Cambridge.

Voronin, L. L. (1976). Microelectrode study of neurophysiological mechanisms of conditioning. In *Soviet Research Reports* (ed. C. D. Woody), Vol. 2, pp. 1–59. Brain Information Service, University of California, Los Angeles.

Wall, P. D. (1970). Habituation and post-tetanic potentiation in the spinal cord. In *Short-term changes in neural activity and behaviour* (eds G. Horn and R. A. Hinde), pp. 181–210. Cambridge University Press, Cambridge.

Weight, F. F. and Erulkar, S. D. (1976). Modulation of synaptic transmitter release by repetitive postsynaptic action potentials. *Science* **193**, 1023–5.

Whitfield, I. C. (1967). *The auditory pathway.* Arnold, London.

Wickelgren, B. G. (1967a). Habituation in spinal motorneurones. *J. Neurophysiol.* **30**, 1404–23.

—— (1967b). Habituation of spinal interneurones. *J. Neurophysiol.* **30**, 1424–38.

Woody, C. D. (1982). *Memory, learning and higher function.* Springer-Verlag, New York.

Young, J. Z. (1939). Fused neurons and synaptic contacts in the giant nerve fibres of cephalopods. *Phil. Trans. R. Soc. B* **229**, 465–503.

# 2
# Biochemical consequences of imprinting

Before the 1960s most theoretical formulations of the neural basis of memory did not take habituation into account. These formulations were, implicitly, concerned with the mechanisms of information storage associated with other, operationally different types of learning (p. 25). Following this precedent, in the discussions which follow the unqualified word 'learning' will refer to forms of learning other than habituation.

There is good experimental evidence that habituation involves a progressive weakening of specific connections between neurones. In contrast, it has for long been believed, in the absence of experimental evidence, that the memory associated with other forms of learning involves a strengthening of specific connections between neurones. This strengthening is considered to increase the likelihood that an impulse in the presynaptic neurone will evoke an impulse in the postsynaptic neurone, facilitating transmission through a particular pathway in the nervous system. The effect could be achieved by strengthening excitatory synapses. A similar strengthening of inhibitory synapses could have a quite different consequence, an impulse in the presynaptic fibre more powerfully inhibiting the postsynaptic neurone. Young (1966) has suggested that learning is achieved by the inhibition of unwanted pathways. An increase in the effectiveness of inhibitory synapses could provide a mechanism for this functional disconnection. Quite possibly both excitatory and inhibitory synapses are involved in learning. The important point, however, is that the requirements of quite different models can be satisfied by one cellular process, a strengthening of synaptic linkages.

The possibility that synaptic changes are involved in memory could be subjected to experimental analysis if the sites of information storage in the central nervous system were known. It is, however, precisely this question of anatomical localization that has proved so difficult to resolve. In order to analyse the cellular mechanisms it is necessary to know the location of these sites. Without this information the highly sophisticated analytic techniques available to the biologist cannot be deployed. For example, the microelectrode and the electron microscope can provide marvellously detailed information about cellular organization, but a prerequisite of using these tools is to know where the electrode is to be directed or which cubic millimetre of brain tissue to remove for sectioning and viewing. Clearly it is critical for further advance to identify the sites at which the postulated changes are occurring. It is perhaps worth emphasizing that the advances which have been made in understanding the neural mechanisms of habituation were contingent on localizing the regions in the nervous system at which decremental neuronal and synaptic changes occurred.

How might regions that are critically involved in memory be identified? The postulated changes in the strength of synaptic linkages could be brought about in many ways. For example, the number of synapses between two cells might increase, or the terminals of the presynaptic axon might expand. In either case the change would have the consequence that an impulse in the presynaptic fibre would exert a greater control over the excitability of the postsynaptic neurone by influencing the permeability of a larger area of its membrane. More subtle ways of increasing synaptic efficiency could be achieved by increasing the number of receptor sites on the postsynaptic membrane or by changing the shape, or conformation, of receptor proteins in this membrane. Indeed, many forms of plastic change at synapses are likely to involve proteins since these macromolecules are fundamental to all aspects of neuronal structure and function. An increased demand for protein may stimulate protein synthesis. Thus the hypothesis that information storage involves the strengthening of synapses has the implication that the rate of protein synthesis is likely to increase in the affected neurones when the synaptic changes occur. This implication provides a promising starting point for an experimental analysis of the neural bases of memory: when animals are trained, the rate of protein synthesis should increase in those regions involved in storage. If such an increase were detected, its precise relationship to the learning process could be investigated. It would, of course, be naive to expect that such an increase would be exclusive to those regions; the best hope is that amongst the regions in which an increase in protein synthesis is detected are those which are involved in storage.

## 2.1 Protein metabolism

Amino acids are the building blocks of proteins. When protein synthesis increases, the uptake of amino acids will also increase. The increased uptake can be detected by using an appropriate radioactively labelled amino acid, which will be incorporated into the newly assembled protein. If the rate of protein synthesis in a region of the brain increases as a result of some training procedure, incorporation of the labelled amino acid should also increase. Accordingly, radioactivity in the region should be higher in the brains of the trained animals than in those of untrained controls.

There are a number of methods for localizing regions responding in this way. A simple method is to divide the brain into a number of samples and measure the amount of radioactivity present in each of them. The values obtained for corresponding samples from the brains of trained and untrained animals could then be compared. This method, which offers a relatively straightforward way of mapping the general metabolic activity of the brain, has the advantage that it is simple to use. The animal is injected with a radioactive amino acid, one which is incorporated into a wide range of proteins. Such an amino acid is lysine. Lysine can be labelled with tritium, $^3H$, which is the radioactive isotope of hydrogen. Soon after the animal has received the injection it can be trained. During this time, some of the circulating [$^3H$]lysine will be incorporated into newly synthesized protein. To determine the amount of the precursor which has been incorporated, the animal is killed and the brain sample quickly removed. The first step in this analysis is to homogenize the sample and to determine the protein content of a portion of the homogenate. Trichloracetic acid is added to another portion of the homogenate. The consequences of adding the acid is that proteins, some of which will contain the [$^3H$]lysine, are precipitated out of solution. The unincorporated [$^3H$]lysine remains in solution (Fig. 2.1). The precipitate, or the acid-insoluble fraction, is then separated from the supernatant and the radioactivity in the acid-insoluble fraction measured. Radioactivity is expressed as the number of disintegrations per minute per milligram of protein (specific activity) and provides a measure of the extent to which the radioactive amino acid has been incorporated into protein.

Not surprisingly, this method has its limitations. For one thing anatomical localization is crude. Another thing is that the relationship between synthesis and incorporation of a labelled precursor is not a simple one so that the

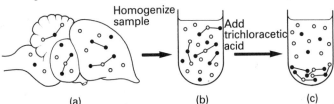

**Fig. 2.1.** Method used for measuring the amount of radioactive lysine incorporated into acid-insoluble substances. The radioactive precursor is injected into the heart region and is distributed throughout the body. A few molecules of radioactive (filled circles) and unlabelled (open circles) lysine are shown distributed in the chick brain (a). Some of the lysine molecules, shown linked together, have been incorporated into proteins which are being synthesized during the time the radioactive precursor is present. A sample of the brain is removed and homogenized (b). Incorporated and unincorporated precursors are separated by adding 10 per cent trichloracetic acid. When this is done the proteins, which are macromolecules, precipitate out of solution (c). The sample is then centrifuged and the precipitate separated from the supernatant fluid. The precipitate is then washed, solubilized, and the radioactivity measured.

results of such studies have to be interpreted with great caution (see Horn, Rose, and Bateson 1973). Nevertheless, if the technique yields encouraging results more refined methods of analysis can easily by employed. These considerations made the method of precursor labelling the one of choice in our first biochemical study of imprinting in the domestic chick (Bateson, Horn, and Rose 1972). The study was a preliminary enquiry into the question of whether any regions of the brain are selectively activated during this learning process.

In this study domestic chicks were hatched and kept in darkness until they were exposed to a conspicuous object at a stage of development when imprinting readily occurs. The incorporation of radioactive lysine into three brain regions of these experimental birds was measured. Corresponding measures were obtained from two control groups of chicks. One of these groups was kept in the light, but not subjected to the imprinting procedure; chicks in the remaining group were kept in darkness. No attempt was made to measure learning directly by giving the experimental group a choice between the imprinting stimulus and a dissimilar object. Learning was presumed to have occurred on the grounds that, in earlier experiments, chicks exposed to the same imprinting stimulus preferred it to a novel object (Bateson and Wainright 1972).

The imprinting stimulus that we used was similar in shape to the one illustrated in Fig. 2.2(a). The two larger surfaces were orange-coloured. The box rotated at 85 revolutions per minute. Approximately 17 hours after hatching the experimental chicks were placed in individual pens in an arena (Fig. 2.3). The floor and three walls of each pen were opaque. The fourth wall facing the centre of the area was made of transparent Perspex through which the chicks could see the flashing orange light. The roof of each pen was open and the whole area illuminated from above by a 60 watt bulb. Chicks in the light control group were placed in pens similar to those in which the experimental chicks were placed, except that the wall facing the flashing light was opaque. The third group of chicks, the dark controls was placed close to the arena and kept in similar pens to those of the other chicks except that the pens were covered by a thick black cloth. Thus all groups of chicks were exposed to the sound of the motor which drove the rotating light, two groups were exposed to the overhead light (experimentals and light controls) but only one group, the experimental chicks, could see the orange box.

In addition to the two control groups a further control procedure was included into the experimental design. The intention of this refinement was to clarify the behavioural significance of any biochemical differences which might be found between the brains of the three groups of chicks. The control procedure introduced was based on the work of Gottlieb (1961). He exposed domestic (Peking) mallard ducklings (*Anas platyrhynchos*) to a model of a mallard drake. Each duckling was subsequently given a choice

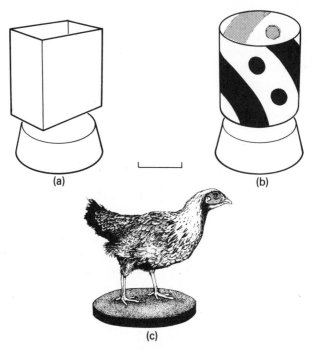

**Fig. 2.2.** Examples of objects which have been used as imprinting stimuli in various experiments described in the text. Stimulus A consists of a 12 V, 45 W lamp over which was placed a coloured filter and round which rotated a plastic box. The two largest surfaces of the box were translucent and the two narrower vertical surfaces blacked out. The object shown in (b) had a similar construction to that shown in (a), but was surrounded by a translucent plastic cylinder painted with two diagonal black stripes between which were two black circular patches. The stuffed jungle-fowl (c) was illuminated by a spot-light, and rotated on a stand. Scale bar 10 cm.

between that model and the model of another mallard duck. Gottlieb showed that the frequency with which the ducklings selectively followed the training model was related to developmental age, calculated from the onset of incubation (Fig. 2.4). If the same phenomenon occurs in domestic chicks, it should be possible to select two groups of chicks according to developmental age and so optimize the chance of successfully imprinting one group exposed to the flashing box, whilst reducing the chance of successfully imprinting the other group of chicks exposed to the same stimulus. If any biochemical changes in the brain are associated with the imprinting process, the changes should be present in the former group of chicks and not present in the latter group. For this reason two sets of chicks were used. Half of the chicks were selected from eggs hatching between 6 and 9 hours before the peak period of hatching and half from eggs hatching at 6–9 hours afterwards. The two sets of chicks were referred to respectively as 'early' and 'late' hatchers.

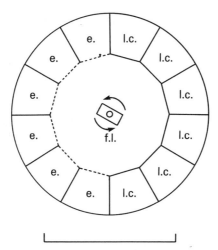

**Fig. 2.3.** Plan view of the pens in which experimental chicks (e.) were exposed to a rotating, flashing light (f.l.) and light control chicks (l.c.) were exposed to an over-head light. The experimental chicks were able to see the flashing light through the transparent Perspex plate (broken lines). All other walls were opaque (continuous lines). The arena was uncovered and was illuminated, with the chicks in the pens, by an overhead electric light. Scale bar 1 m. (After Bateson *et al.* 1972.)

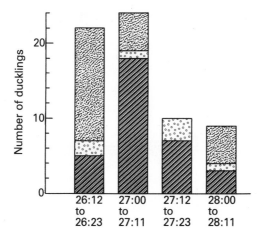

**Fig. 2.4.** Results of test in which ducklings were given a choice between the familiar mallard decoy and a strange mallard decoy. Occurrence of following and imprinting as a function of developmental age and training. The numbers below the bars give the days and hours from the beginning of incubation until training. Ducklings were considered to follow (circled bars) if they approached both decoys or the unfamiliar decoy only. A duckling which followed the familiar model more strongly was con-sidered to be imprinted (striped bars). The length of each section of a bar in the figure represents the number of ducklings in the stated category, for example the length of a mottled bar corresponds to the number of ducklings that did not follow either of the two models in the test. (After Gottlieb 1961.)

The experimental design was the same for early and late hatchers. The experimental chicks were trained by exposing them to the flashing light. The light controls did not see this stimulus, but their pens were illuminated by the electric bulb suspended above the centre of the arena. The total period of exposure of both groups of chicks was 115 minutes. During this time the dark controls were in the covered pens. Forty minutes before the end of this period each chick was briefly removed from its pen and given an injection of 20 microcuries of [$^3$H]lysine into the heart region. After the end of the 115-minute period the chicks were placed in a dark incubator where they remained for 40 minutes. The chicks were then given a 2-minutes test. In this test each chick was placed in an alley at one end of which was a flashing orange light identical to the one to which the experimental chicks had been exposed. The numbers of 'distress' peeps and 'contentement' twitters (Collias and Joos 1953; Andrew 1964) emitted by each chick were recorded.

After the chicks had been killed the brain was quickly removed and divided into three regions (Fig. 2.5). The forebrain hemispheres were

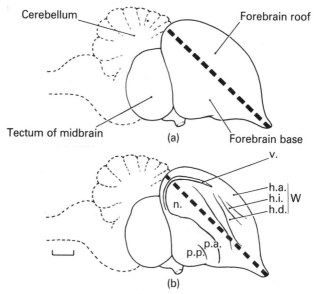

**Fig. 2.5.** Side view of a chick brain. (a) The regions used for studying the incorporation of radioactive lysine into proteins were: (i) the dorsal part ('roof') of the forebrain, separated from (ii) the ventral part ('base') by a cut along the plane indicated by the broken line; (iii) the midbrain which included the optic tectum. The structures discarded are indicated by thin broken lines. (b) Some major telencephalic areas included in the forebrain samples are drawn in outline and are based on sections cut parallel and just lateral to the midline. Abbreviations: h.a., hyperstriatum accessorium; h.d., hyperstriatum dorsale; h.i., hyperstriatum intercalatus. These three structures together comprise the visual Wulst (W). n., neostriatum; p.a., paleostriatum augmentatum; p.p., paleostriatum primitivum; v., ventricle. Scale bar 2 mm.

divided into two parts by an oblique cut extending from the posterior to the anterior poles of the hemispheres. The reason for choosing this plane of section was that the forebrain roof, dorsal to the cut, included the major components of the hyperstriatum, with the associated visual projection areas (the visual Wulst). The midbrain was separated from the forebrain and the hindbrain, by two vertical cuts one placed immediately in front and the other immediately behind the large lobes of the optic tectum. The midbrain with its optic tectum, which receives a major input from each retina, was retained; the hindbrain and the cerebellum were discarded. The brain samples were frozen separately in pots on frozen carbon dioxide and kept at $-20$ degrees Celsius until they were assayed. Each pot was given a code so that the biochemical analyses was performed without knowledge of the behavioural experience of the chick from which the sample was taken. The specific activity of the acid-insoluble residue was determined. This value provided a measure of the amount of radioactive precursor which had been incorporated into protein.

The experiments were conducted over several weeks, so that the chicks came from several batches of eggs. In order to eliminate variability between batches, the specific activity of the acid-insoluble residue was divided by the mean for all brain samples from the dark controls in that batch. The results, standardized in this way, were expressed as percentages of the mean for the dark control group.

In the brief test at the end of the experiment the early hatching chicks gave significantly fewer distress peeps and more contentment twitters than the late hatchers. The high rate of distress peeps in the late hatchers suggested that at the time of the experiment they had already passed the optimum stage of development for imprinting.

The standardized specific activities for the acid-insoluble material are shown in Fig. 2.6. An effect of exposure to the imprinting stimulus was found in only one set of chicks, the early hatchers, and in only one brain region, the forebrain roof. In this region incorporation in the experimental group was significantly higher than in that of the dark controls. Standardized specific activity of the light control group was intermediate between the other two groups (Fig. 2.6(a)).

Two other results of the experiments are particularly interesting. The optic tectum comprised a relatively large part of the midbrain sample. In the chicks exposed to the flashing light and to a lesser extent in the light controls, the optic tectum must have been bombarded by a barrage of impulses from the retina, and probably transmitted impulses onward to the brainstem and forebrain (see Appendix Section, A.3.1 and Fig. A.5). It is unlikely that the discharge from the retina of chicks maintained in darkness throughout the experiment reached the same level as that in the experimental chicks. Yet the incorporation of radioactive lysine into the midbrain was virtually the same for all three groups, both amongst early and late hatchers;

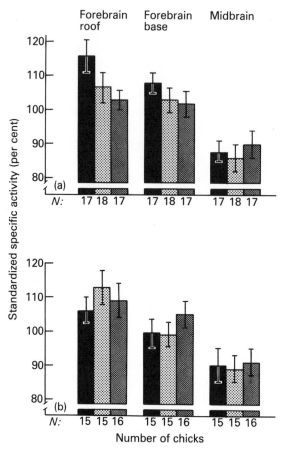

**Fig. 2.6.** Standardized specific activities (means ± standard error of means, S.E.M.) for [³H]lysine-containing proteins of three brain regions for experimental (black bars), light controls (lightly stippled bars) and dark controls (heavily stippled bars). (a) Early hatching chicks. The forebrain roof of the experimental group was higher than that of the dark control group ($P < 0.05$). There were no other significant differences between the groups. (b) Late hatching chicks. There were no significant differences between the groups for any brain region. The value of $N$ below a bar in this and in all other bar diagrams is the number of chicks used in that group. (After Bateson *et al.* 1972.)

that is, differences in visual evoked impulse activity, admittedly inferred, were not associated with differences in the incorporation of the precursor into brain samples each of which contained a large visual projection area. The second, related point concerns the forebrain roof. Both early and late hatching experimental chicks were exposed to the flashing light. Yet only in the early hatchers was this experience associated with a significant increase in the incorporation of radioactive lysine. Again, as in the midbrain, visual experience *per se* was not sufficient to bring about a relative increase in the incorporation of the radioactive amino acid.

It is tempting to suppose that the enhanced incorporation of radioactive lysine into the forebrain roof of early hatching birds and the absence of this effect in late hatching birds is evidence of a specific effect of the imprinting procedure. This supposition cannot, however, be justified on the basis of these experiments alone. For example, the early hatching chicks might have been more active than the late hatching chicks (see Davies and Payne 1982). If so, the differential biochemical changes observed in the early hatching chicks may have been a consequence of this higher level of locomotor activity; the changes might have had little or nothing to do with imprinting. There is thus an ambiguity in interpreting the behavioural significance of the biochemical results. The ways in which we reduced this ambiguity are described in Chapter 3. There are other grounds for caution in interpreting the results of the study, not the least of which is that incorporation of radioactive lysine was found to proceed rapidly in the absence of visual stimulation. This finding indicated that the rate of incorporation of the precursor was a relatively insensitive measure of possible changes in protein synthesis brought about by the imprinting procedure. A more sensitive measure of biochemical change was clearly required.

## 2.2 RNA metabolism

Ribonucleic acid molecules are crucial for the synthesis of proteins. Amino acids are linked to transfer RNA for assembly on ribosomes. These are large complexes of protein associated with several structural RNA molecules. Transfer RNA molecules each carrying a single amino acid arrange themselves on a ribosome to read the genetic information encoded in messenger RNA. The genetic message specifies the sequence and the number of amino acids in the protein macromolecules. With such a central role of RNA in protein synthesis it is likely that changes in protein synthesis will be accompanied and preceded by changes in RNA metabolism. Such changes would be expected as a consequence of imprinting if the increased incorporation of radioactive lysine into acid-insoluble substances reflected changes in protein synthesis (Section 2.1). Accordingly we directed our attention to RNA.

Ribonucleic acid is a macromolecule which is composed of a number of ribonucleotides. Each ribonucleotide contains a molecule of the sugar ribose, a molecule of phosphate, and one of four bases (adenine, guanine, cytosine, or uracil). Although the first three of the bases are also present in DNA, uracil is not. Preliminary studies disclosed that, in the absence of visual stimulation, radioactive uracil was incorporated much more slowly and hence was likely to prove a more sensitive measure of incorporation

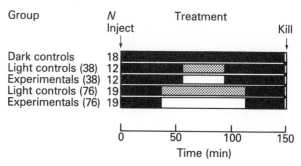

**Fig. 2.7.** Design of the experiment in which radioactive uracil was used as precursor. All chicks were kept in a dark incubator (black bars) after they had been injected with 20 μCi of [³H]uracil and before their final test with the flashing light. The period that the experimental chicks spent exposed to the overhead light and to the flashing light is indicated by the white bars. The period that the light control group spent exposed to the overhead light is indicated by stippled bars. The experimental and light control groups exposed for 76 min were placed in their respective pens 37 min after injection; those exposed for 38 min were placed in their pens 56 min after injection. The time from injection to killing was 150 min. *N* is the number of chicks in each group. (After Bateson *et al.* 1972.)

than radioactive lysine. For these reasons radioactive uracil was selected as precursor in the next experiment, the design of which is shown in Fig. 2.7.

Experimental, light control, and dark control chicks were subjected to stimulus conditions similar to those used in the earlier experiment. The chicks were not divided into early and late hatchers but were selected from the early and middle parts of the hatch. Both experimental and light control chicks were exposed to their respective conditions for either 38 minutes or 76 minutes. These two times were chosen because chicks exposed for 30 minutes to stimuli similar to the one employed in the arena (Figs 2.2(a), 2.3) did not form a preference for the training object and failed, therefore, to show evidence of being imprinted. In contrast, chicks which had been trained for 60 minutes did form a preference and hence had been imprinted (Bateson 1974). Therefore, if incorporation changes were not present after 38 minutes of exposure they might be expected after 76 minutes. At the end of the experiment the brain samples were removed and coded. The subsequent biochemical analysis was similar to that described in the [³H]lysine study since RNA is found in the acid-insoluble fraction of the brain homogenate.

The incorporation of radiolabelled uracil into acid-insoluble material was increased above that of the dark controls in only one group of chicks and in only one brain region. The increase was found in chicks which had been exposed to the imprinting stimulus for 76 minutes (Fig. 2.8). This group of chicks might reasonably be expected to have been imprinted. The increase

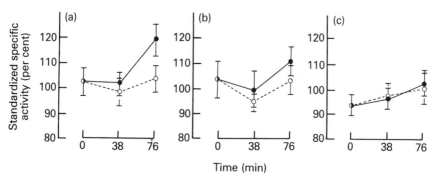

**Fig. 2.8.** Standardized specific activities (means ±s.e.m.) for radioactive uracil incorporated into the roof (a), base (b), and midbrain (c) of experimental (solid circles) and light control (open circles) chicks. Incorporation into the roof of the experimentals exposed for 76 min was significantly higher than that in the roof of the corresponding group of light controls, and the dark controls ($P < 0.05$, one-tailed; $P < 0.05$ respectively). (After Bateson *et al.* 1972.)

was confined to the forebrain roof, the region which had been implicated in the previous experiments (Section 2.1).

## 2.3 Some ambiguities of interpretation

The positive findings of the two experiments were that biochemical changes were associated with exposure to a visually conspicuous object and that these changes occurred in a particular sample of the brain. Before considering the behavioural implications of these findings it is worth considering their biochemical significance. Although one experiment supported the other, there are certain ambiguities of interpretation which are central to data derived from incorporation studies. Whilst increased synthesis of protein will lead to an increased incorporation of the appropriate radioactive amino acid, an increased incorporation of radioactive amino acid into acid-insoluble substances does not necessarily imply increased protein synthesis. At best, incorporation of precursor is a measure of turnover and not of net synthesis. Another difficulty derives from the fact that the immediate precursors to the macromolecules are within the cell. The radioactive precursor must gain access to the interior of the neurone. The labelled precursor reaches the cell surface in the blood stream. The blood flow of a region varies over a wide range of physiological conditions. Accordingly there would be variations in the extent to which the surface of the cell is exposed to the radioactive precursor and, possibly, corresponding fluctuations in the amount of radioactive precursor available for incorporation. Variation in uptake mechanisms across cell membranes and in the pool of the unlabelled precursor all further complicate interpretation.

Some of these difficulties can be circumvented by using *in vitro* methods of analysis. This method has the advantage of eliminating fluctuations in pool size which bedevil incorporation studies conducted *in vivo*. Using such a method Haywood and his colleagues (1970) found evidence that imprinting was associated with an increased RNA synthesis in the forebrain roof, but not in the forebrain base or the midbrain.

Taken at face value the biochemical results together are consistent with the following sequence of changes: experience → impulse activity impinging on neurones in forebrain roof → transcription of DNA message into messenger RNA → protein synthesis.

Events leading to increased protein synthesis are also triggered by certain steroid hormones such as oestrogen, a female sex hormone. It is important, however, to emphasize that the sequence outlined is largely inferential in the case of imprinting (see Horn *et al.* 1973). Certainly RNA polymerase activity was enhanced after 30 minutes of exposure to the flashing light, incorporation of [$^3$H]uracil into RNA occurred after 76 minutes of exposure and changes in the incorporation of [$^3$H]lysine into protein appeared after 115 minutes of training. But the sequence may be more apparent than real: although the time-course of the RNA changes were analysed by varying the times of exposure to the training object, no comparable time-course analysis was made in the study of protein metabolism. Whether or not the model is correct, the relationship of the biochemical changes to the imprinting process is ambiguous. The nature of this ambiguity, and the steps we took to reduce it, are discussed in the next chapter.

## 2.4 Summary

Many forms of learning involve the elaboration of a response to or the association of a response with a particular experience. In such 'incremental' forms of learning the neural change frequently postulated to underlie information storage is the strengthening of synaptic linkages between neurones. This hypothesis has the plausible, though not a necessary, implication that in regions of the brain in which storage occurs there will be an increase in protein synthesis. Studies of imprinting in the domestic chick demonstrated that exposure to a visually conspicuous object was associated with an increased incorporation of a radioactive amino acid into protein, and of radioactive uracil into RNA. Some biochemical ambiguities of these results are discussed.

## References

Andrew, R. J. (1964). Vocalization in chicks and the concept of 'stimulus' contrast. *Anim. Behav.* **12**, 64–76.

Bateson, P. P. G. (1974). Length of training, opportunities for comparison, and imprinting in chicks. *J. comp. physiol. Psychol.* **86,** 586–9.

—— and Wainwright, A. A. P. (1972). The effects of prior exposure to light on the imprinting process in domestic chicks. *Behaviour* **42,** 279–90.

——, Horn, G., and Rose, S. P. R. (1972). Effects of early experience on regional incorporation of precursors into RNA and protein in the chick brain. *Brain Res.* **39,** 449–65.

Collias, N. and Joos, M. (1953). The spectrographic analysis of sound signals of the domestic fowl. *Behaviour* **5,** 175–87.

Davies, D. C. and Payne, J. (1982). Variation in chick sex ratios during hatching. *Anim. Behav.* **30,** 931–2.

Gottlieb, G. (1961). Developmental age as a baseline for determination of the critical period in imprinting. *J. comp. physiol. Psychol.* **54,** 422–7.

Haywood, J., Rose, S. P. R., and Bateson, P. P. G. (1970). Effect of an imprinting preference on RNA polymerase activity in the chick brain. *Nature, Lond.* **228,** 373–4.

Horn, G., Rose, S. P. R., and Bateson, P. P. G. (1973). Experience and plasticity in the central nervous system. *Science* **181,** 506–14.

Young, J. Z. (1966). *The memory system of the brain.* Oxford University Press, London.

# 3
# Real effects of learning?

The finding that biochemical changes are associated with imprinting is consistent with the view that learning involves changes in neural connectivity. However, the biochemical changes could have arisen in a variety of ways and could be attributable to a variety of processes of which learning is only one. Chicks that were exposed to the flashing light may have moved about more, may have been more alert, more excited, and even more stressed than the dark-reared controls. Furthermore these controls, unlike the trained chicks, had little or no visual experience. Any one of these factors, or a combination of all of them, could account for the biochemical differences in the forebrain roof region between the two groups of chicks. For example protein and RNA metabolism of the brain are affected by stress (Bryan *et al.* 1967; Jakoubek *et al.* 1970). Stress is likely to affect the rate of secretion of, for example, adrenaline, growth hormone, adrenocorticotrophin, and cortisol. These hormones may in turn influence the rate of incorporation of amino acids into protein and the rate of synthesis of RNA (Wagle 1963; Jakoubek *et al.* 1972). Thus, whilst changes in neuronal organization associated with learning processes might contribute to the biochemical differences between dark-reared and trained chicks, the attribution of these differences solely, or indeed even partly, to learning processes might be illusory.

All this may seem obvious, but it has proved to be extraordinarily difficult to tease apart neural changes which are the exclusive effect of learning from those 'side-effects', which are not. Progress in distinguishing between these different neural consequences of training is inevitably slow. An experiment which, for example, is designed to control for differences in motor activity between trained animals and their untrained controls, might not control for differences in the amount or complexity of sensory stimulation each group received. A control for differences in sensory stimulation might not control for differences in the motivational state of the two groups of animals. And so on. No single experiment can control for all the side-effects of training. It is possible, however, through a *series* of experiments to reduce the likelihood that particular side-effects entirely account for an observed change in the state of the brain. Accordingly we devised a number of control procedures to determine whether or not the biochemical changes associated with imprinting (Chapter 2) were specific to this learning process.

## 3.1 Dividing the brain

Protein and RNA metabolism in the central nervous system may be affected by motor activity (Hydén 1943; Jakoubek *et al.* 1968) and by stress. If the increased incorporation of radioactive uracil into the forebrain roof of chicks exposed to the flashing light is a consequence of these factors, then the increase should not occur if these factors are controlled. Suppose, for example, that the biochemical differences between the dark-reared chicks and the chicks which had been exposed to the imprinting stimulus resulted solely from stress-induced changes in hormone levels in the trained birds. Suppose, further, that it is possible in an individual chick to 'train' one side of the brain and not the other. Would the trained sides of such brains have a higher level of incorporated precursor due to hormone action than the untrained sides? Probably not because hormones are secreted into the bloodstream, and each side of the brain would be exposed to their actions. Thus, if incorporation was higher in the trained side than in the untrained side, the biochemical effects of exposing chicks to the imprinting stimulus could not easily be accounted for in terms of changes in hormone levels in the blood. Clearly chicks with unilaterally trained brains could serve as useful controls for such non-specific consequences of training.

Following the early work of Myers, Sperry, and Henson (Myers and Sperry 1953; Myers 1956; Myers and Henson 1960) there is now abundant evidence that learning can be restricted, operationally at least, to one side of the brain. The procedure necessary to achieve this restriction in birds was introduced by Cuenod and Zeier (1967) and later exploited by Meier (1971) in his studies of pigeons (*Columba livia*). In these birds the optic chiasma is completely crossed (Cowan *et al.* 1961) so that fibres from the left eye pass to structures in the right side of the brainstem (Appendix, Fig. A.5). The greater part of the onward projection to the forebrain remains crossed (Fig. A.5(a)), but a component crosses the midline in the dorsal supraoptic commissure (Fig. A.5(b)). There are two major visual projection areas in the forebrain. Of these the ectostriatum receives input only from the contralateral eye. The other area, the visual Wulst, receives input from both eyes. If the dorsal supraoptic commissure is cut, then a given hemisphere would receive input from only the contralateral eye.

Meier (1971) took advantage of these anatomical arrangements in his studies of learning in the pigeon. He first covered up one of a bird's eyes. The pigeon was then trained, using the open (first) eye, to discriminate between two shapes (Fig. 3.1). The bird was required to peck one stimulus (the positive stimulus) for food reward. Training was conducted over several days and the learning criterion was 90 per cent correct responses in the first twenty trials of two successive sessions. After having reached criterion the bird was tested using only the originally occluded (second) eye.

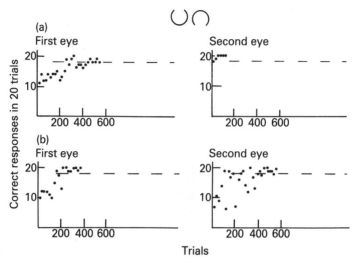

**Fig. 3.1.** Learning curves for pattern discrimination in an intact (a) and a commissurotomized (b) pigeon. The stimuli to be discriminated are shown above the curves. The pigeons learned the discrimination with one eye (the first eye), the other eye being occluded. After criterion (broken line) had been reached, training was continued with only the originally occluded eye (second eye) open. When the intact control (a) used only the second eye, discrimination performance was immediately at criterion, indicating the successful transfer of learning. In the pigeon (b) with the dorsal supraoptic commissure divided, the training period using only the second eye was almost as long as with the first eye. Similar results werre obtained for forty-six control pigeons and for nine pigeons in which the dorsal supraoptic commissure had been sectioned. (After Meier 1971.)

In all birds tested the criterion was reached in fewer trials than was necessary using the first eye (Fig. 3.1(a)). There had thus been a 'transfer of learning'. Meier then repeated the experiment, but this time used birds in which the dorsal supraoptic commissure had been cut (Fig. 3.1(b)). The number of trials to reach criterion using the first eye was similar to that of intact control birds. However, when the lesioned birds were tested with the second eye, which had been occluded during training, no savings were observed. These results together suggest that when intact pigeons learn to discriminate certain patterns using only one eye-system, there is a transfer of learning to the other eye-system. This transfer does not occur if the dorsal supraoptic commissure is cut.

Impulse activity evoked in, say, the left optic nerve by a visual image falling on the left retina reaches both forebrain hemispheres (Perisic *et al.* 1971; Brown and Horn 1979). Hence when an intact pigeon is trained monocularly with the left eye, signals reach both sides of the brain. It is not, therefore, surprising that when the bird is tested monocularly with the right eye, the bird shows great saving in the number of trials to criterion: the right eye is connected to both hemispheres and these connections provide a route of access to information stored in the hemispheres. The situation is quite different when the dorsal supraoptic commissure is cut. Signals originating in the left eye during monocular training pass directly to the right forebrain, not to the left. When the right eye is tested monocularly it has access to the visually deprived left forebrain; they eye does not have access to the visually experienced right hemipshere. Put another way, it is as if the right eye has access to the 'naive' hemisphere and no access to the 'trained' hemisphere and to the information stored there. Not surprisingly, therefore, birds with lesions of the dorsal supraoptic commissure failed to show evidence to transfer. It is perhaps worth remarking that the ipsilateral forebrain could receive visual information by some route other than through the dorsal supraoptic commissure. There are several commissural pathways linking the left and right sides of the brain in birds (see, for example, Zeier and Karten 1973). Furthermore, a small ipsilateral projection from the retina to the thalamus and midbrain of young domestic chicks has recently been described (O'Leary *et al.* 1983). It is thus possible for the 'untrained eye' to gain access to information available to the 'trained eye' using one of these routes. In the experiments of Meier, however, such pathways were unable to support transfer.

It would be wrong to infer from these studies that there is transfer for all visual discrimination habits (see Zeier 1975; Graves and Goodale 1979) or that section of the dorsal supraoptic commissure always prevents transfer when this is known to occur in the intact bird. None the less Meier's results demonstrate conclusively that, in certain tasks, transfer does occur and that this transfer may be prevented by cutting the dorsal supraoptic commissure. In effect, by using this procedure it is possible to train one side of the brain leaving the other side naive. We used this procedure in the imprinting situation with the object of enquiring whether there are differences between the trained and untrained sides of the brain in the incorporation of radioactive uracil into RNA (Horn, Rose, and Bateson 1973).

Between 1 and 4 hours after hatching domestic chicks were anaesthetized and the dorsal supraoptic commissure divided. The chicks were then maintained in a dark incubator for 18–24 hours. An opaque rubber cap was placed over one eye. Shortly afterwards each chick received an injection of radioactive uracil and was then placed in front of a rotating flashing yellow light, similar to that illustrated in Fig. 2.2(a). Instead of using the arrangements for exposure illustrated in Fig. 2.3, each chick was placed in a running wheel facing the training object. The wheel had opaque sides and a wire mesh floor on which the chick stood (Fig. 3.2(a)). The chick could turn the wheel freely but stayed in a constant position approximately 50 centimetres from the light. Rotations of the wheel were automatically counted using magnetic switching devices. The chick was exposed to the training object for a total of 60 minutes.

Since it was essential to know whether these chicks developed a preference for the training object, and if so, whether the preference was restricted to the trained side of the brain, it was necessary to measure the strength of imprinting. The apparatus used to obtain this measure is illustrated in Fig. 3.2(b),(c). The chick was placed in a running wheel similar to that in which it had been trained. This running wheel was mounted on a small trolley which moved on two rails. At one end of the 250 centimetre length of rail stood the 'familiar' flashing yellow light, and at the other end a

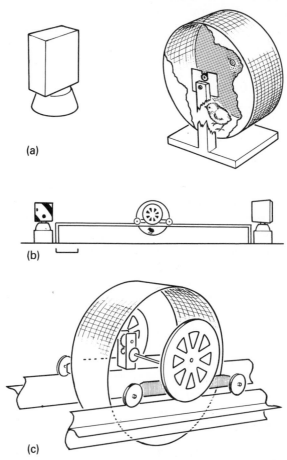

(a)

(b)

(c)

**Fig. 3.2.** Training and test apparatus. (a) Chick in running wheel facing the training object some 50 cm away. For the purpose of illustration one of the opaque sides of the wheel is shown partly removed. The chick ran on the wire mesh. (b) Apparatus used in the choice test. Scale 30 cm. (c) details of running wheel in the apparatus shown in (b). When a bird placed in a running wheel attempted to move in one direction the trolley, and therefore the chick, moved in the opposite direction. ((b) and (c) after Bateson and Wainwright 1972.)

rotating red flashing light (Fig. 2.2(b)). The running wheel was connected to the trolley in such a way that when the chick attempted to approach one object the trolley, together with the chick, moved in the opposite direction. The gearing was such that a chick walking the equivalent of 100 centimetres was carried approximately 18 centimetres the other way. As the chick attempted to approach the object, that object became smaller and less attractive. The apparatus could thus be used for a form of 'behavioural titration' since the point can be measured at which the chick's readiness to approach one stimulus is balanced by its readiness to approach the other stimulus. When a chick attempts to approach the familiar yellow light, say, it is carried towards the other red light. For most chicks there is a point at which it turns round and attempts to approach the red light. It was found that the longer the bird had been exposed to one stimulus before the test the further it travelled away from that stimulus before it turned round and attempted to approach the unfamiliar stimulus. In all choice tests the chick was placed in a running wheel halfway between the two flashing lights. The greatest distance travelled by the wheel away from this midpoint provided the measure of preference. The score was rated positive if the direction travelled was away from the familiar object; that is, the greater the positive score, the stronger the preference for the training object.

In the experiment in which the brain had been divided thirty-six chicks were trained and tested but only twelve were used for biochemical analysis. In six of these the left eye was exposed to the yellow flashing light and in the other six the right eye. The criteria for selection were first that each bird should show visual orientation to a looming object, and second that they should show no motor impairment. Third and most important of all the chicks had to show a clear preference for the flashing yellow light using the eye which had been exposed during training and no clear preference when the other eye alone was used in the test. Biochemical analyses were not performed on chicks that failed to meet these criteria.

Immediately after the final choice test and 150 minutes after injection, chicks which had met the criteria were killed. The brains were rapidly removed, dissected, frozen, and analysed in the ways described in Chapter 2.

The effects of training on the incorporation of radioactive uracil into RNA were investigated. This was done by calculating the difference in the standardized specific activities between trained and untrained sides of the brain (Fig. 3.3). The only significant difference occurred in the roof region of the forebrain. The trained side was higher than the untrained side, the mean difference being 15.2 per cent. There were no significant regional differences in pool size between the two sides of the brain (see pp. 45–6). This finding ruled out the possibility that incorporation of the labelled base into macromolecules could be ascribed to asymmetric changes in pool size resulting, for example, from differences in cerebral blood flow such as might be

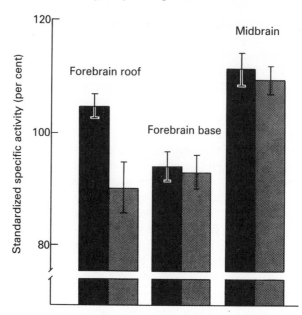

**Fig. 3.3.** Standardized specific activity (mean ±s.e.m.) of RNA from trained sides (black bars) and untrained sides (stippled bars) of the forebrain roof, forebrain base, and midbrain of chicks in which the dorsal supraoptic commissure had been divided. The trained side was contralateral to the exposed eye. Incorporation was significantly higher on the trained side only in the forebrain roof sample ($P < 0.02$). (After Horn *et al.* 1971.)

brought about by exposure to patterned visual stimuli (Bondy and Morelos 1971).

The forebrain roof was the region in which there was a higher incorporation of radioactive lysine into protein in the trained chicks than in the dark-reared controls (Section 2.1). It was also the region where the most rapid incorporation of radioactive uracil into RNA occurred as a consequence of exposing chicks to the training object (Section 2.2). The close agreement between these findings were encouraging. Furthermore, the study using the 'split-brain' chick had reduced the possibility that the biochemical effects of the imprinting procedure were attributable to certain non-specific consequences of training. For example, the biochemical differences between the brains of the trained chicks and their dark-reared controls (Chapter 2) may have resulted from differences in locomotor activity or stress. Such differences cannot readily account for the biochemical differences between the trained and untrained sides of the brain in the split-brain birds. Other non-specific consequences of training are not, however, disposed of by this control procedure.

The combined effect of cutting the dorsal supraoptic commissure and of occluding one eye during training was largely or wholly to deprive one fore-brain hemisphere of visual input. Although impulse activity occurs in the visual pathways even in chicks maintained in darkness the rate of discharge is increased by visual stimulation (Brown and Horn 1979). The consequent higher level of synaptic activity in the non-deprived hemisphere, with the resulting increased demand for transmitter substances, may in turn have increased the demand for proteins and so stimulated protein synthesis. Differences in the amount of impulse traffic reaching the two hemispheres, rather than differences in information storage, could then account for the higher levels of precursor uptake in the roof region of the trained side of the brain. A similar explanation could account for the two earlier biochemical studies of imprinting (Sections 2.1 and 2.2). The biochemical differences between chicks which had been exposed to a flashing light, and their dark-reared controls might have resulted from differences in evoked impulse activity and might have had little to do with learning.

## 3.2 Controlling for some effects of sensory stimulation

In an attempt to resolve some of the ambiguities referred to above, we sought to distinguish short-term changes that might arise through sensory stimulation from longer lasting effects of training (Bateson, Rose, and Horn 1973). In doing so advantage was taken of the evidence that, with various qualifications, the strength of imprinting gradually increases with the duration of exposure to the training object (Sluckin and Salzen 1961; Connolly 1968; Zajonc *et al.* 1973; Bateson and Jaeckel 1976). However, the strength of imprinting cannot be expected to increase indefinitely with the duration of exposure. Accordingly we assumed that the relationship between the cumulative amount learned and the period of exposure to the training object was curvilinear (Fig. 3.4). Such a relationship implies that when chicks are first exposed to the training object they learn relatively little about it. As the period of exposure is extended the rate of learning increases so that the slope of the cumulative learning curve steepens. Thereafter, as the rate of learning declines, presumably because the chicks have progressively less to learn about the training object, the cumulative learning curve gradually flattens off. A property of such a curve is that a given 'movement', say $\Delta t$, along the abcissa may correspond to different movements along the ordinate, depending on where $\Delta t$ is sampled. Consider Fig. 3.4. When the chick is learning at its fastest, the slope of the cumulative learning curve is steepest. At this time a relatively large amount will be learned ($\Delta y_1$) by the chick in the interval $\Delta t$ which immediately follows $t_1$. Later, at say $t_2$, when the rate of learning has declined, the chicks will learn much less about the training object in the interval $\Delta t$; that is, $\Delta y_2$ will be less than $\Delta y_1$. If the neural consequences of training follow a similar curve, a

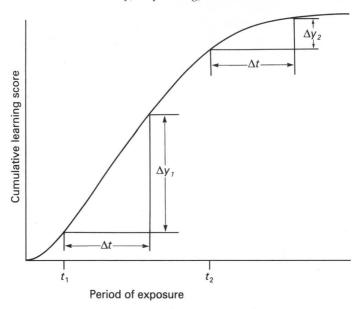

**Fig. 3.4.** Inferred learning curve. The cumulative measure of learning plotted against period of exposure to the training object is assumed to be sigmoid. For further discussion see text.

similar argument holds; for a given period of exposure, $\Delta t$, the neural change after $t_1$ should exceed that after $t_2$.

Suppose that two groups of chicks are exposed to a training object, but one group is exposed for $t_1$ minutes whereas the other group is exposed for longer, say $t_2$ minutes (Fig. 3.4). In this hypothetical experiment the two groups of chicks are injected on the following day with radioactive uracil, and once again exposed to the original stimulus. On this second occasion the exposure period for the two groups is the same, $\Delta t$. When the chicks see the stimulus again, those which had previously seen it for only a short time, $t_1$, should still have something to learn about it. Indeed, for a given period, $\Delta t$, these chicks should learn more about the stimulus than chicks which had previously seen it for the longer time, $t_2$ (Fig. 3.4 $\Delta y_1$ is greater than $\Delta y_2$). Therefore, if incorporation of radioactive uracil is exclusively related to learning, the amount incorporated should be higher in those chicks originally exposed for $t_1$ minutes than in the chicks originally exposed for $t_2$ minutes; that is, incorporation should be related inversely to the duration of the prior period of exposure to the imprinting stimulus. In contrast, if incorporation of radioactive uracil is attributable to short-lasting effects of visual experience, there should be no difference in incorporation between the two groups of chicks: during the period in which the radioactive precursor is being incorporated, the two groups of chicks are exposed to the same stimulus for the same length of time, $\Delta t$. This armchair experiment yields a different prediction for each hypothesis. On the one hand, if the biochemical changes are specifically related to the imprinting process, then incorporation, measured over the second exposure period $\Delta t$, should be lower in the chicks which had initially been trained for the longer period, $t_2$. On the other hand, if the biochemical changes represent short-lasting consequences of visual stimulation, then incorporation should be the same in the two groups of birds.

In the experiments which were designed to distinguish between the two hypotheses, four, instead of two, groups of chicks were used. A few hours after hatching the socially isolated chicks were exposed to constant overhead light for 60 minutes. The 'priming' was done to maximise the effects of subsequent training (Bateson and Wainwright 1972). The chicks were placed in running wheels between 24 and 27 hours after hatching and trained with an orange, flashing, rotating light. The exposure times, $t_i$ were 20, 60, 120, or 240 minutes. Apart from the periods of exposure to light, the chicks were kept in dark incubators in social isolation and were handled in dim green light. The extent to which the four groups approached the stimulus during training is shown in Fig. 3.5(a). As the chicks ran, the activity wheel rotated. Since the diameter of this wheel was 30 centimetres the chicks ran approximately 94 centimetres toward the imprinting object for each complete revolution of the wheel. This object was strongly attractive to the chicks: those exposed to it for 120 minutes ran, on average, well over half a kilometre, whilst those exposed to the object for 240 minutes ran in excess of 1 kilometre.

The chicks' preference for the training object were measured in a choice test using the same apparatus and the same novel object as has been described above (pp. 52–3). The mean preferences of the four groups are shown in Fig. 3.5(b). The strength of their preferences for the training object is correlated with the length of exposure to it. After the test, chicks were returned to the dark incubator.

On the second day after hatching all the chicks were given an injection into the heart region of 20 microcuries of radioactive uracil and returned to a dark incubator for approximately three-quarters of an hour. They were then exposed to the original flashing light for a further 60 minutes (see Fig. 3.4, $\Delta t$). The approach activity of the chicks during the second period of training is shown in Fig. 3.5(c). Birds trained for the two longer periods on the previous day tended to be more active, but the trend was not statistically significant. The chicks were killed 150 minutes after injection, and the brains were dissected as shown in Fig. 2.5(a), except that the forebrain roof was further subdivided. The line of section was transverse and divided the forebrain roof approximately into an anterior two-thirds and a posterior one-third. The brain samples were frozen, coded, and analysed for acid-insoluble radioactivity. To eliminate variability between sets of samples

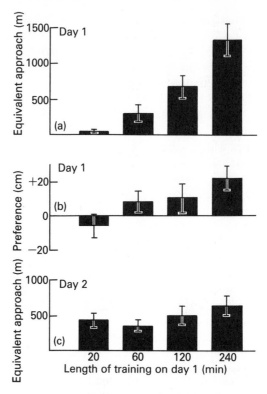

**Fig. 3.5.** Mean and standard errors for chicks' approach activity toward an orange flashing light and for their preferences for it in a choice test. (a) Approach activity expressed as the total distance moved by the running wheel as the chicks ran toward, but did not get closer to the training object. (b) Preference for the familiar object. A chick's preference was the maximum distance travelled from the midpoint on the railway between the familiar light and the novel one. A positive value represents a preference for the training object, a negative value a preference for the novel. Preference for the familiar object was correlated with the length of exposure (Spearman $r_s=0.325$; $P<0.01$). (c) Approach activity during the second period of exposure, on the second day of hatching. (After Bateson *et al.* 1973.)

analysed at different times, each measure of incorporation was expressed as standardized specific activity, that is as a percentage of the mean for all the brain samples in the set from which the sample was analysed.

In the anterior part of the forebrain roof, the incorporation of radioactive uracil into RNA (Fig. 3.6(a)) was negatively correlated with the length of training on the previous day. The difference in the anterior roof region between the group trained for 60 minutes and the group trained for 240 minutes was also statistically significant ($P<0.05$). None of the other differences in the other brain regions was statistically significant.

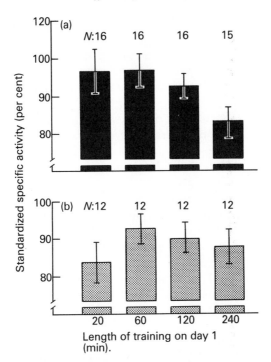

**Fig. 3.6.** Standardized specific activity of radioactive uracil incorporated into RNA in the anterior forebrain roof of 2-day-old domestic chicks (means ±S.E.M.). The experimental birds (a) were trained with an imprinting stimulus for varying amounts of time on the first day after hatching and were all retrained for 60 min on the second day. The control birds (b) received the same treatment on the first day but were left in the dark on the second. The decline in the experimentals as training on day 1 increased from 20 to 240 min is statistically significant (Spearman $r_S = -0.311$; $P < 0.02$) whereas no such relationship was detected in the controls (Spearman $r_S = +0.106$). The number of chicks in each group is given above the corresponding bar. (After Bateson *et al.* 1973.)

The effect of training on day 1 on uracil incorporation into the anterior roof on day 2 could have occurred regardless of whether or not the birds had been trained on day 2. For example, incorporation may have been depressed for a long time as a result of the first period of training; and the longer this training period the greater might have been the depression. An experiment was therefore conducted in which control chicks were trained for 20, 60, 120, or 240 minutes on the first day after hatching. However, on the second day, when incorporation of radioactive uracil was measured, they were not exposed to the stimulus again, but remained throughout in darkness. In every other respect the control birds were treated in the same way as the experimental birds. The approach of these controls during training, as well as their preferences, did not differ from that of the experimental birds. In the control chicks, no significant differences were found between any of the groups in any of the brain regions (Fig. 3.6(b)). Thus the duration of training on day 1 had no effect on incorporation into macromolecules on day 2 if the birds received no further training. This result contrasts markedly with that found in birds trained for 60 minutes on the second day after hatching.

It seemed reasonable to infer that those chicks trained for longer periods had learned more than those trained for shorter periods, because preference for the familiar object continued to be strengthened over the first 240 minutes of training (Fig. 3.5(b)). If this inference is correct, it is also reasonable to assume that the experimental birds trained for longer periods on day 1 had less to learn on day 2 about the object to which they were becoming attached than had those trained for the shorter period on day 1.

It is, of course, possible that when the well trained chicks saw the training stimulus for the second time they were less attentive to it and therefore received less visual stimulation than the birds which had been trained for shorter periods on day 1. However, this possibility is implausible because, if anything, the birds trained for the longer period on day 1 approached the familiar object more on day 2 than did the birds trained for the shorter periods.

When the data from this experiment are considered together with those of previous experiments, particularly those from split-brain chicks, they provide evidence that the biochemical changes occurring in the anterior part of the forebrain roof are linked with acquisition processes involved in imprinting rather than with more general side-effects of training such as short-lasting effects of sensory stimulation.

It remained possible, however, that general neuronal differentation in the anterior forebrain roof was affected by the imprinting procedure: the further the development of the region had proceeded on the first day, the less might have occurred on the second day when the experimental birds were once again trained. It is easy enough to envisage such a process. For example, Valverde (1971) reared mice in darkness to the age of 20 days. He then exposed them to light for various periods of time and subsequently examined the morphology of neurones in the visual cortex. The dendrites of these neurones posses small swellings known as dendritic spines. The spines receive one or more terminals of presynaptic fibres to form 'spine synapses'. Valverde counted the number of dendritic spines per unit length of the apical dendrites of certain cells in the visual cortex. The number of spines per unit length of dendrite increased with the duration of exposure to light. Such an effect might, in principle, occur in the chicks of the two-day experiments described above. Spine frequency might increase to a maximum amongst neurones in the forebrain roof after 240 minutes of exposure on day 1. Subsequent exposure of those chicks on day 2 would not be associated with an increase in spine frequency. If incorporation of radioactive uracil into RNA reflected these growth processes then there would be little incorporation at the time of the second exposure. The situation would be different for chicks which had been exposed to the imprinting stimulus for, say, 60 minutes on day 1. The hypothetical increase in dendritic spine frequency might be sub-maximal after this period of training. Subsequent exposure to the stimulus would be expected to increase the number of dendritic spines per unit length of dendrite. This increase should be associated with a corresponding elevation of incorporation of radioactive uracil into RNA. Hence incorporation in this group of chicks would be higher than in the chicks that had been exposed on day 1 for 240 minutes. Although subsequent experiments (Bradley *et al.* 1981; Horn *et al.* 1985*a,b*) failed to provide evidence of such effects of exposure to an imprinting stimulus on dendritic spine frequency, the general argument is a valid one. The next experiments (Bateson, Horn, and Rose 1975) were therefore undertaken to clarify the interpretation of the results of the two-day study which has been described above.

### 3.3 Biochemical and behavioural variations

When a group of chicks is exposed to an imprinting object for a fixed interval of time, there is a wide variation in the strength of the preference the birds form for the familiar object. There is also a wide range of variation in the amount of radioactive uracil incorporated into the brain. These natural variations in behaviour and brain biochemistry were exploited: if incorporation of radioactive uracil into acid-insoluble substances is closely related to the imprinting process, chicks which form the stronger preferences should have the higher incorporation. If incorporation is related to non-specific neural growth resulting from visual stimulation, then, provided that the chicks are alert, no systematic differences between them would be expected since they would all have been exposed to the stimulus for the same length of time.

One hundred and six chicks were injected with radioactive uracil on the day of hatching and exposed to a yellow (Fig. 2.2(a)) or red (Fig. 2.2(b)) rotating flashing light for a total of 72 minutes. As in earlier experiments the chicks were trained in running wheels which faced the imprinting stimulus. About 20 mintues after the chicks had been trained in this way they were given a choice in the test apparatus (Fig. 3.2(b)) between the familiar rotating light and a novel rotating light. Various measures of each chick's behaviour were recorded and these measures are set out in Table 3.1. After death the brain was divided as before (Fig. 2.5(a)), the forebrain, in addition, being sub-divided into anterior and posterior parts. The incorporation of radioactive uracil into the acid-insoluble fractions of these brain regions was measured.

Preference for the familiar, the only direct measure of learning, was positively correlated with incorporation into the anterior roof of the forebrain:

**Table 3.1** *Summary of the behavioural measures recorded in the experiments of Bateson, Horn, and Rose (1975)*

| | | |
|---|---|---|
| *Training* | Training approach latency | Time from beginning of training to first approach movement |
| | Initial approach | Amount of approach movements during training within 20 min after first approach movement |
| | Total approach | Total amount of approach movements throughout training period |
| *Test* | Test latency | Time from beginning of test to first attempted approach movement |
| | Peep calls | Number of 'distress' calls given in first minute of test |
| | Test movement | Total disturbance travelled on railway by trolley during choice test |
| | Preference for familiar | Greatest overall excursion of trolley from midpoint on the rails during choice test; the greater the excursion away from the familiar object the stronger the preference for the familiar |

the more the birds learned, the higher was the incorporation of precursor into RNA in this region alone. However, this association was weak (Table 3.2). It seemed possible that the relationship between preference for the familiar and the incorporation of radioactive uracil into the anterior forebrain roof might be partially obscured by another factor. Those birds that were quick to respond during training showed a low incorporation into acid-insoluble fractions in the midbrain and forebrain base as well as in the anterior roof of the forebrain (Table 3.2). Since the birds which approached most were in general those that learned most (Bateson and Jaeckel 1974), incorporation into the anterior forebrain roof may have been the result of two opposed effects. One of these effects, shared with other brain regions, may have been to reduce incorporation into the acid-insoluble fraction; the other, specific to the anterior roof, may have been to increase incorporation into this fraction. The presumed negative and general effects of high activity during training were eliminated by expressing the specific radioactivities for the two roof regions as percentages of the specific radioactivities from the forebrain base and midbrain in the same bird. The correlation between the values for the two roof regions and eight behavioural measures are shown in Table 3.3. The only statistically significant correlation coefficient in this table is for the association between preference for the familiar and incorporation into the anterior part of the forebrain roof. This correlation is

**Table 3.2** *Correlations between behaviour and incorporation of radioactive uracil into acid-insoluble material in four brain regions; Spearman correlation coefficients are given (after Bateson et al. 1975)*

|  | Midbrain | Base | Posterior roof | Anterior roof |
|---|---|---|---|---|
| Training approach latency | 0.353** | 0.231* | 0.091 | 0.229* |
| Initial approach | −0.224* | −0.088 | −0.148 | 0.021 |
| Preference for the familiar | −0.150 | −0.182 | 0.093 | 0.181§ |

$*P<0.05; **P<0.001; §P<0.05$ for one-tailed test.
The positive correlations between training approach latency and incorporation indicate that the longer chicks took to approach, the higher was incorporation into RNA. The negative correlation with initial approach indicates that the more chicks approached in the first 20 min after they had started to approach, the lower was incorporation into RNA in the midbrain.

positive and highly significant (see Fig. 3.7). In other words, of all the behavioural measures, only the index of imprinting was positively correlated with the incorporation of radioactive uracil into RNA in the anterior forebrain roof. The association between preference for the familiar and incorporation into the posterior forebrain was not statistically significant.

Do not the results of these experiments lend support for the hypothesis that the biochemical changes are a consequence of some general effect of training on neuronal growth and development? A prediction of this hypothesis was that there should have been no systematic differences in the incorporation of radioactive uracil between birds, provided that they were

**Table 3.3** *Correlations between behavioural measures and incorporation of radioactive uracil into the anterior and posterior roof regions of the forebrain of 116 chicks; Spearman correlation coefficients are given (after Bateson et al. 1975)*

| Phase of experiment | Behaviour | Posterior roof | Anterior roof |
|---|---|---|---|
| Training | Approach latency | −0.136 | −0.062 |
|  | Initial approach | 0.006 | 0.151 |
|  | Total approach | −0.024 | 0.096 |
| Test | Latency | −0.082 | −0.092 |
|  | Peep calls | −0.011 | 0.063 |
|  | Movement | −0.129 | −0.010 |
|  | Preference for familiar | 0.178 | 0.316* |

$*P<0.001.$

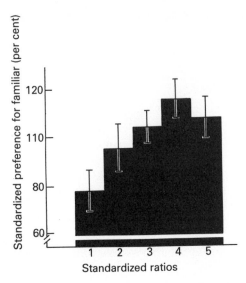

**Fig. 3.7.** Preference for familiar scores (means ±S.E.M.) plotted against incorporation of radioactive uracil into acid-insoluble material in the anterior forebrain roof. The preference score was standardized to eliminate batch differences and differences between the training conditions (yellow or red imprinting object). The specific radioactivity for the anterior forebrain roof of a bird was divided by the mean specific radioactivity of the midbrain and forebrain base for that bird. These standardized ratios, expressed as percentages, were then rank ordered and divided into five groups with twenty-one chicks in each group except for group 5 which contained twenty-two chicks. The Spearman correlation coefficient of 0.316 was highly significant, $P < 0.001$. (After Bateson *et al.* 1975.)

alert during the period of exposure. This stipulation is an important one. If some chicks were drowsy, with their eyelids fully or partially closed, they would have received less retinal stimulation than alert chicks, and there would have been correspondingly less impulse traffic in their visual pathways. Furthermore, subtle physiological processes operate when the degrees of behavioural arousal and alertness vary. There is much evidence to show that variation in these two states is associated with variation in the transmission of evoked activity in the visual pathways, at least in some mammals (for reviews see Horn 1976; Wurtz *et al*, 1980; Rizzolatti 1983) and it would be prudent to suppose that similar processes also operate in birds. Variations in external visual conditions are know to affect the structure of neurones in a visual area of the brain (p. 60; for a review see Lund 1978). It could be argued, therefore, that the more alert the young chick is, the greater will be the influx of visual evoked activity in the forebrain. This high level of impulse activity could powerfully stimulate neuronal growth and RNA synthesis. Since alert chicks would also be expected to have high preference scores, there should be a correlation between preference and incorporation. There should, however, also be a correlation between incorporation and certain other measures of the chicks' behaviour if alertness influences the incorporation of radioactive uracil into RNA. For example, latency to approach the training stimulus provides a measure of alertness since it measures the chicks' quickness to respond to the training object. However, there was no correlation between latency to approach, either in the training or test situation, and incorporation into the anterior part of the forebrain roof. Indeed, none of the measures of behaviour obtained during training was correlated with incorporation into this region of the brain (Table 3.3). Nor, for that matter, was any measure of responsiveness, activity, or distress in the test correlated with the biochemical measure. These results suggest that none of these aspects of the chicks' behaviour could easily account for the changes occurring in the anterior roof region. The natural variability of the birds had been used, therefore, to dissasociate many of the factors which are normally confounded with the storage of information during imprinting.

## 3.4. Comment

The biochemical studies of imprinting had three major objectives: (i) to enquire whether biochemical changes occurred in the brain after chicks had been exposed to an imprinting stimulus; if such changes were found, (ii) to determine whether they had some trivial explanation and (iii) to attempt to localize, albeit crudely, the biochemical changes. The first objective had been achieved (see Chapter 2). So far as the second objective was concerned evidence was gradually accumulating that the rapidly occurring biochemical changes in the anterior part of the forebrain roof could not be attributed to any of the more obvious behavioural side-effects of the training procedure. So far as the third objective was concerned, the early studies had implicated the forebrain roof region and later studies narrowed the focus of interest on the anterior two-thirds of this structure. Progress in reaching the third objective had therefore been only modest. Yet if the biochemical changes were restricted to particular structures in the brain, it was essential to identify these structures. As discussed above (pp. 34–5), further advances would be greatly facilitated by, or might only be possible if there is such localization.

## 3.5 Summary

The biochemical changes which were described in Chapter 2 could have been brought about by a variety of side-effects of the training procedure. Chicks which had been exposed to the imprinting stimulus might have been more alert, more excited, more active, and received more sensory stimulation than their controls. Three experiments are described which were designed to control for these various factors. (i) By dividing the dorsal supraoptic commissure it was possible to 'train' one side of the brain. It was found that the incorporation of radioactive uracil into RNA in the forebrain roof region was higher in the trained side than in the untrained side. (ii) Short-lasting effects of visual stimulation were controlled in an experiment in which different groups of chicks were trained for different lengths of time on the day of hatching and for equal lengths of time on the following day. The results provided no evidence that short-lasting effects of sensory stimulation could account for the biochemical changes observed. (iii) The amount of radioactive uracil incorporated into the anterior two-thirds of the forebrain roof was correlated with the chicks' preferences for the familiar object, a measure of the strength of imprinting, but not with other measures of the chicks' behaviour. The possibility that the biochemical changes reflected some aspect of information storage occurring during the imprinting process was not excluded by these control procedures whereas certain other explanations were.

## References

Bateson, P. P. G. and Jaeckel, J. B. (1974). Imprinting: correlations between activities of chicks during training and testing. *Anim. Behav.* **22**, 899–906.

—— and Jaeckel, J. B. (1976). Chicks' preferences for familiar and novel conspicuous objects after different periods of exposure. *Anim. Behav.* **24**, 386–90.

—— and Wainwright, A. A. P. (1972). The effects of prior exposure to light on the imprinting process in domestic chicks. *Behaviour* **42**, 279–90.

——, Rose, S. P. R., and Horn, G. (1973). Imprinting: lasting effects on uracil incorporation into chick brain. *Science* **181**, 576–8.

——, Horn, G., and Rose, S. P. R. (1975). Imprinting: correlations between behaviour and incorporation of [$^{14}$C]uracil into chick brain. *Brain Res.* **84**, 207–20.

Bondy, S. C. and Morelos, B. S. (1971). Stimulus deprivation and cerebral blood flow. *Exp. Neurol.* **31**, 200–6.

Bradley, P., Horn, G., and Bateson, P. (1981). Imprinting: an electron microscopic study of chick hyperstriatum ventrale. *Exp. Brain Res.* **41**, 115–20.

Brown, M. W. and Horn, G. (1979). Neuronal plasticity in the chick brain: electrophysiological effects of visual experience on hyperstriatal neurones. *Brain Res.* **162**, 142–7.

Bryan, R. N., Bliss, E. L., and Beck, E. C. (1967). Incorporation of uridine.$^3$H into mouse brain RNA during stress. *Fedn Proc. Fedn Am Socs exp. Biol.* **26**, 709.

Connolly, K. (1968). Imprinting and the following response as a function of amount of training in domestic chicks. *Quart. J. exp. Psychol.* **9**, 453–60.

Cowan, W. M., Adamson, L., and Powell, T. P. S. (1961). An experimental study of the avian visual system. *J. Anat.* **95**, 545–63.

Cuenod, M. and Zeier, H. (1967). Transfert visuel interhemispherique et commissurotomie chez le pigeon. *Archs suisses Neurol. Neurochirg. Psychiat.* **100**, 365–80.

Graves, J. A. and Goodale, M. A. (1979). Do training conditions affect interocular transfer in the pigeon. In *Structure and function of cerebral commissures* (eds

I. Steele Russell, M. W. van Hof, and G. Berlucchi), pp. 73–86. Macmillan, London.

Horn, G. (1976). Physiological studies of attention and arousal. In *Mechanisms of transmission of signals for conscious behaviour* (ed. T. Desiraju), pp. 285–99. Elsevier, Amsterdam.

——, Horn, A. L. D., Bateson, P. P. G., and Rose, S. P. R. (1971). Effects of imprinting on uracil incorporation into brain RNA in the 'split-brain' chick. *Nature, Lond.* **229**, 131–2.

——, Rose, S. P. R., and Bateson, P. P. G. (1973). Monocular imprinting and regional incorporation of tritiated uracil into the brains of intact and 'split-brain' chicks. *Brain Res.* **56**, 227–37.

——, Bradley, P., and McCabe, B. J. (1985*a*). Morphological correlates of imprinting. *Behav. Brain Res.* (in press).

——, Bradley, P., and McCabe, B. J. (1985*b*). Changes in the structure of synapses associated with learning. *J. Neurosci.* in press.

Hydén, H. (1943). Protein metabolism in the nerve cell during growth and function. *Acta physiol. scand.* **6**, Suppl. 17, 1–136.

Jakoubek, B., Horácková, M., and Gutman, E. (1968). Changes of protein metabolism during increased functional activity in spinal motoneurones and sciatic nerve. *Proc. Int. Union Physiol. Sci.* **7**, 2150.

——, Semiginovsky, B., Krauss, M., and Erdossová, R. (1970). The alteration of protein metabolism of the brain cortex induced by anticipation stress and ACTH. *Life Sci.* **9**, 1169–80.

——, Buresová, M., Hájek, I., Etrychová, J., Pavlik, A., and Dedicova, A. (1972). Effect of ACTH on the synthesis of rapidly labelled RNA in the nervous system of mice. *Brain Res.* **43**, 417–28.

Lund, R. D. (1978). *Development and plasticity of the brain.* Oxford University Press, New York.

Meier, R. E. (1971). Interhemispharischer Transfer visueller Zweifachwahlen bei kommissurotomierten Tauben. *Psychol. Forsch.* **34**, 220–45.

Myers, R. E. (1956). Function of corpus callosum in interocular transfer. *Brain* **79**, 358–63.

—— and Henson, C. O. (1960). Role of corpus callosum in transfer of tactuokinesthetic learning in chimpanzee. *Archs Neurol. Psychiat. Chicago* **3**, 404–9.

—— and Sperry, R. W. (1953). Interocular transfer of a visual form discrimination in cats after section of the optic chiasma and corpus callosum. *Anat. Rec.* **115**, 351–2.

O'Leary, D. D. M., Gerfen, C. R., and Cowan, W. M. (1983). The development and restriction of the ipsilateral retinofugal projection in the chick. *Dev Brain Res.* **10**, 93–109.

Perisic, M., Mihailovic, J., and Cuenod, M. (1971). Electrophysiology of contralateral and ipsilateral visual projections to the Wulst in pigeon (*Columba livia*). *Int. J. Neurosci.* **2**, 7–14.

Rizzolatti, G. (1983). Mechanisms of selective attention in mammals. In *Advances in vertebrate neuroethology* (eds J.-P. Ewert, R. R. Capranica, and D. J. Ingle), pp. 261–95. Plenum Press, New York.

Sluckin, W. and Salzen, E. A. (1961). Imprinting and perceptual learning. *Quart. J. exp. Psychol.* **13**, 65–77.

Valverde, F. (1971). Rate and extent of recovery from dark rearing in the visual cortex of the mouse. *Brain Res.* **33**, 1–11.

Wagle, S. R. (1963). The influence of growth hormone, cortisol and insulin on the incorporation of amino acids into protein. *Archs Biochem.* **102**, 373–8.

Wurtz, R. H., Goldberg, M. E., and Robinson, D. L. (1980). Behavioural modulation of visual responses in the monkey: stimulus selection for attention and movement. *Progr. Psychobiol. physiol. Psychol.* **9**, 44–83.

Zajonc, R. B., Reimer, D. J., and Hausser, D. (1973). Imprinting and the development of object preference in chicks by mere repeated exposure. *J. comp. physiol. Psychol.* **83**, 434–40.

Zeier, H. (1975). Interhemispheric interactions. In *Neural and endocrine aspects of behaviour in birds* (eds P. Wright, P. G. Caryl, and D. M. Vowles), pp. 163–80. Elsevier, Amsterdam.

—— and Karten, H. J. (1973). Connections of the anterior commissure in the pigeon (*Columba livia*). *J. comp. Neurol.* **150**, 201–16.

# 4

# Cerebral localization

The distinguished neuropsychologist Karl Lashley invested many years of work 'in search of the engram', as he himself put it. Toward the end of his life he wrote, 'I sometimes feel, in reviewing the evidence on the localization of the memory trace, that the necessary conclusion is that learning just is not possible' (Lashley 1950, pp. 477–8). Part of the evidence on which this ironical conclusion is based derived from Lashley's studies of maze learning in rats. So far as learning performance was concerned, he considered one part of the cerebral cortex to be more or less equivalent to any other (Lashley 1929). What mattered was the mass of cortex that was intact after he had made his brain lesions, not which particular part had been removed.

In spite of this heritage, neurophysiological studies of habituation in the early 1960s demonstrated that response decrement did not occur at every synaptic junction between the sensory receptors receiving the repeated stimulus and the muscles involved in the initial response. Transmission failed at particular junctions in this pathway. In other words evidence was accumulating that, in the case of a simple form of learning, the neural changes were localized; one piece of neural tissue was not the equivalent of any other. The same message appeared to be coming out of the work on imprinting. Biochemical changes closely related to this process were not uniformly distributed amongst the various blocks of brain studied. The changes were consistently found in the forebrain roof, more particularly in the anterior two-thirds of this region.

The anterior part of the forebrain roof is a relatively large mass of tissue. It contains millions of neurones and includes a number of anatomically distinct regions. Are the training-dependent changes in the incorporation of radioactive uracil uniformly distributed throughout the anterior forebrain roof or are they localized to one or more of its constituent regions? The techniques which had been employed to study imprinting (Chapter 2) were not well suited to answer this question for a simple practical reason: it would have been necessary to dice the anterior forebrain roof into tiny fragments, each of which would have had to be identified, and to measure the incorporation of the labelled precursor into each one of them. This formidable procedure would have had to be repeated for each chick in the study. An alternative approach to the localization problem was needed. The technique of autoradiography appeared to be suitable, for it provided a sensitive method of detecting a radioisotope whilst allowing good preservation of the histological structure of the brain.

To use the autoradiographic technique a radioisotope is first introduced into the tissue. The tissue must then be fixed to preserve its structure and thin sections of the tissue cut, though the fixing and cutting procedures may be carried out in the reverse order. The tissue sections are then covered with a photographic emulsion in the dark. As the radioisotope decays, charged particles are emitted. Compounds labelled with radioactive carbon, $^{14}C$, were used in the experiments described below. This radioactive isotope, like tritium, emits negatively charged beta particles. The tissue sections, mounted on glass plates, and covered with photographic emulsion are left in darkness for days or even months. Where the isotope lies in close apposition to the emulsion some of the ejected beta particles will pass into it and strike some of the silver halide crystals. When the emulsion is later developed, crystals which have been struck are converted into visible grains of silver.

The autoradiographic technique can be used for localizing radioisotopes at the light-microscopic and electron-microscopic levels. However, such cellular and sub-cellular localization would provide too fine a level of resolution for the imprinting studies, simply because there are so may cells in the anterior part of the forebrain roof. What was needed was a 'macroautoradiographic' technique that could be used to enquire whether changes in incorporation are localized to particular histological *regions* of this piece of forebrain. If the changes proved to be localized in this way then a more refined autoradiographic technique could be employed to study their cellular distribution. Macroautoradiography involves precisely the same principles as microautoradiography though there are, of course, differences in technique. For example, in macroautoradiography the mounted tissue sections are often covered with a plate of film rather than being dipped in photographic emulsion. The emulsion on X-ray film is admirable for these purposes. Compared with the nuclear emulsions used for light and electron microscope work, X-ray emulsions have relatively large crystal diameters. As a result fewer grains per unit area are needed to give a blackening on film that is visible to the naked eye.

### 4.1. Probing with radioactive uracil

The method, as it was applied to the chick brain, is illustrated in Fig. 4.1. $[^{14}C]$uracil was injected into the heart region of a chick. After training, instead of removing the brain and dividing it up (Fig. 2.5(a)) the brain was frozen and cut into sections. These were mounted on glass slides and X-ray film was placed over the slides in darkness and left in place for several weeks. The film was then developed. The degree of blackening of the film

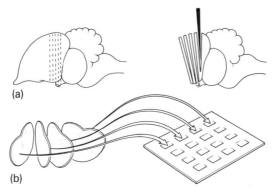

(a)

(b)

**Fig. 4.1.** Diagram of some stages in the preparation of autoradiographs. Radioactive uracil was injected into the heart region and the chick exposed to the imprinting object. Two and a half hours after injection the chick was killed and the brain removed and frozen. Thin sections, 15 μm thick were cut (a) and mounted on glass slides (b). X-ray film was placed over the slides in darkness. Slides and film were left in darkness and the film subsequently developed.

provided an index of radioactivity: the darker the region of film the greater the radioactivity in the corresponding part of the brain section (Fig. 4.4). The degree of blackening of the selected area of the film was determined by placing the film over a small light spot and measuring the optical density of that patch of film. Optical density is a measure of how much the light intensity is reduced by the image on the film.

The optical density of a film image can be determined to a high degree of accuracy. Hence even small differences between imprinted chicks and their controls in the incorporation of a radioactive precursor into a particular region could in principle be detected. The drawback is that the differences could be spurious for a number of quite simple reasons. When tissue is prepared for autoradiography it must be fixed to preserve its histological structure. Fixation has the effect of precipitating macromolecules so that they are stabilized and locked in position in the tissue. After fixation, water is withdrawn from the tissue by immersing it in increasing concentrations of alcohol. These procedures are usually assumed to remove small molecules but to leave macromolecules in the tissue. These assumptions are reasonable safe ones to make if all the experimenter is interested in is the qualitative distribution of a radiolabelled precursor. They are not safe assumptions for quantitative work. Certain fixatives have the effect of binding soluble precursors to the fixed and precipitated macromolecules. A consequence of this fixative action would be to increase the amount of precursor which appeared, spuriously, to be incorporated into the macromolecules. Another difficulty is that some fixatives are associated with a variable loss both of RNA and protein (see Rogers 1973). The consequence of such loss would be to reduce the amount of labelled macromolecules in the tissue. Both of these artefacts of fixation—spurious increases and spurious decreases in the incorporation of radioactive precursors—are severe handicaps for quantitative autoradiography.

In order to overcome these drawbacks a technique was developed for preparing macroautoradiographs which reliably reflected the incorporation of radioactive uracil into acid-insoluble subtances in the brain (Horn and McCabe 1978). The method involved removing the brains of chicks some 2.5 hours after the chicks had received an injection of radioactive uracil. The brain was frozen and sections cut at −30 degrees Celsius. These fresh sections were mounted on slides, immersed in trichloracetic acid, and then washed in distilled water. The object of placing the brain sections in acid was to precipitate the macromolecules (Chapter 2) and so to bind them in position. The object of washing in water was to remove from the sections ions and small molecules which included the unincorporated radioactive uracil. The method was effective in achieving both of these objectives. There was no detectable retention of acid-soluble radioactivity in sections treated in this way, nor was there a detectable loss of acid-insoluble radioactivity from the sections.

With these technical difficulties overcome it was possible to proceed with the enquiry into the possible cerebral localization of biochemical changes resulting from imprinting (Horn, McCabe, and Bateson 1979). Because the autoradiographic technique is time-consuming it was desirable to avoid using brains from chicks that had learned relatively little during training. Chicks that are behaviourally active are likely to learn more quickly than chicks that are inactive. To take advantage of this relationship it was necessary to devise a method for selecting active birds. The method had to be applied to both experimental and control chicks in order to reduce ambiguities in the interpretation of any autoradiographic differences between the two groups. For example, if the brains of behaviourally active imprinted chicks were compared with those of dark-reared chicks selected at random and therefore including inactive chicks, differences between the brains of the two groups could arise from the greater behavioural activity of the imprinted birds and so be confused with an effect of imprinting. This possibility is not merely a theoretical one: the incorporation of radioactive uracil into macromolecules in the midbrain is dependent on the approach activity of chicks (Table 3.2).

The design of the autoradiographic study was based upon the experiment in which groups of chicks were trained for different periods of time on the first day of hatching (day 1) and for an equal period of time on the following day (Section 3.2). With this design, chicks could be selected and matched in pairs on a basis of their activity on day 1. The design also led to the prediction that chicks which had been trained for the longest period on day 1 should have the lowest incorporation on day 2 (see Fig. 3.6(a)).

All chicks were primed by exposing them to a static overhead white light for 30 minutes prior to training (p. 57). Each chick was later placed in a running wheel facing the training stimulus. This consisted of a moving horizontal yellow slit. The slit could be seen in a window and moved upwards at the rate of four slits per second. Above this flashing light was a loudspeaker which emitted the maternal call of the domestic hen. The call was introduced because the tendency to follow moving objects is markedly enhanced if the object makes intermittent sounds resembling the maternal call characteristic of the species (Gottlieb 1971, Chapter 7). The procedure is known to accelerate imprinting on a visual stimulus (Smith and Bird 1963). Chicks were exposed to the training stimulus for either 45 minutes ('undertrained', control chicks) or 180 minutes ('overtrained', experimental chicks) on day 1. The chicks were matched in pairs on the basis of their weight and approach activity during training. Ten pairs of chicks were selected in this way (for one of these pairs the undertrained bird was exposed for 60 minutes and the overtrained bird for 240 minutes). After training the chicks were returned to a dark incubator and, on the following day, given an injection of radioactive uracil. Each chick was subsequently placed in a running wheel and exposed to the training stimulus for 63 minutes. Because this stimulus had been found in other experiments to be an effective imprinting stimulus (Bateson 1979), the chicks were not given a preference test.

The chicks were killed 150 minutes after injection and the whole brain was dissected out and frozen on solid carbon dioxide. Each brain was placed into a jar and given a code number; all subsequent procedures were conducted 'blind'. Serial sections of the forebrain were cut and alternate pairs mounted on glass slides. These sections were prepared for autoradiography using the method outlined above. The sections were then placed against X-ray film. All the films from any one pair of chicks were exposed for the same time, and then developed and fixed under standard conditions.

The optical density of the autoradiographs was measured using a microdensitometer. The selection of sites for making the measurements was done on theoretical grounds and also on the basis of a pilot experiment. In this experiment, six pairs of chicks were trained on a schedule similar to that of the chicks in the main experiment. The section autoradiographs were studied by visual inspection and the training schedule, unknown to the observer, of each bird of a pair was predicted. No decision could be reached for one pair of chicks. Of the remaining five pairs the training schedules were correctly predicted in four of them. In all of these four pairs of chicks the medial part of the hyperstriatum ventrale (see Fig. 4.2) especially its intermediate region, between the anterior and posterior poles of the cerebral hemispheres, was darker in the undertrained than in the overtrained chicks. No other differences between pairs of brains was predictive of behaviour. The results of using the hyperstriatum ventrale as predictor,

*Memory, Imprinting, and the Brain*

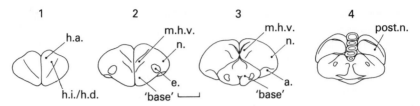

**Fig. 4.2.** Tracings of section autoradiographs showing the sites of measurements for representative slabs. Tracing 1 is a section taken from the anterior part of the forebrain. The remaining tracings are from progressively more posterior sections. Abbreviations: a., archistriatum; e., ectostriatum; h.a., hyperstriatum accessorium; h.i./h.d., hyperstriatum intercalatus/hyperstriatum dorsale; m.h.v., medial hyperstriatum ventrale; n., neostriatum; post.n., posterior neostriatum. Scale bar 3 mm. (After Horn *et al.* 1979.)

though not statistically significant, were suggestive. For this reason the optical density of the medial part of the hyperstriatum ventrale was measured in the main experiment. In addition, the hyperstriatum accessorium, the hyperstriatum intercalatus/hyperstriatum dorsale and the ectostriatum were sampled since these are visual projection areas (Fig. 4.2; Appendix, Fig. A.5). Measurements were made from the neostriatum, a component of the forebrain that has been compared to parts of the mammalian neocortex (Cohen and Karten 1974). The optical density of the archistriatum was also measured. This is a complex of nuclei (Zeier and Karten 1971) which can easily be identified in the section autoradiographs, but it did not prove possible to distinguish the individual components of the complex. Finally, measurements were made of the optical density of a region situated in the ventromedial part of the hemisphere, well within the forebrain 'base' (Fig. 2.5(a)).

Each anatomical region selected for measurement was subdivided into one or more coronal 'slabs', approximately 0.6 millimetres thick and corresponding to eighteen section autoradiographs from a brain. For each region, the number of slabs was the same for all brains. Within each slab, measurements on ten section autoradiographs were averaged and the mean value was then standardized by expressing is as a percentage of the mean of all measurements for that brain. The standardization procedure controlled for differences that might arise from, for example, differences between chicks in the amount of radioactive uracil injected. Only after all measurements had been made was the code, with which the brains were numbered, broken.

Standardized mean optical density was significantly greater in undertrained than in overtrained chicks in a part of the medial hyperstriatum ventrale which extended across two adjacent slabs. The approximate positions of these slabs are shown in Fig. 4.3(a). Sample autoradiographs from the slabs are shown in Fig. 4.4. No such differences between undertrained

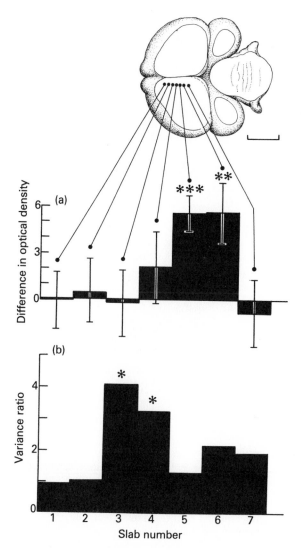

**Fig. 4.3.** (a) Mean differences ±s.e.m. (undertrained minus overtrained) in standard-ized optical density at sampling sites within the medial hyperstriatum ventrale. The approximate locations of the sampling sites are shown on the diagram of a chick brain viewed from above, the dorsal surface having been removed (scale bar 4 mm). **$P < 0.01$; ***$P < 0.001$. (b) Variance ratios calculated from the standardized data for each of the seven slabs within the medial hyperstriatum ventrale. The ordinate indicates variance of the data from undertrained chicks divided by the variance of the data from the overtrained chicks. *$P < 0.05$. (After Horn *et al.* 1979.)

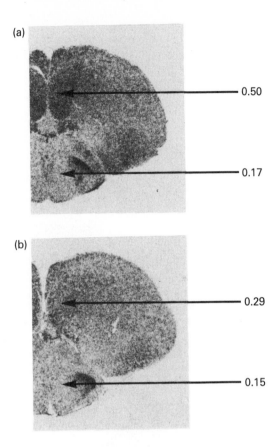

**Fig. 4.4.** Autoradiographs of sections from overtrained and undertrained chicks of a matched pair. Functional activity is measured by the amount of radioactive uracil incorporated into a region. Areas of high incorporation are darker than those with lower incorporation: the higher the value for optical density, the higher the incorporation. The autoradiograph from the overtrained bird (b) is slightly lighter overall than that from the undertrained bird (a). This effect, suggesting a lower incorporation of radioactive uracil into all areas of the overtrained chick, was not consistently distributed between chick pairs. The difference could be due to a variety of factors such as small differences in the amount of precursor injected. Variation due to such factors was eliminated by the standardization procedure used. The medial part of the hyperstriatum ventrale (upper arrow for each autoradiograph) is darker relative to surrounding regions in the autoradiograph from the undertrained chick (upper) compared with that of the overtrained (lower). The lower arrows (optical densities 0.17 and 0.15 respectively) point to the region selected for measurement in the forebrain base region. Optical density measurements were made from a small area immediately to the left of the arrow tips.

and overtrained birds were found for other brain slabs. However, inspection of the data from some of the slabs suggested that the individual values were more variable in the undertrained chicks than in the overtrained chicks. To examine this possibility quantitatively a variance ratio was calculated by dividing the variance of data from the undertrained chicks by the variance of data from the overtrained chicks. The ratios are plotted in Fig. 4.3(b). In slabs 3 and 4 the variances for the undertrained chicks were significantly greater than those for the overtrained chicks. These slabs lay immediately anterior to those in which there were significant differences between mean values from the two groups of birds (Fig. 4.3(a)).

The results of this study suggest that while changes are almost invariably produced in some parts (slabs 5 and 6) of the medial hyperstriatum ventrale by the imprinting procedure, other parts (slabs 3 and 4) are implicated only in some individuals. The four slabs occupy a region which is about 2.4 millimetres long. The anterior boundary of the region lies immediately in front of the midpoint of a line drawn between the anterior and posterior poles of the forebrain hemispheres. The region is referred to as the 'intermediate and medial part of hyperstriatum ventrale' (IMHV).

No other significant differences between the two groups of chicks were found in any other anatomical region measured, including the major visual projection areas, the hyperstriatum accessoruium, the hyperstriatum intercalatus/hyperstriatum dorsale, and the ectostriatum.

The results of the autoradiograph study were consistent with previous work on imprinting in two important ways. Firstly, the IMHV lies within the anterior part of the forebrain roof, a part of the cerebral hemispheres which was implicated by two different experiments (Sections 3.2 and 3.3). Secondly, the direction of the changes was similar to that of an earlier study (Section 3.2): the higher level of incorporation was found in the brains of chicks which had been undertrained on the day of hatching.

These points of consistency suggest that the changes in incorporation are related in some way to the imprinting process. There is, however, another interpretation of the autoradiographic work. In this experiment the maternal call of a domestic hen had been presented together with the visual stimulus. The overtrained birds were therefore exposed to the sound for a longer time on day 1 than the undertrained birds. An auditory projection area, field L, lies in the posterior part of the neostriatum, below and to the lateral side of the hyperstriatum ventrale (Fig. A.6). The two structures are separated by a clearly defined lamina. The optical density measurements of the medial hyperstriatum ventrale were made above and medial to this lamina, well clear of field L. Nevertheless, in the guinea-fowl (*Numida meleagris*) and in the domestic chick, field L is connected to the hyperstriatum ventrale (Bonke *et al.* 1979; Bradley *et al.* 1985), so that cells in this structure could be influenced by auditory stimulation. Even the most caudal part of the hyperstriatum ventrale receives a projection from field L.

However, incorporation into this part was not affected by the different behavioural experiences of the overtrained and undertrained birds (Fig. 4.3, slab 7). This result is not consistent with the 'auditory experience' hypothesis; nor, for that matter, are the results of the split-brain study (Section 3.1). In this study there was an hemispheric asymmetry in the incorporation of radioactive uracil into RNA in the forebrain roof region. This hemispheric asymmetry cannot be accounted for by differences in auditory stimulation since both ears were uncovered during training.

## 4.2 Probing with radioactive 2-deoxyglucose

Soon after the results of the autoradiographic study described above had appeared, Kohsaka and his colleagues (1979) published their own study of imprinting in the domestic chick. This was an autoradiographic analysis, but the authors did not use radioactive uracil as precursor, they used radioactive 2-deoxyglucose. This technique was first introduced by Sokoloff and his colleagues in 1977 and is based on the fact that under most circumstances glucose is taken up by neurones and used as a fuel. When neurones are active, energy is required, amongst other things to restore and maintain ion concentrations and to synthesize transmiter substances in nerve terminals. These energy demands are met by glucose. 2-Deoxyglucose, an analogue of glucose which lacks oxygen on the second carbon atom, is taken up by a cell in the same way as glucose is taken up. However, unlike glucose, 2-deoxyglucose is barely metabolized and remains trapped in the cell (Sokoloff *et al.* 1977; see also Hawkins and Miller 1978). Sokoloff and his colleagues (1977) labelled 2-deoxyglucose with radioactive carbon-14. When tracer doses of this radioactive molecule were injected into rats, regional increases in neural activity could be identified by exposing sections of the brain to film and so preparing autoradiographs. The Sokoloff technique can be used to reveal brain regions in which neuronal impulse activity results in immediate energy demands. The radioactive uracil technique allows the identification of regions in which there is a change in synthesis or in turnover of macromolecules, most probably RNA. These changes are unlikely to reflect immediate consequences of neuronal impulse activity; the radioactive uracil technique more probably detects indirect consequences of this activity, such as neurosecretion or growth. Although the two techniques do not measure the same aspect of neural metabolism, the aspects they measure may be complementary.

Kohsaka and his colleagues hatched and raised chicks in darkness until they were between 8 and 12 hours old. Each chick was then placed in an arena and exposed to the imprinting object, a red balloon 15 centimetres in diameter. The balloon was moved around the area for 45 minutes. After chicks had been trained in this way they were returned to dark individual cages for 2 days. On the third day each chick was placed once again in the arena for 45 minutes together with the red balloon. Chicks which followed the moving object for 20 minutes were considered to be imprinted upon it, those chicks which followed for less than 5 minutes were considered not to be imprinted. The chicks were returned to the dark incubator for another day. On the fourth day after hatching each chick was given an injection of radioactive 2-deoxyglucose and exposed to the moving red ballon for 45 minutes. This procedure was intended to excite activity in the visual system and in the neural networks that might have been formed through the imprinting process. The radioactive molecules should be trapped in the activated cells, so that the location of these cell systems could be identified on autoradiographs. These were prepared by sectioning the brain and placing the sections on X-ray film.

Kohsaka and his collaborators reported significantly higher incoporation in the medial part of the hyperstriatum ventrale in the imprinted chicks compared with their non-imprinted controls. The region of hyperstriatum ventrale implicated lay approximately half-way between the anterior and posterior poles of the cerebral hemispheres, and therefore appeared to correspond to the IMHV. In the same plane of section there was also a higher level of incorporation into the lateral part of the neostriatum in the imprinted birds. The possible role in imprinting of the lateral part of the cerebral hemisphere is discussed elsewhere (pp. 99–101). No other regional differences between the two groups of chicks were significant.

The interpretation of the experiments of Kohsaka and his colleagues is not straightforward. For example, the authors do not say whether chicks trained in the way they described had formed a preference for the training stimulus. The chicks were not given a choice between the red balloon and some other object which they had not previously seen. Unless this test is done either in the experiments they described, or in some other experiment, it is not possible to be sure that the chicks which followed the moving balloon were imprinted on it. The chicks which followed this object may have been active birds which found the red balloon attractive enough to follow without any need of their having been exposed to it. However, if the results are taken at their face value and treated with appropriate caution they provide additional evidence, using very different measures of brain activity and behaviour, of changes in the IMVH associated with imprinting.

Maier and Scheich (1983), in their studies of guinea-fowl chicks, also found an increased incorporation of radioactive 2-deoxyglucose in the medial part of hyperstriatum ventrale associated, they believed, with acoustic imprinting. The area appears to overlap the most anterior part of the IMHV. Increased incorporation was also found in the lateral parts of both the neostriatum and the hyperstiatum ventrale as well as in the hyperstriatum accessorium. In these experiments young chicks were exposed for 2 hours to tone bursts of either 1.8 kilohertz or 2.5 kilohertz. Preferences were tested in a Y-shaped maze. A box was placed at the far end of each branch of the Y. A loudspeaker, which was situated behind each box, delivered either the 1.8 kilohertz tone or the 2.8 kilohertz tone. A chick was placed in the stem of the Y and was considered to be imprinted if it approached to criterion the side from which the training sound was being emitted. The criterion was three out of three or three out of four correct choices. The preferences of eleven chicks trained on the 1.8 kilohertz tone (group I), and four chicks trained on the 2.5 kiloherztz tone (group II) were tested. Eight of the chicks in group I approached the correct box and three chicks failed to do so. In group II, three chicks made the correct choice and one chick did not. These respective performances are not significantly different from chance. There is no good evidence, therefore, that the chicks were imprinted; so the biological significance of the differences in incorporation between 'trained', and control brains is not clear.

A puzzling aspect of the study by Maier and Scheich is their report of an increased incorporation of radioactive 2-deoxyglucose into the visual Wulst. Control chicks were not given a training session. They were injected with radioactive 2-deoxyglucose and exposed to a 1.8 kilohertz tone just before they were killed. Incorporation was higher in the hyperstriatum accessorium of the 'trained' birds than in the controls. The visual experience of the controls prior to their exposure to the 1.8 kilohertz tone is not given. It is important to have this information: the higher level of incorporation into the visual projection area may have little to do with acoustic imprinting, but might reflect, for example, difference visual experiences of the 'trained' birds and their controls.

The results of Maier and Scheich's work are tantalizing since they raise the possibility that part of the IMHV may be implicated in acoustic imprinting in guinea-fowl chicks as well as in visual imprinting in domestic chicks. It is important therefore that the ambiguities in the guinea-fowl work are quickly resolved.

### 4.3 Some unanswered questions

The autoradiographic studies go some way to answering the questions of whether the biochemical changes associated with imprinting in domestic chicks are uniformly distributed throughout the anterior forebrain roof region or are localized within it. The finding of localized changes does not, however, preclude the possibility of changes occurring in regions not measured, or of changes occurring which have different time course from those which were studied (see Chapter 7). Furthermore it is logically possible that there are both local and diffuse changes, the latter falling below the 'noise' level of the experiment. Clearly it is necessary to keep an open mind on these possibilities.

The finding of a localized change makes it possible to ask many questions and to apply a wide range techniques in the further analysis of imprinting.

The autoradiograhic technique used did not permit localization at a cellular level. Presumably incorporation was mainly into cell bodies lying within the IMHV since it is in the cell bodies that the great bulk of ribosomes, on which amino acids are assembled, is concentrated. If structural changes in neurones accompany or follow the increased levels of uracil incorporation, it is important to know where these changes are to be found, whether for example in the dendritic and axonal arborizations of neurones wholly restricted to the IMHV and/or in the terminal arborizations of neurones that project outside this region. It is also essential to know the routes by which information flows to and from the IMHV, the physiological transformation of signals that take place in the IMHV, its cellular architecture, the transmitter substances that it contains, the effects on behaviour of removing or stimulating the region, its functions in relationship to other regions with which it is connected and so on. The list of questions is almost endless, but many need to be answered in order to gain insight into the neural bases of imprinting.

## 4.4 Summary

The anterior part of the forebrain roof, which is implicated in the imprinting process (Chapter 3), is a relatively large structure. Autoradiographic techniques were used to enquire whether the whole of the structure or only restricted parts of it are specifically involved in the process. In one study the tracer molecule was radioactive uracil. Changes in incorporation associated with training were found in only a restricted part of the forebrain roof, the hyperstriatum ventrale. The change was confined to that part of the structure lying close to the midline. The region, referred to as the IMHV, is approximately 2.4 millimetres long and is centred approximately on the midpoint between the anterior and posterior poles of the cerebral hemispheres. Similar changes were found in the brains of domestic chicks when the tracer was radioactive 2-deoxyglucose.

## References

Bateson, P. (1979). Brief exposure to a novel stimulus during imprinting in chicks and its influence on subsequent preferences. *Anim. Learn. Behav.* **7**, 259–62.

Bonke, B. A., Bonke, D., and Scheich, H. (1979). Connectivity of the auditory forebrain nuclei in the Guinea Fowl (*Numida meleagris*). *Cell Tissue Res.* **200**, 101–21.

Bradley, P., Davies, D. C., and Horn, G. (1985). Connections of hyperstriatum ventrale in the domestic chick (*Gallus domesticus*). *J. Anat.* (in press).

Cohen, D. H. and Karten, H. J. (1974). The structural organization of the avian brain: an overview. In *Birds, brain and behaviour* (eds I. J. Goodman and M. W. Schein), pp. 29–73. Academic Press, New York.

Gottlieb, G. (1971). *Development of species identification in birds: an inquiry into the prenatal determinants of perception.* Chicago University Press, Chicago.

Hawkins, R. A. and Miller A. L. (1978). Loss of radioactive 2-deoxy-D-glucose-6-

phosphate from brains of conscious rats: implications for quantitative autoradiographic determination of regional glucose utilization. *Neuroscience* **3**, 251–8.

Horn, G. and McCabe, B. J. (1978). An autoradiographic method for studying the incorporation of uracil into acid-insoluble compounds in the brain. *J. Physiol., Lond.* **275**, 2–3P.

——, ——, and Bateson, P. P. G. (1979). An autoradiographic study of the chick brain after imprinting. *Brain Res.* **168**, 361–73.

Kohsaka, S., Takamatsu, K., Aoki, E., and Tsukada, Y. (1979). Metabolic mapping of chick brain after imprinting using [$^{14}$C]2-deoxyglucose technique. *Brain Res.* **172**, 539–44.

Lashley, K. S. (1929). *Brain mechanisms and intelligence: a quantitative study of injuries to the brain.* Chicago University Press, Chicago.

—— (1950). In search of the engram. *Symp. Soc. exp. Biol.* **4**, 454–82.

Maier, V. and Scheich, H. (1983). Acoustic imprinting leads to differential 2-deoxy-D-glucose uptake in the chick forebrain. *Proc. natn. Acad. Sci. U.S.A.* **80**, 3860–4.

Rogers, A. W. (1973). *Techniques of autoradiography* (2nd edn). Elsevier, Amsterdam.

Smith, F. V. and Bird, M. W. (1963). The relative attraction for the domestic chick of combinations of stimuli in different sensory modalities. *Anim. Behav.* **11**, 300–5.

Sokoloff, L., Reivich, M., Kennedy, C., Rosiers, M. H. D., Patlak, C. S., Pettigrew, K. D., Sakurada, O., and Shinohara, M. (1977). The $^{14}$C-deoxyglucose method for the measurement of local cerebral glucose utilization: theory, procedure, and normal values in the conscious and anaesthetized albino rat. *J. Neurochem.* **28**, 897–916.

Zeier, H. and Karten, H. J. (1971). The archistriatum of the pigeon: organization of afferent and efferent connections. *Brain Res.* **31**, 313–36.

# 5
# Brain lesions, acquisition, and retention

The experiments described in Chapter 3 went some way towards answering the question posed by the first biochemical studies: are the biochemical changes associated with imprinting exclusive to it? If, as the results implied, the IMHV is necessary for imprinting, then this behaviour should not be possible if the IMHV is destroyed. This strong prediction can be tested by placing lesions in the IMHV and exposing chicks to an imprinting stimulus. Attractively simple as such a test is, there are a number of drawbacks to it. On the one hand, if the lesion is placed in the brain of a young animal it is possible that some other region will take over the function of the damaged part. A failure to find the expected result might not be because the prediction is wrong, but rather a testimony to the plasticity of the developing brain. On the other hand, if the expected result is obtained it would certainly suggest that the IMHV is necessary for imprinting, but the structure may be necessary in only a trivial way. For example, if lesions to the IMHV made the chicks sleepy or inattentive, poorly motivated or blind, they would be unlikely to learn much, or anything at all, about the training object. Furthermore, the IMHV might be necessary for imprinting in the way that any other bit of brain may be necessary for this process—just as any part of a serially arranged circuit must be intact if the circuit is to operate at all. These limitations of the lesioning technique are substantial. Nevertheless, we considered that the positive reasons for using the technique to study imprinting were compelling.

## 5.1 Lesions to the IMHV, and the acquisition of a preference

In the experiments designed to investigate the effects of lesions to the IMHV on the acquisition of a preference, two groups of chicks were used (McCabe, Horn, and Bateson 1981). The IMHV of each chick in one group was lesioned; chicks in the other group served as controls. On the day of hatching chicks were reared in darkness, exposed for half an hour to a stationary overhead light and then placed for 30 minutes in the running wheels facing the imprinting object (Fig. 5.1). The purpose of exposing both groups of chicks to the imprinting stimulus before placing lesions was to

**Fig. 5.1.** Summary of events in the experiment designed to analyse the effects of bilateral lesions to the IMHV on the acquisition of a preference through imprinting (McCabe *et al.* 1981). The numbers above the upper line are the approximate times at which the various interventions occurred given in hours after the estimated time of hatching (0 h). The times also apply to the corresponding events on the lower line. During the period indicated by the continuous line the chicks were individually housed in a dark incubator. The chicks were given a preference test when they were approximately 47 h old. All chicks were primed, P, for 30 min before being exposed to the imprinting object on the day of hatching (day 1). Sequence of procedures: (a) Chicks with lesions of the IMHV. The filled square indicates a lesioned IMHV. During the period indicated by the broken line ⊣ ⊢ the chicks were exposed to a training stimulus. (b) Sham-operated control chicks. During the period shown by the open rectangle these chicks were anaesthetized and the scalp incised and then sutured. All of these conventions apply to similar figures elsewhere in the text.

select only active chicks and thereby to minimize the number of non-learners in the experiment (see p. 72). Chicks were matched in pairs on the basis of their activity during this 30 minute period (Fig. 5.2, training period 1). One chick of the pair was assigned to the lesion group and the other to the control group. A potential disadvantage of this selection procedure was that the birds might have formed a preference during the half hour of exposure. However, in a pilot experiment we found that chicks trained in this way for 30 minutes showed no preference when given a choice between the training stimulus and a novel stimulus on the following day.

Half of the chicks were exposed to a box (Fig. 2.3(a)) red on its two largest surfaces and rotating at 28 revolutions per minute. The other half was exposed to a different stimulus (Fig. 2.3(c)), a rocking stuffed jungle-fowl (*Gallus gallus*), the species considered to be ancestral to the domestic fowl (see Zeuner 1963). During exposure, the recording of a hen's maternal call was played to the chicks. Both chicks of a pair (lesioned and control) were exposed to the same imprinting object.

After a pair of chicks had been trained for half an hour, both chicks were anaesthetized. A small window was made in the skull of one chick and a needle, insulated except for a small zone at the tip, inserted into the brain so that the tip lay within the IMHV. A radiofrequency current was turned on and the brain tissue around the electrode tip was coagulated. This procedure was carried out for the IMHV of the left and right hemispheres. After the operation the skin over the skull was closed with sutures. The skin over the skull of the control chicks was incised and then sutured in the same way as that of the lesioned birds. The two birds, as they lay anaesthetized, were indistinguishable. Each was given a code number and all training and testing procedures were carried out without the experimenter knowing which bird had received the lesions.

On the day after the operation, when the chicks had recovered from the anaesthetic, training was continued for a total of 2.5 hours using the stimulus to which they had previously been exposed. Subsequently (Fig. 5.1) the preferences of all the chicks were measured by comparing their approach to the training stimulus with that to a second novel stimulus, the red box or the jungle-fowl, whichever the chick had not previously seen. The test differed from the one that had been used in earlier experiments. The new test involved placing the chick in a running wheel and exposing the chick for 4 minutes to the training object and to the novel object in a balanced sequence. A preference score was calculated. This score gave the fraction, expressed as a percentage, of all approach counts in the test which were directed to the training stimulus; the score provided a measure of the attractiveness of this stimulus relative to that of the novel stimulus. The score was calculated from the following expression:

$$\frac{100 \times \text{approach counts to training stimulus}}{\text{approach counts to training stimulus} + \text{approach counts to novel stimulus}}$$

The preference score ranged from zero (approach directed entirely to the novel stimulus through 50 (no preference) to 100 (approach directed entirely to the training stimulus).

During the training periods the approach of the sham-operated control chicks increased and then levelled off. The effect can be seen in Fig. 5.2. Approach, expressed as revolutions of the running wheel per hour, was low in period 1. During the first hour of training on day 2 the approach increased, continued to increase for the next hour and then levelled off. For the lesioned chicks, approach counts in period 1 were almost identical with those of the controls, demonstrating that experimental and control chicks were well matched for approach activity in the preoperative period of exposure on day 1. This was the only period in which the approach counts of the two groups of birds were similar. The median approach counts of the lesioned chicks did not increase over time and were consistently below those of the controls. In this measure of behaviour, as in all others, data for chicks trained on the red box were combined with those for chicks trained on the jungle-fowl: the appropriate analysis of variance failed to provide evidence that the means differed according to the object used for training.

The preference scores of the two groups of chicks are shown in Fig. 5.3. The sham-operated control chicks showed a strong preference for the training stimulus. The lesioned birds showed no such preference, achieving a mean score that was not significantly different from 50.

It can be seen from the expression used to calculate the preference score

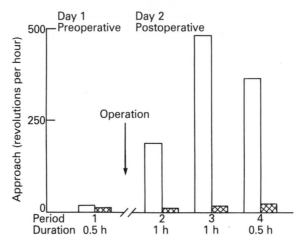

**Fig. 5.2.** Approach score for lesioned and control chicks during the four training periods. Approach scores are expressed as revolutions of the running wheel per hour. Median values are given. For sham-operated controls (open bars) the approach scores during period 2 were significantly greater than in period 1 (Wilcoxon $T=3$; $P<0.01$) and those in period 3 were greater than those in period 2 ($T=5$, $P<0.01$). Data from sham-operated controls in periods 3 and 4 were not significantly different from each other. On day 2 the approach of lesioned chicks (cross-hatched bars) was significantly less than that of controls during all three periods. (After McCabe *et al.* 1981.)

that it could be reduced in three ways: (i) by a reduction in approach to the training object; (ii) by an increased approach to the novel object; or (iii) by a combination of (i) and (ii). The mean approach counts of the lesioned and sham-operated control chicks are shown in Table 5.1. The sham-operated chicks approached the novel stimulus in the test much less than they approached the training stimulus. In contrast, the approach of the lesioned chicks to the training stimulus was not significantly different from their

**Table 5.1** *Approach during preference test; mean $\pm$ s.e.m. numbers of revolutions toward the training object and novel object respectively (data from McCabe et al. 1981)*

| Treatment | Approach during preference test | |
|---|---|---|
| | To training object | To novel object |
| Sham-operated control chicks | 28.92±9.72 | 5.83±5.14 |
| Chicks with lesions of IMHV | 9.42±5.35 | 4.08±4.09 |

The sham-operated chicks approached the training object significantly more than they approached the novel object ($t=3.36$, $P<0.01$).

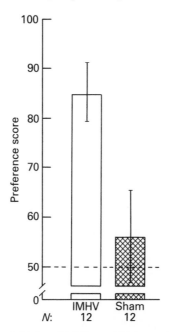

**Fig. 5.3.** Preference scores of chicks with bilateral lesions of the IMHV and of sham-operated ('Sham') chicks after exposure to an imprinting stimulus for 2.5 h on the day after hatching. The mean preference score of the lesioned chicks was $56.58 \pm 9.67$ (S.E.M.). This score was not significantly different from 50, but differed significantly from that of the sham-operated control birds ($t=2.93$; $P<0.02$). In this figure, as in all figures in which the ordinate is preference score, the broken line represents the no preference level unless otherwise stated. (After McCabe *et al.* 1981.)

approach to the novel stimulus. The lower preference score of the lesioned birds was mainly attributable, therefore, to a reduction in their approach to the training object. They treated this object much as the controls treated the novel object. These results provided no evidence that the lesioned birds had learned anything about the stimulus to which they had been exposed.

Many explanations can be invoked to account for these results (see, for example p. 83). The impaired imprinting ability of chicks with lesions of IMHV was not, however, due to a reduced activity in the test since the preference score is independent of overall activity: the score gives the percentage of the total activity that is directed towards the training object. Furthermore the lesioned chicks' approach to the novel object was similar to that of the control chicks' approach to the novel object (Table 5.1). Was the impairment of approach activity during testing and training due to sensory or motor defects in the lesioned animals? A test was set up that might reveal gross changes in these functions. After the preference test had been completed the chick was placed in an incubator. A rod with a small shining tip was introduced into the incubator and moved from side to side at a distance of 30 centimetres from the chick. The time taken for the chick to approach and peck the rod was measured. The times taken by the lesioned birds (median time of 39.5 seconds) did not differ significantly from those of the sham-operated birds (median time 45.5 seconds). This test of visuomotor coordination did not allow the experimenters to discriminate between the lesioned and sham-operated birds. In a final test an experimental chick together with its sham-operated control was placed on a laboratory table on which stood various objects including beakers, pipettes, tools, books, pens and so on. A 'clinical' impression of each chick was formed based on its general behaviour—the extent to which it pecked at objects, the degree to which it avoided obstacles, and the general amount of movement. The IMHV-lesioned chicks could not be distinguished from their controls.

The location and extent of the lesions were reconstructed from serial section of the brains (Fig. 5.4). Part of the hyperstriatum ventrale was destroyed in each chick. That part of hyperstriatum ventrale which comprises the IMHV lies between section outlines numbered 4 and 7 in Fig. 5.4. The region was extensively damaged in all experimental chicks.

Approach activity to a stimulus increases as chicks learn the characteristics of that stimulus (Salzen and Sluckin 1959; Horn *et al.* 1973). Hence the lower approach activity of the lesioned birds during training could be a consequence of an impaired ability to learn; that is, the observed differences in behaviour during training and in the test could derive from a single deficit in the lesioned birds, namely an inability to learn the characteristics of the stimulus to which they were exposed.

The lesion experiments were conducted to test the prediction that, if the IMHV is necessary for imprinting, imprinting should not be possible if this brain region is destroyed. The results of these experiments are consistent with this prediction, and so give some support for the underlying assumption of a specific role for the IMHV in the imprinting process. However, as discussed above (p. 83), caution is necessary in interpreting the results of experiments involving damage to the brain and the results of this study are, by themselves, no exception to this rule.

If bilateral damage to the IMHV impairs the acquisition of a preference through the imprinting procedure, does such damage after imprinting impair retention? The next set of experiments was designed to answer this question (McCabe, Cipolla-Neto, Horn, and Bateson 1982).

## 5.2  Lesions to the IMHV, and the retention of a preference

The effects of lesions to the IMHV on retention were examined in an experiment the design of which is outlined in Fig. 5.5. Chicks were trained by exposing them to the stimuli which had been used in the previous lesion study, with the difference that the stuffed jungle-fowl, instead of rocking,

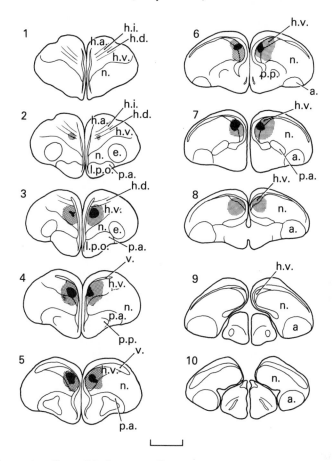

**Fig. 5.4.** Reconstruction of lesions on diagrams of coronal sections of the chick brain. The diagrams represent sections approximately 500 μm apart, the most anterior being diagram 1. Black areas depict regions that were destroyed in all twelve chicks. Stippled areas depict regions that were destroyed in more than a quarter of the chicks (that is, three of the twelve) but in less than all twelve of them. The left hemisphere is shown on the left side of each outline section. Abbreviations: a., archistriatum; e., ectostriatum; h.a., hyperstriatum accessorium; h.d., hyperstriatum dorsale; h.i., hyperstriatum intercalatus; h.v., hyperstriatum ventrale; l.p.o., lobus paraolfactorius; n., neostriatum; p.a., paleostriatum augmentatum; p.p., paleostriatum primitivum; v., ventricle. Scale bar 3mm. (After McCabe *et al.* 1981.)

rotated at the same rate as the box, 28 revolutions per minute. The chicks were exposed to this object or to the rotating, flashing red box for two periods of 60 minutes, separated by a 70 minute period in darkness. The chicks were anaesthetized approximately 3 hours after training. Bilateral lesions were placed in the IMHV and the scalps of the sham-operated chicks were incised and sutured as had been done for the lesioned birds. Two more

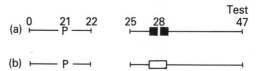

**Fig. 5.5.** Outline of events in the experiments designed to investigate the effects of lesions to the IMHV on the retention of a preference acquired through imprinting. Sequence of procedures: (a) for birds receiving lesions; (b) for sham-operated controls.

groups of chicks were used. In the previous study (Section 5.1) there had been no control for the non-specific consequences of brain damage. Lesions were therefore placed in the visual Wulst in the hope that chicks with such lesions would provide the necessary controls. This expectation was based on two pieces of information. No changes associated with imprinting had been found in the region in either of the two autoradiographic studies (Horn *et al.* 1979; Kohsaka *et al.* 1979) and Salzen and his collaborators (1975, 1978) had shown that lesions placed in the visual Wulst of domestic chicks had little or no effect on imprinting. Finally, a group of chicks was included in order to follow up the report by Salzen and his colleagues (1975, 1978, 1979) that imprinting was affected by lesions placed in the lateral regions of the forebrain; this result was consistent with the findings of Kohsaka and his collaborators (1979) who reported autoradiographic changes in this region of the forebrain. Lesions were therefore placed in the lateral cerebral area of the forebrain of a group of chicks. On the day following the operations the preferences of all the chicks were measured using the sequential test of the earlier lesion experiment, and the preference scores were calculated (p. 85).

Since all the chicks were intact during the training period the approach counts of the four groups were, not surprisingly, statistically homogenous (Table 5.2). Approach increased from the first to the second training period.

The preference scores were not significantly affected by the object on which the chicks had been trained. For this reason the preference score of the chicks which had been trained on the red box were combined with those of chicks which had been trained on the jungle-fowl. The mean preference scores for each of the four groups of chicks are shown in Fig. 5.6. Of the three lesioned groups only the chicks with lesions in the IMHV had a lower preference score than the sham-operated controls. The chicks with lesions in the IMHV also had a lower preference score than chicks with lesions in the Wulst. Whilst all other groups of chicks had a preference score that was well in excess of the chance level, the score for chicks with lesions in the IMHV was not significantly different from a score of 50. In other words chicks with lesions in the IMHV were, by one criterion or another, the 'maverick' group.

**Table 5.2** *Approach counts (mean ± S.E.M.) during training (after McCabe et al. 1982)*

| Group | Training session 1 | 2 | N |
|---|---|---|---|
| Sham | 338.42 ± 40.20 | 504.44 ± 44.09 | 48 |
| IMHV | 392.06 ± 65.41 | 604.94 ± 73.52 | 16 |
| LCA | 322.19 ± 69.37 | 538.00 ± 84.79 | 16 |
| W | 251.44 ± 51.13 | 460.31 ± 71.09 | 16 |

There were no significant differences between the experimental (lesioned) groups. Approach during the second session was significantly greater than that during the first session ($P < 0.001$). For key to abbreviations see legend to Fig. 5.6.

If a preference score significantly in excess of 50 implies the retention of a preference in trained chicks, then chicks with lesions in the IMHV showed no retention. A preference score of 50 does not, of course, provide unequivocal evidence of amnesia; evidence, that is, that the chicks had 'lost their memory' of the object on which they had been trained. They may, for example, have had perfectly good memories for that object, but the lesion

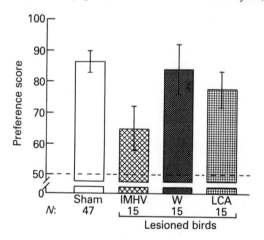

**Fig. 5.6.** Preference scores for the four experimental groups of chicks. Mean ±S.E.M. preference scores are shown according to treatment. Sham, IMHV, W, and LCA refer respectively to the sham-operated controls, chicks with lesions of the IMHV, the Wulst, and the lateral cerebral area. The mean preference scores of the following groups exceeded 50 by (i) sham-operated controls, 36.5±3.28 ($t=11.13$, $P<0.001$); (ii) W, 34.0±7.9 ($t=4.30$, $P<0.01$); (iii) LCA, 27.8±5.61 ($t=4.96$, $P<0.01$). The preference score of the IMHV group did not differ significantly from 50 (mean difference=14.4±7.53, $t=1.91$), and was significantly less than that of the sham-operated controls ($t=3.15$, $P<0.01$) and of the chicks with lesions in the Wulst ($t=2.26$, $P<0.05$). (After McCabe *et al.* 1982.)

may have interfered with their ability to recall it. Amnesia due to defective recall can often be reversed by giving the subject a cue or a prompt of some sort. Lewis and his colleagues (1968), for example, have devised a method for assessing a deficit in recall in rats rendered amnesic by electroconvulsive shocks. The technique involves giving the subject a 'reminder trial' before the recognition test. The preference test used here is a form of recognition test, providing a measure of the chick's response to two stimuli only one of which the chick has seen before. In the preference test the chicks were exposed to the training stimulus and a novel stimulus for a total of 8 minutes. The order of exposure is shown in Table 5.3. One half (Table 5.3, I) of the chicks saw the training object first, the other half (Table 5.3, II) saw the novel object first. If brief exposure had reawakened recognition in IMHV-lesioned chicks, some aspect of the preference score of chicks in half I should be different from that of chicks in half II. To investigate this possibility, two subdivided preference scores were calculated for each chick. One subdivided preference score was calculated from the first 4 minutes of test and one for the second 4 minutes. If the first exposure to the training stimulus in the test had reminded the chicks of its characteristics, the subdivided preference score D (Table 5.3) should have been higher than score A. Score D was calculated for chicks which, in the second 2-minute period of the test, had been exposed to the training object; score A was calculated for chicks which before the test had been in the dark incubator and therefore had not benefited from a reminder trial. There was no significant difference between scores A and D for the IMHV-lesioned chicks, nor, for that matter, between any of the subdivided preference scores. These measures, at least, provided no evidence of defective in recall in the chicks with lesions of the IMHV, or indeed in any other group of chicks.

There are other reasons why the IMHV-lesioned chicks might have had low preference scores, and being drowsy in the test is an obvious one. If

**Table 5.3** *Order in which chicks were exposed to the two stimuli (training and novel) in the preference test*

| Half | Two minute period | | Subdivided preference score | Two-minute period | | Subdivided preference score | Total time (min) |
|------|-------|--------|-------|-------|--------|-------|------|
| | First | Second | | Third | Fourth | | |
| I | Training | Novel | A | Novel | Training | B | 8 |
| II | Novel | Training | C | Training | Novel | D | 8 |

Half (I) of all the chicks in the experiment of McCabe and his co-workers (1982) were tested in the sequence shown in the upper line of the table and half (II) in the sequence shown on the lower line. Subdivided preference scores for each 4 min of the test were calculated from the expression:

$$\frac{100 \times \text{approach to training stimulus}}{\text{approach to training stimulus} + \text{approach to novel stimulus}}$$

they were indeed drowsy they would be expected to have moved less than other birds with lesions. In fact the total activity, that is the sum of approach and withdrawal counts, during the preference test did not differ significantly between the experimental groups.

A number of other tests were used in these experiments to measure the general behavioural state of the chicks. After the preference tests, the chicks were returned to the dark incubator. Subsequently each chick was placed in a vertical cylinder of white cardboard. The cylinder was 25 centimetres high so the bird could not look over the top. Through a slit in the wall a small red bead protruded into the cylinder just above the floor. (Fig. 5.7(a)). The bead rocked slowly and the time taken for the chick to peck it was recorded. There were no significant differences between any of the groups in the mean time taken to peck the bead (Fig. 5.7(b)), a result which suggests that there was no gross impairment of visuomotor coordination in any of the lesioned groups of birds.

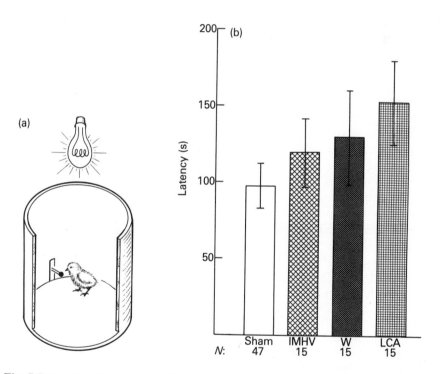

**Fig. 5.7.** Rocking bead test. (a) The white cardboard cylinder in which the chick was placed has been cut away for the purposes of illustration. During the test the chick was observed through the open top of the cylinder. The red bead was mounted on a motor and rocked up and down at a rate of one oscillation per second, and with an excursion of 1 cm. The time taken for the chick to peck the bead was recorded. (b) The time taken in seconds (means ±s.e.m.) by each group of chicks to peck the rocking bead is shown. Abbreviations as in Fig. 5.6.

Further support for this conclusion came from another pecking test. Some hours after the rocking bead test had been completed each chick was placed in an illuminated incubator on the floor of which millet seed had been scattered. The chicks remained in this incubator for half an hour. The number of times the chick pecked was counted and a note made of whether or not it hit or missed the seed. The percentage of pecking movements which were hits was calculated. For all chicks, just over 80 per cent of pecks were accurate hits, and there were no significant differences between the four groups of birds.

After all the procedures in this experiment had been completed (see also Section 6.1) the brains were removed. Four brains were selected at random from each group of lesioned birds and processed for histology. Serial sections were cut and from these sections the lesions were reconstructed by projecting the images of the sections on drawings from an atlas of the brain. The areas occupied by the lesions were measured using a planimeter and the volumes of brain damaged were calculated. As in the earlier lesion study, the IMHV was extensively damaged, the zone of destruction being fairly well circumscribed (Fig. 5.8(a), sections 4 and 5). The lesion in the Wulst (Fig. 5.8(b)) damaged mainly the anterior half of the hyperstriatum accessorium and encroached on the underlying hyperstraitum intercalatus and the hyperstriatum dorsale. The hyperstriatum ventrale was virtually untouched by this lesion. The laterally placed lesion (Fig. 5.8(c)) invaded the lateral parts of the hyperstriatum ventrale and neostriatum, especially in the intermediate region of the cerebral hemispheres.

Could the consequences on imprinting of the various lesions be accounted for by a variation in the size of the lesion, that is, a 'mass action' effect? The volumes of the lesions, expressed as percentages of the volumes of the forebrain, are given in Fig. 5.9. The three mean values are almost identical so that an explanation based on a mass action effect is virtually excluded.

## 5.3 One IMHV for acquisition and retention

A further refinement to the lesion studies was introduced in the next set of lesion studies (Horn, McCabe, and Cipolla-Neto 1983). Previous experiments had shown that destruction of the IMHV in the two cerebral hemispheres prevented the acquisition and the retention of a preference for a visually conspicuous object. In the next experiment we enquired whether a preference could be established when only one IMVH was intact during training. If a preference could be established under these conditions, was retention impaired when that IMHV was subsequently destroyed?

The procedures used to investigate these questions were similar to those of the earlier lesion studies. The particular sequence of events in the experi-

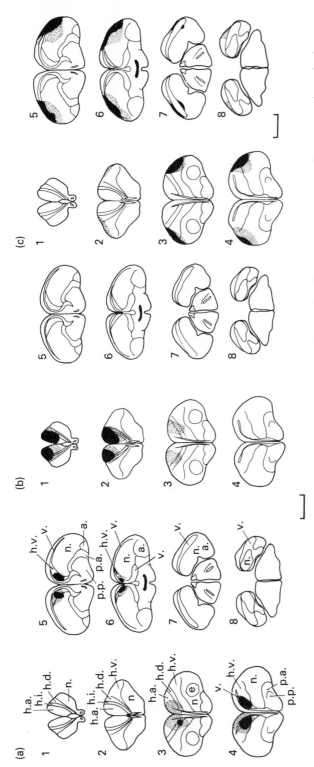

**Fig. 5.8.** Histological reconstructions of brain lesions drawn on outline sections. The diagrams represent sections approximately 1 mm apart. Section 1 is anterior and section 8 is posterior. The black areas indicate tissue destroyed in all four brains examined. The shaded areas denote tissue destroyed in more than one brain. The left hemipshere is shown on the left side of each outline section. (a) Lesions in the IMHV; (b) lesions in the Wulst; (c) lesions in the lateral cerebral area. Abbreviations: a., archistriatum; e., ectostriatum; h.a., hyperstriatum accessorium; h.d., hyperstriatum dorsale; h.i., hyperstriatum intercalatus; h.v., hyperstriatum ventrale; n., neo-striatum; p.a., paleostriatum augmentatum; p.p., paleostriatum primativum; v., ventricle. Scale bar 3 mm. (After McCabe *et al.* 1982.)

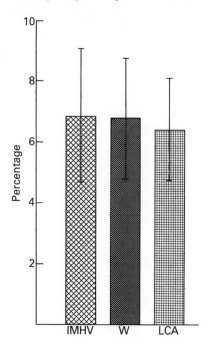

**Fig. 5.9.** Volume of lesions expressed as a percentage of the volume of the forebrain. Figures from right and left hemispheres were combined. Means±s.e.m. are given. IMHV, W, and LCA refer respectively to chicks with lesions in the IMHV, the Wulst, and in the lateral cerebral area. Data were derived from measurements of the brains of four birds in each group. (Data from McCabe *et al.* 1982.)

ments are outlined in Fig. 5.10. The dark-reared chicks were anaesthetized in pairs approximately 12 hours after hatching. One member of a pair served as the sham-operated control. The other member was the experimental bird and a lesion was placed in one of four regions. These regions were the right IMHV, the left IMHV, the right Wulst, and the left Wulst. After the operation the chicks were returned to the dark incubator. The fol-

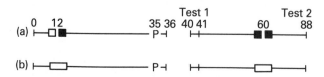

**Fig. 5.10.** Summary of events in the experiments designed to investigate acquisition and retention when the IMHV of only one hemisphere was intact during exposure training. Two preference tests were given. Sequence of procedures: (a) For chicks in which lesions were placed either in the IMHV or in the Wulst. The first lesion was unilateral; after the second lesion, the damage was bilateral. (b) For sham-operated controls. (After Horn *et al.* 1983.)

lowing day each chick was placed in the running wheel and exposed to the training stimulus, the red box, or the rotating stuffed jungle-fowl, for two periods each of 1 hour. Later the chicks were given a sequential preference test. Sometime after this test had been completed each chick was again anaesthetized and, in the experimental birds, the remaining IMHV or Wulst was lesioned. The second preference test was conducted on the following day, when the chicks were approximately 88 hours old.

The behavioural results for chicks with lesions placed first in the left side of the brain were not significantly different from those of chicks with lesions placed first on the right side. This was true whether the lesions were in the Wulst or in the IMHV. Accordingly, data from the chicks receiving the first lesion in the right or left IMHV were combined into one group and data from chicks receiving the first lesion in the right or left Wulst were combined into another. Because there was no statistical evidence that the preference scores of chicks trained on the red box were different from those of chicks trained on the jungle-fowl, the two sets of preference scores were combined.

Chicks trained with IMHV or the Wulst of only one hemisphere intact achieved mean preference scores which were well above chance and indistinguishable from those of the sham-operated controls (Fig. 5.11(a)). Clearly acquisition is not impaired if one or other of these two brain regions is lesioned before training is begun. The high preference scores in the experimental groups were achieved even though, during training, the chicks in these two groups were less active and approached the training stimulus significantly less than the sham-operated birds (Horn *et al.* 1983).

If the IMHV which was present during training is necessary for retention, then its demise should be followed by a fall in the preference score to the chance level. This is precisely what was found. The mean preference score of chicks which had received the second lesion in the IMHV (Fig. 5.11(b), IMHV) was 60.31. This score was less than one standard error away from 50 and so was not significantly different from chance performance. In contrast, the mean preference score of the chicks which received the second lesion in the Wulst was well above chance and almost identical with that of the sham-operated controls (Fig. 5.11(b)). The scores of these two groups were significantly greater than those of the IMHV-lesioned birds.

The subdivided preference scores (Table 5.3) attained in test 2 were uninfluenced by the familiar, 'reminder', stimulus or by the novel stimulus coming first for any of the groups of chicks. Once again there was no evidence that the effects of the lesion to the IMHV on preference score could be ascribed to defective recall.

It was concluded, on the basis of this study and the two earlier studies of brain lesions, that at least one IMHV must be intact for the acquisition of a preference by imprinting, and it does not matter whether the intact IMHV is the left or the right. It was also concluded that if only one IMHV region is present during training it must also be present for recall.

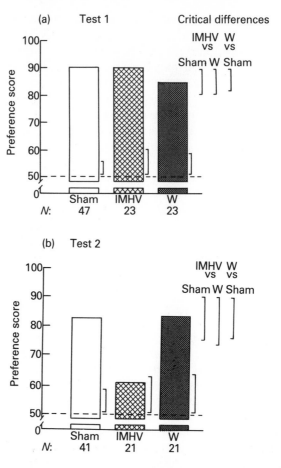

**Fig. 5.11.** Mean preference scores of three experimental groups of chicks. To the right of each mean value and just above the broken line is given the critical difference ($P=0.05$) for the comparison of that mean value with the no preference score of 50. If a mean value differs from 50 by more than this critical difference, it is significantly different from 50. Also given are critical differences ($P=0.05$) for comparisons between the mean scores attained in a particular test. 'Sham', sham-operated chicks; W, chicks with lesions in the Wulst; IMHV, chicks with lesions to the IMHV. Some deaths occurred in the course of the experiment so that there was a short-fall in the original numbers, 48 shams and 24 chicks in each of the other groups. (After Horn *et al.* 1983.)

## 5.4  Other lesion studies

The experiments that have been described so far in this chapter were undertaken to test certain predictions which arose out of earlier biochemical and autoradiographic studies. Other workers have examined the effect of damage to the forebrain on various aspects of approach behaviour and imprinting. Is there any consistency in the result of these several investigations?

Collias (1980) investigated the effects of partial or complete decerebration on 'early socialization' in domestic chicks. The operation was performed within an hour of hatching. Decerebration involved the bilateral removal of the forebrain hemispheres. In chicks which were partially decerebrate some 75 per cent of the telencephalon was removed; the intact portion comprised the basal structures of the hemispheres and included the paleostriatal complex (see Fig. 5.8, regions p.a. and p.p.). The responsiveness of the chicks was tested in two ways. In the first, each chick was placed in a 10 foot long runway with a loudspeaker at either end. The clucking sound of a hen was played through one or other of the loudspeakers. The chick was placed in the middle of the runway and its approach response to the clucking was recorded. Normal control chicks approached the sound on 80 per cent of the occasions on which it was presented on the first two days after hatching. Decerebrate chicks did not approach the sound though they could walk and could assume an alert posture in response to a loud noise. The incompletely decerebrate chicks approached the clucking sound about as often as did the normal chicks. Furthermore the partially decerebrate birds, like the intact birds followed Collias as he walked away from them. The decerebrate birds did not do so.

These tests of early socialization were not tests of imprinting since the chicks were not required to discriminate between a novel stimulus and the stimulus to which they had been exposed. The tests used by Collias demonstrate that young decerebrate chicks do not exhibit approach responses, whereas partially decerebrate chicks do.

More direct studies of the influence of brain lesions on imprinting are those of Salzen and his colleagues (1975, 1978, 1979). These workers were following up an earlier observation by Benowitz (1972) who had shown that a lesion of the posterior and lateral part of the telencephalon resulted in a complete loss of the ability of young domestic chicks to learn and retain a taste avoidance response. Salzen and his colleagues found that lesions of the lateral side of the forebrain hemisphere (see Fig. 5.12) prevented both the acquisition and the retention of a preference for an object through exposure to it. By contrast a lesion of the anterior part of the forebrain hemispheres, in which the visual Wulst was severely damaged, had relatively little effect on either of these two aspects of the learning process. In all of the experiments of this group of workers IMHV was spared.

There is, then, general agreement that damage to the Wulst has little or no effect on imprinting. Is there a discrepancy between the results of Salzen and his colleagues (1978) and those described above (Section 5.2) on the effect of lateral forebrain lesions on retention? Probably not. There are several reasons for this view. We had found that chicks with lesions placed in the lateral cerebral area after training preferred the familiar object to one

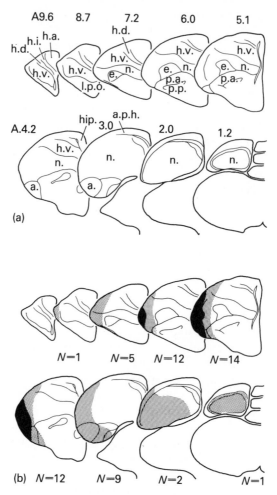

**Fig. 5.12.** (a) A series of transverse sections taken from a stereotaxic brain atlas for domestic chicks prepared by Salzen and Williamson. (b) Lateral forebrain lesions in 14 chicks. The stippled area indicates the group total of tissue removed bilaterally, while the dark area shows the common area damaged in 75 per cent of the cases. The figures below each section indicate the number of chicks with damage in that plane of section. Stereotaxic coordinates are in millimetres, 9.6 being the most anterior. Abbreviations for the forebrain structures are: a., archistriatum; a.p.h., area parahippocampalis; e., ectostriatum; h.a., hyperstriatum accessorium; h.d., hyperstriatum dorsale; h.i., hyperstriatum intercalatus; hip., hippocampus; h.v., hyperstriatum ventrale; l.p.o., lobus paraolfactorius; n., neostriatum; p.a., paleostriatum augmentatum; p.p., paleostriatum primitivum. (After Salzen *et al.* 1978.)

they had not previously seen (Fig. 5.6). This behaviour contrasted with that of the chicks with lesions of the IMHV since these chicks failed to score significantly above chance level. However, chicks with lesions of the lateral cerebral area achieved a mean preference score which was not significantly different either from that of the sham-operated controls or from that of the chicks with lesions of the IMHV; that is, the lateral cerebral group fell between the groups with the two extreme mean preference scores. In this study damage to the lateral cerebral area was a little less extensive than that in the experiments of Salzen and his co-workers (1978). In these experiments the lesion involved part of the archistriatum, a structure which was not damaged in the experiments of McCabe and his colleagues (1982). The differences in the size and position of the lesions can readily be seen by comparing Fig. 5.8(c) with that of Fig. 5.12(b). It is possible, therefore, that had the lateral cerebral lesion shown in Fig. 5.8(c) involved the archistriatum the mean preference score of the birds might have approximated more closely to that of the chicks with IMHV lesions. Clearly this question can be resolved experimentally, but it is of particular interest that the IMHV projects to the lateral cerebral area and to the archistriatum (Bradley and Horn 1979; Bradley *et al.* 1985).

There are other differences between the experiments of the two groups of workers. Salzen and his colleagues reared each operated chick in a box containing an object hung from the roof. The object, a yellow sponge or a green stuffed cloth ball, was free to sway in the centre of the box. The chicks were housed in this box for between 3 and 10 days. The discrimination test was conducted in a simple enclosure in which the two objects were hung against one wall. The chick was placed at the centre of the opposite wall facing them. The experimenter noted which of the objects the chick approached. The chicks in these experiments were therefore older than the chicks in the experiments described in Sections 5.2 and 5.3, and were exposed for a much longer period of time to very different stimuli. These factors are important when analysing the neural basis of the imprinting process (Chapters 7 and 8).

## 5.5  Evaluating the evidence of lesion studies

The method of studying residual function after the brain has been injured by pathological processes, by accident or by design, must be amongst the crudest available to neurobiologists. Some of the limitations of the method have already received comment, and have been discussed explicitly by Gregory (1961). This having been said, the history of neurobiology would probably be quite different, and probably in a less advanced state than it is now, if the technique had not been used. In some circumstances it is the only method available and observations based on it have often laid the foundations for subsequent, more refined analyses. Examples are not hard to find. The first inroads into the experimental analysis of spinal cord function relied heavily on the method (see Liddell 1960). Early studies of asymmetry in cerebral function in humans depended on relating unilateral lesions of the cerebral hemispheres to impairment in the ability to speak or to comprehend the spoken or written word (Broca 1865; Wernicke 1874; Dejerine 1891). More recently the lesion studies of Scoville and Milner (1957) gave great impetus to interest in the hippocampus and stimulated much fruitful experimental investigations into the functions of this structure (see Ciba Foundation Symposium 1978; Seifert 1983). A role of the inferior temporal lobe of the primate brain in visually guided behaviour first clearly became apparent through the ablation experiments of Chow (1952), Mishkin (1954), and Mishkin and Pribram (1954), and these studies have been effectively exploited at the electrophysiological level by many workers (see, for example, Bruce *et al.* 1981; Perrett *et al.* 1982). The discovery of 'blind sight' depended on a perspicaceous analysis of the consequences of brain lesions on residual visual capacities (Weiskrantz 1980; Zihl and Werth 1984), and observations of the effects of lesions to the parietal lobe of humans (see Critchley 1953) laid the foundation for elegant electrophysiological analyses of attention in monkeys (see Lynch *et al.* 1977; Wurtz *et al.* 1980; Bushnell *et al.* 1981).

If knowledge of function rested solely on information derived from ablation experiments, then the explanatory power of such knowledge would, of course, be quite limited. In the case of imprinting, the lesion studies discussed in detail in this chapter are not the sole source of knowledge about the role of the IMHV in this behaviour. Rather the results of these studies give support to predictions, based largely on biochemical evidence, that the IMHV plays a critical role in the imprinting process. The severe disruption of this process by lesions is unlikely to have arisen from defects in visuomotor coordination, locomotor activity, alertness, or in the capacity to make visual discriminations since the chicks performed quite as well as sham-operated birds on tests of perceptual and motor performance (see also Chapters 6, 7, and 8). It is also unlikely that chicks with lesions of IMHV suffer from defective recall (p. 92). Gentle and his collaborators (1978) suggested that ablations which involve the ventral hyperstriatum of adult domestic hens make the birds less reactive to frightening stimuli. Young chicks which are imprinted on a particular visual object do not approach and may actively avoid other objects. If lesions to IMHV of young chicks made them less fearful, then, in the preference test, approach to the novel object might be expected to increase. This was not the case. The approach made by chicks to the novel stimulus was unaffected by the lesion to the IMHV (Table 5.1; see also Horn and McCabe 1984). It is unlikely therefore that the consequences of lesions can be ascribed to a general reduction in fearfulness. Another explanation is that chicks with these lesions are simply not interested in approaching the training object, the lesion in some way impairing their motivation to do so. This is a difficult argument to refute, but several lines of evidence suggest that it is not a plausible explanation of the lesioned birds' behaviour. One line of evidence, certainly indirect, comes from the 'two-day' biochemical study described in Section 3.2. In those experiments four groups of chicks were trained for various periods of time on the day of hatching. On the following day, day 2, all groups were exposed to the training object for 60 minutes. It was found that the incorporation of radioactive uracil into the anterior part of the forebrain roof on day 2 was lowest in those chicks which had been trained for the longest period on day 1. The low level of incorporation might have reflected a relatively low motivational state, which in turn should have been expressed in some aspect of the chicks' behaviour. The chicks which had been exposed to the training stimulus longest on day 1 had learned most about it (Fig. 3.5(b)). When they saw that stimulus on the following day they may have 'lost interest' in it and so might not be expected to approach it with much vigour. This did not happen. In fact (see Fig. 3.5(c)) the birds trained for the longer period on the previous day tended to run more toward the training object than other groups of chicks, though this tendency did not achieve statistical significance. Other evidence that chicks with lesions in the IMHV are not suffering from a motivational defect is that they show normal pecking and feeding behaviour (pp. 88 and 93). Furthermore certain other behaviours are not affected by the lesion (see Chapter 6 and Sections 7.4, 8.1, and 8.4.1).

The effect on imprinting of lesions to the IMHV could be interpreted as an impairment of access to a store; that is, during training and subsequent recognition tests information passes through the region without being stored there. The results of the autoradiographic study (Horn *et al.* 1979) could then be attributed to a sort of 'use hypertrophy', the region being used when the information, stored elsewhere, is being accessed. In the early stages of imprinting the access point might show heightened biochemical activity because of say, growth occurring there. However, many other parts of the brain were examined in the autoradiographic study, including two visual projection areas and areas considered to be involved in the control of motor activity. None of these regions behaved in a similar fashion to the IMHV. Hence 'use' *per se* does not lead to localized autoradiographic changes. These considerations reduce the plausibility of the 'access' hypothesis.

The results of the first biochemical study of imprinting (Chapter 2) were, inevitably, beset with difficulties of interpretation. Through a series of control procedures involving further biochemical measures of brain function and through a series of lesion studies it was possible progressively to reduce the earlier ambiguities. The evidence, taken together, suggests that the IMHV is critical for the storage of information having a direct influence on filial preferences. The evidence also suggests that, when young chicks are exposed to a visually conspicuous object, changes occur in the neural organization of the IMHV which form the basis of some aspect of the chicks' memory of the object. Whether this involvement of IMHV in information storage is limited to imprinting or extends to other forms of learning is an issue which is considered in the next chapter. Within the context of imprinting, it is an open question as to whether the suggested storage function of the IMHV is restricted to certain kinds of stimuli towards which filial responses are be directed. This question is considered in Chapter 8.

## 5.6 Summary

Experiments which were reviewed in Chapters 2, 3, and 4 suggested that a part of the forebrain, particularly the IMHV, is critically implicated in the storage of information acquired by young chicks when they are exposed to a visually conspicuous object. The implication has the consequence that the acquisition and retention of a preference through the imprinting process should not be possible if the IMHV is destroyed. The experiments described in this chapter show that, if the IMHV is destroyed bilaterally before training, the chicks fail to develop a preference for the training object. If the region is destroyed bilaterally after training is complete, retention is severely impaired. By a process of exclusion is seems probable that the IMHV is critical for the storage of information having a direct influence on filial preferences.

## References

Benowitz, L. (1972). Effects of forebrain ablations on avoidance learning in chicks. *Physiol. Behav.* **9**, 601–8.
Bradley, P. and Horn, G. (1979). Efferent connections of hyperstriatum ventrale in the chick. *J. Anat.* **128**, 414–5.
——, Davies, D. C., and Horn, G. (1985). Connections of the hyperstriatum ventrale in the domestic chick (*Gallus domesticus*). *J. Anat.* **140**, 577–89.
Broca, P. (1865). Sur la faculté du language articulé. *Bull. Soc. Anthropol., Paris* **6**, 337–93.
Bruce, C., Desimone, R., and Gross, C. G. (1981). Visual properties of neurons in a polysensory area in superior temporal sulcus of the macaque. *J. Neurophysiol.* **46**, 369–84.
Bushnell, M. C., Goldberg, M. E., and Robinson, D. L. (1981). Behavioral enhancement of visual responses in monkey cerebral cortex. I. Modulation in posterior parietal cortex related to selective visual attention. *J. Neurophysiol.* **46**, 755–72.
Chow, K. L. (1952). Further studies of selective ablation of associative cortex in relation to visually guided behaviour. *J. comp. physiol. Psychol.* **45**, 109–18.
Ciba Foundation Symposium (1978). *Functions of the septo-hippocampal system*, Ciba Foundation Symposium No. 58, Excerpta Medica, Amsterdam.
Collias, N. E. (1980). Basal telencephalon suffices for early socialization in chicks. *Physiol. Behav.* **24**, 93–7.
Critchley, M. (1953). *The parietal lobes*. Arnold, London.

Dejerine, J. (1891). Sur un cas de cécité verbale avec agraphie, suivi d'autopsie. *Mem. Soc. Biol.* **3**, 197–201.

Gentle, M. J., Wood-Gush, D. G. M., and Gordon, J. (1978). Behavioural effects of hyperstriatal ablation in *Gallus domesticus. Behav. Process.* **3**, 137–48.

Gregory, R. L. (1961). The brain as an engineering problem. In *Current problems in animal behaviour* (eds E. H. Thorpe and O. L. Zangwill), pp. 307–30. Cambridge University Press, Cambridge.

Horn, G. and McCabe, B. J. (1984). Predispositions and preferences. Effects on imprinting of lesions to the chick brain. *Anim. Behav.* **32**, 288–92.

——, Rose, S. P. R., and Bateson, P. P. G. (1973). Experience and plasticity in the central nervous system. *Science* **181**, 506–14.

——, McCabe, B. J., and Bateson, P. P. G. (1979). An autoradiographic study of the chick brain after imprinting. *Brain Res.* **168**, 361–73.

——, ——, and Cipolla-Neto, J. (1983). Imprinting in the domestic chick: the role of each side of the hyperstriatum ventrale in acquisition and retention. *Exp. Brain Res.* **53**, 91–8.

Kohsaka, S.-I., Takamatsu, K., Aoki, E., and Tsukada, Y. (1979). Metabolic mapping of chick brain after imprinting using [$^{14}$C]2-deoxyglucose. *Brain Res.* **172**, 539–44.

Lewis, D. J., Misanin, J. R., and Miller, R. R. (1968). Recovery of memory following amnesia. *Nature, Lond.* **220**, 704–5.

Liddell, E. G. T. (1960). *The discovery of reflexes.* Clarendon Press, Oxford.

Lynch, J. C., Mountcastle, V. B., Talbot, W. H., and Yin, T. C. T. (1977). Parietal lobe mechanisms for directed visual attention. *J. Neurophysiol.* **40**, 362–89.

McCabe, B. J., Horn, G., and Bateson, P. P. G. (1981). Effects of restricted lesions of the chick forebrain on the acquisition of filial preferences during imprinting. *Brain Res.* **205**, 29–37.

——, Cipolla-Neto, J., Horn, G., and Bateson, P. P. G. (1982). Amnesic effects of bilateral lesions placed in the hyperstriatum ventral of the chick after imprinting. *Exp. Brain Res.* **48**, 13–21.

Mishkin, M. (1954). Visual discrimination performance following partial ablation of the temporal lobe. II. Ventral surface vs. hippocampus. *J. comp. physiol. Psychol.* **47**, 187–93.

—— and Pribam, K. H. (1954). Visual discrimination performance following partial ablations of the temporal lobe. I. Ventral vs. lateral. *J. comp. physiol. Psychol.* **47**, 14–20.

Perrett, D. I., Rolls, E. T., and Caan, W. (1982). Visual neurones responsive to faces in the monkey temporal cortex. *Exp. Brain Res.* **47**, 229–38.

Salzen, E. A. and Sluckin, W. (1959). The incidence of the following response and the duration of responsiveness in domestic fowl. *Anim. Behav.* **7**, 172–9.

——, Parker, D. M., and Williamson, A. J. (1975). A forebrain lesion preventing imprinting in domestic chicks. *Exp. Brain Res.* **24**, 145–57.

——, ——, —— (1978). Forebrain lesions and retention of imprinting in domestic chicks. *Exp. Brain Res.* **31**, 107–16.

——, Williamson, A. J., and Parker, D. M. (1979). The effects of forebrain lesions on innate and imprinted colour, brightness and shape preferences in domestic chicks. *Behav. Process.* **4**, 295–313.

Scoville, W. B. and Milner, B. (1957). Loss of recent memory after bilateral hippocampal lesions. *J. Neurol. Neurosurg. Psychiat.* **20**, 11–21.

Seifert, W. (ed.) (1983). *Neurobiology of the hippocampus.* Academic Press, London.

Weiskrantz, L. (1980). Varieties of residual experience. *Quart. J. exp. Psychol.* **32**, 365–86.

Wernicke, C. (1874). *Der aphasische Symtomen Komplex*. Cohn and Weigert, Breslau.

Wurtz, R. H., Goldberg, M. E., and Robinson, D. L. (1980). Behavioral modulation of visual responses in the monkey: stimulus selection for attention and movement. *Progr. Psychobiol. physiol. Psychol.* **9**, 43–83.

Zihl, J. and Werth, R. (1984). Contribution to the study of 'blindsight'. I. Can stray light account for saccadic localization in patients with postgeniculate field defects? *Neuropsychologia* **22**, 1–11.

Zeuner, F. E. (1963). *A history of domesticated animals*. Hutchinson, London.

# 6
# Imprinting and associative learning

Chicks with lesions of the IMHV appear to behave remarkably like normal chicks except that they give no evidence of remembering an object which they have had an opportunity of seeing for some time. It is possible that the lesions had other subtle effects on behaviour, effects that may have gone undetected by the simple observations of visuomotor coordination that had been made. For example, it is not difficult to envisage a situation in which damage to the brain is compatible with chicks pecking at small bright objects or at particles of food but being totally incapable of learning anything at all about their world. One way of investigating such a possibility is to enquire whether damage to IMHV impairs other sorts of learning abilities besides imprinting. Such an investigation was undertaken in two sets of experiments both of which were designed to enquire whether chicks will learn to make particular responses if they are rewarded for doing so. In other words, do lesions of the IMHV impair associative learning?

## 6.1 Working for a reward of warm air

It is common practice to use food or water to reward an animal for making a particular response. Such rewards serve to strengthen, or increase the frequency of responses and are termed reinforcers. However, food and water exert very little control over the behaviour of young chicks which use the yolk sac for nutrition during the first few days of life. Zolman (1968; 1969) has shown that heat can successfully be used to reinforce approach responses in young chicks. In the first of these two studies young chicks, up to 3 days of age, were required to approach a red circle. The circle, mounted on a plastic rod was placed, in a counterbalanced sequence, in one of two goal boxes. The whole apparatus in which the experiment was conducted was maintained at a chilly temperature of 10 degrees Celsius. Correct approaches were reinforced by a 15-second pulse of heat delivered by an infra-red lamp. Each chick was given twenty trials. The chicks made significantly more correct choices as the training progressed. This result provided evidence that, under appropriate conditions, chicks will learn to associated

107

a reward of heat with approach to a particular stimulus. Can chicks with lesions of the IMHV also perform such a task?

The chicks used to investigate this question had also been used in the experiments described in Section 5.2 (McCabe, Cipolla-Neto, Horn, and Bateson 1982). These experiments need be referred to only briefly here. Bilateral lesions were placed in IMHV in one group of chicks, in the Wulst of another and in the lateral cerebral area of a third group. All chicks, including the sham-operated birds, had been exposed to the red box or to the jungle-fowl before the surgical intervention. Preference for the training object was impaired only in chicks with lesions in IMHV. This group of chicks, like other chicks with lesions, pecked at a moving red bead as quickly and as accurately as the sham-operated controls; and there were no significant differences between the four groups in the number or accuracy of pecking movements made to millet seeds scattered on the floor of the incubator.

After the pecking tests were complete the chicks were returned to the dark incubator for up to 15 hours. At this time, when the chicks were between 2.5 and 3 days old, the next phase of the experiment was begun; the chicks were required to discriminate between two visual patterns to obtain a reward of warm air. The experiment was conducted in a cold room maintained at 12 degrees Celsius. The apparatus used is illustrated in Fig. 6.1. Above each goal box was a fan by means of which a stream of warm air could be introduced into the box. The chick was transferred in a black box from its dark incubator to the experimental room and left in the box, at room temperature, for a short time. Thereafter training was begun. Twenty-four trials were run for each bird. Half of the birds were rewarded if they approached the blue and black pattern, the remaining birds being rewarded if they approached the yellow and black pattern. The position of the stimulus to be rewarded (that is, right or left goal box in each of the twenty-four trials) was determined by a schedule which safeguarded against conditioned responses being set up for right or left position or for alternation between right and left sides.

The groups did not differ in the time taken to leave the start box and run down the alley (Table 6.1). Figure 6.2 shows, for each group, the number of birds giving correct and incorrect responses in the first and last trials. In the first trial performance was not significantly better than chance in any of the groups (Fig. 6.2(a)). In contrast, the proportion of correct to incorrect choices in the last trial was significantly better than chance in each group (Fig. 6.2(b)). Approximately half of the chicks in each group achieved a criterion of eight consecutive correct responses. The number of trials taken to reach this criterion did not differ significantly between the groups (Table 6.1). Thus, as witnessed by a variety of criteria, all groups of chicks learned the simultaneous visual discrimination task within twenty-four trials; and

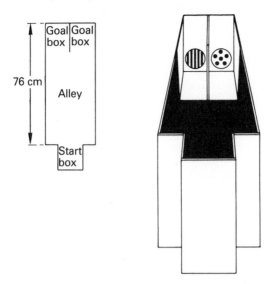

**Fig. 6.1.** Apparatus for the heat reinforcement experiment. The dimensions in the left inset are scaled relative to the length of 76 cm. The floor and side walls of the goal box were painted white and the alley and start box black. The stimulus patterns were back-projected on to the Perspex rear walls as circles of light 10 cm in diameter. One stimulus pattern comprised black bars 1.3 cm wide separated by the same interval on a yellow background. The other stimulus pattern was composed of black spots, each 2.5 cm, on a blue background. (After McCabe *et al.* 1982.)

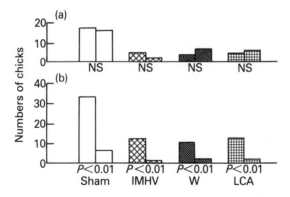

**Fig. 6.2.** Simultaneous visual discrimination task. Number of chicks making correct (left-hand bars) and incorrect responses (right-hand bars) in the first trial (a) and in the last, the twenty-fourth, trial (b). Below each pair of bars is the result of a one-tailed binomial test of the null hypothesis that correct and incorrect choices have equal probabilities. NS, not significant. The data are shown according to treatment group (see legend to Fig. 5.6). (After McCabe *et al.* 1982.)

**Table 6.1** *Data from the simultaneous visual discrimination task (after McCabe et al. 1982)*

| Group | Number of trials to criterion | Time to leave start box and run down alley (s) | $N$ |
|---|---|---|---|
| Sham | 15.15±1.14 (0.57) | 44.81± 5.79 | 47 |
| IMHV | 13.71±1.77 (0.47) | 54.43±11.27 | 15 |
| LCA | 18.10±1.57 (0.67) | 58.87±10.31 | 15 |
| W | 16.13±1.95 (0.53) | 43.75± 9.64 | 15 |

The criterion referred to in the second column was eight consecutive correct responses; the proportions of chicks which attained this criterion are given in brackets. There were no significant differences either in the proportion of birds in each group which reached criterion or in the number of trials to criterion. The time taken to leave the start box and run down the alley has been averaged over the twenty-four trials. If a chick did not enter a goal box within 120 s it was assigned a value of 120 s. Means ±s.e.m. are given. The experimental groups did not differ significantly. For abbreviations see legend to Fig. 5.6.

there were no significant differences between the groups for any of the criteria.

These results greatly strengthen the conclusion derived from other tests that the IMHV lesions do not disrupt in a general way the perceptual or motor capacities of the chicks. But could it be argued from these experiments that the IMHV is not involved in a heat-reinforced visual discrimination? Although the results are consistent with this view, they are also open to other interpretations. The heat-reinforced task involved simultaneous visual discrimination which may have been easier for the chicks than the successive discrimination required after imprinting. Furthermore the visual stimuli used in the heat-reinforcement task were different from, and may have been easier to discriminate than the stimuli used in the imprinting experiment. An additional complication is that the heat-reinforced task was used some 30 hours after the imprinting procedure. As chicks grow older they may learn to discriminate between stimuli in a more efficient or different manner. Clearly an experiment was needed which circumvented these difficulties, an experiment which would allow a more direct comparison of the effects of lesions to the IMHV on the acquisition of information through an imprinting procedure and the acquisition of information through the different procedure of instrumental conditioning.

## 6.2 Working for a view

Ducklings (*Anas rubripes tristis* and *Anas platyrhynchos*) which have been imprinted on an object will learn to peck a disc in order to see that object (Peterson 1960). These studies show that once ducklings have been imprinted on a conspicuous object, that object has the properties of a reinforcer (see also Campbell and Pickleman 1961; Hoffman *et al.* 1966). It has also been shown that an object which is effective as an imprinting stimulus is also effective as a reinforcer as imprinting occurs (Bateson and Reese 1969). These workers found that day-old chicks quickly learned to press a pedal in order to be presented with either a red or blue flashing light. After reaching criterion on this associative task the chicks were given a choice test. The blue and red flashing lights which had served as reinforcers were placed at either end of an alley. Each chick was placed in the middle of the alley and its approach behaviour was recorded. The chicks were found to approach the light which they had seen during training. These experiments demonstrated that a conspicuous object could reinforce behaviour in young chicks which, prior to training, were visually naive. Furthermore, the experiments showed that as the chicks learned to associate the pedal press with a view of the flashing object, the chicks also learned the characteristics of that object and were subsequently able to recognize it. Since the two processes of recognition and association occurred concurrently, the training procedure appeared to be an appropriate one to enquire whether or not the processes could be dissociated by lesions of the IMHV (Johnson and Horn 1984, 1985).

The operant training apparatus used is illustrated in Fig. 6.3. Three walls of the box were painted matt black. The remaining side was made of wire mesh in front of which stood the reinforcing object, either the red box or the stuffed jungle-fowl. In the floor of the box were set two conspicuous pedals painted in a black and white chequer-board pattern. The chicks could press the pedals merely by stepping on them. Pressing one of the pedals activated a relay which resulted in the illumination and rotation of the reinforcing object for so long as the chick remained on the pedal. The 'activated' object was now attractive to the chick which moved toward it, and in doing so, moved off the pedal. As a result, the object ceased to be illuminated and stopped moving. Pressing the other pedal had no effect. In order to counteract any left/right bias the position of the 'active' pedal was varied systematically between different birds. For a given bird the active pedal was consistently on the right or on the left side of the floor of the box. Thus the chicks were required to go to a certain place in order to be rewarded by a view of the activated object.

Two groups of chicks were used, sham-operated controls and chicks with lesions placed bilateraly in IMHV. The chicks were hatched and reared in darkness until they were approximately 12 hours old. Sham-operated controls were anaesthetized; the scalp was incised and then sutured. The methods used to place lesions in IMHV were similar to those which have already been described (Section 5.1). During the operation the chicks were coded and, as before, all subsequent procedures were conducted without the experimenter knowing the surgical history of the chicks. Operant training began when the chicks had fully recovered from surgery and were

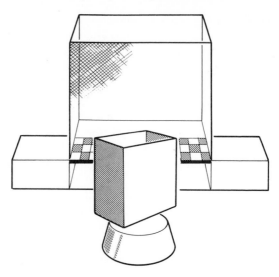

**Fig. 6.3.** Diagram of the operant training apparatus with one of the reinforcing stimuli in front of the open mesh side. The mesh side measures 42 cm×30 cm. The stimulus was placed 35 cm in front of the apparatus. (After Bateson and Reese 1969.)

20–24 hours old. For half of the chicks the reinforcing object was the illuminated, rotating red box; for the other half it was the illuminated, rotating stuffed jungle-fowl.

The two groups did not differ in the mean time to make the first pedal press (Fig. 6.4(a)). Some 70 per cent of the birds in each group reached the criterion of nine out of ten successive presses of the active pedal in one of the two training sessions (Fig. 6.4(b)). There were no significant differences in the mean time taken by each group of chicks to reach the criterion, and in both groups the criterion was reached sooner in the second operant training session than in the first (Fig. 6.4(c)). Furthermore, the two groups of chicks did not differ in the amount of time spent on the active pedal. Thus chicks with lesions in IMHV did not differ significantly from the sham-operated controls in any measure of performance, and both groups learned to press the pedal in order to gain a view of the training object which they approached.

Two hours after the second session in the operant training apparatus the chicks were given a simultaneous choice test (pp. 52–3 and Fig. 3.2(b)). The trolley (Fig. 3.2(c)) stood on the railway, midway between the jungle-fowl and the red box. Each chick was placed in the running wheel which was mounted on the trolley. The stimuli were then switched on. As the chick attempted to approach a stimulus the running wheel rotated and the trolley was displaced on the railway. The distance which the trolley moved in 4

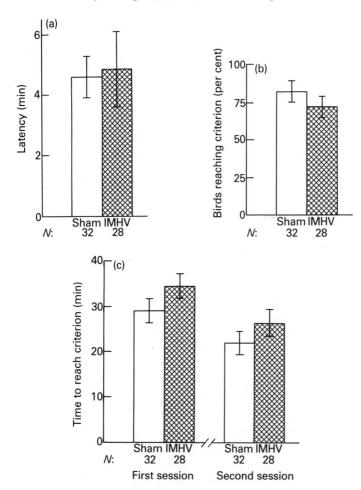

**Fig. 6.4.** Operant training task. Means ± s.e.m. (a) Latency to make first pedal press. (b) Percentage of birds reaching criterion in one of the two training sessions. The birds came from seven batches and the percentage of birds in each batch to reach criterion was calculated. The overall mean and standard error of these seven mean values were calculated and are shown. (c) Time taken to reach criterion according to training session. The mean time taken in the second session was significantly shorter than that in the first session for both the sham-operated controls and for the IMHV-lesioned chicks ($P < 0.005$). (After Johnson and Horn 1985.)

minutes was used as a basis for calculating the preference score (see legend to Fig. 6.5). This score provided a measure of the percentage of the total activity in the test which was directed towards the training object. The sham-operated chicks prefered the object which had been used as the rein-forcer; chicks with bilateral lesion of the IMHV performed at chance, show-ing no greater preference for the reinforcing object than for the novel

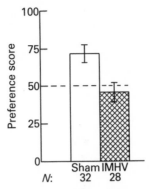

**Fig. 6.5.** Preference scores of chicks which had been trained on the operant task. Means ± s.e.m. The objects which had been used as the reinforcers (either the rotating red box or the rotating jungle-fowl) were placed at either end of the railway (see Fig. 3.2(b)). The preference score was calculated from the expression

$$\frac{100 \times \text{distance travelled by trolley as chick attempted to approach the reinforcer}}{\text{total distance travelled by trolley}}$$

The sham-operated control chicks preferred the visually conspicuous object which they had seen as reinforcer, and their mean preference score was significantly greater than 50 ($P < 0.01$). The mean preference score of the lesioned birds was significantly less than that of their controls ($P < 0.01$), and was not significantly different from 50. (After Johnson and Horn 1985.)

object. The mean score achieved by the controls was significantly greater than that achieved by the lesioned birds (Fig. 6.5).

For the sham-operated controls the data give strong support for the observation that chicks learn the characteristics of the reinforcing stimulus as they learn to press the pedal that activates it (Bateson and Reese 1969). Lesions to the IMHV dissociate these two processes. In such chicks an object may serve as a reinforcer in an operant task, but the chicks fail to 'recognize' that object in a preference test. In order to gain some insight into the nature of this defect, it is necessary to consider a chick's behaviour when it selectively approaches an object to which it has previously been exposed, and also to consider what may be meant by the term 'recognition' in such situations.

Besides approaching the object, the chick may also emit contentment calls; and if the object is removed, the chick may emit distress calls. It is commonplace, in the imprinting literature, to refer to such objects as 'familiar'. By the same token a novel object, one which the chick has never seen before, is 'unfamiliar'. The test used to measure the strength of imprinting involves exposing the chicks to the familiar object and to a novel object. This preference test may be considered to be a form of recognition test (Sluckin 1972). The ability to discriminate between familiar and unfamiliar stimuli is considered to be based on recognition memory both in studies of human (see Baddeley 1976) and of animal (see Gaffan 1974, 1983) behaviour. The 'memory' is inferred because a particular past experience exerts a specific effect on behaviour; the word 'recognition' is used because the subject discriminates on the basis of familiarity.

Is it reasonable to infer that a chick has a defect of recognition memory if, in a preference test, the chick fails to approach selectively the object to which it has previously been exposed? The chick may have a defect of recognition memory, but it need not have. There are a number of ways of accounting for a failure to approach selectively the training object, and the failure may only be ascribed to a defect of recognition memory if there are good grounds for doing so. For chicks with lesions of the IMHV explanations in terms of changes in motor or sensory functions, alertness, motivation, and a variety of other factors are not consistent with the available evidence (see Sections 5.5, 7.4, and 8.1). This view is supported by the experiments described above in which a conspicous reinforcing object was illuminated and rotated when chicks stood on the correct pedal. When the reinforcing object was activated in this way the control chicks moved off the pedal to approach the object. Not only did the IMHV-lesioned chicks learn to press the correct pedal as quickly as the controls, but they also moved off the pedal as quickly. In the preference test the lesioned bird were no less active than the controls; but unlike the controls the lesioned birds did not direct their movements more to the reinforcing object than to the novel object.

The failure of IMHV-lesioned chicks selectively to approach in a preference test an object which they have previously seen, and which is selectively approached by trained control chicks may tentatively be taken as evidence that the IMHV is involved in recognition memory. Further evidence in support of this view is given in later chapters. Lesions to the IMHV dissociate this memory from the memory required to perform an associative learning task.

## 6.3 Recognition memory and associative learning

At first sight it may seem strange that a chick will work in order to see a stimulus and later fail to recognize it (Johnson and Horn 1984, 1985), or that a chick which has been exposed to an object for 2 hours and then fails to recognize it is nonetheless able to learn a visual discrimination task (McCabe *et al.* 1982). Yet this remarkable behaviour is reminiscent of a syndrome which has been described in human patients, and more recently in monkeys (see Horn 1983).

In 1957 Scoville and Milner reported the case of a patient, H.M., who suffered from severe epilepsy. In an attempt to alleviate his epileptic symptoms, the medial part of the temporal lobe, including the hippocampus, was removed bilaterally. Whilst the symptoms of epilepsy gradually subsided another pathology supervened. H.M. developed a severe amnesia which has persisted ever since the operation. Milner (1966) described the clinical picture he presented and recorded his mother's observations about him. H.M. would do the same jigsaw puzzles day after day without showing any practice effect and he would read the same magazines over and over again without ever finding their contents familar. The same forgetfulness applied to people he had met since the operation, even to neighbours who had been visiting the house regularly for several years (Milner 1966). In spite of H.M.'s severely defective recognition memory, he was able to learn new motor skills such as mirror drawings. However, on each occasion that he performed such a task he denied having done it on previous occasions; the learning was unaccompanied by any feeling of familiarity (Milner 1962). H.M. is able to learn to perform certain visual discrimination tasks. One of these tasks if particularly interesting since it shares some features of the visual discrimination tasks which chicks with damage to the IMHV are able to perform (Section 6.1). H.M. was required to distinguish between a circle and ellipses simultaneously presented (Sidman *et al.* 1968). The figures were projected from the rear on to a panel of small screens placed in front of him. If he pressed the screen on which the circle was present, he was rewarded with a penny. He performed this task successfully.

Another organic amnesia, similar in some ways though not symptomatically identical with that associated with medial temporal lobe lesions, is found in some chronic alcoholics; some of the symptoms of their amnesia may be induced, reversibly, by drugs (Brown *et al.* 1982, 1983). This syndrome, which is associated with chronic alcoholism, was first described by Korsakoff toward the end of the last century (see Zangwill 1983). In Korsakoff patients brain damage may often be extensive, but a common feature is that pathological changes are found in the hypothalmus and part of the thalmus (Brierley 1977; Mair *et al.* 1979). Accordingly the syndrome is sometimes referred to as 'diencephalic amnesia' (see p. 253 and Section 12.1.1.). Korsakoff patients are defective in recognition memory, especially so if the object to be remembered is seen out of context (Huppert and Piercy 1976). These patients are, however, able to form associations. The first report of this ability is that of Claparède (1911, quoted by MacCurdy 1928). Claparède hid a pin between his fingers and pricked the hand of a Korsakoff patient. She claimed she remembered no more about this experience but when Claparède moved his hand close to hers she pulled her hand away. The patient appeared to have associated Claparède's hand movement with a pin prick so that a sensory-motor associative link of some kind may be inferred; yet the patient did not know why she had withdrawn her hand.

Weiskrantz and Warrington (1979) were able to establish reliable, stable conditioned responses in two patients with memory defects. The conditioned stimulus was a compound auditory and visual signal. The sound source and the visual stimulus, a small pilot lamp, was placed just below and in front of the patient's left eye. A brief puff of air served as the unconditioned stimulus. The air puff was directed to the right eye and yielded a blink each time the puff was delivered. The apparatus had a very distinctive and unusual appearance and remained visible throughout the sessions and during the rest breaks. After a number of pairings of the compound light and sound stimulus with the air puff, the compound stimulus alone evoked an eye-blink response. Retention of the conditioned eye-blink response persisted across intervals of 10 minutes and 24 hours. However, the subjects appeared to be unfamiliar with the essentials of the procedure and appeared not to recognize the nozzle of the air puffer or the light and the buzzer used as the compound conditioned stimulus. These results are in line with other findings from many amnesic patients. They perform badly in tasks which require recognition of objects or events (see Gaffan 1972; Warrington 1974) although they show reasonable visual discrimination and motor skill learning (Talland 1965; Sidman *et al.* 1968; Gaffan 1972; Warrington and Weiskrantz 1979). It would be wrong to suppose that all of these patients necesarily have the same clinical signs of memory loss and the same cerebral pathology (see above). It is, however, heuristically valuable to search for common symptoms and to enquire whether patients having them also have in common a similar pattern of brain damage.

Once some of the features which characterized H.M.'s amnesia were recognized and interest in early descriptions of Korsakoff's syndrome re-awakened (see Zangwill 1966), the search was on for animal models of these amnesias. However, it is clearly important to know for what one is searching; the verbal denial of familiarity by human amnesics is not a response that is available to the experimenter studying amnesia in animals. With certain exceptions (Harlow and Zimmerman 1959) recognition tests have not been used extensively outside the fields of imprinting and human neuropsychology. An important step forward was taken when, in 1974, Gaffan introduced such a test designed for use with macaque monkeys. The test was straightforward. A tray with three food wells was presented to the monkey. On the 'sample' trial a single object was presented. The object covered the central food well which contained a morsal of food. After the monkey had displaced the object and retrieved the bait a screen was lowered between the monkey and the food wells. At the matching trial, which occurred 10 seconds after the animal had responded to the sample, the same object was presented again. This time it was over a baited well on the right- or left-hand sides. The opposite food well was covered by a second object which the monkey had not seen before. The well covered by this novel object was not baited. The animal was allowed to choose one of the objects, and collected the bait by moving the object it had previously seen. This 'matching to sample' is a test of familiarity. These trials may be repeated many times provided that there is a sufficient array of objects. The task can also be made increasingly difficult by, for example, increasing the number of novel objects present with the familiar object during the test.

These and other tests of recognition (see Mishkin and Delacour 1975) have been used to study the effects of brain lesions on memory. The lesions were placed in the diencephalon (Aggleton and Mishkin 1983*a,b*) or the medial part of the temporal lobe (Zola-Morgan and Squire 1984; Mahut and Moss 1985). As described above, damage to these brain regions is often associated with amnesia in human patients. Monkeys with these lesions are impaired in tasks which involve object recognition, but much less impaired in tasks which involve visual discrimination learning. Thus, specific brain damage in monkeys and humans and damage to the IMHV in chicks appear to have similar consequences: there is a dissociation between the memory necessary for recognition and the memory necessary for associative learning. These issues are considered again below and will also be considered when discussing the role of the IMHV in memory (Section 11.3).

### 6.4 Is there a special relationship between imprinting and the IMHV?

The experiments described in Sections 6.1 and 6.2 might suggest that the IMHV has a function which is specific to imprinting. In order to assess the plausibility of this suggestion it is necessary to take into account a variety of factors.

Objects which serve as suitable imprinting stimuli exert several effects on young precocial birds. In addition to eliciting a following response, such a stimulus acts as a reinforcer and also initiates in the nervous system changes which enable the chick subsequently to recognize that object. The effect of such an object on following can be observed directly. The operation of an imprinting stimulus as a reinforcer is deduced: reinforcing stimuli are those which strengthen certain responses and since an imprinting stimulus has this effect (see Section 6.2) it is, by definition, a reinforcing stimulus. The capacity of an imprinting object to leave in the nervous system some sort of 'trace' is inferred if the young bird comes to prefer the object to which it has been exposed over some other visually conspicuous object which it has not seen before. Another consequence of young birds being imprinted upon a particular object is that the birds may actively avoid other visually conspicuous objects. This consequence can, of course, be observed directly in the birds' behaviour.

Clearly different procedures—observational, deductive, and inferential— are used to characterize the effects of exposing young, visually naive, nidifugous birds to certain objects. This characterization is useful for the further analysis of the underlying neural mechanisms, for it implies that several neural processes may be involved. Thus an imprinting stimulus (i) elicits approach responses in naive birds, (ii) acts as a reinforcer, (iii) evokes processes which lead to the formation of a neural representation of the stimulus, and (iv) may result in the chick avoiding other conspicuous objects.

In so far as an imprinting stimulus elicits approach activity in visually naive birds it acts as an unconditioned stimulus in the Pavlovian sense; that is, as a stimulus which unconditionally elicits a response or set of responses (see Mackintosh 1974). When imprinting objects strengthen an operant response, they act as reinforcers. Do the reinforcing properties of imprinting objects influence the chicks' responses to these objects? The experiments of Hoffman and his collaborators (1972) suggest that this is the case. These workers showed that the distress calls of young ducklings were suppressed by a moving stimulus from the first time that it was presented to them. If the stimulus was stationary, distress calls were not suppressed. Hoffman and his colleagues arranged for presentations of the stationary stimulus to be intermixed with presentations of the same stimulus in motion. Under these conditions the stationary stimulus acquired the ability to suppress the distress vocalizations. This result suggests that the reinforcing properties of the moving stimulus, which unconditionally evoked a filial response, the suppression of distress calls, brought this response under the control of other features of the stimulus. Hoffman and Ratner (1973) developed the general case that the reinforcing aspects of an imprinting stimulus facilitated the development of familiarity with other characteristics of the stimulus.

Some of the neural processes implicated in imprinting (see p. 118) and the way that these processes might interact may usefully described by constructing a simple model. An outline of such a model is given in Fig. 6.6(a). A chick is exposed to stimulus 'I' which is an effective artificial imprinting object. Not all visual stimuli elicit filial behaviour, for example stimuli which are the size of millet seeds evoke pecking responses. Hence the existence of a filter between the sensory input and the motor system controlling approach may be inferred. Such a filter is represented diagrammatically as F in Fig. 6.6(a), but, for simplicity, is omitted in the other diagrams shown. In the model, stimulus I activates several neural pathways. Evoked activity in one of these pathways weakly excites neurones (Fig. 6.6, 'Ap.') controlling approach, the unconditioned response. This approach is not specific to a particular object. The imprinting stimulus also acts as a reinforcer and this operation is assumed in the model to be mediated by an incentive system (see also Chapter 9). A neural pathway activated by stimulus I leads to a store. A neural representation of the stimulus in the store is gradually formed during the period of exposure. A necessary condition for the formation of this representation is the presence of an input from the incentive system. As the representation builds up, the output from the store is considered to increase and as a result the chick's approach to stimulus I is strengthened. The processes by which chicks come to avoid novel objects

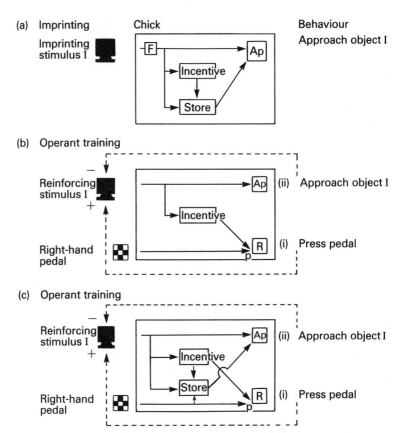

**Fig. 6.6.** Diagrammatic representation of some events occurring during training. The large rectangle represents the chick's central nervous system. Boxes within the rectangle refer to neuronal systems having the specified functions. The arrows within the large rectangle refer to interactions taking place within the chick; arrows outside the rectangle indicate the consequences of the chick's behaviour. Stimulus I, a rotating box illuminated red on its two larger surfaces, is used throughout and is an effective, artificial, imprinting object. Diagram (a) represents events that may occur during the course of exposure to stimulus I in an imprinting situation. F represents a filter. It is shown only in this diagram and is present to emphasize the point that not all visual stimuli elicit approach responses. Ap represents the neuronal system controlling approach. (b) The chick is in the operant training apparatus (Fig. 6.3). As the chick moves about it stands on the right-hand, active pedal in the floor of the apparatus. This pedal has the chequer-board pattern illustrated. R in the diagram represents a system of neurones which controls the behaviour of walking to the right and standing on the active pedal. The consequence of this act is to turn on (+) stimulus I. When this stimulus appears the chick approaches it ((b), (ii)) and steps off the pedal. As a result stimulus I is switched off (−). The processes indicated in diagrams (a) and (b) will be occurring simultaneously during operant training and are shown together in diagram (c). For further discussion see text.

are not shown in the model. Such avoidance behaviour is a consequence of filial attachment to a particular object: as the chick becomes progressively more familiar with that object it avoids objects that are very different from it. It is as if, once the neural representation of stimulus I has been formed, 'not I' objects are avoided (see Fig. 7.10 and 7.11). The developing avoidance behaviour could be based on a neural matching system: a strong mismatch between the stored information and the activity evoked in the nervous system by a novel object results in the activation of an avoidance system. However, even if such an matching system is involved, little is known of the mechanism by which it might operate, although this subject has been a matter of speculation for some years (Horn 1952, 1967; Sokolov 1960; Vinogradova 1970; Palm 1982; see Fig. 1.12).

The models shown in Fig. 6.6 may also be used to consider, in a simplified form, the neural processes engaged in the performance of the operant task used by Johnson and Horn (Section 6.2). The right-hand pedal in the floor of the training box was painted with a different chequer-board pattern from that on the left-hand pedal (Fig. 6.3). Suppose that a chick moves about the training box more or less at random. By chance the chick stands on the active pedal, say the one on the right-hand side of the box. Activity will be evoked in the sensory pathways by the right chequer-board pattern. This activity will coincide with activity in the system of neurones controlling the behaviour of the chick moving to the right pedal and standing on it (Fig. 6.6(b), R). When the chick stands on the pedal stimulus I is turned on. The incentive effect of this stimulus might facilitate transmission at junction p (Fig. 6.6(b)) when fibres in the sensory pathways and the neurones in the R system are active together (Hebb 1949). Once stimulus I has been turned on it elicits an approach response. As the chick approaches it leaves the pedal and stimulus I is turned off. The chick then walks round the floor of the box. If it steps on the left-hand pedal stimulus I is not activated. If the chick stands on the right-hand pedal, the incentive effect of stimulus I will again facilitate transmission at junction p. As this process is repeated this link becomes progressively strengthened and the right-hand chequer-board pattern progressively increases its control over the 'press-right pedal' system. The 'habit' of pressing the right pedal become established. The neural basis of this habit resides in the postulated facilitation of transmission at junction p in Fig. 6.6(b),(c). It is worth emphasizing that this mechanism is only one of a number that could account for the formation of the habit. The 'memory' for the associative learning task is peripheral, at the point at which transmission is facilitated (p). In the model, this memory is deliberately not re-represented in the central store shown in Fig. 6.6.

During the time that stimulus I is activated signals evoked by it pass to the store and to the incentive system so that a representation of the stimulus is built up in the store (Fig. 6.6(a)). The processes and interactions occurring within the chick and outlined in Fig. 6.6(a) and (b) occur throughout the period of operant training and are diagrammatically presented in combined form in Fig. 6.6(c). When the chick is given a preference test after operant training, the bird approaches stimulus I which it recognizes, since there is a representation of the stimulus in the store. The model accounts for the major consequences of removing the store prior to training on the operant task. The effect of such an experimental manipulation would be to reduce the processes from those illustrated in Fig. 6.6(c) to those in Fig. 6.6(b) where no store is shown. In these circumstances the chicks would be quite capable of learning the operant task, but they would not be expected to approach the reinforcing stimulus more than any other imprinting stimulus of similar attractiveness. Clearly this scheme is over-simplified if only because in intact chicks it is to be expected that, as operant training proceeds, the tendency to approach stimulus I should increase. As a result, the chicks would spend less time on the pedal. Less time on the pedal would have the consequence of less reinforcement. Hence the chicks must in some way optimize these conflicting interests.

Which of the various processes illustrated in Fig. 6.6 might be affected by bilateral lesion of the IMHV placed before or soon after training? If these lesions were to destroy the incentive system a representation of stimulus I would not be formed and the chick would not recognize it. That is, of course, the consequence of such a lesion (Sections 5.2 and 5.3). In addition, the stimulus could not be used as a reinforcer (Fig. 6.6(b)). Hence chicks with this lesions should not learn the operant task. Since they do, it may be concluded that the lesion does not affect the incentive system. Does the lesion to the IMHV effect the capacity of the imprinting stimulus unconditionally to evoke an approach response? Evidently not, since chicks with these lesions will approach visually conspicous objects. This result implies that removal of the IMHV does not interfere with the integrity of the pathway which is shown in Fig. 6.6(a) as carrying the input evoked by stimulus I directly to the approach system.

When the IMHV was removed bilaterally before chicks were exposed to an imprinting stimulus, approach activity, though present, was not strengthened during the course of training as it was in control chicks (Section 5.1 and Fig. 5.2). These results suggest that the incentive system does not operate by facilitating transmission in the direct pathway to the approach system (Fig. 6.6(a)). Chicks with lesions of the IMHV fail to recognize the object I to which they have been exposed, either in an imprinting situation or during training on the operant task. Such an effect would be achieved by destroying the store. This intervention would not affect the capacity of visually conspicuous objects to evoke an approach response or to act as a reinforcer; destruction of the IMHV affects neither of these capacities. These considerations suggest that the IMHV resembles the store more closely than any other function in the model. The IMHV may operate as a store itself or provide an access route for a store elsewhere. Arguments have been presented for supposing that the access hypothesis is inadequate to account for the experimental evidence (see p. 103).

Kossut and Rose (1984) found that the incorporation of radioactive 2-deoxyglucose was increased in the medial part of hyperstriatum ventrale in young chicks trained on an associative learning task. The region appeared to overlap the posterior boundary of the IMHV. Kossut and Rose used a passive avoidance task (Lee-Teng and Sherman 1966; Cherkin 1969). In this procedure a small bead, between 2 and 4 millimetres in diameter, is dipped into methylanthranilate, a liquid which to a human has a highly unpleasant taste. When chicks peck such a bead most of them show signs of aversive behaviour such as closing the eyes whilst opening the beak or shaking the head. When chicks are presented with a similar dry bead within the next few hours many will avoid pecking it. This avoidance behaviour is not shown by control chicks which had previously pecked a bead which had been dipped in water.

It may be inferred that, to chicks which had pecked the bead dipped in methylanthranilate, the bead became a predictor of an unpleasant experience; that is, the chicks had formed an association between the act of pecking the bead and the aversive experience which accompanied and followed this act. Hence the passive avoidance task is an associative learning task. This particular task involves the IMHV (Kossut and Rose 1984; Stewart *et al.* 1984), a finding which at first sight appears to be at odds with the results, described in Sections 6.1 and 6.2, that lesions of the IMHV are without effect on associative learning. If associative learning can occurr in the absence of the IMHV, then surely it is surprising to find cellular changes there following the acquisition of a task involving this kind of learning?

In the experiments described in Section 6.1 and 6.2 the reinforcing stimuli were rewarding; in the experiments using methylanthranilate the reinforcing stimuli were aversive. As a result of pecking the bead which had been dipped in this substance, the chicks withheld a response which they tend to emit without training: their tendency to peck bright objects was reduced. This behaviour may be a clue as to what is happening. Gaffan and his colleagues (1984) have looked in some detail at the effects of sectioning the fornix on associative learning in macaque monkeys. The fornix is a fibre bundle containing axons which project from the hippocampus and associated structures to targets, especially in the diencephalon. Recognition memory appears to be impaired by lesions of the fornix (Gaffan 1974; Gaffan and Weiskrantz 1980). In contrast, the memory necessary to perform some associative learning tasks is spared (Gaffan 1974). This statement implies that the lesion does not affect some forms of associative learning. Which forms are affected and which are not? Gaffan and his colleagues (1984) concluded from an extensive series of experiments that fornix transection did not impair performance on associative task involving 'natural' response tendencies, such as a tendency to look for food; but the lesion affected performance when the task to be acquired was the reverse of the animal's 'spontaneous tendency' (see Douglas 1967). In chicks, the two associative tasks that were unaffected by lesions to the IMHV both involved 'natural' responses. In the heat reinforcement task, the reward was a current of warm air (Section 6.1). The room in which the experiment was conducted was cold, so that the chicks may be considered to have worked in order to get warm. In the experiments described in Section 6.2 (Johnson and Horn 1984, 1985) the reinforcing stimulus was a visually conspicuous object which chicks will approach without any training. In contrast to these two studies, the passive avoidance task involved suppressing a strong tendency to peck small bright objects; here the acquired behaviour was incompatible with the chicks' predisposition to peck. These considerations suggest that the fornix/hippocampal system of primates on the one had and the IMHV system of chicks on the other are implicated in recognition memory and appear to be implicated in some, but not all forms of associative learning. This is a minimal position. The experimental evidence does not preclude the possibility that these systems play a role of some kind in all forms of associative learning.

When an animal learns to associate a stimulus with a reward two things may happen. A habit is established and need consist of little more than the strengthening of connections between receptors activated by the stimulus and neurones controlling the response which the animal emits (see also Section 12.1.1). In the normal course of events it is likely that, in addition, the animal recognizes the stimulus which it associates with the response—just as a normal patient might *both* avoid the approach of Claparède's hand *and* recognize Claparède as the man who hid a pin between his fingers. The memory necessary for the withdrawal response, the habit, appears to have been dissociated from the memory necessary for recognition in Claperède's amnesic patient. For normal subjects, neural changes might be expected in the memory systems supporting both of these components of behaviour. This view implies that, in associative learning, the two memory systems are in parallel. Such an effect would be achieved if, for example (Fig. 6.6(c)), the signals evoked by the chequer-board pattern were recorded in the central store as well as being recorded as a strengthening of the junction p between afferent input and the 'press right pedal' system. These points are made explicit in Fig. 6.7. The peripheral memory is represented as a strengthening of the junction p in the sensory-motor pathway. The box marked 'Store' in the figure corresponds to a central memory system in which the characteristic of the chequer-board pattern are represented. With such an arrangement the central store could be destroyed without interfering with the habit, which would be impaired if the sensory-response pathway were interrupted. There is some evidence to support such a notion. On the one hand, Benowitz (1972) found that lesions which appeared to encroach on

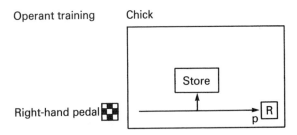

**Fig. 6.7.** Simple diagram to illustrate two memory systems which might be formed during the acquisition of an operant learning task. The operant task described in Section 6.2 is used as the example. The figure is based on a simplified version of Fig. 6.6(c). Operant training is assumed to lead to a strengthening of the link p (see Fig. 6.6(b), (c)). This strengthening is the basis of the peripheral, or sensory-response memory. A neural representation of the conditioned stimulus, the chequer-board pattern, may also be formed in the central store during the course of training. This representation lies in parallel with the peripheral representation. The central store is shown as registering only the conditioned stimulus. However, the outcome of the stimulus–response association (the switching on of the reinforcing object; see Fig. 6.6(b), (c)) may also be registered centrally. For further discussion see text.

IMHV did not impair retention in chicks trained on the passive avoidance task described above: the chicks continued to perform this habit. If this is indeed the case, and if the cellular changes in this brain region (Kossut and Rose 1984; Stewart *et al.* 1984) reflect a storage function for the region in passive avoidance learning, then this store must lie in parallel with the store that supports the habit, or the sensory-motor component of the passive avoidance response. On the other hand, lesions of the lateral cerebral area severely impaired retention of passive avoidance learning (Benowitz 1972); this lesion was without effect on the retention of a preference acquired through imprinting (Section 5.2).

It would certainly be unifying if the IMHV played a role in recognition memory irrespective of whether the memory is acquired through imprinting or through other forms of learning. If this proved to be the case, then the IMHV system might have a very general function in memory. Information stored about events may not only involve a neural representation of particular objects, but also the rules that relate that representation to the outcome of the animal's response to an object—whether, for example, a small bead is aversive or not. A bird which has pecked the aversive bead may be reluctant to peck similar beads which may turn up in quite different contexts. Such reluctance suggests that the information initially stored about the bead, and the outcome of pecking it, can be used in other situations (see Dickinson 1980, especially Chapter 3). These considerations will be the subject of further discussion (Sections 7.3, 11.3, and 12.1.1). It is, however, clear that to understand the role of the IMHV in associative learning much more experimental evidence is required; but the evidence already available suggests that the IMHV plays a role in learning processes beyond that of imprinting.

## 6.5 Summary

Visually conspicuous objects act (i) as unconditioned stimuli eliciting approach in visually naive chicks, (ii) as reinforcers, and (iii) to initiate processes which lead to the formation of neural representations of the objects (recognition memory). Evidence is presented that bilateral lesions of IMHV do not interfere with functions (i) and (ii). The lesions impair object recognition memory (iii) without impairing certain forms of associative learning. Evidence of an apparently similar dissociation between recognition memory and visual discrimination learning in humans and other primates is reviewed.

## References

Aggleton, J. P. and Mishkin, M. (1983a). Visual recognition impairment following medial thalmic lesions in monkeys. *Neuropsychologia* **21**, 189–197
——, —— (1983b) Memory impairments following restricted medial thalamic lesions in monkeys. *Exp. Brain Res.* **52**, 199–209.
Bateson, P. P. G. and Reese, E. P. (1969). The reinforcing properties of conspicuous stimuli in the imprinting situation. *Anim. Behav.* **17**, 692–9.
Baddeley, A. D. (1976). *The psychology of memory.* Harper and Row, New York.
Benowitz, L. (1972). Effect of forebrain ablations on avoidance learning in chicks. *Physiol. Behav.* **9**, 601–8.
Brierley, J. B. (1977) Neuropathology of amnesic states. In *Amnesia* (2nd edn) (eds C. W. M. Whittey and O. L. Zangwill), pp. 199–243. Butterworth, London.
Brown, J., Lewis, V., Brown, M., Horn, G., and Bowes, J. B. (1982). A comparison between transient amnesias induced by two drugs (diazepam and lorazepam) and amnesia of organic origin. *Neuropsychologia* **20**, 55–70.
——, Brown, M. W., and Bowes, J. B. (1983). Effects of lorazepam on rate of forgetting, on retrieval from semantic memory and on manual dexterity. *Neuropsychologia* **21**, 501–512.
Campbell, B. A. and Pickleman, J. R. (1961). The imprinting object as a reinforcing stimulus. *J. comp. physiol. Psychol.* **54**, 592–6.
Cherkin, A. (1969). Kinetics of memory consolidation: role of amnesic treatment parameters. *Proc. natn. Acad. Sci. U.S.A.* **63**, 1094–101.
Claparède, E. (1911). Récognition et moiïté. *Archs Psychol., Genève* **11**, 79–90.
Dickinson, A. (1980). *Contemporary animal learning theory.* Cambridge University Press, Cambridge.
Douglas, R. T. (1967). The hippocampus and behavior. *Psychol. Bull.* **67**, 416–42.
Gaffan, D. (1972). Loss of recognition memory in rats with fornix lesions. *Neuropsychologia* **10**, 327–41.
—— (1974). Recognition impaired and association intact in the memory of monkeys after transection of the fornix. *J. comp. physiol. Psychol.* **86**, 1100–9.
—— (1983). Animal amnesia: some disconnection syndromes? In *Neurobiology of the hippocampus* (ed. W. Seifert), pp. 513–28. Academic Press, New York.

—— and Weiskrantz, L. (1980). Recency effects and lesion effects in delayed non-matching to randomly baited samples by monkeys. *Brain Res.* **196**, 373–86.

——, Saunders, R. C., Gaffan, E. A., Harrison, S., Shields, C., and Owen, M. J. (1984). Effects of fornix transection upon associative memory in monkeys: role of hippocampus in learned action. *Quart. J. exp. Psychol.* **36**, 173–221.

Harlow, H. F. and Zimmerman, R. R. (1959). Affectional responses in the infant monkey. *Science* **130**, 421–32.

Hebb, D. O. (1949). *The organization of behavior.* John Wiley, New York.

Hoffman, H. S. and Ratner, A. M. (1973). A reinforcement model of behavioural control by a stationary imprinting stimulus. *Psychon. Rev.* **80**, 527–44.

——, Schiff, D., Adams, J., and Searle, J. L. (1966). Enhanced distress vocalization through selective reinforcement. *Science* **151**, 352–4.

——, Eiserer, L. A. and Singer, D. (1972). Acquisition of behavioural control by a stationary imprinting stimulus. *Psychon. Sci.* **26**, 146–48.

Horn, G. (1952). The neurological basis of thought. *Mermaid* **18**, 17–25.

—— (1967). Neuronal mechanisms of habituation. *Nature, Lond.* **215**, 707–11.

—— (1983). Information storage in the brain. A study of imprinting in the domestic chick. In *Advances in vertebrate neuroethology* (eds J.-P. Ewert, R. R. Capranica, and D. J. Ingle), pp. 511–41. Plenum Press, New York.

Huppert, F. A. and Piercy, M. (1976). Recognition memory in amnesic patients: effect of temporal context and familiarity of material. *Cortex* **12**, 3–20.

Johnson, M. H. and Horn, G. (1984). Differential effects of brain lesions on imprinting and an associative learning task. *Neurosci. Lett.* Suppl. 18, S131.

——, —— (1985). Dissociation of recognition memory and associative learning by a restricted lesion of the chick forebrain. *Neuropsychologia* (in press).

Kossut, M. and Rose, S. P. R. (1984). Differential 2-deoxyglucose uptake into chick brain structures during passive avoidance training. *Neuroscience* **12**, 971–7.

Lee-Teng, E. and Sherman, S. M. (1966). Memory consolidation of one-trial learning in chicks. *Proc. natn. Acad. Sci. U.S.A.* **56**, 926–31.

McCabe, B. J., Cipolla-Neto, J., Horn, G., and Bateson, P. P. G. (1982). Amnesic effects of bilateral lesions placed in the hyperstriatum ventrale of the chick after imprinting. *Exp. Brain Res.* **48**, 13–21.

MacCurdy, J. T. (1928). *Common principles in psychology and physiology.* Cambridge University Press, London.

Mackintosh, N. J. (1974). *The psychology of animal learning.* Academic Press, London.

Mahut, H. and Moss, M. (1985). Consolidation of memory—the hippocampus revisited. In *Neuropsychology of memory* (eds N. Butters and L. Squire), in press. Guildford Press, New York.

Mair, W. G. P., Warrington, E. K. and Weiskrantz, L. (1979). Memory disorder in Korsakoff's psychosis. A neuropathological and neuropsycholigical investigation of two cases. *Brain* **102**, 749–83.

Milner, B. (1962). Les troubles de la mémoire accompagnant des lésions hippocampiques bilatérales. In *Physiologie de l'hippocampe,* Colloques Internationaux No. 107, pp. 257–72. Paris: CNRS.

—— (1966). Amnesia following operation on the temporal lobes. In *Amnesia* (eds C. W. M. Whitty and O. L. Zangwill), pp. 109–33. Butterworth, London.

Mishkin, M. and Delacour, J. (1975). An analysis of short-term visual memory in the monkey. *J. exp. Psychol.: Anim. Behav. Process.* **1**, 326–34.

Palm, G. (1982). *Neural assemblies.* Springer, Berlin.

Peterson, N. (1960). Control of behaviour by presentation of an imprinted stimulus. *Science* **132**, 1395–6.

Scoville, W. B. and Milner, B. (1957). Loss of recent memory after bilateral hippocampal lesions. *J. Neurol. Neurosurg. Psychiat.* **20**, 11–21.

Sidman, M., Stoddard, L. T. and Mohr, J. P. (1968). Some additional quantitative observations of immediate memory in a patient with bilateral hippocampal lesions. *Neuropsychologia* **6**, 245–54.

Sluckin, W. (1972). *Imprinting and early learning*. Methuen, London.

Sokolov, E. N. (1960). Neuronal models and the orienting reflex. In *The central nervous system and behavior* (ed. M. A. B. Brazier), pp. 187–276. Josiah Macey Jr. Foundation, New York.

Stewart, M. G., Rose, S. P. R., King, T. S., Gabbot, P. L. A., and Bourne, R. (1984). Hemispheric asymmetry of synapses in chick medial hyperstriatum ventrale following passive avoidance training: a stereological investigation. *Devl. Brain Res.* **12**, 261–9.

Talland, G. A. (1965). *Deranged memory: a psychonomic study of the amnesic syndrome*. Academic Press, New York.

Vinogradova, O. (1970). Registration of information and the limbic system. In *Short-term changes in neural activity and behaviour* (eds G. Horn and R. A. Hinde), pp. 95–140. Cambridge University Press, Cambridge.

Warrington, E. K. (1974). Deficient recognition memory in organic amnesia. *Cortex* **10**, 289–91.

Weiskrantz, L. and Warrington, E. K. (1979). Conditioning in amnesic patients. *Neuropsychologia* **17**, 187–94.

Zangwill, O. L. (1966). The amnesic syndrome. In *Amnesia* (eds C. W. M. Whitty and O. L. Zangwill). Butterworth, London.

Zangwill, O. L. (1983). Disorders of memory. In *Handbook of psychiatry: 1. General psychopathology* (eds M. Shepherd and O. L. Zangwill), pp. 97–113. Cambridge University Press, Cambridge.

Zola-Morgan, S. and Squire, L. R. (1984). Preserved learning in monkeys with medial temporal skills: sparing of motor and cognitive skills. *J. Neurosci.* **4**, 1072–85.

Zolman, J. F. (1968). Discrimination learning in young chicks with heat reinforcement. *Psychol. Rec.* **18**, 303–9.

Zolman, J. F. (1969). Stimulus preferences and form discrimination learning in young chicks. *Psychol. Rec.* **19** 407–16.

# 7

# How many stores? Cerebral asymmetry and imprinting

The first hint that the right and left cerebral hemispheres may play different roles in the process of imprinting on simple, artificial objects came from an electron microscope study of the IMHV. This study is discussed in detail in Section 10.2. Briefly, it was found that training was associated with a change in the structure of synapses in the left IMHV, but was not associated with any statistically significant change in the right IMHV. This evidence of hemispheric asymmetry in the imprinting process, though unexpected, was not inconsistent with the results of the other experiments on imprinting which were reviewed in earlier chapters. The first biochemical studies (Chapters 2 and 3) examined changes in brain samples which included both the left and right IMHV; the two regions were sampled in the autoradiographic study without regard to side (Chapter 4); and the IMHV was destroyed in both hemispheres in the lesion experiments outlined in Chapter 5. It is possible therefore that the left IMHV was the active region in all of these studies and that the inclusion of the right IMHV was without effect on the outcome of an experiment, or served only to dilute any effect that was present. A set of experiments was therefore designed specifically to follow up the morphological evidence of cerebral asymmetry by investigating the roles of the right and left IMHV in the retention of a preference.

## 7.1 Sequential lesion studies

If there is a difference in the functions of the right and left IMHV in the process of imprinting, then the selective destruction of these regions should have different effects on imprinting. For example, if the synaptic changes observed in the left IMHV underlie the chicks' recognition memory for the training object, the destruction of this region should impair retention. By the same token, if the right IMHV is not involved in information storage then its destruction should not impair retention. This line of enquiry, which has the virtue of simplicity, as well as the inevitable danger of being oversimple, was followed in the next set of experiments (Cipolla–Neto, Horn and McCabe 1982).

By assuming a model in which the left IMHV has a storage function, but the right has not, the outcome of various surgical interventions may be pre-

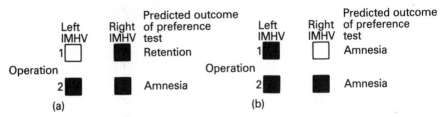

(a)                                        (b)

**Fig. 7.1.** In this model it is assumed that only the left IMHV has a storage function and that the chicks have been trained before any operative intervention. The effects on retention of various interventions are predicted. The boxes represent the right and left IMHV. (a) In the first operation (1) the right IMHV is removed, and after recovery from the operation the chicks' preferences are measured. The left IMHV is then removed at a second operation (2) and the chick's preferences measured in a second test. Birds receiving this sequence of operations are referred to as RIMHV birds, the right IMHV being the first to have been removed. (b) In this sequence the left IMHV is first removed (1) and then the right (2). These birds are referred to as LIMHV birds. For further discussion, see text.

dicted (Fig. 7.1). For example, if the right IMHV of trained chicks is removed, they should recognize the object on which they were trained (Fig. 7.1(a), 1). However, if the left IMHV of these chicks is then removed, they should fail to show a preference for the training object and, in this sense, be amnesic (Fig. 7.1(a), 2). In Fig. 7.1(b), the expected outcomes of removing first the left IMHV and then the right are shown. These various predictions were tested in an experiment the design of which is illustrated in Fig. 7.2. The training procedures were similar to those used in previous lesion studies (Section 5.1 and 5.2). Dark-reared chicks were primed for half an hour when they were approximately 19 hours old. The birds were then trained by exposing them for a total of 2 hours to either the rotating red box or to the rotating stuffed jungle-fowl. Approximately 3 hours after the end of training, the chicks were anaesthetized and assigned to various groups. In one group the lesion was placed in the right IMHV and in another group in the left IMHV. Other groups of chicks served as controls. In one group lesions were placed in the Wulst of the left hemisphere, whilst in another group the

**Fig. 7.2.** Design of the sequential lesion experiment. (a) The procedure for chicks lesioned first in the right IMHV and then in the left. The times were the same for other groups of chicks which received lesions. (b) Procedure for sham-operated controls. For details of symbols see the legend to Fig. 5.1. (After Cipolla-Neto *et al.* 1982.)

lesions were placed in the Wulst of the right hemisphere. Sham-operated chicks were treated as before (p. 84) the scalp being incised and then sutured, but the brain left intact. After the chicks had recovered from the operation they were given a sequential preference test (test 1) and a preference score was calculated (p. 85). After this test, the chicks were again anaesthetized and those with unilateral lesions were subjected to a second operation. In this operation the corresponding structure (the IMHV or the Wulst) in the intact hemisphere was lesioned. After this operation, therefore, the lesions (to the IMHV or to the Wulst) were bilateral. The chicks were returned to the dark incubator, and when they had recovered from the anaesthetic, they were given a second preference test (test 2). Whilst each chick was anaesthetized it was assigned a number and all behavioural test were conducted 'blind'.

An analysis of variance performed on the data failed to disclose a significant difference between the preference scores of chicks trained on the box and those of chicks trained on the fowl. The preference scores for a given group of chicks (for example, sham-operated controls) trained on the box were therefore combined with the preference scores of the corresponding group of chicks which had been trained on the fowl. There were no significant differences between the chicks lesioned first in the right Wulst and those lesioned first in the left, so that the data from these two groups of chicks were combined.

The results of the preference tests are shown in Fig. 7.3. Sham-operated controls preferred the training stimulus in both tests. For these chicks, the mean preference score in test 2 was slightly, but significantly, smaller than in test 1. The scores of chicks with lesions in the Wulst resembled those of the sham-operated controls in tests 1 and 2: in both tests the lesioned birds preferred the training object and achieved scores which were not significantly different from those of the sham-operated controls. However, the mean preference scores of birds with lesions of the Wulst, unlike those of the controls, remained stationary from test 1 to test 2.

Chicks with unilateral lesions of the right IMHV were expected to prefer the training stimulus in test 1 (Fig. 7.1(a), 1). They did so (Fig. 7.3(a), 'RIMHV'). The mean preference score of these chicks was not significantly different from that of the sham-operated controls or of the chicks with unilateral lesions of the Wulst. The predicted outcome of the second operation, in which the remaining left IMHV was removed, is shown in Fig. 7.1(a), 2. These chicks should lose their preference for the training object. They did so. Their mean preference score in test 2 was not significantly different from the chance score of 50 (Fig. 7.3(b), RIMHV). Their score in this test was also significantly less than those of the sham-operated controls, and of the chicks with lesions in the Wulst. These results, therefore, are consistent with the model on which Fig. 7.1 is based, namely that the left IMHV has a sto-

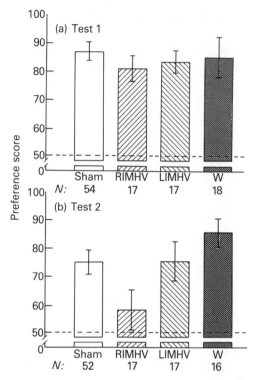

**Fig. 7.3.** Preference scores for various groups of chicks. Means ± S.E.M. are shown. Data from chicks with lesions in the right and left Wulst (W) were combined. RIMHV refers to those chicks in which the lesion was placed in the right IMHV at the first operation; LIMHV refers to those chicks in which the lesion was placed in the left IMHV at the first operation. There were no significant differences between any of the mean values in test 1. In test 2 the mean preference score of the RIMHV chicks was significantly less than that of the (i) sham-operated controls ($P < 0.05$), (ii) chicks with lesions in the Wulst ($P < 0.005$), and (iii) LIMHV chicks ($P < 0.05$). The RIMHV chicks' mean preference score was not significantly different from 50 in test 2. The mean preference scores of all the other groups of chicks were significantly greater than this chance score and did not differ significantly from each other. (After Cipolla-Neto *et al.* 1982.)

rage function, but that the right IMHV does not. The results certainly do not allow this model to be rejected.

In the simplest version of the model only the left IMHV stores the information which is necessary for the recognition of the training object. If this version of the model is correct the chicks should be amnesic if the left IMHV is removed after training (Fig. 7.1(b), 1). This result was not obtained. Chicks with lesions placed in the left IMHV soon after they had been trained, strongly preferred the training object (Fig. 7.3(a), LIMHV). This result demonstrates that the information necessary for recognition cannot be stored exclusively in the left IMHV. Perhaps, notwithstanding the morphological evidence given in Section 10.2, the left and right are both involved, each being capable of supporting a preference established through training: so long as one IMHV is intact chicks will continue to prefer the training object. It would then follow that if that IMHV is removed, the chicks These chicks continued to prefer the training object (Fig. 7.3(b), LIMHV). The mean preference score of these birds was not significantly different left IMHV had first been removed and then the right IMHV removed? These chicks continued to prefer the training object (Fig. 7.3(b), LIMHV). The mean preference score of these birds was not significantly different from those of the sham-operated controls, and of the chicks with lesions in the Wulst. What is more, in test 2, the mean score of the LIMHV birds was significantly greater than that of the RIMHV birds (Fig. 7.3(b)). These results do not support the notion that the right and left IMHV store information. In fact, neither of the two models, that the store is exclusively in the left IMHV or that it is in both the left and the right IMHV, can explain all of the results.

The difficulty for either model is emphasized by the fact that when test 2 was performed, the IMHV region in both groups of chicks was destroyed bilaterally. Yet one group (LIMHV) maintained a clear preference for the training stimulus and the other group (RIMHV) performed at chance level. If it is reasonable to assume the existence of a recognition memory in chicks which prefer the training object, it follows that, for chicks in the LIMHV group, the recognition memory was accessible in the absence of both right and left IMHV.

A clue as to what might be happening comes from two sources. The first is that the chicks which ended up with bilateral lesions in IMHV reached this state in different ways. In one group, the left IMHV was lesioned first and in the other group the right IMHV was lesioned first. The second clue comes from two previous lesion studies. Bilateral lesions of the IMHV placed *before* training prevented the acquisition of a preference (Section 5.1). In such chicks the preference score was close to the chance score of 50 (Fig. 5.3). When bilateral lesions were placed shortly *after* training the mean preference score was $64.6 \pm 7.53$. This score is not significantly different from 50 (Student's $t$-test, $t=1.91$). The probablility of obtaining this $t$ value by chance is greater than one in twenty, but less than one in ten. In other words, the difference was close to significance and suggested that some information about the training object may have been retained. Is it possible that the IMHV is involved both in acquisition and retention, but that the information gradually passes out of the IMHV with the lapse of time after training? In other words, is there a dynamic element in storage which is not included in either of the models proposed above?

A model that is consistent with the results of the two earlier lesion studies as well as with those of the sequential lesion study is shown in Fig. 7.4. In

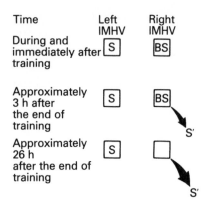

**Fig. 7.4.** Model of the role of the left and right IMHV in the retention of a preference. Information necessary for the recognition of the training object is considered to be stored in both the left and right IMHV. The left IMHV is considered to be a permanent store (S) for at least the period of the experiments described in the text. The right IMHV is considered to function as a buffer store (BS), slowly transferring information to another store, S'. Relatively little has been transferred by approximately 3 h after training; transfer is complete within 26 h after training.

this model it is assumed that, during training, information is stored in the left IMHV and also in the right. Destruction of these two regions prior to training would be expected to eliminate the store so that a preference would not be, and indeed is not, formed. Information storage in the left IMHV is considered to be 'permanent', at least for the duration of the experiments. The right IMHV is considered to be a 'buffer' store, which passes information on to some other store, S'. If the right *and* left IMHV are removed after training the strength of retention would depend on how much information had been transferred to S'; the longer the interval, the stronger would be the chick's preference for the training object. Experimental evidence suggests that when the interval is approximately 3 hours, the amount of information transferred is not quite sufficient to support a preference for the training object (Fig. 5.6, IMHV). Removal of *one* IMHV approximately 3 hours after training would therefore be expected to be associated with full retention. In terms of the model (Fig. 7.4), if the right is removed 3 hours after training the buffer store would be removed so that no further information could be transferred to S'. Recognition of the training object would then depend mainly on the store in the left IMHV. If this region is then removed at a second operation, the mean preference score should be close to 50, depending on how much information had been transferred to S'. The observed mean score (Fig. 7.3(b), RIMHV) was not significantly greater than 50, a result which again suggests that relatively little information may have been transferred to the postulated S' in the 3 hours following training. If only the left IMHV is removed 3 hours after training the buffer store in the right IMHV would remain intact and information would continue to be transferred to S'. Is transfer complete and if so, when? When the second lesion was placed, in the right IMHV, approximately 26 hours after the end of training (Fig. 7.2) the chicks' mean preference for the training object was almost identical with that of the controls (Fig. 7.3(b), LIMHV). This result suggests that when 26 hours have elapsed after the end of training, transfer is complete. Transfer may be complete before this time, though transfer is, at best, only partial when 3 hours have elapsed after training.

A prediction of the model illustrated in Fig. 7.4 is that after transfer to the postulated S' is complete, bilateral removal of IMHV should not affect the retention of an acquired preference. This prediction was tested in the experiment outlined in Fig. 7.5. The hatching, rearing, and training conditions of these chicks were the same as for chicks in the sequential lesion

**Fig. 7.5.** Design of the experiment in which chicks were trained, returned to the dark incubator, and lesions subsequently placed bilaterally in the IMHV. Procedures for lesioned chicks (a) and for sham-operated controls (b). (After Cipolla-Neto *et al.* 1982.)

study described above. Approximately 21 hours after training had been completed the chicks were given a preference test (Fig. 7.5, test 1) after which they were returned to the dark incubator until they were anaesthetized approximately 26 hours after training. Thirty chicks served as sham-operated controls. Lesions were placed bilaterally in the IMHV of thirty experimental chicks. The chicks recovered in the dark incubator, and were given a preference test some 68 hours after hatching (Fig. 7.5, test 2).

Preference scores are shown in Fig. 7.6. The mean scores for the two groups of chicks in test 1, conducted before the chicks were anaesthetized, were not significantly different from each other. In test 2, the mean preference scores of each group was significantly less than the respective scores achieved in test 1. Although the mean score in test 2 for the lesioned chicks was slightly smaller than that of the sham-operated controls, the difference was not statistically significant. The lesioned chicks, as predicted by the model preferred the training stimulus at a high level of significance ($P<0.001$).

The model accounts reasonably well for most of the experimental data and one of the predictions based on the model was met. It is, however, worth emphasizing that it is only a model. The assumptions made for the

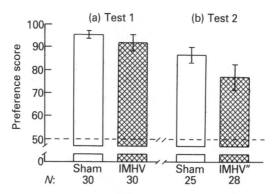

**Fig. 7.6.** Preference scores (means ± s.e.m.). The mean preference score for each group in test 2 was significantly less than the corresponding score in test 1 ($P < 0.05$). (After Cipolla-Neto *et al.* 1982.)

left IMHV are reasonably well supported by experimental evidence (Chapters 4 and 5). The existence of S′, however, is inferred from behavioural evidence alone: bilateral removal of the IMHV achieved at a single operation made some 26 hours after training, or by the appropriate sequence of lesions to left and right IMHV, did not impair retention. It follows from these experimental results that there must be a storage system outside IMHV. Storage in this system is not complete if the right IMHV is removed soon after training (Fig. 7.3(b), RIMHV). These results suggest that storage within S′ can only be achieved if the right IMHV is present, an experimental finding that generated the idea of a buffer store in the right IMHV.

There are many aspects of the model which are incomplete. For example there is no experimental evidence to suggest where S′ is except that it is not in the IMHV, though it would make good sense to direct efforts in search of S′ to those regions to which the IMHV projects. Furthermore, it is assumed that the right IMHV does not normally function as a permanent store because no statistically significant changes in the structure of synapses have been found there after chicks had been imprinted (Section 10.2). This negative evidence, is necessarily, not strong: further studies might, after all , disclose such changes. However, in the absence of evidence to the contrary it is assumed that the right IMHV serves as a buffer store, which temporarily retains information and transfers it to other storage systems.

The idea that memories may be shifted about is not strange to the computer sciences, for buffer stores, which temporarily retain information and then transfer it to other storage systems, are commonplace in computers. The notion may, however, sound outlandish in the neurosciences, but it is not new. For example Marr (1970, 1971) proposed different roles for the mammalian neocortex and the archicortex, which includes the hippocampus, in memory. He suggested that the archicortex stored 'simple' memory, a simple form of associative memory. Marr proposed that information in permanent memory is stored in the neocortex. He suggested that information is transferred from the archicortex to the neocortex during sleep. This suggestion implies that Marr's simple memory store must be capable of holding events for at least 1 day. Although Marr's model remains speculative, the concept of a temporary store from which information is transferred to a permanent store is not wholly foreign to neurobiology.

The time taken to transfer information to S′ is relatively long and the physiological processes by which it might be accomplished are not known. Until relatively recently neural events having such a long time-course would have been puzzling. Now, whilst such observations are a challenge, they are not beyond physiological comprehension. For example, peptides are present in many neurones and it is likely that they serve as chemical messengers in the central nervous system. Neuropeptides differ from a number of transmitters such as acetylcholine in that they are not recycled and hence replenished at the synapse. Neuropeptides are manufactured in the cell body and are transported peripherally along the axon. Thus it is possible that peptidergic neurones present in the right IMHV are excited by particular afferent fibres. This input might induce or change the rate of synthesis of the messenger RNA coding for the peptide. The peptide would then be transported along the axon and be released at its terminals. The peptide may then bind to receptors locally, on the postsynaptic neurone, and even bind to receptors on other neurones, reaching them by diffusion. Activation of the receptors could induce metabolic changes in these post-synaptic neurones, leading for example to a change in the density of receptors in the sub-synaptic membranes. All this is of course speculation. But the point is worth making because many of the physiological events referred to have been observed in the central (Potter *et al.* 1981; Chen *et al.* 1983) and autonomic (Zigmond and Chalazonitis 1979) nervous systems. The postulated series of events, from the arrival of the afferent impulses in the right IMHV through to the change in production of a peptide, its transport along the axon, its liberation and action of the postsynaptic cell, could well take many hours to be completed. The long time-course of storage in the postulated S′ is not, then, so mysterious as it might at first seem to be.

## 7.2 Modification of hemisphere function

All of the surgical interventions carried out in the sequential lesion study (Fig. 7.2) were performed on chicks which had previously been trained. A different set of results emerged when the first intervention in the two-stage operation on the IMHV was made *before* training. It will be recalled (Section 5.3) that chicks could form a strong preference for a training object when only one IMHV was intact. It did not matter whether the intact IMHV was the left one or the right one. This result would be expected from the model illustrated in Fig. 7.4: if only the left IMHV is intact during training it could provide a store, if only the right IMHV is intact during training the right IMHV and/or S′ could provide a store. In the experiment described in Section 5.3 the chicks, which had been trained with only one IMHV intact, were anaesthetized for a second time and the intact IMHV was lesioned (Fig. 5.10). According to the model (Fig. 7.4) the left IMHV is a store; if this IMHV is the only one present during training its destruction after training should result in amnesia. This result was obtained (Fig. 7.7(b), L). Thus whether the right IMHV is removed before training (Horn *et al.* 1983) or shortly after training (Cipolla–Neto *et al.* 1982) retention depends critically on the presence of the left IMHV. This evidence is consistent with the model. What would be predicted from this model if chicks are trained with only the right IMHV intact and this structure is lesioned? If enough time has elapsed from the end of training to the time that the lesion is made, storage in S′ should be complete and be sufficient to support a preference.

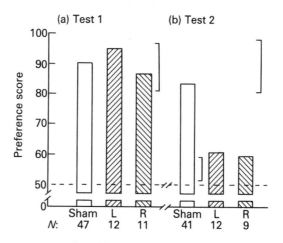

**Fig. 7.7.** Preference scores for chicks trained with only one IMHV region intact (means ± s.e.m.). The design of this experiment is given in Fig. 5.10. Unlike Fig. 5.11 the mean preference score for chicks with lesions in the IMHV are given according to whether the left (L) or right (R) IMHV was intact during training and in test 1. This test was conducted shortly after training was complete. The critical difference ($P=0.05$) for comparing a mean value against 50 is given to the right of the Sham preference score in (b). The critical difference ($P=0.05$) for comparing left and right IMHV against Sham scores is shown as the vertical bar to the right of each diagram. (a) All preference scores were significantly greater than 50 ($P<0.005$) and none were significantly different from each other. (b) Mean preference scores achieved in test 2, performed when the chicks had recovered from the operation to remove the IMHV which had been intact during training. The sham-operated chicks preferred the training object. The lesioned chicks did not prefer the training object and their mean preference scores were not significantly greater than chance. The mean preference scores of the two groups of lesioned birds differed significantly from that of the sham-operated controls. (Data from Horn *et al.* 1983.)

The consequence of placing this lesion approximately 20 hours after the end of training is shown in Fig. 7.7(b), R. The mean score of these chicks was not significantly different from chance. Under these experimental conditions therefore, there are no grounds for supposing that a store in S' had been formed.

The apparent failure to establish a store in S' could be because the right IMHV was removed before this store was fully established. In a previous study it was shown that this postulated store is able to support a preference if the right IMHV had remained intact for approximately 26 hours after the end of training (Fig. 7.3(b), LIMHV). Perhaps 20 hours is too short for the store in S' to be established? When the right (together with the left) IMHV was removed approximately 3 hours after training the preference score was $64.4 \pm 7.53$ (Fig. 5.6, IMHV). This score was not significantly different from the no preference level of 50. If the presence of the right IMHV alone for approximately 20 hours allowed some transfer of information to S', the mean preference score measured after the right IMHV had been removed should be in excess of 64. In the event, the observed mean preference score was $59.39 \pm 9.73$ (Fig. 7.7(b), R). There is no evidence therefore of a store in S' being formed under these conditions. To summarize (Fig. 7.8(b)): when only the right IMHV is intact during training (i) it becomes crucial for retention and appears to take on a storage function which is normally taken on by the left IMHV and (ii) storage within S', functioning independently of the IMHV, does not occur.

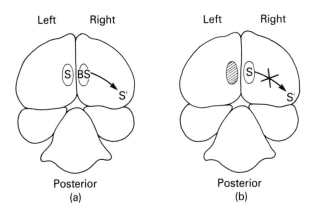

**Fig. 7.8.** Diagrammatic view of chicks' forebrain hemipsheres viewed from above. The oval outline in each hemisphere represents the IMHV. Model of memory systems formed during training (a) and their modification by lesions (b). (a) The left IMHV is crucial for one of the systems (S). Information is transferred to S' under the influence of the right IMHV which serves as a buffer store (BS). See also Fig. 7.4. (b) Consequence of removing the left IMHV (cross-hatched area) before training. Transfer to the second storage system S' appears not to occur, and the right IMHV becomes crucial for retention. (After Horn *et al.* 1983.)

The finding in the domestic chick that right hemisphere function can be modified by a lesion placed in the left hemisphere may have parallels in other species. Nottebohm and his colleagues (1976) have shown that the most caudal part of the hyperstriatum ventrale (HVc) is involved in song control in the canary (*Serinus canarius*). HVc is a specialized nucleus which is present in some song birds, but does not appear to have a counterpart in the hyperstriatum ventrale of the domestic chick. Nottebohm and his collaborators have suggested that the left HVc plays a dominant role in song learning (Nottebohm and Nottebohm 1976; Nottebohm *et al.* 1976). Following destruction of the left HVc, the right HVc and its efferent pathway take over and redevelop normal song. It is thus possible to induce a reversal of hemispheric dominance by destroying the left HVc (see Nottebohm 1980). A comparable result has been found in humans, in which the left hemisphere is usually dominant for speech. If this hemisphere is removed or appropriate regions damaged in the adult, the patient suffers a severe impairment of speech and recovery is usually minimal (for a review see Moscovitch 1977). In young children, in contrast, when the left hemisphere is removed or severely damaged, linguistic functions can be subversed by the right hemisphere (see Dennis and Kohn 1975; Hécaen 1976; Trevarthen 1983). The right hemisphere thus develops a function which is normally characteristic of the left, but only does so if damage to the left hemisphere occurs early in life.

In the chick there appears to be a cost to right hemisphere function if the left IMHV is removed before the chicks are trained: the store in S' fails to become established. There may be also a cost to right hemisphere function in the human brain as a consequence of the abnormal demand made on it by lesions to the left hemisphere early in life. The right hemisphere of the human adult appears to be superior to the left in visuospatial abilities (for a review see Levy 1974). These right hemisphere abilities may be degraded if this hemisphere takes on linguistic functions (see Levy 1969).

### 7.2.1 A neuronal model

The evidence that removal of the left hemisphere modifies the function of the right suggests that there is an interaction between the two sides of the brain. Virtually nothing is known of the cellular basis of this interaction. It is not, however, difficult to speculate about possible mechanisms and to do so may be experimentally fruitful. Consider for example the circuit drawn in Fig. 7.9. The cell bodies of N, P, I, and Q are all contained within the right IMHV. How might the circuit operate (i) in the intact chick (Fig. 7.8(a)), when the right IMHV appears to serve as a buffer store and to transfer information to S', and (ii) when the left IMHV is removed prior to training (Fig. 7.8(b)) and the right appears to act as a permanent store, S' not being formed? In considering the model shown in Fig. 7.9 the mechanism by which a neural representation of a stimulus is formed is not considered (see Section 10.3). It is sufficient to assume that a trace of the stimulus is left in

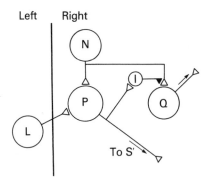

**Fig. 7.9.** Scheme to illustrate possible neuronal interactions which could account for the influence of the left IMHV on the right in the formation of memory. Open triangles represent excitatory synapses, the closed triangle an inhibitory synapse. The output of cell Q would be to other neurones in the right IMHV or to other brain regions, possibly those controlling approach/avoidance behaviour. For further discussion see text.

the nervous system if that stimulus induces changes in specific groups of neurones, changes which outlast the presentation of that stimulus. The trace would be temporary if the changes were reversible over a relatively short time, and permanent if they were stable over a relatively long time.

Each cell drawn in Fig. 7.9 represents a population of cells. Cell P is connected to neurones in S′. Cell P would only discharge if it is excited by inputs from both cells N and L. Cell N is an output neurone of the buffer store in the right IMHV. Cell L is connected directly or indirectly with the left IMHV. This cell serves to control the firing of cell P and thereby controls the transfer of specific information to cells in S′. During the period of exposure to an imprinting stimulus cells N and L are jointly active. Cell P fires and continues to do so for as long as the chick is exposed to the stimulus. Cell P has the properties described above (p. 137), namely that when it is adequately excited the rate of synthesis of peptide messenger RNA is increased. The newly synthesized peptide is then transported along the axon of cell P and released from its synaptic terminals. The peptide binds with receptors on neurones in S′ and so initiates plastic changes which form a basis of permanent memory. In the circuit shown in Fig. 7.9, cell N is also excitatory to cell Q. Cell P excites cell I through a recurrent collateral. Transmission at this junction is considered to be fast-acting and 'conventional': it is assumed that cell I does not have receptors for the peptide secreted by cell P. Cell I liberates an inhibitory transmitter at its terminals which blocks transmission between cells N and Q. Thus when cell P discharges, cell Q does not fire. Suppose, now, that the left IMHV has been removed prior to training. Cell L will, of course, cease to function. Cell P will not fire since excitation from cell N is subthreshold for the discharge of cell P. Because cell P is silent the store in S' is not formed. Also because cell P is silent the input from cell N excites cell Q. This discharge in Q is assumed to lead to structural changes at the synaptic junction between cell N and cell Q (see Section 10.3.4). These changes provide a basis for a permanent store in the right IMHV. In the absence of the left IMHV, therefore, information is retained in the right IMHV and there is no transfer to S'.

This speculative scheme would yield, at the macroscopic level of the lesion studies, the consequences illustrated in Fig. 7.8(b). Removal of the left IMHV *after* training would not influence the formation of S' since the necessary trigger events in cell P would have been completed during the training period. The scheme can also account for the results of the other lesion studies. Bilateral removal of the IMHV prior to training would remove the whole of the assembly shown in Fig. 7.9, so that S' could not be formed. Removal of the right IMHV (with or without the left) after training would have consequences which would depend on several factors. These include the time taken to increase synthesis of the peptide, the rate of transport of the peptide along the axon of cell P, the distance the peptide must travel and the time taken to exert an effect on the target cell in S'. Assume, for example, an axonal transport rate of 2 millimetres per hour (see Thoenen and Kreutzberg 1981) and a transport distance of 6 millimetres, the distance of the farthest point of any region in the right hemisphere from the centre of the right IMHV. The time for the wave of newly synthesized peptide to reach the most distal target would be 3 hours. If it is assumed either that there is no peptide in the terminal of cell P prior to the arrival of this wave or too little significantly to affect the cells in S', then the modifying effect of activity of cell P on S' would begin some 3 hours after the wave of peptide had been synthesized. A lesion placed in the right IMHV would destroy the body of cell P and would stop, or retard transport along its axon. Hence if a lesion is placed in the right IMHV some 3 hours or more after the end of training the first wave of peptide would have arrived at S' and some changes would have begun there. If the lesion is placed after the last stimulus-induced wave of peptide has reached and acted on cell S', then the store in S' should go on to completion. Bilateral removal of IMHV after this time, and 26 hours may be a generous delay, would allow the store to support an acquired preference. In the light of these speculations it is of interest that cell bodies containing the peptide methionine-enkephalin are present in IMHV. Some of these cells have axons which are approximately 5 millimetres long (McCabe and Hunt 1983).

There are many ways in which the scheme described above and illustrated in Fig. 7.9 could be tested. For example, a necessary condition for the scheme to work is that the left and right IMHV are interconnected in order for the two regions to interact. There is no evidence that the two are directly interconnected although there is an abundance of indirect connections (Bradley *et al.* 1985). Are those connections functional and is the left IMHV excitatory to some neurones in the right IMHV? Are there neurones, such as cell P, which will discharge only if there is an input from the left IMHV *and* from within the right IMHV. Will the selective block of particular neuropeptides also block the formation of a store in S′ even though both right and left IMHV are intact during training and remain intact for 26 hours afterwards? The scheme may, of course, prove to be wrong. But for the present it provides a way of thinking about a complex set of experimental results in terms of neurones with known or plausible properties.

## 7.3 How many stores and what are they for?

Within the context of the lesion experiments described above there is evidence of two storage systems, S and S′. The evidence that store S is contained within a system of which the left IMHV is a critical part, or may actually be within the left IMHV, has been given in Section 7.1, in Chapter 5, and elsewhere (Chapters 6 and 10), and is referred to again below. The location of S′, if indeed it is localized, is not known, though the lateral parts of the forebrain damaged by Salzen and his colleagues (1975, 1978) might be implicated. However, the involvement of this area in S′ is only one of a number of possibilities. Any or all of the areas to which IMHV projects are plausible candidates. One of these areas, the paleostriatum augmentatum (p. 243) is part of a complex that has been implicated in learning in pigeons (Mitchell and Hall 1984), and in imprinting in chicks (Davies *et al.* 1985; see section 9.3). These studies did not distinguish between the right and left sides of the brain. N. McCabe and Rose (1985) found metabolic changes in the right but not in the left forebrain base, which included the paleostriatal complex, following the acquisition of a passive avoidance task (see p. 123). The results provide at best only rough clues to the location of S′, and cannot of course substitute for a direct experimental analysis of this putative system.

The evidence available suggests that S and S′ are independent storage systems. Admittedly the left IMHV appears to exert a permissive role in the transfer of signals to S′; but the left IMHV need not transfer specific information to S′, and is not considered to do so in the scheme set out in Fig. 7.9. The information passed on to S′ is transferred from the buffer store. If this scheme is correct then S and S′ are parallel stores which, over the time course of these studies, are stable.

The notion that there are multiple permanent memory stores is not new (see Baddely 1976; Warrington 1979). Perhaps more interesting is the question which asks what functions these systems serve. Before training, chicks will approach a wide variety of objects. As a result of being exposed to one object, chicks direct their social responses to it. After this period of training the range of objects which they approach narrows down: the training object and stimuli resembling it may be approached and dissimilar objects avoided. These behaviours appear to follow simple rules. Before training the rule is 'approach visual objects within a certain range of size, colour, contrast, speed of movement . . .'. Training modifies this rule which now has two components: (i) approach training object or objects resembling it; (ii) avoid objects that do not resemble it. A simple algorithm for this behaviour is given in Fig. 7.10. The formation of such rules may be considered to comprise part of a 'reference' memory (see Honig 1978) and their neural bases might be very simple. An example of a hypothetical mechanism whose operations would generate such a rule is illustrated in Fig. 7.11. The arrangement of this figure is similar to that of Fig. 6.6(a), although the 'incentive system' has been ommitted in Fig. 7.11 and an avoidance control system has been added. Objects (A–Z) which are satisfactorily imprinting stimuli are considered to activate neural pathways leading to the circuits controlling approach and avoidance behaviour, and to a store. In a naive chick (Fig. 7.11, 1) any of these objects, say A, activates the approach system more strongly than the avoidance system. As a result of continued exposure to this object a neural representation of it is established in the store. When the object is presented after training (Fig. 7.11, 2) the neural representation is activated, there is an output from the store and the chick approaches the object vigorously (for further discussion see Section 6.4). If object Z is now presented to a chick which has formed a strong attachment

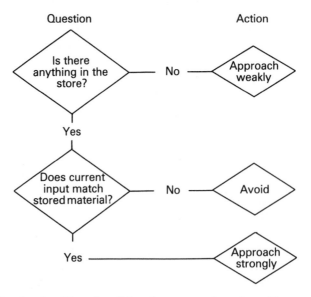

**Fig. 7.10.** Simple algorithm describing the approach and avoidance responses of chicks before and after imprinting.

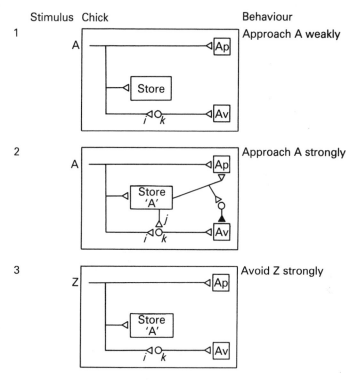

**Fig. 7.11.** Diagrammatic representation of some neural processes that may govern approach and avoidance behaviour before and after imprinting. The large rectangle represents the chick's nervous system. Boxes within the rectangle represent neural systems having the specified function. Ap represents approach and Av represents avoidance control systems. $i/k$ is a synapse which transmits inefficiently in naive chicks. Open triangles represent excitatory inputs, the filled triangle represents an inhibitory input. (1) a naive chick is exposed to stimulus A. There is not representation of stimulus A in the store and accordingly no output from the store to the approach system. The direct line to the approach system transmits more efficiently than the line to the avoidance system. (2) after training on object A. When this object is presented to the chick a neural representation of it in the store is activated. As a result there is an output from the store. The approach system is strongly excited. During training an increasing output from the store serves to strengthen synapse $i/k$. After training, when A is presented the avoidance system is also activated through this synapse. However, the inhibitory link from the output of the store blocks the excitatory input to the avoidance system. Where a chick, imprinted upon A, is shown stimulus Z, the chick avoids it. For further discussion see text.

to object A, the chick avoids Z (Fig. 7.11, 3). This behaviour contrasts sharply with that of naive chicks which weakly approach Z. One way of accounting for this change is to suppose that synaptic junction $i/k$ transmits inefficiently in naive birds. During training there is an output along $j$ from the store to cell $k$ (Fig. 7.11, 2). The two active inputs, $i$ and $j$, to cell $k$

summate, causing the latter to discharge. The occurrence of conjoint activity in pre- and postsynaptic elements of synapse $i/k$ is assumed to increase, irreversibly, the efficiency of transfer across this synapse (Hebb 1949). When Z is presented after prolonged exposure to A, the approach system is only weakly activated, just as it would be in a naive bird. There is no match between the information in store, which contains the neural representation of object A, and the incoming pattern of signals evoked by object Z. Hence there is no output from the store to the approach system. However, transmission across synaptic junction $i/k$ is effective and the avoidance system is strongly activated. Such a system would provide a rule or reference memory for approach and avoidance, but whether a similar mechanism operates in the real nervous system is not known. And, as remarked earlier (p. 121), the mechanism by which an incoming signal is compared with the stored information in the brain has also been the subject of, as yet, unresolved speculation.

The evidence reviewed in Section 7.1 suggests that both the S system associated wtih the left IMHV and the S′ system support a recognition memory and a reference memory. To that extent they are similar. but is it possible that they differ in some way?

An obvious possibility is that the storage capacity of the two systems is different. If S′ had the larger capacity, then information in it, more effectively than in S, may be 'updated' by being modified or extended through subsequent experience, and be used more flexibly, as in transferring experience gained in one situation to solving problems in another situation (see Polt 1969). These issues, which are taken up again later (Section 12.1.1) will doubtless be resolved by further experiments.

If it is legitimate to raise the functional question of the roles of S and S′ in memory it is also legitimate to enquire the function of the proposed buffer store associated with the right IMHV. Might the information within this store be used for some particular behavioural purposes? The question is worth raising even though there is as yet no answer to it. One possiblity is that informaton stored there is used during the performance of a particular trial or sequence. Such a store is known as 'working memory' (Baddeley 1976; Honig 1978; Olton *et al.* 1979; Olton and Feustle 1981; see also Konorski 1967). Working memory is considered to provide a store for information needed to complete successfully the trial in question; information is not stored there from one trial to the next, since previous records may serve only to confuse the animal. Although detailed information about a trial may be erased when the trial is complete, certain kinds of information acquired during the trial may be worth retaining. Thus, information about events which are particularly aversive or particularly rewarding may be passed on from the working memory system to a more permanent storage system. The right IMHV may be, or be part of, the former system, S′ the latter.

The concept of a working memory has been applied to the behaviour of birds as well as to the behaviour of mammals (Honig 1978). The concept is particularly useful in analysing foraging behaviour. When a bird searches for food or recovers food which it has previously stored it is important for the bird to remember where it has just been. There is good evidence of this behaviour in several species (for example Kamil 1978; Sherry *et al.* 1981; Vander Wall 1982; Sherry 1984). The concept of working memory has not been used in the context of imprinting though it might be fruitful to do so. For example, if a chick wanders away from its mother it is important for the chick to remember where the mother is in order to return to her. This information may not be worth committing to permanent memory.

Much of what has been written about the functions of S, S′, and the buffer store are necessarily speculative, not least because the experimental results from which they are inferred are relatively new. The field is likely to be a fruitful one for experimental exploitation.

### 7.4 Lesions, motivation, and stimulus–response pathways

Several reasons have been given for attributing the biochemical changes in the IMHV and the effects of lesions to these structures to some aspects of memory function rather then, for example, to changes in arousal or attention or to alterations in sensory and motor functions (see Chapters 3 and 5 and Sections 6.1, 6.2, and 8.1). The experiments described in the present chapter have a bearing on these issues, particularly on the question of motivation. Do lesions to the IMHV influence the chicks in such a way that they cease to be motivated to approach the training object? In the sequential lesion study (Section 7.1 above) both groups of chicks had bilateral lesions of the IMHV when their preferences were measured in test 2. One group performed at chance level and the other group showed full retention. It is difficult to see how such a result could be expected if the lesions affected motivational systems. Another difficulty for the 'motivational' explanation is that chicks prefer the training objects if the right and the left IMHV are removed on the day after training (Fig. 7.6(b)); they do not have such a preference if the bilateral operation is performed within 3 hours after training (Fig. 5.6). Other results also impinge on the explanatory power of the motivational hypothesis. As will be seen in the next chapter, when lesions to the IMHV affect performance the effect is subtantial in chicks trained on the box and small for chicks trained on the fowl. If the lesions to the IMHV affect motivation they do so for one group of chicks and not the other. These results, together with those described in earlier chapters and sections referred to above, suggest that the effect of lesions of the IMHV on preferences cannot easily be explained in terms of alterations in motivational state.

Some of the results which have been described in this chapter also impinge on another general issue. Is it at all likely that the sensory neurones which respond to a suitable imprinting object are connected to the neurones controlling approach in a way which may be represented as a single straight line linking the sensory neurones to the motor neurones? If this were so, then exposure to the training object might serve to strengthen the stimulus–response link and be tantamount to establishing a simple reflex arc. Interrupting the arc before training would prevent this strengthening and so prevent acquisition. Interrupting the arc after strengthening had occurred would sever the link between the sensory and motor neurones; the training object could not then elicit an approach response. This behaviour might be interpreted as a defect of retention. If the IMHV were a component of such an arc, even a special component with a storage function, then the effect of damaging it need not be different from the effect of damaging any other part of the arc. Now if the idea of such an arc is correct then destruction of IMHV should always impair an acquired preference for the training object. This is not the case (see Fig. 7.3, LIMHV chicks, and Fig. 7.6(b)). IMHV cannot therefore be considered simply as a part of the stimulus–response arc. If there is such an arc, IMHV must lie in parallel with it (see Fig. 6.6 and Fig. 7.11). Studies of the effects of lesions to the IMHV on associative learning (McCabe *et al.* 1982) point in the same direction: the acquisition of a selective approach response to one of two visually conspicuous objects is not impaired by lesions of the IMHV if the correct approach is rewarded. It is difficult to see how much such an operant response could be acquired if the IMHV were part of a simple, linearly connected afferent–efferent pathway.

### 7.5 Summary

Evidence is presented which suggests that there is a hemispheric asymmetry in the roles of the right and left IMHV in the imprinting process. It is suggested that the left IMHV has a storage function and may itself be a store. The left IMHV is not, however, the only store. Under special circumstances the right and left IMHV may be removed, and yet the chick retains the previously acquired preference. On the basis of these results the existence of another store is inferred. This store is referred to as S′. The store appears to be formed slowly under the control of the right IMHV which may act as a buffer store. A neural model of the interaction between right and left IMHV and the inferred store S′ is given. The evidence for multiple memory systems in other animals, including humans, is given. The possible functions of the memory systems of the chick are discussed.

### References

Baddeley, A. D. (1976) *The psychology of memory.* Harper and Row, New York.

Bradley, P., Davies, D. C., and Horn, G. (1985). Connections of the hyperstriatum ventrale of the domestic chick (*Gallus domesticus*). *J. Anat.* **140**, 577–89.

Chen, C. L. C., Dionne, F. T., and Roberts, J. L. (1983). Regulation of the pro-opiomelanocortin in mRNA levels in rat pituitary by dopaminergic compounds. *Proc. natn. Acad. Sci. U.S.A.* **80**, 2211–15.

Cipolla-Neto, J., Horn, G., and McCabe, B. J. (1982). Hemispheric asymmetry and imprinting: the effect of sequential lesions to the hyperstriatal ventrale. *Exp. Brain Res.* **48**, 22–7.

Davies, D. C., Horn, G., and McCabe, B. J. (1985). Noradrenaline and learning: the effects of the noradrenergic neurotoxin DSP4 on imprinting in the domestic chick. *Behav. Neurosci.* (in press).

Dennis, M. and Kohn, B. (1975). Comprehension of syntax in infantile hemiplegics after cerebral hemidecortication: left-hemisphere superiority. *Brain and Language* **2**, 472–82.

Hebb, D. O. (1949). *The organization of behavior*. John Wiley, New York.

Hécaen, H. (1976). Acquired aphasia in children and the ontogenesis of hemispheric functional specialization. *Brain and Language,* **3**, 114–34.

Honig, W. K. (1978). Studies of working memory in the pigeon. In *Cognitive processes in animal behaviour* (eds S. H. Hulse, H. Fowler, and W. K. Honig), pp. 211–48. Erlbaum, Hillsdale, N.J.

Horn, G., McCabe, B. J., and Cipolla–Neto, J. (1983). Imprinting in the domestic chick: the role of each side of the hyperstriatum ventrale in acquisition and retention. *Exp. Brain Res.* **53**, 91–8.

Kamil, A. C. (1978). Systematic foraging by a nectar-feeding bird, the Amakikhi (*Loxops virens*). *J. comp. physiol. Psychol.* **92**, 388–96.

Konorski, J. (1967). *Integrative activity of the brain.* University of Chicago Press, Chicago.

Levy, J. (1969). Possible basis for the evolution of lateral specialisation of the human brain. *Nature, Lond.* **224**, 614–15.

—— (1974). Psychobiological implications of bilateral asymmetry. In *Hemisphere function in the human brain* (eds S. J. Dimond and J. G. Beaumont), pp. 121–83. Elek (Scientific Books), London.

Marr, D. (1970). A theory for cerebral cortex. *Proc. R. Soc. B* **176**, 161–234.

—— (1971). Simple memory: a theory for archicortex. *Phil. Trans. R. Soc.* **262**, 23–81.

McCabe, B. J., Cipolla–Neto, J., Horn, G., and Bateson, P. P. G. (1982). Amnesic effects of bilateral lesions placed in the hyperstriatum ventrale of the chick after imprinting. *Exp. Brain Res.* **48**, 13–21.

—— and Hunt, S. P. (1983). Peptides and biogenic amines in the telencephalon of the domestic chick. An immunocytochemical study. *Neurosci. Lett.* Suppl. 14, S242.

McCabe, N., and Rose, S. P. R. (1985). Passive avoidance training increases fucose incorporation *in vitro. Neurochem. Res.* (in press).

Mitchell, J. A. and Hall, G. (1984). Paleostriatal lesions and instrumental learning in the pigeon. *Quart. J. exp. Psychol.* **36B**, 93–117.

Moscovitch, M. (1977). The development of lateralization of language functions and its relation to cognitive and linguistic development: a review and some theoretical speculations. In *Language development and neurological theory* (eds S. J. Segalowitz and F. A. Gruber), pp. 193–211. Academic Press, New York.

Nottebohm, F. (1980). Brain pathways for vocal learning in birds: a review of the first 10 years. *Prog. Psychobiol. physiol. Psychol.* **9**, 85–124.

—— and Nottebohm, M. (1976). Left hypoglossal dominance in the control of canary and white-crowned sparrow song. *J. comp. Physiol. A* **108**, 171–92.

Nottebohm, F., Stokes, T. M., and Leonard C. M. (1976). Central control of song in the canary, *Serinus canarius. J. comp. Neurol.* **165**, 457–86.

Olton, D. S. and Feustle, W. A. (1981). Hippocampal function required for non-spatial working memory. *Exp. Brain Res.* **41**, 380–9.

——, Becker, J. T., and Handelmann, G. E. (1979). Hippocampus, space and memory. *Behav. Brain Sci.* **2**, 313–65.

Polt, J. M. (1969). Effect of imprinting experience on discrimination learning in chicks. *J. comp. physiol. Psychol.* **69**, 514–8.

Potter, E., Nicolaisen, A. K., Ong, E. S. Evans, R. M., and Rosenfeld, M. G. (1981). Thyrotropin-releasing hormone exerts rapid nuclear effects to increase production of the primary prolactin in RNA transcript. *Proc. natn. Acad. Sci. U.S.A.* **78**, 6662–6.

Salzen, E. A., Parker, D. M., and Williamson, A. J. (1975). A forebrain lesion preventing imprinting in domestic chicks. *Exp. Brain Res.* **24**, 145–57.

——, Parker, D. M., and Williamson, A. J. (1978). Forebrain lesions and retention of imprinting in domestic chicks. *Exp. Brain Res.* **31**, 107–16.

——, Williamson, A. J. and Parker, D. M. (1979). The effects of forebrain lesions on innate and imprinted colour, brightness and shape preferences in domestic chicks. *Behav. Process.* **4**, 295–313.

Sherry, D. (1984). Food storage by black-capped chickadees: memory for the location and contents of caches. *Anim. Behav.* **32**, 451–64.

Sherry, D. F., Krebs, J. R., and Cowie, R. J. (1981). Memory for the location of stored food in marsh tits. *Anim. Behav.* **29**, 1260–6.

Thoenen, H. and Kreutzberg, G. W. (eds) (1981). The role of fast transport in the nervous system. *Neurosci. Res. Program Bull.* **20**, 1–138.

Trevarthen, C. (1983). Development of the cerebral mechanisms for language. In *Neuropsychology of language, reading and spelling* (ed. U. Kirk), pp. 47–82. Academic Press, London.

Vander Wall, S. B. (1982). An experimental analysis of cache recovery in Clark's Nutcracker. *Anim. Behav.* **30**, 84–94.

Warrington, E. K. (1979). Neuropsychological evidence for multiple memory systems. In *Brain and mind*, Ciba Foundation Symposium no. 69 (New Series), pp. 153–66. Excerpta Medica, Amsterdam.

Zigmond, R. E. and Chalazonitis, A. (1979). Long-term effects of preganglionic nerve stimulation on tyrosine hydroxylase activity in the rat superior cervical ganglion. *Brain Res.* **164**, 137–52.

# 8

# Predispositions and preferences

Although young chicks and ducklings will follow a wide range of visual stimuli the range is not unlimited and some objects are more effective than others at eliciting approach. Fabricius and Boyd (1952/53) found that objects smaller than a match-box were ignored by ducklings or pursued by them as food, and were relatively ineffective as imprinting stimuli. Schaefer and Hess (1959) showed that a following response is more effectively elicited in chicks by blue and red than by yellow or white stimuli, and Kovach (1971) found that green was less effective than certain other colours in eliciting approach behaviour. Size, shape, contrast, the presence or absence of movement as well as its direction, all influence the effectiveness of a stimulus in evoking approach and this list is far from exhaustive (for reviews see Sluckin 1972; Kovach 1983).

In analysing the features of stimuli which elicit approach in young birds artificial objects rather than natural parents have been used in most experimental studies. The advantages of this strategy are clear enough. Stimulus parameters can be manipulated in the case of artificial objects in ways that would be quite impossible to do using a live parent; and an artificial object does not vary in its behaviour to young chicks in a way that a parent might. The strategy has the disadvantage that it does not allow an inquiry into the question of whether there is something special about the process by which the young of some species of birds learn the visual characteristics of their own kind. Stuffed animals or simple models of animals have been used to elicit approach in many experiments and it necessary to turn to these studies to pursue the inquiry. In doing so the obvious must be borne in mind, that no animal model is identical to a living animal. Accordingly these studies must be interpreted with caution in seeking to elucidate the problem of species identification.

Johnston and Gottlieb (1981) investigated this problem using domestic (Peking) and semi-wild mallard ducklings (*Anas platyrhynchos*). When the ducklings were 24 hours old they were allowed to follow for 20 minutes one of a number of objects: a stuffed mallard hen or a stuffed hen of one of two other species of waterfowl, or one of two geometric forms. The chicks were subsequently given a choice test in which the training model and one of the other models were simultaneously present. The upshot of these experiments was that the ducklings behaved *as if* they had a predispositon to

approach their own kind. This predisposition could be overridden by training the ducklings with a geometric form; the predispositon could be
partially offset, but not overridden, by exposing the ducklings to one or
other of the two species of waterfowl. Johnston and Gottlieb, who were cautious in interpreting their results and did not offer a 'predispositions'
explanation for them, concluded by warning against '. . . an oversimplified
approach to the species-identification problem . . .'. It is difficult not to
agree with them, the more so since the problem appeared to arise, albeit in a
modified form, in studying the effects of brain lesions on imprinting.

### 8.1 Brain lesions and preferences

In each of the studies designed to investigate the effects of brain lesions on
imprinting, the training objects were either a rotating flashing red box or a
stuffed hen jungle-fowl (Fig. 2.2(a) and (c) respectively). The jungle-fowl
either rocked or rotated about its own axis. Lesions were placed before,
after or both before and after the training session (Chapter 5 and Section 7.1).
After a chick had been exposed to the training object its preference for this
object over some other object was measured. The novel object was the box
or the fowl, whichever the chick had not previously seen. During the test the
chicks were exposed successively, and in balanced order, to the box and to
the fowl. In each study at least two groups of chicks were used, those with
lesions of the IMHV and sham-operated controls. In none of the studies
was there a significant difference between the preference scores of chicks
trained on the jungle-fowl and those of chicks trained on the box, although
evidence for such an effect was specifically sought in the statistical test
used, an analysis of variance. Nevertheless, when the mean preference
scores from each of the experiments were set out (Table 8.1), those of the
lesioned chicks trained on the box were, unexpectedly, consistently below
those of the lesioned chicks trained on the fowl (Horn and McCabe 1984).

An analysis of variance was performed on the original preference scores
from which the means in Table 8.1 were calculated. The overall mean preference score (Fig. 8.1) of the sham-operated control chicks trained on the
box (78.68) was very similar to that of the controls trained on the jungle-
fowl (83.49). Lesioned chicks which had been trained on the box showed
no preference for the training stimulus: the overall mean preference score of
these chicks was 50.68. In contrast, lesioned chicks which had been trained
on the jungle-fowl preferred the training stimulus. The overall mean preference score (72.19) for these chicks was significantly different both from the
chance score of 50 and from the overall mean preference socre of lesioned
chicks trained on the box. Do these results imply that lesions to the IMHV
were without effect on the preferences of chicks trained on the fowl? The
overall mean preference score of controls trained on this stimulus was
83.49. This score is significantly greater than that achieved by the lesioned

**Table 8.1** *Mean preference scores of chicks with lesions of the IMHV and of sham-operated controls (after Horn and McCabe 1984)*

| Source | Trained on rotating flashing red box | | Trained on stuffed jungle-fowl | | Approximate time elapsing between end of training and the start of testing (h) |
| --- | --- | --- | --- | --- | --- |
| | IMHV-lesioned chicks | Sham-operated controls | IMHV-lesioned chicks | Sham-operated controls | |
| McCabe et al. (1981) | 47.51 (6) | 83.20 (6) | 73.99 (6) | 85.16 (6) | 2 |
| McCabe et al. (1982) | 55.90 (8) | 82.60 (23) | 72.80 (7) | 90.50 (24) | 23 |
| Cipolla-Neto et al. (1982) (RIMHV chicks)* | 52.06 (9) | 70.41 (27) | 64.83 (8) | 77.97 (25) | 44 |
| Horn et al. (1983) | 47.76 (12) | 83.74 (21) | 77.05 (9) | 81.46 (20) | 48 |
| Overall mean values | 50.68 (35) | 78.68 (77) | 72.19 (30) | 83.49 (75) | — |
| Standard errors | ±4.73 | ±2.99 | ±5.88 | ±2.72 | — |

The data are set out according to the object on which the chicks had been trained. The numbers in brackets indicate the numbers of chicks used in the stated category. The results are from all experiments in which preference scores were impaired by lesions to the IMHV. The standard errors given in the table are used to compare the overall mean values against a preference score of 50. For comparisons between means, standard errors derived from the analysis of variance performed on the transformed data (see Horn *et al.* 1983) were used. There was a significant effect of lesions to the IMHV on the preference score ($F_{1,181} = 27.67$; $P < 0.001$). There was a significant interaction between treatment (lesion and control) and training object ($F_{1,181} = 5.92$; $P < 0.025$). The overall mean preference score of chicks trained on the jungle-fowl was significantly different from (i) 50 ($P < 0.001$), (ii) the overall mean preference score of the lesioned chicks trained on the box ($P < 0.001$), and (iii) the overall mean of control chicks trained on the jungle-fowl ($P < 0.01$). The preference scores did not differ significantly between experiments.
*Chicks which received lesions first in the right IMHV and then the left (see Section 7.1).

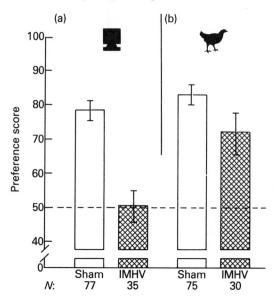

**Fig. 8.1.** Summary of data from experiments in which preference scores were impaired by lesions of the IMHV. The scores for chicks with lesions of the IMHV and sham-operated controls are set out according to the stimulus to which the chicks were exposed during the training period. Means ± s.e.m. for chicks trained with the box (a) and with the jungle-fowl (b). The standard errors may be used to compare the means against the chance, no preference score of 50. Data obtained from Table 8.1.

chicks trained on the jungle-fowl ($P < 0.01$). Thus lesioned chicks trained on the jungle-fowl showed a small, but statistically significant deficit.

The reduced preference scores of IMHV-lesioned birds may have contained a component attributable to some non-specific effects of the brain lesions. This is unlikely to be so. The last three experiments cited in Table 8.1 contained additional controls which received lesions to the Wulst. The mean preference scores of the box-trained and fowl-trained chicks with these lesions were not significantly different from those of their respective controls (Fig. 8.2).

Since a reduction in preference score can be achieved in several ways (see p. 86) the approach counts to the two objects used in the preference test were analysed, combining the data from all the experiments in Table 8.1. The only significant effect was found in the IMHV-lesioned chicks trained on the box. These chicks approached the training object significantly less than did the sham-operated controls ($P < 0.05$); that is, the effect of the lesion was not to reduce the chick's fear of strange objects. If this had been the case the lesioned chicks would have been expected to run more towards the novel object than did their controls. Instead the lesioned chicks behaved

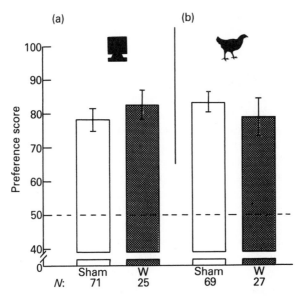

**Fig. 8.2.** Effects of lesions to the Wulst on chicks' preferences. Data for lesioned birds (W) and their controls (Sham) are from the last three experiments cited in Table 8.1. Lesions to the Wulst were without significant effect on the mean preference scores of chicks trained on the box or of chicks trained on the fowl compared to those of their respective controls. Means±s.e.m.. Chicks trained with the box (a) or with the jungle-fowl (b).

as if they were unfamiliar with the training object, as if, that is, their memory of it was impaired.

The results set out in Table 8.1 are strikingly consistent across the four studies. Sham-operated control chicks trained on the box or on the jungle-fowl achieved high preference scores and the two overall mean values were almost identical. In the experiments in which damage to IMHV impaired the chicks' preferences for a training stimulus, the preferences both of the chicks trained on the stuffed jungle-fowl and of those trained on the box were significantly reduced. But the effect on the latter group was profound whereas the effect on chicks trained on the stuffed jungle-fowl was relatively weak.

Perhaps the most straightforward interpretation of these results relates to the differences in complexity of the two training objects, the jungle-fowl being richer in many stimulus dimensions, such as colour and spatial contrast, than the red box. Because of these differences information about the rotating box may take up relatively little storage 'space' and may be contained in the neural networks located within the IMHV. In contrast, information about the jungle-fowl may take up a relatively large amount of storage space and the neural networks involved may be more widely distributed in the brain. A lesion to the IMHV would then disrupt the recognition system for the box, but be too small to cause a corresponding disruption of the recognition system for the jungle-fowl.

A quite different interpretation of the results takes account of the possible biological significance of the stuffed jungle-fowl. Lesions to the IMHV have an effect, albeit a small one, on the preferences of chicks trained on this object. This result may imply that a substantial part of the neural recognition system for the jungle-fowl lies outside the IMHV. Is it possible that there are two systems concerned in the recognition of the jungle-fowl, one within the IMHV and the other outside it and that the two systems have different functions? If so, is the system outside the IMHV concerned with the recognition of some *general* features of congeners and conspecifics, and the system within the IMHV involved with the recognition of *individual* conspecifics, such as the mother, storing information about her particular colours, markings, plumage, and so on? The profound effects of lesions to the IMHV on the preferences of chick trained on the red box, suggest that this region is also involved in the recognition of objects other than individual members of the species. These considerations lead to provocative speculations which, for heuristic purposes, are worth setting out explicitly, bearing in mind of course that they are indeed speculations: (i) the IMHV is involved in the recognition of objects which chicks learn about, including the characteristics of individual conspecifics as well as the characteristics of other objects. Learning is assumed to imply that there is no neural representation—'trace' or 'engram'—of the object prior to exposure to it, and that exposure to the object is necessary for the particular neural representation to be formed. This second requirement may seem pedantic, but, as will become clear (Section 8.2), it is not. (ii) A system exists outside the IMHV which is concerned with recognizing some general features of the chick's own kind, congeners or even conspecifics.

## 8.2 Behavioural analysis of preferences

On the evidence available, the 'stimulus complexity' interpretation of the lesion data (p. 155) is a simpler one than the 'dual recognition' interpretation referred to above. Furthermore, if the dual recognition view is correct, then it is curious that no behavioural evidence of a stronger preference for the jungle-fowl, or a selective predisposition to approach it, had been found over the years of studying intact chicks. Such a predisposition might have been present but gone undetected if the sequential tests, which had been used in all save one of the lesion studies, were insufficiently sensitive. There are indeed grounds for supposing that this test is a good deal less sensitive than the simultaneous choice test (Fig. 3.2(b), (c)). In the sequential test approach was measured in terms of rotation of the running wheel.

As the circumference of the running wheel is 94 centimetres, a chick must run on average at least half this distance, 47 centimetres, for a count to be registered. In contrast, movement of the trolley in the simultaneous test is measured to the nearest centimetre. A 1 centimetre movement of the trolley on the railway corresponds to a movement by the chick of 5.7 centimetres on the circumference of the running wheel. On average a chick should run just over half this distance, for the trolley movement to be recorded as 1 centimetre. Thus the unit of measurement in the sequential test corresponds to a movement by the chick of more than 47 centimetres, but less than 141 centimetres on the circumference of the running wheel; the corresponding movement in the simultaneous choice test is in excess of 2.85 centimetres but less than 8.5 centimetres. Other things being equal, therefore, the simultaneous test is over sixteen times more sensitive than the sequential test. In addition there are reasons for supposing that a simultaneous discrimination task is easier to perform than a sequential discrimination task (see Mackintosh 1974). Thus the simultaneous choice test is more sensitive and may reveal more subtle changes in preference than the sequential test. The simultaneous test, with the red box at one end of the railway and the jungle-fowl at the other, was used in the studies of chicks preferences which are described below.

### 8.2.1 Interaction between acquired preferences and predispositions.

In the first set of experiments (Johnson, Bolhuis, and Horn 1985) chicks were given an opportunity to see either the rotating jungle-fowl or the rotating red box by pressing a pedal in the operant training apparatus (see Section 6.2 and Fig. 6.3). The chicks were then returned to the dark incubator. Their preferences were tested either some 2 hours later (test 1) or some 24 hours later (test 2, see Fig. 8.3). The preference scores of all four groups of chicks are shown in Fig. 8.4(a),(b). When tested approximately 2 hours after the chicks had last seen a conspicuous visual object,

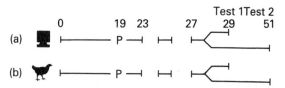

**Fig. 8.3.** Outline of the experiences of experimental chicks in the study of acquired preferences and predispositions (Johnson *et al.* 1985). At P chicks were primed for half an hour. Approximately 4 h later they were given two sessions of training in an operant box (see Fig. 6.3), the sessions being separated by an interval of 2 h. By pressing the active pedal in this box approximately half of the chicks (a) saw the illuminated rotating red box and the other chicks (b) the illuminated rotating jungle-fowl. The preferences of approximately half of the chicks were measured (test 1) 2 h, and that of the remaining chicks (test 2) 24 h after the end of training. Preferences were measured in the simultaneous choice test (Fig. 3.2(b), (c)).

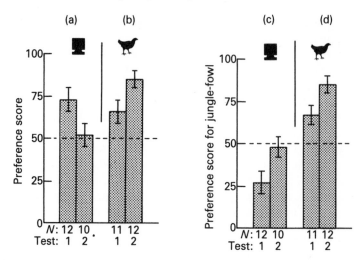

**Fig. 8.4.** Mean preference scores (±s.e.m.) in Test 1 and Test 2 for box-exposed ((a), (c)) and fowl-exposed ((b), (d)) chicks. In (a) and (b), preference scores were calculated from the expression

$$\frac{100\times \text{distance travelled by trolley as chick attempted to approach the familiar conspicuous object}}{\text{total distance travelled by the trolley}}.$$

In (c) and (d) the preference scores in (a) and (b) were expressed as preferences for the stuffed jungle-fowl (see legend to Fig. 8.6). (Results based on data from Johnson *et al.* 1985.)

the chicks preferred that object, whether it had been the jungle-fowl or the red box. These preferences were not significantly different from each other. When tested 24 hours after exposure the situation had changed. The mean preference of the fowl-exposed chicks had strengthened significantly whereas that of the box-exposed chicks had weakened significantly to the chance level of 50.

Since the box and the fowl are both present in the simultaneous choice test, preference can be expressed in terms of approach to the jungle-fowl irrespective of a chick's prior experience. Mean scores expressed as preferences for the jungle-fowl are plotted in Fig. 8.4(c),(d). Chicks which had been exposed to the box and which preferred this object in test 1 necessarily had a low preference for the jungle-fowl. All chicks tested approximately 24 hours after training, however, showed a significantly greater preference for the jungle-fowl than those tested at approximately 2 hours, regardless of the training stimulus.

The increased strength of preference for the jungle-fowl need not be remarkable for chicks which had had prior experience of this object. But it was surprising to find some evidence of a similar trend in chicks which had seen the box, but had not seen the jungle-fowl prior to the preference test. If 'consolidation' is invoked to account for the improvement in the fowl-exposed chicks, consolidation would also have to be invoked for the box-exposed chicks. Accordingly, the preferences of these chicks for the familiar should have been higher in test 2 than test 1. This was not the case. Perhaps the scores of these birds had fallen to chance and the apparent strengthening of their preference for the jungle-fowl was an unwarranted interpretation of the data? Clearly it was necessary to look for evidence which could clarify these issues.

Evidence as to what might be going on came from a study the design of which is illustrated in Fig. 8.5. Chicks were maintained in darkness until they were primed. The birds were then divided into two groups. Chicks in one of these groups (Fig. 8.5(a)) were placed individually in running wheels housed in cabinets the walls of which were painted matt black. A dim over-head light was switched on and remained on whilst the chicks were in the wheels. No training object was present in the relatively featureless black cabinet. After this experience, the light-exposed chicks were returned to individual compartments in the dark incubator. The other group of chicks remained in social isolation within their dark incubator. These chicks were the dark-primed group (Fig. 8.5(b)). Two hours (test 1) after their period in the running wheels some of the light-exposed chicks together with some of the dark-primed chicks were given the preference test. The remaining birds in each group were given the test (test 2) 24 hours after the light-exposed chicks had been removed from the wheels. The dark-primed chicks showed no preference for the box or for the fowl in either of the two tests (Fig. 8.6). The light-exposed chicks at test 1 behaved in a similar way. At test 2, how-ever, these birds strongly preferred the jungle-fowl, even though they had not seen it before the test.

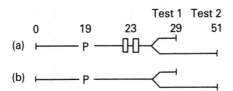

**Fig. 8.5.** Outline of the experiences of control chicks in the study of acquired prefer-ences and predispositions (Johnson *et al.* 1985). When the light-exposed chicks (a) were approximately 23 h old they were placed individually in running wheels housed in an illuminated cabinet. The total period of exposure was 2 h divided into two sessions of 1 h. These sessions are indicated by the open rectangular blocks. Between sessions the chicks spent 1.5 h in the dark incubator. Approximately 2 h *or* 24 h after the second session the chicks were given a preference test (test 1 or test 2 respec-tively). Dark-primed chicks (b) remained in the incubator until they were tested. Whilst in the incubator the chicks were in darkness save for the half-hour period of priming (P) when an overhead light was switched on.

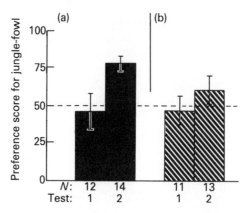

**Fig. 8.6.** Preference scores (means ± s.e.m.) of light-exposed and dark-primed chicks. Test 1 was conducted approximately 2 h and Test 2 approximately 24 h after chicks in the light-exposed group (a) had been removed from the running wheels. The dark-primed chicks (b) were approximately the same age as the light-exposed chicks. Preference scores were calculated from the expression

$$\frac{100 \times \text{distance travelled by trolley as chicks attempted to approach the jungle-fowl}}{\text{total distance travelled by the trolley}}$$

Thus 100 signifies that all approach was directed towards the fowl, 0 that approach was directed towards the box. (After Johnson *et al.* 1985.)

The usual method of measuring preferences has been to relate a given preference score to a baseline level of 50. An alternative method of measuring preferences is to use as baseline the mean preference scores of the light-exposed group. By using this preference score account is taken of the shift in preference toward the jungle-fowl. This convention is followed in Fig. 8.7. The data shown in Figs 8.4(c), (d) and 8.6(a) are plotted together in Fig. 8.7. In this figure the preferences of all these groups, the light-exposed 'control' and the box-exposed and the fowl-exposed 'experimental' groups are expressed as preference scores for the jungle-fowl. The magnitude of the shift in baseline level is given the value $\Delta y$. The difference between the mean preference score of an experimental group and that of a light-exposed group is $k_i$. This difference provides a measure of the preferences acquired by the chick for one of the conspicuous objects as a result of being exposed to it during the performance of the operant task.

In test 1 the mean preference score of the chicks exposed to the box was less than that of the light-exposed controls by 19.2 per cent (Fig. 8.7, $k_1$). The corresponding difference for the chicks exposed to the fowl is almost identical, 20.7 per cent (Fig. 8.7, $k_2$) but in the opposite direction on the scale used in this figure. The preferences of all three groups of chicks shift toward the jungle-fowl from test 1 to test 2. Is this shift associated with the

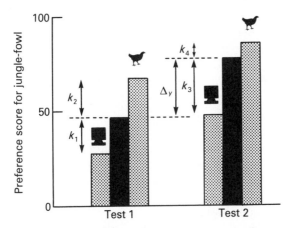

**Fig. 8.7.** A model for the interaction between acquired preferences and a developing predisposition. Preference score values are taken from the data in Figs 8.4(c), (d) and 8.6(a). All mean preference scores are expressed as preferences for the stuffed jungle-fowl. Broken lines represent baselines in test 1 and test 2 set by the respective groups of light-exposed chicks. $\Delta y$ represents the difference in mean preference score between the light-exposed birds in test 1 and in test 2. $k_1$–$k_4$ represent the effects of prior exposure to the red box or to the jungle-fowl. See text for further discussion. (After Johnson *et al.* 1985.)

loss of an acquired preference or is this preference retained? If the acquired preference is lost, it would be expected (Fig. 8.7) that $k_3 < k_1$ and $k_4 < k_2$. In order to test this hypothesis the mean preference score of the light-exposed control birds in each test was subtracted from the preference score of each trained bird at the same test. The resulting adjusted scores were subjected to an analysis of variance. The adjusted scores of the experimental birds were not significantly affected by the time of testing (test 1 or test 2). This result implies that the acquired preferences were stable over the period studied. This finding, when considered together with the evidence that the relative preference for the jungle-fowl increased from test 1 to test 2, suggests that the preferences of the experimental chicks are affected by two underlying processes: (i) a developing predisposition which becomes apparent as an increasing preference for the jungle-fowl in the light-exposed chicks and (ii) a learning process through which chicks come to recognize particular objects to which they have been exposed. If this object is a jungle-fowl, the predisposition appears to be strengthened; if the object is the red box the predisposition is obscured, but not eliminated.

This view is consistent with the findings of Johnston and Gottlieb (p. 152), that the preference of mallard ducklings for conspecifics could be overridden or partially offset by exposing the young ducklings to geometric forms or to some other species of waterfowl. The view is also consistent with other evidence that the development of visually guided behaviour, and of some of the neural processes which may underlie it are affected both by experience and by maturational processes (see for example Klopfer 1967; Gottlieb 1976; Bateson 1978; Wiesel 1982; Kovach 1985).

### 8.2.2 Conditions for the emergence of a predisposition

The evidence provided by the light-exposed control group of chicks suggested that some aspect of their experience contributed to the emergence of a preference for the jungle-fowl at test 2. But what aspect? Whatever it was, it was not shared by the dark-primed chicks since these birds did not express a preference in either test 1 or test 2 (Fig. 8.6(b)). The dark-primed and the light-exposed chicks differed in at least two ways. The light-exposed chicks had two more hours of visual experience than the dark-primed chicks and had also spent 2 hours in the running wheel. Which of these experiences, if either, was necessary for the preference for the jungle-fowl to emerge at test 2? It is difficult to isolate the effects of light exposure: chicks move about more in light than in darkness (Bolhuis *et al.* 1985), so that the effects of light-exposure and of movement are confounded. It is, however, easy enough to exclude light and to study the effects of keeping chicks in the running wheels for 2 hours.

To investigate these effects three groups of chicks were used (Bolhuis, Johnson, and Horn 1985). Chicks of one group (dark-primed) remained in individual compartments in the incubator which, except for the half hour of priming, was kept in darkness (Fig. 8.8(a)). The treatment which these chicks received was similar to that of one of the groups of chicks used by

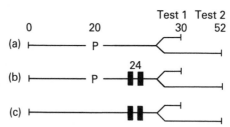

**Fig. 8.8.** Experiment designed to investigate some factors involved in the emergence of a preference for the jungle-fowl (Bolhuis *et al.* 1985). Chicks in treatment groups (a) and (b) were primed for half an hour. Chicks in treatment groups (a) (dark-primed) remained individually housed in the dark incubator at all other times. Chicks in treatment group (b) (wheel-primed) were treated in the same way except for two 1 h sessions during which they were in the running wheel in darkness. These sessions are indicated by the filled black rectangles. A period of 1.5 h intervened between the two sessions. Chicks in treatment group (c) (wheel-dark) remained socially isolated in the dark incubator except for the two sessions, each of 1 h, when the chicks remained in darkness but were kept individually in the running wheels. Preferences of all chicks were tested when the chicks were either approximately 30 h old or when they were approximately 52 h old.

Johnson and his collaborators (Fig. 8.5(b)). Another group of chicks (wheel-primed) was treated in a similar way except that these chicks spent a total of 2 hours in the running wheels in darkness (Fig. 8.8(b)). Any behavioural differences between the chicks which received treatment (a) and chicks which received treatment (b) (Fig. 8.8) was likely to be related in some way to the experience or lack of experience of the running wheel. To assess the effects of priming, a third group of chicks was used (Fig. 8.8(c)). Chicks in this group (wheel-dark) were in darkness throughout and remained individually housed in their incubator except when they were in the running wheels.

As in the earlier study (Fig. 8.6(b)), the dark-primed chicks which remained in the incubator did not develop a preference either for the box or for the fowl (Fig. 8.9(a)). Chicks which had been primed and placed in the running wheel, remaining there in darkness for 2 hours, preferred the jungle-fowl at test 2, but expressed no preference at test 1 (Fig. 8.9(b)). Finally, chicks which remained in darkness throughout the experiment, but spent 2 hours in a running wheel, also developed a preference for the fowl in the second test (Fig. 8.9(c)). The activity in the running wheels of a given group of chicks in test 2 was not significantly different from the activity of the corresponding group in test 1.

The results of these experiments suggest that experience of the running wheel, and/or of some associated experience such as handling, is sufficient for the preference to appear 24 hours later. Furthermore, the experiments demonstrate that the preference can appear in the absence of visual experience.

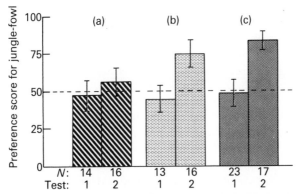

**Fig. 8.9.** Preferences of chicks which received the treatments indicated in Fig. 8.8(a), (b), and (c) respectively. Preference scores were calculated from the expression given in the legend to Fig. 8.6. (a) Chicks in treatment group (a) were dark-primed and remained in the incubator until their preferences were tested. (b) The wheel-primed chicks of treatment group b spent two hours in the running wheel. (c) Chicks in treatment group c were maintained in darkness until given the choice test. These chicks spent 2 hours in the running wheel. (Results based on data from Bolhuis *et al.* 1985).

**Fig. 8.10.** This complex visual pattern covered two walls of a cabinet in which one group of chicks was trained. The pattern was visible to each chick whilst it was in the running wheel. Scale 3 cm. (After Bolhuis *et al.* 1985.)

It would be a mistake to conclude from this experiment that 'general' visual experience is without influence on the emerging preference for the jungle-fowl. Indeed such an effect was demonstrated in an experiment in which two groups of chicks were used (Bolhuis *et al.* 1985). One group was treated in a similar way to that of the light-exposed chicks of Johnson and his colleagues (Fig. 8.5(a)). The treatment of the other group was slightly different. Whilst in the running wheel each chick in this group saw a complex visual pattern (Fig. 8.10). As in the previous study (see Fig. 8.6(a)), chicks in the light-exposed group developed a preference for the jungle-fowl 24 hours after having been removed from the wheel. These chicks showed no preference in the earlier test (Fig. 8.11(a)). In contrast, chicks which had seen the complex geometric pattern expressed a preference for the fowl 2 hours after having been removed from the wheel (Fig. 8.11(b)). The different preferences of the two groups do not have much to do with differences in locomotor activity since the two groups were equally active during the time that they were in the wheel and during the tests. These experiments suggest, therefore, that experience of a complex visual pattern can advance the time of appearance of the preference for the fowl. Evidently, non-specific visual experience as well as the non-specific experience associated

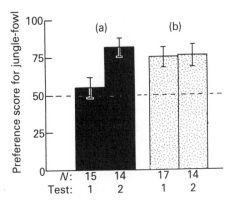

**Fig. 8.11.** Preference of two groups of light-exposed chicks. Preference scores were calculated from the expression given in the legend to Fig. 8.6. (a) These chicks were subjected to the same procedures as those outlined for the light-exposed chicks in Fig. 8.5(a). The chicks showed no preference (relative to a score of 50) in test 1 but a significant preference for the jungle-fowl in test 2 ($P<0.01$). (b) These chicks followed the same treatment regime as chicks in treatment group (a) above, but saw the complex visual pattern (Fig. 8.10) whilst they were in the running wheels. These chicks preferred the jungle-fowl both in test 1 and in test 2 ($P<0.01$). (After Bolhuis *et al.* 1985.)

with being in a running wheel can influence the development of a seemingly specific preference for the fowl over the box. Since the chicks had not seen the fowl before the test they had no opportunity to learn anything about it. Prior exposure to the jungle-fowl is not necessary, therefore, for chicks to prefer it to the box.

The experiments described in this section and in Section 8.2.1 provided evidence which had been lacking (see p. 156): that under appropriate circumstances, a predisposition for the jungle fowl can be demonstrated in young chicks. However, this predisposition did not override the effects of training in the experiments cited in Table 8.1. In those studies, preferences were measured using the sequential test. It was earlier suggested (pp. 156–7) that the failure to detect an emerging preference for the fowl in those studies may have been because the sequential test is insufficiently sensitive to have done so. Evidence that this is so comes from an unpublished experiment in which dark-reared chicks were placed in running wheels for 2 hours. The preferences of one group of chicks were tested 2 hours later and those of another group 24 hours later. At each time, half the chicks were given the sequential test and half the simultaneous test. Chicks given the sequential test preferred neither the box nor the fowl on either occasion. In contrast, chicks given the simultaneous choice test developed the expected preference for the fowl 24 hours after having been removed from the running wheel. These results suggest that the emerging preference for the jungle-fowl is too weak to 'surface' in the sequential test. The preference is strong enough consistently to be detected in the simultaneous choice test; and it may be strong enough therefore to introduce an important bias in the behaviour of the young birds (p. 171).

## 8.3  Predisposition to what?

Does the emerging preference for the jungle-fowl express a growing attraction for objects which possess some of the features of conspecifics, or a growing attraction for complex forms over simple forms? None of the experiments which have been described so far help to resolve this questions, so a further set of experiments was designed (Johnson and Horn 1985*a*). These experiments would have been easy to do if the stuffed fowl had been two-dimensional for it would then have been possible to cut the drawing up so that it ceased to resemble the jungle-fowl. Such a picture would certainly be visually complex. But if chicks prefer conspecifics, the 'scrambled' drawing should not be as attractive to them as the 'unscrambled' version. However, the stuffed jungle-fowl is a three dimensional object so that a different approach to the problem was necessary; it was also necessary to proceed economically since jungle-fowl skins are not easy to come by.

The behavioural method used was the simple one in which dark-reared chicks were placed in running wheels for 2 hours. The experimental design was similar to that illustrated in Fig. 8.8(c). In that experiment the objects used in the choice test were the red box and the jungle-fowl. In the new experiment the jungle-fowl was retained, but the red box was replaced by one of the objects illustrated in Fig. 8.12. The chicks' preferences were tested at either 2 hours or 24 hours after the end of the 2-hour period spent in darkness in the running wheel. When the red box had been used as the alternative object to the jungle-fowl, a preference for the latter appeared at the second test, but not at the first (Fig. 8.9(c)). If the alternative object was treated by the chicks as if it were the whole jungle-fowl, then their preference scores should not differ significantly from 50 at either test.

The object illustrated in Fig. 8.12(a) was a stuffed jungle-fowl with various parts of the body placed in unnatural positions. To a human observer, nevertheless, the object looked unmistakably like a jungle-fowl. Apparently it also does to young chicks. They showed no preference for the whole jungle-fowl over the modified version either in test 1 or test 2 (Fig. 8.13(a)). The pattern of results was very similar when the alternative object was a partially disarticulated stuffed fowl (Fig. 8.12(b)). The chicks showed a weak preference for the whole fowl, their preferences in tests 1 and 2 being almost identical (Fig. 8.13(b)). The object represented in Fig. 8.12(c) was composed of large chunks of the jungle-fowl, and was also well balanced for preferences at tests 1 and 2 (Fig. 8.13(c)). Finally, the skin was cut up into pieces and stuck on to the two larger surfaces of the box (Fig.

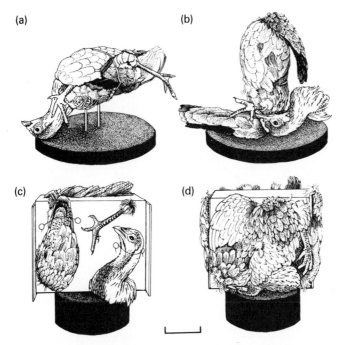

**Fig. 8.12.** Objects used as alternatives to the stuffed jungle-fowl. (a) A stuffed jungle-fowl with head, wings, and legs in anatomically grotesque positions. (b) A stuffed jungle-fowl from which various parts of the body had been removed and placed on the rotating base. (c) Large pieces of the jungle-fowl mounted on each side of the box. (d) The jungle-fowl skin 'scrambled' so that few whole elements were distinguishable by the experimenter. Scale bar 6 cm.

8.12(d)). The chicks did not express a preference at test 1 but at test 2 they clearly preferred the whole jungle-fowl (Fig. 8.13(d)).

The emerging preference (Fig. 8.13(d)) does not appear to be cued by the greater textural complexity of the whole fowl since the textural complexity of the objects shown in Fig. 8.12(a) and (b) was similar to that of the object shown in Fig. 8.12(d). It is also unlikely that chicks prefer at test 2 the more complex outline of the fowl to the outline of the box: chunks of fowl were mounted on the box to construct the object shown in Fig. 8.12(c), yet this object was as attractive to the chicks at test 2 as was the whole fowl (Fig. 8.13(c)).

The results of these experiments suggest that differences in visual complexity between an object and the jungle-fowl cannot easily account for the emerging preference for the fowl. The results raise the possibility that this preference is directed to objects which possess sufficient stimulus elements to allow the objects to be identified as conspecifics or congeners. This possibility was examined by giving chicks a choice between the stuffed

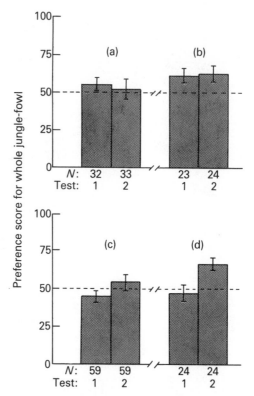

**Fig. 8.13.** Preference scores of chicks (means ± s.e.m.) given a choice between a rotating stuffed jungle-fowl and one of the objects illustrated in Fig. 8.12. The outcome of each preference test is shown, the letters corresponding to the object used as the alternative to the whole fowl. The experimental design was similar to that shown in Fig. 8.8(c). Test 1 was conducted 2 h and test 2 was carried out 24 h after chicks had been removed from the running wheels. Only the score in test 2 for the object shown in Fig. 8.12(d) was significantly greater than the score in test 1 ($P < 0.001$). (After Johnson and Horn 1985a.)

jungle-fowl and a stuffed bird of another genus (Johnson and Horn 1985*a*). The bird was a Gadwall duck (*Anas strepera*). The experimental design was the same as that described above. The chicks showed no preference for the jungle-fowl over the duck at test 1 or at test 2. The same pattern of results was obtained when the choice was between the jungle-fowl and a stuffed carnivorous mammal, a polecat (*Mustela putorius*).

These experiments provide no support for the view that the emerging preferences is *restrictively* directed to conspecifics or congeners. The results suggest that this preference is directed to some stimulus elements which are shared by the whole and by the partially scrambled, stuffed animals (Fig. 8.12(a)–(c)) but not shared by them and the red box or the scrambled skin illustrated in Fig. 8.12(d). What these elements may be is not known, but they could be relatively simple (see Marr and Nishihara 1978), and may even be as highly specific as the eyes and face (see Tinbergen and Perdeck 1950; Tinbergen 1951; Hinde 1954; Coss 1972).

## 8.4 What role for the IMHV in the preference for the jungle fowl?

### 8.4.1 Emerging preferences

The experiments which disclosed the presence of an emerging preference for the fowl were conducted on intact chicks. Does the IMHV play a role in this emerging preference? Or does this preference still appear when the IMHV has been destroyed, as might be expected if the changing preference is an expression of a change in state of the postulated recognition system lying outside the IMHV (p. 156).

As chicks learn to press a pedal in order to illuminate an object and cause it to rotate, they also learn the characteristics of this reinforcing object (see Section 6.2). Chicks with lesions of the IMHV learned to perform this operant task (see p. 112 and Fig. 6.4). They showed no signs, however, of having learned much about the reinforcing object when their preferences were tested 2 hours after training (Fig. 6.5). These results, broken down according to the reinforcing object used during operant training, are shown in Fig. 8.14(a). Preferences for the reinforcing object were impaired by lesions to the IMHV though preference for the red box appeared to be more affected by the lesion than preferences for the jungle-fowl. After this first preference test had been completed the chicks were returned to their dark incubator. Their preferences were measured again in a second test conducted 24 hours after the end of training (Fig. 8.14(b)). The preferences of the sham-operated chicks shifted towards the jungle-fowl from test 1 to test 2, whether the chicks had been exposed to the box or to the fowl. This shift also occurred in the lesioned birds. The emerging preference does not therefore depend on the integrity of the IMHV.

### 8.4.2 Recognition of individuals

In order to investigate the possibility that the IMHV is implicated in individual recognition (p. 156), three groups of chicks were used (Johnson and Horn 1985c). Bilateral lesions were placed in the Wulst of sixteen chicks and in the IMHV of another sixteen soon after hatching. Fifty-two chicks served as sham-operated controls. On the following day, when the chicks were approximately 30 hours old they were placed individually in running wheels and exposed to a stuffed jungle-fowl for a total period of 200 minutes. Two fowls were used (Fig. 8.15), half the chicks in each group being exposed to one and a half to the other. The chicks' preferences were measured in the simultaneous choice apparatus, the two jungle-fowls being placed at either end of the railway. The test was given

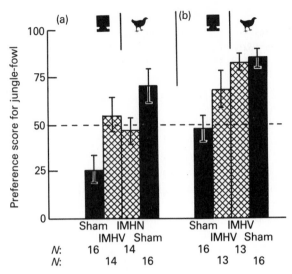

**Fig. 8.14.** Preference scores of chicks exposed to the box or the fowl during the performance of an associative learning task (see Section 6.2). The chicks' preferences were tested both 2 h (a) and 24 h (b) after training. Lesions were placed bilaterally in the IMHV before training. The preference score was calculated from the expression given in the legend to Fig. 8.6 and provides a measure of the chicks' preferences for the jungle-fowl. A score significantly below 50 indicates a preference for the red box and a score significantly above 50, a preference for the jungle-fowl. When tested 2 h after training (test 1) each group of sham-operated chicks preferred the conspicuous object they had previously seen ($P < 0.05$). The score of lesioned chicks which had been exposed to the box was significantly different from that of their controls ($P < 0.02$). The corresponding difference for chicks which had been exposed to the jungle-fowl was almost significant ($t = 1.91$; $0.1 < P > 0.05$). When preferences were measured again in test 2 a significant increase in preference for the jungle-fowl was present in all groups (matched samples $t$; $P < 0.01$ in all cases). (After Johnson and Horn 1985$b$.)

less than 3 hours after training. Sham-operated control chicks with lesions of the Wulst both preferred the familiar, stuffed jungle-fowl, their mean scores (63.6 and 69.7 respectively) being significantly greater than the chance level of 50 ($P < 0.05$). In contrast, the mean score (38.3) of chicks with lesions of the IMHV was not significantly different from 50. Their mean score was significantly less than those of the other two groups of chicks ($P < 0.02$ in each case). The results of this experiment suggest that intact chicks, as well as chicks with lesions of the Wulst, learn something about a jungle-fowl when they are exposed to it, and that they are subsequently able to recognize that individual. The IMHV appears to be necessary for this recognition process.

The results described in this section and in Sections 8.2, 8.3, and 8.4.1 are consistent with the hypothesis that there is a special-purpose system of

**Fig. 8.15.** Line drawing of the two stuffed jungle-fowls used in the experiment designed to study the role of the IMHV in individual recognition. Scale 10 cm.

neurones outside the IMHV which supports a predisposition to approach objects possessing certain morphological features. The putative system does not appear to be operational at the time of hatching, but may be rendered operational by various procedures such as keeping the chick in a running wheel for 2 hours or by exposing the chick to a complex visual pattern. Klopfer (1967) also found evidence of a need to activate a predisposition in Peking ducklings. He wrote, 'It looked as if some kind of innate preference existed that had to be activated by the experience of following . . .'. Just what the mediating physiological processes may be and how they are triggered by the seemingly non-specific behavioural experiences are issues which are discussed elsewhere (Sections 9.6, 10.3.7, and 12.2.2).

The emerging preference may have an important functional role to play in the early life of the chick. It is possible that, once exposed to the visual complexity of their natural environment, or as a result of moving about even in darkness, chicks quickly develop a preference for certain features or stimulus elements, such as the eyes and face of their mother. It may be that these elements are possessed by other animals as well, but the mother is the animal that the young chicks are most likely to encounter soon after hatching. The preference may be relatively weak to start with (p. 165), but it may be quite sufficient to bias the chicks' approach towards their own kind. Learning processes may then restrict this preference to a particular individual. Thus the initial preference of the chick would 'guide' it to the appropriate object, which is most likely to be an adult member of its own species. Learning processes could then be seen as an aid to the recognition of individual features of the chick's mother. Thus, in the early hours and days of a young chick's life non-specific experiences may activate a system through which the chick comes to recognize its own kind; specific experiences, which involve learning processes, may allow the chick to recognize its kin. The IMHV appears to be implicated in this learning process.

## 8.5 S' and the jungle-fowl

Evidence has been presented to show that a second store, S', outside the IMHV is gradually formed in the course of imprinting (see Chapter 7). Since a recognition system capable of supporting a preference for the jungle-fowl also exists outside the IMHV (Sections 8.1 and 8.4.1) it is necessary to enquire whether the two systems are one and the same. There are reasons for believing them to be independent.

In each of the experiments cited in Table 8.1 lesions to the IMHV reduced the preference score significantly below that of the controls only for birds which had been trained on the box. When destruction of the IMHV was without significant effect on chicks' preferences (Section 7.1 and Fig. 7.3, LIMHV group) the result was anomalous only for chicks which had been trained on the box. Hence the initial reason for postulating a store S' outside the IMHV was to account for the behaviour of these birds. The postulate was supported by the finding that bilateral lesions of the IMHV placed approximately 26 hours after training did not significantly affect the preference scores (Figure 7.6(b)). Subsequent analysis of the data plotted in this figure has shown that lesioned chicks had as strong a preference for the object on which they had been trained, whether it was the box or the fowl, as had their controls. S' may thus store information about objects which the chicks learn to recognize; and there are no grounds for supposing that S' has anything to do with the putative system, also outside the IMHV, which supports a predisposition to approach certain objects, including those which resemble conspecifics.

These considerations greatly simplify the general properties of S and S' (Section 7.3 and Fig. 7.8(a)): they are involved in the storage of information acquired through learning processes.

## 8.6 Summary

In experiments in which damage to the IMHV impaired chicks' preferences for a training stimulus, the preferences both of chicks trained on the jungle fowl and of chicks trained on the red box were reduced. The effect on the box-trained chicks was profound whereas the effect on the chicks trained on the jungle fowl was relatively weak. These results are discussed within the context of species identification. Using a sensitive test for measuring chicks' preferences it was shown that chicks increasingly prefer the jungle fowl to the box over the first 2 or 3 days after hatching. The emerging preference could be detected in chicks which had been exposed to the box as well as to chicks which had been exposed to the fowl. This preference for the fowl appeared in visually experienced chicks which had seen neither of these objects before their preferences were measured. Furthermore, the preference emerged even in dark-reared chicks provided that they had been kept in a running wheel for 2 hours. The preference did not appear in chicks which were left individually housed in the dark incubator. The results suggest that the preferences of young chicks are affected by two underlying processes. There is (i) a developing predisposition which becomes apparent as an increasing preference for the jungle fowl. The predisposition can be activated by non-specific experiences, and once activated interacts with (ii) a learning process through which chicks come to recognize particular objects to which they have been exposed. The IMHV is concerned with the second process. Some structure or structures outside the IMHV are concerned with the first: the emerging preference for the fowl occurs in chicks with bilateral lesions of the IMHV. It is shown that the emerging preference does not express a predisposition for visually complex objects over simple objects, nor for morphological features which are unique to the chick's own kind.

# References

Bateson, P. P. G. (1978). Early experience and sexual preferences. In *Biological determinants of sexual behaviour* (ed. J. B. Hutchinson), pp. 29–53. John Wiley, Chichester.

Bolhuis, J., Johnson, M. H., and Horn, G. (1985). Effects of early experience on the development of filial preferences in the domestic chick. *Devl Psychobiol.* **18** (in press).

Cipolla-Neto, J., Horn, G., and McCabe, B. J. (1982). Hemispheric asymmetry and imprinting: the effect of sequential lesions to the hyperstriatum ventrale. *Exp. Brain Res.* **48**, 22–7.

Coss, R. G. (1972). Eye-like schemata: their effect on behaviour. PhD dissertation, University of Reading.

Fabricus, E. and Boyd, H. (1952/53). Experiments on the following reactions of ducklings. *Wildfowl Trust Ann. Rep.* **6**, 84–9.

Gottlieb, G. (1976). The roles of experience in the development of behavior and the nervous system. In *Studies in the development of behavior and the nervous system*, Vol. 3, *Neural and behavioral specificity* (ed. G. Gottlieb), pp. 25–54. Academic Press, New York.

Hinde, R. A. (1954). Factors governing the changes in strength of a partially inborn response, as shown by the mobbing behaviour of the chaffinch (*Fringilla coelebs*). I. The nature of the response, and an examination of its course. *Proc. R. Soc. B* **142**, 306–31.

Horn, G. and McCabe, B. J. (1984). Predispositions and preferences. Effects on imprinting of lesions to the chick brain. *Anim. Behav.* **32**, 288–92.

——, ——, and Cipolla-Neto, J. (1983). Imprinting in the domestic chick: the role of each side of the hyperstriatum ventrale in acquisition and retention. *Exp. Brain Res.* **53**, 91–8.

Johnson, M. H. and Horn, G. (1985*a*). An analysis of a predisposition in the domestic chick. *Behav. Brain Res.* (in press).

——, —— (1985*b*). Dissociation of recognition memory and associative learning by a restricted lesion of the chick forebrain. *Neuropsychologia* (in press).

——, —— (1985*c*). Is a restricted brain region of domestic chicks involved in the recognition of individual conspecifics? *Behav. Brain Res.* (in press).

——, Bolhuis, J. J., and Horn, G. (1985). Interaction between acquired preferences and developing predispositions during imprinting. *Anim. Behav.* **33**, 1000–6.

Johnston, T. D. and Gottlieb, G. (1981). Development of visual species identification in ducklings. *Anim. Behav.* **29**, 1082–99.

Klopfer, P. H. (1967). Is imprinting a Cheshire cat? *Behav. Sci.* **12**, 122–9.

Kovach, J. K. (1971). Effectiveness of different colors in the elicitation and development of approach behavior in chicks. *Behaviour* **38**, 154–68.

—— (1983). Perceptual imprinting: genetically variable response tendencies, selective learning, and the phenotypic expression of colour and pattern preferences in quail chicks (*C. coturnix japonica*). *Behaviour* **86**, 72–88.

—— (1985). Behavioral genetics and the search for the engram: genes, perceptual preferences and the mediation of stimulus information. In *Behavior genetics: principles and applications II* (eds J. L. Fuller and E. C. Simmel), Erlbaum, Hillsdale, N.J. (in press).

McCabe, B. J., Cipolla-Neto, J., Horn, G., and Bateson, P. P. G. (1982). Amnesic effects of bilateral lesions placed in the hyperstriatum ventrale of the chick after imprinting. *Exp. Brain Res.* **48**, 13–21.

——, Horn, G., and Bateson, P. P. G. (1981). Effects of restricted lesions of the chick forebrain on the acquisition of filial preferences during imprinting. *Brain Res.* **205**, 29–37.

Mackintosh, N. J. (1974). *The psychology of animal learning.* Academic Press, London.

Marr, D. and Nishihara, H. K. (1978). Representation and recognition of the spatial organization of three-dimensional shapes. *Proc. R. Soc. B* **200**, 269–94.

Tinbergen, N. (1951). *The study of instinct.* Clarendon Press, Oxford.

—— and Perdeck, A. C. (1950). On the stimulus situation releasing the begging response in the newly hatched herring gull chick (*Larus a. argentatus* Pont). *Behaviour* **3**, 1–39.

Schaefer, H. H., and Hess, E. H. (1959). Color preferences in imprinting objects. *Z. Tierpsychol.* **16**, 161–72.

Sluckin, W. (1972). *Imprinting and early learning,* Methuen, London.

Wiesel, T. N. (1982). Postnatal development of the visual cortex and the influence of environment. *Nature, Lond.,* **299**, 583–91.

# 9
# Physiological constraints on memory and imprinting

In Chapter 6 it was suggested that information about an imprinting object is recorded only if the storage system receives the sensory input evoked by the object, together with an input from an 'incentive' system (Section 6.4). If this suggestion is correct then nothing should be recorded if the storage system receives only the sensory input. Suppose that it were possible to conduct an experiment in which the input was restricted in this way, and the chicks subsequently presented with an object which evoked this input. Since nothing had been stored, the chicks would not be expected to express a preference for the object. A study has recently been conducted which contained some of the features of this experiment (McCabe, Horn, and Bateson 1979). The study was designed to investigate the possibility of introducing information directly into the IMHV by artificial means to see whether this procedure influenced the chicks' preferences; if the procedure was successful, the result would provide further evidence for the involvement of IMHV in imprinting.

## 9.1 Effects of stimulating the brain

Chicks are able to distinguish between lights flashing at 4.5 and 1.5 herz. In the experiments demonstrating this ability, the flashing effect was achieved by means of a rotating cylinder (Fig. 9.1). It was found that chicks must be exposed to one of these frequencies for 5 hours for a preference to be established. From a neurophysiological point of view a flashing light is a particularly useful stimulus for two reasons. Firstly is it possible to search for evoked responses corresponding to the stimulus frequency and so trace the paths taken by these 'frequency-labelled' responses in the nervous system. Secondly it is easy to deliver electrical pulses at a particular frequency to a site in the nervous system and subsequently to enquire whether the animal's preferences are biased toward a light flashing at that frequency. The latter method was exploited to determine whether stimulating the IMHV in this way influenced chicks' subsequent approach behaviour.

Chicks were hatched and reared in darkness until they were approximately 10 hours old. The chicks were then anaesthetized and bipolar stimulating electrodes were introduced into both hemipsheres in the follow-

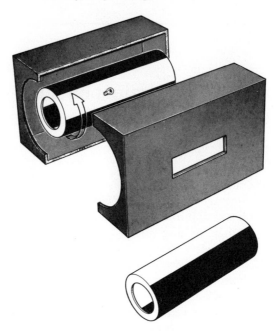

**Fig. 9.1.** Exploded diagram of visual stimulus used in the choice test. The inside of the cylinder was illuminated by a 48 W bulb. The light was diffused by tracing paper covering the cylinder. One cylinder was painted with one black stripe, the other with three black stripes. When the cylinder was rotated at a given rate the effect viewed through the slit was of light flashing at 1.5 Hz or 4.5 Hz depending on the number of stripes. The slit, measuring 15 cm×5 cm, was cut in a black matt surface. (After McCabe *et al.* 1979.)

ing regions: (i) the IMHV or (ii) the hyperstriatum accessorium or (iii) the ectostriatum. The latter two placements were for control purposes. Both are visual projection areas, and it was assumed that any visual input to the IMHV is likely to involve one or both of these regions (see Section 11.1.1). Some 16 hours after the operation, two chicks were placed individually in separate running wheels, the two wheels being housed in a sound-proof box. The centre of each running wheel was 50 centimetres away from a vertical black matt surface behind which was a striped cylinder (Fig. 9.1). Whilst in the running wheel the brain region of each chick was stimulated with trains of electrical pulses delivered at the rate of either 1.5 or 4.5 trains per second. During the time that the pulses were being delivered the box was illuminated so that the chick could see the cylinder through the slot in the black surface. The cylinder was also illuminated, from within, and the translucent stripes appeared yellow. The cylinder was stationary throughout the period of cerebral stimulation. The chicks were placed in a running wheel and exposed to the stationary yellow stimulus in this way to acclimatize them to the type of environment that they would encounter in the preference test. Intracerebral stimulation continued for a total of 5 hours. At the end of this time each chick's preference was tested in the simultaneous choice test apparatus. A visual stimulus (Fig. 9.1) stood at either end of the railway. Each stimulus generated a flashing red light, one at 4.5 hertz and the other at 1.5 hertz.

The results for the chicks with electrodes implanted bilaterally in the IMHV are shown in Fig. 9.2. Chicks which had been stimulated at 1.5 trains per second preferred the light flashing at 1.5 hertz; and chicks which had been stimulated at 4.5 trains per second preferred the light flashing at 4.5 hertz. For the sixteen chicks with electrodes implanted bilaterally in either the hyperstriatum accessorium or in the ectostriatum and stimulated electrically, no significant effects of train frequency on preference for the flashing lights were observed.

The hyperstriatum accessorium projects directly to the IMHV and the ectostriatum is linked to the IMHV over a multi-synaptic pathway (Section 11.1.1). Yet electrical stimulation of these two visual areas failed to influence the chicks' preferences whereas direct stimulation of the IMHV did so. These results suggest that (i) input to the IMHV from a visual pathway alone is not sufficient for chicks to use, in subsequent behavioural tests, the temporal information contained within that input and therefore (ii) for the

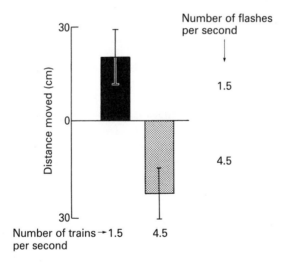

**Fig. 9.2.** Preferences of chicks stimulated in the IMHV (mean ± s.e.m.). The maximum distance moved by the trolley from the midpoint of the railway in 10 min was taken as the chick's preference (Bateson and Wainwright 1972). The horizontal line on the ordinate indicates no preference. Twelve chicks were stimulated at 1.5 trains per second and thirteen chicks were stimulated at 4.5 trains per second. (After McCabe *et al.* 1979.)

information to be used in this way, input from at least one other system is necessary. Presumably the electrical stimulation of the IMHV activated the two proposed inputs, or directly excited the postsynaptic elements in the IMHV on which these two inputs impinge. The two suggestions ((i) and (ii)), based on the outcome of the brain stimulation experiments, are similar to those put forward in Section 6.4 (see also Fig. 6.6(a)), though they derive from an entirely different experimental approach. It is certainly attractive to think of a non-sensory system which provides an input to the IMHV and mediates the reinforcing or incentive effect of an imprinting stimulus; but are there any grounds for supposing that a visually conspicuous object would excite such a system?

A visual stimulus would evoke activity in the optic nerve and so excite neurones in the thalamus and in the optic tectum. The optic tectum projects to the ectostriatum via a synapse in the thalamus (Appendix, Section A3.1). The optic tectum also projects to other regions of the brain including the brainstem core (Bradley *et al.* 1985; for a review see Pearson 1972). Cell groups in the brainstem core project to many areas of the central nervous system. In mammals, and probably also in birds, one of the cell groups with extensive projections to the forebrain is the locus coeruleus, the cells of which are rich in noradrenaline (Section A.4). The visual stimulus would not only evoke activity in the visual areas of the forebrain, but would also be expected to excite cells in the brainstem core (see, for example, Watabe *et al.* 1982). Thus if a neurone in the forebrain receives an input from a visual projection area, that neurone may also receive, at the same time or shortly afterwards, an input from the brainstem core. Could such an indirect input mediate the reinforcing action of a visual imprinting stimulus?

Some years ago Young (1963) suggested that, for certain kinds of learning, 'registration in memory' is dependent on the occurrence of signals evoked by reinforcing stimuli. Griffith (1966), starting from the assumption that memory is mediated by changes in synaptic strength, proposed a cellular mechanism by which the reinforcing signals might influence this change. But what neural systems might be engaged by reinforcing stimuli? Kety (1967) drew attention to the widespread distribution of monoamines in the mammalian brain. He pointed out that drugs which modify the levels of these amines, especially the catecholamines dopamine and noradrenaline, have profound affects on mood in humans and on diverse behaviours in other mammals. In the light of these considerations he suggested that the catecholamines and especially noradrenaline play an important role in affective and arousal states. Both Kety (1970, 1972) and Crow (1968) went on to propose that the effects of reinforcing stimuli on the synaptic mechanisms assumed to underlie memory are mediated by neurones in the noradrenergic system, the cell bodies of which lie in the brainstem core. Kety (1970) predicted that drugs which '. . . deplete or bock norepinephrine (noradrenaline) in the brain should retard consolidation and prevent acquisition'. In order to test the hypothesis that noradrenaline-containing neurones innervating the cerebral cortex form an essential component of the learning mechanism, Anlezark and his co-workers (1973) placed lesions in the locus coeruleus of rats. These lesions resulted in a reduction in the concentration of noradrenaline in the cerebral cortex to approximately one-third of that found in controls. The ability of the lesioned rats to learn a simple approach task for food reward was severely impaired. However, in spite of the promise of this early work, many later studies failed to find a general impairment of learning ability after severe depletion of noradrenaline in the brain (for a review see Mason 1984).

The effects on learning abilities of manipulations which reduce brain noradrenaline levels are difficult to interpret. Where an effect on acquisition has been demonstrated, the effect may be brought about by an indirect action on behaviour and be consequent upon changes in arousal, attention, distractability, motivation, and locomotor activity—factors which complicate the interpretation of a change in behaviour following almost any experimental interference with the physiological state of an animal (see Chapter 5). A change in behaviour associated with low noradrenaline levels may also be brought about in a physiologically indirect way. For example, noradrenergic neurones in the locus coeruleus may be implicated in the release of the adrenocorticotrophic hormone—ACTH (Amaral and Sinnamon 1977). Damage to this system of neurones may modify learning abilities indirectly through a primary effect on the ability of an animal to adapt to stressful conditions. In addition, when neurotoxins are used to impair the functions of the noradrenergic system, the toxin may have side-effects which have their own behavioural consequences. Clearly there are many interpretations of results which demonstrate that the acquisition of certain behaviours is impaired when brain noradrenaline levels are reduced.

A similar ambiguity exists in the interpretation of experiments which *fail* to find a relationship between brain noradrenaline levels and the acquisition or retention of new behaviours. For example, experimental manipulations of noradrenaline levels do not eliminate all of this amine from the forebrain. If the amount of putative plastic changes in the brain varies according to the difficulty of the task to be learned, then the residual concentration of noradrenaline in the brain may be adequate to support the acquisition and maintenance of relatively simple behaviours, but be inadequate to support more complex behaviours. In addition, the way in which noradrenaline depletion is achieved, the age at treatment, and the time-lag between noradrenaline depletion and the start of behavioural testing may all be important factors influencing the outcome of the treatment. Indeed Bear and his colleagues (1983) pointed out that the effects of chronic noradrenaline depletion may subsequently be masked by, for example, an increase in the density of β-adrenergic receptors (Sporn *et al.* 1977; Harik *et al.* 1981). Thus, if training is undertaken at the appropriate time, the change in density

of these receptors may compensate for the reduced levels of available noradrenaline.

In contrast to the confused relationship that exists between learning
abilities and brain noradrenaline concentrations, Kasamatsu and his co-
workers have provided convincing evidence for a role of noradrenaline in
neuronal plasticity (see Kasamatsu 1983). Approximately 80 per cent of
neurones in the visual cortex of the normal cat can be excited by the appropriate stimuli delivered to either eye and in this sense the neurones are
binocular (Hubel and Wiesel 1962). However, if the lid of one eye is
sutured early in life, neurones in the visual cortex of kittens become domi-
nated by the originally open eye and the majority can only be excited by
stimuli delivered to it (Wiesel and Hubel 1963; Hubel and Wiesel 1970).
These physiological changes are accompanied by morphological changes.
Axons carrying input from the one open eye appear to innervate a larger
territory of cortex than would be expected from studies of kittens raised
with both eyes open (see Wiesel 1982). The shift in 'ocular dominance' can
be prevented if 6-hydroxydopamine (6-OHDA), a drug which destroys
noradrenaline- and dopamine-containing neurones, is infused directly into
the visual cortex (Kasamatsu *et al.* 1979; Daw *et al.* 1983; Bear *et al.* 1983).
Cortical plasticity can be restored in kittens treated with 6-OHDA if noradrenaline is infused directly into the visual cortex (Kasamatsu *et al.* 1979).
Even more remarkable were the findings of Kasamatsu and co-workers
(1979) using older kittens or adults cats. Kasamatsu and his colleagues
(1979) took advantage of the evidence that the period over which unilateral
eyelid suture can affect ocular dominance is limited to a short time in the
first three months of life (Hubel and Wiesel 1970); unilateral eyelid
suture much after this time has little or no effect on ocular dominance.
Kasamatsu and his colleagues showed that when this operation was performed on the older animals and the visual cortex infused with
noradrenaline, a shift in ocular dominance occurred. In other words,
plasticity had been restored by infusing noradrenaline into the adult cortex.

The evidence suggesting that noradrenaline may be involved in the neural
events underlying shifts in ocular dominance, together with the original
speculations of Crow (1968) and Kety (1970) that noradrenaline may influence learning through a primary effect on synapses, led us to investigate the
effects on imprinting of reducing the levels of noradrenaline in the brain
(Davies, Horn, and McCabe, 1985). Such a study should be promising not
only because some aspects of imprinting involve learning processes, but
also because imprinting is associated with changes in the morphology of
synapses within the IMHV (Section 10.2). As a preliminary step we
enquired whether catecholamines are present in specific regions of the chick
forebrain, and if so, whether the concentrations of these amines vary with
age and with visual experience (Davies, Horn, and McCabe 1983).

## 9.2 Effects of age and visual experience on catecholamine levels in parts of the chick forebrain

The concentrations of dopamine and noradrenaline were measured in three regions, taken from each hemisphere of the chick forebrain. The regions were (i) the Wulst, (ii) medial forebrain comprising mainly the IMHV, and (iii) basal forebrain comprising mainly paleostriatum augmentatum (see Fig. A.3). The samples were taken from chicks immediately after hatching and from other chicks at 12, 22, 26, 29 and 50 hours after hatching, respectively. One group of chicks was dark-reared throughout. Eight chicks from this group were killed and brain samples removed at each of these ages. Another group of chicks was reared in darkness until they were 21 hours old when they were primed (see p. 57) for half an hour. These chicks were returned to the dark and forebrain samples were taken from eight of them when they were 22 hours old. The remaining primed birds were exposed to the rotating red box for a total of 2 hours. Brain samples were removed from eight of these chicks immediately after training, when the chicks were 26 hours old. The remaining twenty-four trained chicks were killed in two groups, one group at 3 hours after training (aged 29 hours) and the other group 24 hours after training (aged 50 hours).

There were not significant hemispheric asymmetries in the concentrations of dopamine or of noradrenaline. The concentration of dopamine, which was highest in the basal forebrain sample and lowest in the Wulst, did not vary with age or with visual experience. At the time of hatching the basal forebrain sample contained the highest level of noradrenaline ($53.13 \pm 7.85$ nanograms per gram of sample) and the medial forebrain sample the lowest ($26.09 \pm 3.75$ nanograms per gram of sample). Noradrenaline concentration increased with age in both the Wulst and the medial forebrain samples (Fig. 9.3). There was no significant change in noradrenaline levels with age in the basal forebrain sample.

An analysis of variance showed that, for all areas combined, the concentration of noradrenaline was significantly greater in visually experienced chicks than in the dark-reared chicks (Fig. 9.4). The magnitude of this difference did not vary significantly between the three regions or with age. Thus exposure to an artificial imprinting stimulus was associated with a widespread elevation of noradrenaline concentrations within the chick telencephalon. Earlier studies had demonstrated that chicks exposed to the rotating red box for 2 hours prefer it to a novel object (see, for example, Section 5.2). It is reasonable, therefore, to assume that in the above study the chicks which had seen this stimulus also formed a social attachment to it.

The results of this study were encouraging, though little more than that.

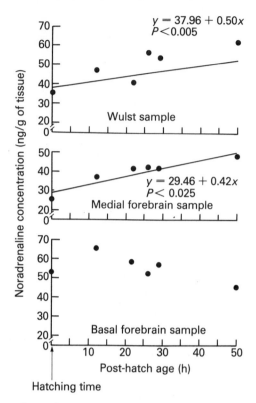

**Fig. 9.3.** Concentrations of noradrenaline in samples from three regions of the forebrain hemispheres of dark-reared chicks. The data for the upper two graphs were fitted adequately by linear regression equations with the stated parameters. The data from the basal forebrain samples did not change significantly with time. Each data point represents the mean for eight chicks. (After Davies *et al.* 1983.)

The finding that dopamine concentration did not change with age or visual experience does not rule out the possibility that this amine is involved in imprinting processes: the levels present at hatching may have been adequate to support these processes. Nor do the findings of a change in noradrenaline concentration with both age and visual experience imply that this amine is involved in some particular way in imprinting. Nevertheless these positive findings served to focus attention on noradrenaline; and some means was required to deplete the forebrain of this amine in order to enquire whether chicks so treated could be imprinted.

The noradrenergic neurotoxin *N*-(2-chloroethyl)-*N*-ethyl-2-bromobenzylamine hydrochloride (DSP4), is a useful drug for investigating some functions of brain noradrenaline (Ross *et al.* 1973; Ross 1976). Following the injection of DSP4 into rats there is a long-lasting depression of nora-

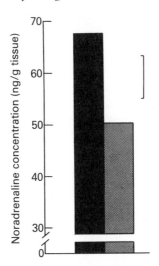

**Fig. 9.4.** The effect of visual experience on the concentration of noradrenaline in the chick telencephalon. The diagram represents combined data from the Wulst, medial forebrain, and basal forebrain samples taken at 22, 26, 29, and 50 h after hatching. Mean noradrenaline levels were significantly higher in visually experienced (black bar) than in dark-reared (shaded bar) chicks ($F_{1,49}=5.57$; $P<0.05$). The vertical line represents the standard error of the difference between the two mean values. There were thirty-two chicks in each of the two groups. (After Davies *et al.* 1983.)

drenaline concentrations in the cerebral cortex and in other parts of the central nervous system (Ross 1976; Jaim-Etcheverry and Zieher 1980). Jonsson and his colleagues (1981) described similar effects of DSP4 on brain noradrenaline levels in mice. These workers concluded that DSP4 produces a relatively selective degeneration of noradrenaline nerve terminals in the mouse and in the rat. For this and other reasons (p. 187) we used this drug to investigate the effects on imprinting of reducing brain noradrenaline levels (Davies *et al.* 1985).

### 9.3  Noradrenaline and imprinting

Immediately after chicks had been hatched they were assigned to one of two groups. Experimental chicks, of which there were forty-eight, were injected with DSP4 in distilled water. The forty-eight control chicks received only distilled water. After injection the chicks were returned to a dark holding incubator and about 30 hours later each chick received a repeat injection. When the chicks were 60 hours old they were primed for 30 minutes. Subsequently each chick was placed in a running wheel and exposed for 1 hour to either the rotating, flashing red box or to the rotating, stuffed jungle-fowl. Two hours after training the chicks' preferences were measured in the sequential test and the preference score calculated (p. 85). Approximately 1 hour after this test the time taken to approach and peck a rocking bead was recorded.

After the testing procedures had been completed twelve experimental and twelve control chicks were killed and the brains quickly removed. Three regions, referred to in Section 9.2 above, were removed from each hemisphere. Since no hemispheric asymmetry in noradrenaline concentration had previously been found for any of the three regions, tissue from corresponding regions of the right and left hemipsheres were combined for subsequent analysis of noradrenaline concentration.

Control chicks trained on the red box developed a clear preference for that stimulus (Fig. 9.5). However, the chicks which had received DSP4 and which had been trained on the box achieved a mean preference score which was well below that of their controls and was not significantly different from chance. In contrast, for chicks trained on the jungle-fowl the preference score of the DSP4-treated birds was almost identical to that of their controls. During the preference test both groups of chicks receiving DSP4 were no less active than their controls and drug treatment did not affect the latency to peck the rocking bead.

DSP4 treatment resulted in a significant reduction in noradrenaline concentration in the three forebrain regions investigated (Fig. 9.6). The percentage reduction (approximately 65 per cent) was similar in each region. Noradrenaline levels in fowl-trained chicks were reduced by the same extent as in box-trained chicks.

Data from each forebrain region were analysed separately to determine

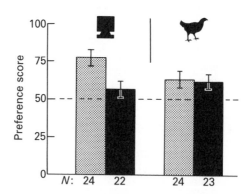

**Fig. 9.5.** The effects of DSP4 on preference score. Mean ± S.E.M. preference score for controls (dotted bars) and DSP4-treated chicks (black bars). The preference score of control chicks trained on the red box was significantly greater than 50 ($P < 0.001$). DSP4 treatment had no significant effect on the preference scores of chicks trained on the jungle-fowl and the preference score of these chicks and of their controls were significantly greater than 50 ($P < 0.02$ for both comparisons). (After Davies *et al.* 1985.)

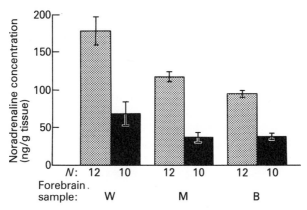

**Fig. 9.6.** The effects of DSP4 on forebrain noradrenaline concentrations. Mean ± s.e.m. noradrenaline concentrations for samples from the Wulst (W), medial forebrain (M), and basal forebrain (B). Dotted bars, control chicks; black bars, DSP4-treated chicks. DSP4 treatment resulted in a significant reduction in forebrain noradrenaline concentration relative to that of controls ($P < 0.01$ in all regions). There was no significant interaction between drug treatment and training stimulus ($F_{1,17} = 0.26$). (After Davies *et al.* 1985.)

whether preference score varied with nordrenaline concentration. There was a significant, positive correlation between preference score and noradrenaline concentration in the medial forebrain sample ($P < 0.05$) and in the basal forebrain sample ($P < 0.01$), but not in the Wulst ($P > 0.2$) of chicks trained on the red box. None of the corresponding correlations for chicks trained on the jungle-fowl were significant ($P > 0.2$ for each region).

The results of this experiment suggested that DSP4 exerted a differential effect on chicks' performance, the effect depending on the object used for training. There could, however, be another explanation for the results. The failure of DSP4 to modify the preferences of chicks trained on the jungle-fowl may have been due to a 'floor' effect. Employing this hypothesis, the observed results would be accounted for in the following way. DSP4 only exerts an effect on chicks which, if untreated, would be expected to have a high mean preference score. Such a score was found in the control chicks trained on the box. A high preference score was not achieved by the control chicks trained on the jungle-fowl: the preference score of these chicks was significantly less than that of control chicks trained on the red box ($P < 0.05$). Hence DSP4 should affect the preference of chicks trained on the box, but have little effect on chicks trained on the fowl.

To distinguish a floor effect from a differential effect of DSP4 according to the training object, a second experiment was conducted. The design of this experiment was similar to that of the previous experiment in which the drug was used, except that, during the training period, a recording of the maternal call was played whenever the red box or jungle-fowl was presented. The procedure accelerates imprinting on a visual stimulus (see p. 73). In addition, the duration of training was increased to a total of 80 minutes. These steps proved to be effective (Fig. 9.7). The mean preference score of the controls trained on the red box was similar to that of the controls trained on the jungle-fowl. Both mean scores were well above the no preference level. This was also true for DSP4-treated chicks trained on the jungle-fowl. Their preference score was not significantly different from that of their controls. In contrast, the mean preference score of DSP4-treated chicks trained on the box was (i) significantly less than that of their controls, (ii) significantly less than that of the DSP4-treated chicks trained on the fowl, and (iii) not significantly different from chance. These results together rule out the floor hypothesis because the high mean preference scores of the two control groups were not significantly different from each other.

To summarize: The preference score was clearly reduced in the DSP4-treated chicks which had been trained on the box. Noradrenaline levels were reduced to a similar extent in all forebrain samples. There was a positive correlation between noradrenaline concentration and preference score in the medial forebrain and the basal forebrain samples only in chicks which had been trained on the red box.

When a drug impairs a particular behavioural response it is important to know, as discussed above, whether the effect is specific or whether it is a

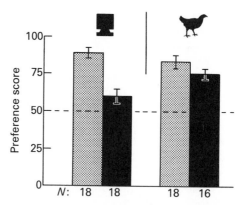

**Fig. 9.7.** Effects of DSP4 on preference scores. Mean ± s.e.m. preference scores for controls (dotted bars) and DSP4-treated birds (black bars). There were no significant differences between the mean scores of the two control groups and both scores were significantly greater than 50 ($P < 0.001$). The mean score of DSP4-treated chicks trained on the jungle-fowl was not significantly different from that of the controls, but was significantly greater than 50 ($P < 0.001$). The mean score of DSP4-treated chicks trained on the red box was significantly less than that of their controls ($P < 0.001$), significantly less than that of the DSP4-treated chicks trained on the jungle-fowl ($P < 0.02$), and not significantly different from 50. (After Davies *et al.* 1985.)

consequence of an action on a subtle aspect of behaviour which secondarily affects the response. Indeed, some drugs which are used to deplete noradrenaline have effects on behaviour which are far from subtle. Sham rage, seizures, incontinence, and compulsive turning followed the injection of 6-OHDA into the ventricles of the brain in the experiments of Kasamatsu and Pettigrew (1979). None of the chicks receiving DSP4 exhibited such abnormal behaviour. These chicks were no less active than their controls in the preference tests, and DSP4 treatment had no significant effect on the latency to peck the rocking bead. None the less, if DSP4 had equally affected the preferences of chicks trained on the jungle-fowl and of chicks trained on the red box, then there would have been no easy way of resolving the behavioural ambiguities that such a result would have presented (see p. 179 above). In the event, the drug affected profoundly the acquisition of a preference in chicks exposed to one stimulus but had little effect on acquisition in chicks exposed to the other. It is therefore unlikely that the drug exerted its action on imprinting through some non-specific influence on behaviour.

For chicks trained on the red box there was a positive correlation between preference score and noradrenaline concentration in the medial forebrain sample, which was composed mainly of the IMHV. This result further strengthens the case for a role of the IMHV in imprinting on artificial objects (see Chapter 8). There was also a positive correlation between preference score and noradrenaline concentration in the basal forebrain sample of chicks trained on the red box. This sample contained mainly the paleostriatum augmentatum, a structure which may be involved in the control of movement (Karten and Dubbeldam 1973; Rieke 1980). It is unlikely, however, that the effect found in the paleostriatum augumentatum for chicks trained on the red box had much to do with locomotor activity. The chicks exposed to the jungle-fowl were not less active than chicks exposed to the red box; but there was no correlation between noradrenaline concentration and preference score for chicks trained on the fowl. Whether the correlation has anything to do with imprinting processes is not known. The paleostriatum augmentatum and the IMHV are reciprocally connected (p. 243) and this relationship may imply some functional interaction between the two systems (Section 7.3). The absence of a correlation between preference score and the noradrenaline content of the Wulst sample is consistent with the results of the lesion studies: extensive damage to the Wulst does not impair the ability of chicks to acquire and retain a preference for a visually conspicuous object through imprinting (see Chapter 5).

The results of the above study (Davies *et al.* 1985) give some support for the involvement of noradrenaline in the process by which chicks learn the characteristics of an artificial object. The support is, necessarily, qualified. For one thing a unique role for noradrenaline in cortical plasticity is open

to question (Sillito 1983). Indeed, Shaw and Cynader (1984) have recently
shown that changes in ocular dominance in monocularly deprived kittens
can be blocked by perfusing the visual cortex with L-glutamate. It is not
known whether this action is mediated through a primary effect on noradrenaline or whether both of these substances affect cortical plasticity
independently. It is possible that plastic changes at a synapse occur only if
there is a conjunction of firing in the pre- and postsynaptic neurones (Hebb
1949). Both glutamate (Shaw and Cynader 1984) and noradrenaline
(Reader 1978; Kasamatsu and Heggelund 1982) modify the discharge of
cortical neurones. Thus these substances might prevent plastic changes by
disrupting the pattern of discharge of cortical neurones. These considerations do not rule out a specific, physiological role for noradrenaline in
neuronal plasticity. In normal animals, noradrenaline might, for example,
stabilize the discharge of neurones so that 'the conditions necessary for
plastic changes to occur may be realized (see also Section 10.3.4). There
are, however, other reasons for reserving judgement about the mode of
action of DSP4. It is possible that the drug exerts its effects on imprinting
not through its action on noradrenaline, but through physiological changes
which co-vary with noradrenaline concentrations. It is also possible that
DSP4, like L-glutamate, directly disrupts the firing pattern of neurones in
the IMHV and in other regions of the chick brain. There is no independent
evidence to exclude these possiblities. The differential effects of DSP4 on
imprinting according to the stimulus used in training is similar to the effects
on this process of lesions to the IMHV (Horn and McCabe 1984). Lesions
to this structure severely impaired imprinting in chicks which were exposed
to the red box but had much less effect in chicks exposed to the jungle-
fowl. Further evidence that the neural consequences of training chicks with
the box can be dissociated from the neural consequences of training with
the fowl came from another set of experiments (Bolhuis, McCabe, and
Horn 1985).

## 9.4 Testosterone and imprinting

Male chicks which have been injected with testosterone are less easily dis-
tracted and more persistent in responding to a variety of stimuli than are
chicks which have not received the hormone (Andrew 1972; Andrew and
Rogers 1972; Archer 1974). In reviewing a number of experiments Andrew
and his collaborators (1981) suggested that testosterone may affect mechanisms common to memory formation and attention. Attention and memory
are involved in imprinting. Is imprinting influenced by this hormone? Testosterone had been shown by James (1962) and by Balthazart and de
Rycker (1979) to affect the approach responses to domestic chicks; but
these workers had not demonstrated an effect of the hormone on chicks'

preferences, a direct measure of the strength of imprinting. We therefore investigated the relationship between testosterone and imprinting (Bolhuis *et al.* 1985).

In these experiments chicks were hatched in darkness and shortly afterwards were sexed (Davies and Payne 1982). Each chick received a single subcutaneous injection of either testosterone enanthate in arachis oil (experimental chicks) or arachis oil alone (control chicks). The doses of testosterone enanthate injected were of 1, 3, or 5 milligrams. This preparation of the hormone was used since it is long-acting and has been shown to maintain steady levels in the blood for at least 24 hours (Andrew 1983). Each dose of testosterone was administered to equal numbers of males and females. After injection, the birds were coded as usual so that the experimental history of each chick was unknown to those conducting the subsequent training, testing, and bioassay procedures.

Approximately 16 hours after the injection and when the chicks were between 22 and 27 hours old they were primed for half an hour. Soon afterwards each chick was placed in a running wheel and exposed for a total period of 2 hours to either the rotating stuffed jungle-fowl or to the rotating red box. At the end of training the chicks were again put into individual compartments in the dark incubator. Two hours later the chicks' preferences were measured in a sequential test. A preference score (p. 85) was calculated for each bird. After testing, the chicks were returned to the dark incubator for half an hour when a blood sample was taken from each chick. The plasma was separated from the sample. The concentration of testosterone in the plasma was measured by radioimmunoassay (see Yalow 1980). Testosterone is not the only male sex hormone (androgen) present in the plasma, and the method used to measure testosterone concentration was sensitive to $5\alpha$-dihydrotestosterone (22.4 per cent cross-reaction). For the sake of brevity, and following others (for example Tanabe *et al.* 1979), the results of the assay are referred to as plasma 'testosterone' concentrations.

There were no sex differences in the concentrations of plasma testosterone or in preference scores. The absence of sex differences in the level of testosterone in the plasma of controls is consistent with the results of Tanabe and his collaborators (1979). These workers showed that plasma testosterone concentration in female chicks did not differ significantly from that of male chicks during the 4 weeks that followed hatching.

The effect of injected, or exogenous testosterone on mean preference score depended on the training stimulus. For this reason the data from the chicks trained on the jungle-fowl were analysed separately from those for chicks trained on the red box. The results for chicks trained on the jungle-fowl are considered first. The overall mean preference score for all birds trained on the jungle-fowl was $61.74 \pm 2.11$. The preference score was affected by exogenous testosterone: the mean score for experimental chicks was $64.52 \pm 2.32$ whereas the mean score for the controls was

54.76±4.30. The two means are significantly different ($P<0.05$). The mean score of the controls was not significantly different from the no preference level of 50. This result was a little surprising given that the chicks had been exposed to the jungle-fowl for 2 hours. Some insight into what might be going on was gained when the preference scores were ranked according to plasma testosterone concentration. The median concentration was 1.07 nanograms per millimetre. The mean preference score of those controls whose testosterone level exceeded the median value was significantly greater than 50 ($P<0.05$). The mean preference score of the remaining control chicks was not significantly different from 50.

These results together suggest that there is a relationship between preference score and plasma testosterone concentration for chicks trained on the jungle-fowl. The evidence for such a relationship was strengthened by the finding of a positive correlation between these two variables. The correlation was significant for the control chicks (Fig. 9.8(a)) and for the experimental chicks (Fig. 9.8(b)) considered separately or together (Fig. 9.9(b)). Thus preference score and testosterone were related both within and beyond the physiological range of plasma testosterone concentrations. The slope of the regression line (Fig. 9.8) relating preference score to testosterone concentration was significantly lower for experimental chicks than for the controls ($P<0.05$.) There was thus a tendency for the relationship between the two variables to level off at higher concentrations of testosterone.

The overall mean preference score for all chicks trained on the red box was 70.14 ± 2.02. The mean preference scores of the experimental and control chicks were not significantly different from each other or from the overall mean. For these box-trained birds there was not a significant correlation between plasma testosterone concentration and preference score either in controls or in experimental chicks considered separately, or when data from both groups were combined.

The mean preference score for all chicks trained on the red box (70.14 ± 2.02) was significantly ($P<0.01$) greater than that of all chicks trained on the jungle-fowl (61.74 ± 2.11). Since preference scores can never be greater than 100, it could be argued that the preferences of chicks trained on the red box are related to plasma testosterone concentrations, but that this putative relationship was obscured because the preference scores of these chicks, being nearer to the theoretical maximum than those of the fowl-trained chicks, were subject to a 'ceiling' effect. In order to examine this possibility the preference scores of chicks trained on the red box were ranked, the birds with the highest preference score eliminated, and the mean of the remaining preference scores determined. This process of eliminating the highest value was repeated until the mean preference score of the restricted group of box-trained birds was as near as possible to that of the chicks trained on the jungle fowl. This point was achieved when twenty-three birds had been eliminated. The mean preference score of this

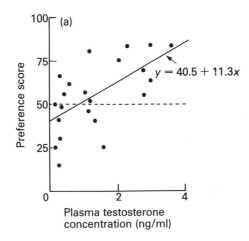

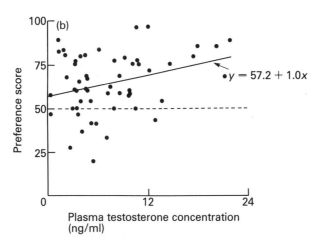

**Fig. 9.8.** Relationships between preference score and plasma testosterone concentration in chicks trained on the jungle-fowl. The data were fitted by linear regression equations with the stated parameters. (a) Control chicks. The correlation coefficient ($r$=0.62, 20 d.f.) was significant ($P$<0.002). (b) Experimental chicks. The correlation coefficient ($r$=0.30, 55 d.f.) was significant ($P$<0.02). (After Bolhuis *et al.* 1985.)

restricted group of box-trained chicks was 61.68 ± 1.93. There was no significant correlation between preference score and plasma concentration in this group of chicks (Fig. 9.9(a)). The slope of the linear regression was significantly lower than the slope of the corresponding line for all chicks trained on the jungle-fowl; that is, the stimulus-dependent disparity persisted, even after matching the mean preference score of the box-trained chicks with that of the fowl-trained chicks.

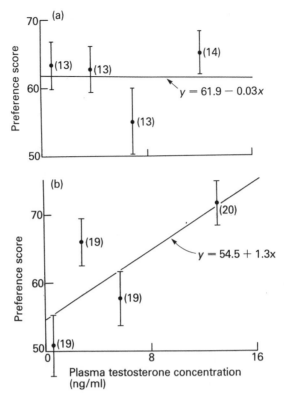

**Fig. 9.9.** Relationships between preference score and plasma testosterone concentration. Data from experimental and control chicks have been combined. The mean preference score of the box-trained chicks was matched (see text) to that of the jungle-fowl-trained chicks. The distribution of the testosterone concentrations was divided by its quartiles and the means of the four resulting sub-groups are plotted. Numbers of chicks are given in brackets. The bars represent $\pm 1$ S.E.M. (a) Chicks trained on the red box ($r = 0.0095$, 74 d.f., NS). (b) chicks trained on the jungle-fowl ($r = 0.34$, 75 d.f., $P < 0.01$). The slopes of the two lines shown in (a) and (b) are significantly different ($P < 0.05$). (After Bolhuis *et al.* 1985.)

Were the effects of exogenous testosterone on the chicks' behaviour non-specific, acting for example on sensory–motor coordination, arousal, and so on, rather than on mechanisms more directly involved in the acquisition of a preference? It is unlikely that testosterone affected chicks' levels of arousal or visuomotor coordination during the preference test: during this test, approach counts to the training and novel objects were not significantly correlated with testosterone concentration. But the strongest argument against a non-specific action of the hormone is that plasma testosterone concentration was related to preference score only in chicks trained on the jungle-fowl and not in chicks trained on the box.

The correlation between preference score and testosterone concentration in chicks trained on the jungle-fowl is not, of course, by itself evidence of a causal relationship between the two variables. Furthermore, even if the relationship is causal the correlation gives no indication of which is cause and which is effect. Does a strong preference for the jungle-fowl lead to the secretion of high levels of testosterone or is a high level of testosterone necessary for the development of a strong preference for the jungle-fowl? If preference for the jungle-fowl increases the secretion of testosterone, the plasma concentration of testosterone in control chicks trained on the fowl should be higher than that of control chicks trained on the box. However, the mean plasma concentrations in the two groups of birds were not significantly different. A direct test of whether preference score depends on testosterone concentration is to inject exogenous testosterone. When this was done plasma testosterone levels increased significantly and so did the mean preference score of chicks trained on the jungle-fowl. For these chicks, therefore, there is evidence of a causal link between the two variables, testosterone concentration in the plasma influencing preference score.

The implication that testosterone influences the acquisition of certain behaviours through an effect on neuronal function is not without precedent. For example, certain brain regions controlling song and other vocalizations have been identified in the canary (Nottebohm *et al.* 1976; Nottebohm 1980; see p. 140). Similar structures are involved in the song system of the zebra finch, *Peophila guttata* (Gurney and Konishi 1980). Song is reduced in zebra finch males after castration and is re-established by the administration of exogenous androgens (Pröve 1974; Arnold 1975). Some of the structures of the song system in this bird accumulate testosterone or its metabolites (Arnold 1980). These studies suggest that target cells for androgens are implicated in the acquisition of song in the canary and zebra finch and that androgens are necessary for this function (Arnold 1981; Nottebohm 1981).

## 9.5 Double dissociation

The preferences of chicks trained on the red box were strongly influenced by DSP4 whereas the preferences of chicks trained on the jungle-fowl were little influenced by this drug. There was thus a 'simple dissociation' between the effects of DSP4 on box-trained and fowl-trained chicks. Another simple dissociation arose out of the studies of testosterone and imprinting. The preferences of chicks trained on the jungle-fowl were influenced by the concentration of testosterone in the plasma; there was no such relationship for chicks trained on the red box. This complementary pattern, a double dissociation (Teuber 1955; Shallice 1979; Jones 1983), suggests that at least some of the neural mechanisms underlying these preferences are subject to different physiological constraints.

## 9.6 Comment and speculation

The experiments which have been described in Sections 9.1 and 9.3 suggest that impulse activity in the sensory pathways is not sufficient for a chick to form a social attachment to an artificial object which elicits this activity. Some additional factors appear to be involved. For chicks trained on the red box a limiting factor may be the concentration of noradrenaline in the forebrain. Within limits, the higher the concentration of this amine in a region consisting largely of the IMHV, the stronger was the box-trained chicks' preference for this stimulus. These results are consistent with the theory of Kety (1970, 1972) and Crow (1968; Crow and Arbuthnott 1972) that the reinforcing effects of a stimulus are mediated by noradrenaline. The results are also consistent with the view that information about an imprinting object is recorded only if the storage system receives both the sensory input evoked by the object and an input from the incentive system. (Section 6.4).

The evidence that noradrenaline may be involved in imprinting does not of course exclude the possibility that other substances may also be involved (see p. 188). Nor does the evidence exclude the possibility that some neural systems may be modified even when the brain has been severely depleted of noradrenaline. Indeed, such a system appears to be implicated in the development of a preference for the jungle-fowl. Chicks which were exposed to the jungle-fowl preferred it to the box, even though brain noradrenaline levels had been reduced by 65 per cent. However, the preference of fowl-trained chicks for their training object was correlated with, and may have been limited by, the concentration of testosterone in the plasma.

Chicks will develop a preference for the jungle-fowl even if they have never seen it before. All that is required is to place chicks, aged 20 hours or so, into a running wheel for a couple of hours. It does not matter whether the chicks are in darkness or in light during this time. But if they are returned to their dark incubator for 24 hours and their preferences tested, they prefer the jungle-fowl to the box (Section 8.2). The preference does not appear if the chicks spend only 2 hours in the incubator after having been removed from the wheel. One way of thinking about these results is to suppose that these various procedures have the effect of 'functionally validating', in the sense of rendering operational, a special-purpose system which supports the preference for the jungle-fowl. Since this preference may be limited by plasma testosterone levels, it is possible that the system is functionally validated by the hormone. This possibility raises a number of issues. Chicks which spend some time in the running wheel are handled more, probably move about more, and whilst in the wheel have different sensory experiences from chicks which have remained in the dark incubator. Do these experiences separately or collectively influence the levels of plasma testosterone in the chicks? There is at present no direct answer to this question. However, Kruhlich and his collaborators (1974) have shown that the secretion of a number of hormones by the anterior lobe of the pituitary gland of laboratory rats is affected by a variety of procedures, including the transfer of the animals from one room to another. One of these hormones, the luteinizing hormone, stimulates the secretion of testosterone. The secretion of luteinizing hormone was increased and did not return to control levels until approximately 1 hour after transfer. The increase in luteinizing hormone might be expected to lead to an elevation in the concentration of plasma testosterone. If a similar sequence of events occurred in chicks placed in the running wheel, the ensuing increase in the secretion of testosterone, from the testes or ovaries (see Tanabe *et al.* 1979), might have been sufficient to validate the putative system supporting the preference for the jungle-fowl, though the validation process must take several hours to be effective.

A mechanism of this kind could account for the emerging preference for the jungle-fowl (Section 8.2). Could such a mechanism account for other results, for example the accelerated preference that appears if the chicks are placed in the running wheel and are able to see a complex pattern or the jungle-fowl itself? It is possible that sensory input and testosterone levels interact within the postulated system. For a given level of testosterone, the functional coupling between neurones might be stronger with optimal sensory inputs than with sub-optimal inputs. A complex visual pattern might provide a more effective excitatory drive to the cells than diffuse illumination, but the jungle-fowl might be more effective still. The stronger the functional coupling between neurones in the system, the more vigorously would the neurones discharge when, in the preference test, the jungle-fowl is presented. Accordingly, the stronger would be the output to the approach motor neurones and the more vigorously would the chick approach the fowl.

How might functional validation be achieved? It is possible, for example, that neurones in the postulated system initially become functionally coupled only in the presence of adequate levels of testosterone (see Section 10.3.7). After functional validation, neurones in the system may respond selectively to certain combinations of stimuli (for example head and eye: see Hinde 1954; Candland 1969; Coss 1972), combinations which are possessed by the stuffed jungle-fowl. If neurones in the system are connected to the motor system controlling approach, the presentation of the jungle-fowl after functional validation would elicit a selective approach response even though the jungle-fowl had never previously been seen by the chick.

The evidence of the lesion studies suggests that the IMHV is not a part of the special-purpose system (Sections 8.1 and 8.4.1). It is, however, possible

that once this putative recognition system outside the IMHV has been functionally validated, in whatever way this has been achieved, chicks will
approach a particular conspecific and learn its characteristics. It has already
been suggested that the IMHV is involved in this learning process (p. 156)
and evidence in support of this suggestion has been given (Section 8.4.2).
The role of the IMHV may be to 'fill out' the specification of the special-
purpose system; the filling out may entail learning the details of individuals.
On this view the special-purpose system, functionally validated by testosterone, is 'used' to guide the chick to a conspecific. Thereafter two things may
happen. Neurones in the system become more efficiently connected because
they are excited by an optimum stimulus; and the information required to
recognize, say, the chick's mother is entered into the IMHV storage system.

If noradrenaline is necessary for storage to occur in the IMHV system, it
follows that the component contributed by this system to the recognition of
the jungle-fowl, in chicks which have been trained on this object, should be
impaired when the forebrain is depleted of noradrenaline. In both experiments in which DSP4 was used to lower noradrenaline levels, the mean
preference scores of fowl-trained chicks were reduced slightly. The mean
reduction of $8.52 \pm 4.73$ per cent in one of these experiments (Fig. 9.7)
was statistically significant ($t=1.80$, $P<0.04$, one-tailed). This percentage
reduction is not very different from that brought about by destroying the
IMHV: when lesions were placed in the IMHV after training, the mean
preference score of fowl-trained chicks was lower than that of their controls
by approximately 11 per cent (Table 8.1).

It would be unwise to suppose that the two substances testosterone and
noradrenaline are respectively the only intervening variables which, in the
alert chick, impose constraints on its predispositions and on the preferences
which develop through exposure to a suitable object. Just as the notion of a
single 'general motivational state' has given way to a healthy plurality of
intervening variables affecting behaviour (see Hinde 1970, 1982), so different physiological factors may impose constraints on different patterns of
behaviour, for example feeding, filial, and, in older birds, predator avoidance and mate selection. And more than one factor may have a part to play
in a given function, including memory (see p. 221).

### 9.7 Summary

Evidence is reviewed that activity in the sensory pathways is not sufficient
for information to be stored. Variables associated with the internal state of
the animal impose constraints on storage. The roles of noradrenaline and
testosterone in imprinting processes are analysed. The concentration of noradrenaline in parts of the forebrain, including the IMHV, appear to limit
acquisition particularly in chicks which have been trained on the box. For
the fowl-trained chicks preference for the jungle-fowl was correlated with the

concentration of testosterone in the plasma. Within the limits of the experiments described, testosterone was without influence on the preferences of the box-trained chicks. It is concluded that at least some of the neural mechanisms underlying the preference for the box and for the fowl, respectively, are subject to different physiological constraints. It is suggested that the emerging preference for the jungle-fowl, described in Section 8.2, results from the activity of a special-purpose system. This system may be rendered operational, or functionally validated, by testosterone.

## References

Amaral, D. G. and Sinnamon, H. M. (1977). The locus coeruleus: neurobiology of a central noradrenergic nucleus. *Progr. Neurobiol.* **9**, 147–96.

Andrew, R. J. (1972). Recognition processes and behaviour, with special reference to effects of testosterone on persistence. *Adv. Study Behav.* **4**, 175–208.

—— (1983). Specific short-latency effects of oestradiol and testosterone on distractibility and memory formation in the young domestic chick. In *Hormones and behaviour in higher vertebrates* (eds J. Balthazart, E. Pröve, and R. Gilles), pp. 463–73. Springer-Verlag, Berlin.

—— and Rogers, L. J (1972). Testosterone, search behaviour and persistence. *Nature, Lond.* **237**, 343–6.

——, Clifton P. G., and Gibbs, M. E. (1981). Enhancement of effectiveness of learning by testosterone in domestic chicks. *J. comp. physiol. Psychol.* **95**, 406–17.

Anlezark, G. M., Crow, T. J., and Greenway, A. P. (1973). Impaired learning and decreased cortical norepinephrine after bilateral locus coeruleus lesions. *Science* **181**, 682–4.

Archer, J. (1974). The effects of testosterone on the distractibility of chicks by irrelevant and relevant novel stimuli. *Anim. Behav.* **22**, 397–404.

Arnold, A. P. (1975). The effect of castration and androgen replacement on song, courtship and aggression in zebra finches (*Poephila guttato*). *J. exp. Zool.* **191**, 309–26.

—— (1980). Quantitative analysis of sex differences in hormone accumulation in the zebra finch brain: methodological and theoretical issues. *J. comp. Neurol.* **189**, 421–36.

—— (1981). Logical levels of steroid hormone action in the control of vertebrate behavior. *Am. Zool.* **21**, 233–42.

Balthazart, J. and de Rycker, C. (1979). Effects of androgens and oestrogens on the behaviour of chicks in an imprinting situation. *Z. Tierpsychol.* **49**, 55–64.

Bateson, P. P. G. and Wainwright, A. A. P. (1972). The effects of prior exposure to light on the imprinting process in domestic chicks. *Behaviour* **42**, 279–90.

Bear, M. F., Paradiso, M. A., Schwartz, M., Nelson, S. B., Carnes, K. M., and Daniels, J. D. (1983). Two methods of catecholamine depletion in kitten yield different effects on plasticity *Nature, Lond.* **302**, 245–7.

Bolhuis, J. J., McCabe, B. J., and Horn, G. (1985). Androgens and imprinting. Differential effects of testosterone on filial preferences in the domestic chick. *Behav. Neurosci.* (in press).

Bradley, P., Davies, D. C., and Horn, G. (1985). Connections of the hyperstriatum ventrale in the domestic chick (*Gallus domesticus*). *J. Anat.* **140**, 577–89.

Candland, D. K. (1969). Discriminability of facial regions used by the domestic chicken in maintaining the social dominance order. *J. comp. physiol. Psychol.* **69**, 281–5.

Coss, R. G. (1972). Eye-like schemata: their effect on behaviour. PhD dissertation, University of Reading.

Crow, T. J. (1968). Cortical synapses and reinforcement: an hypothesis. *Nature, Lond.* **219**, 736–7.

—— and Arbuthnott, G. W. (1972). Function of catecholamine-containing neurones in mammalian central nervous system. *Nature new Biol.* **238**, 245–6.

Davies, D. C. and Payne, J. K. (1982). Variation in chick sex ratios during hatching. *Anim Behav.* **30**, 931–932.

——, Horn, G., and McCabe, B. J. (1983). Changes in telencephalic catecholamine levels in the domestic chick. Effects of age and visual experience. *Dev. Brain Res.* **10**, 251–5.

——, ——, ——, (1985). Noradrenaline and learning: the effects of the neurotoxin DSP4 on imprinting in the domestic chick. *Behav. Neurosci.* **99** (in press).

Daw, N. W., Rader, R. K., Robertson, T. W., and Ariel, M. (1983). Effects of 6-hydroxy dopamine on visual-deprivation in the kitten striate cortex. *J. Neurosci.* **3**, 907–14.

Griffith, J. S. (1966). A theory of the nature of memory. *Nature, Lond.* **211**, 1160–3.

Gurney, M. E. and Konishi, M. (1980). Hormone-induced sexual differentiation of brain and behavior in zebra finches. *Science* **108**, 1380–3.

Harik, S. I., Duckrow, R. B., LaManna, J. C., Rosenthal, M., Sharma, V. K., and Banerjee, S. P. (1981). Cerebral compensation for chronic noradrenergic denervation induced by locus ceruleus lesion: recovery of receptor binding, isoproterenol-induced adenylate cyclase activity, and oxidative metabolism. *J. Neurosci.* **1**, 641–9.

Hebb, D. O. (1949). *The organization of behavior.* John Wiley, New York.

Hinde, R. A. (1954). Factors governing the changes in strength of a partially inborn response as shown by the mobbing behaviour of the chaffinch (*Fringilla coelebs*). I. The nature of the response, and an examination of its course. *Proc. R. Soc. B* **142**, 306–31.

—— (1970). *Animal behavior (2nd end).* McGraw-Hill, New York.

—— (1982) *Ethology: its nature and relations with other sciences.* Fontana, London.

—— and McCabe, B. J. (1984). Predispositions and preferences. Effects on imprinting of lesions to the chick brain. *Anim. Behav.* **32**, 288–92.

Hubel, D. H., and Wiesel, T. N. (1962). Receptive fields, binocular interaction and functional architecture in the cat's visual cortex. *J. Physiol., Lond.* **160**, 106–54.

——, —— (1970). The period of susceptibility to the physiological effects of unilateral eye closure in kittens. *J. Physiol., Lond.* **206**, 419–36.

Jaim-Etcheverry, G. and Zieher, L. M. (1980). DSP4: a novel compound with neurotoxic effects on noradrenergic neurons of adult and developing rats. *Brain res.* **188**, 513–23.

James, H. (1962). Imprinting with visual flicker: effects of testostrone cyclopentylpropionate. *Anim. Behav.* **10**, 341–6.

Jones, G. V. (1983). On double dissociation of function. *Neuropsychologia* **21**, 397–400.

Jonsson, G., Hallman, H., Ponzio, F., and Ross, S. (1981). DSP4 (*N*-(2-chloroethyl)-*N*-ethyl-2-bromobenzylamine)—a useful denervation tool for central and periperhal noradrenaline neurons. *Eur. J. Pharmac.* **72**, 173–88.

Karten, H. J. and Dubbeldam, J. L. (1973). The organization and projections of the paleostriatal complex in the pigeon (*Columba livia*). *J. comp. Neurol.* **148**, 61–90.

Kasamatsu, T. (1983). Neuronal plasticity maintained by the central norepinephrine system in the cat visual cortex. *Progr. Psychobiol. physiol. Psychol.* **10**, 1–112.

—— and Heggelund, P. (1982). Single cell responses in cat visual cortex to visual stimulation during iontophoresis of noradrenaline. *Exp. Brain Res.* **45**, 317–27.

—— and Pettigrew, J. D. (1979). Preservation of binocularity after monocular deprivation in the striate cortex of kittens treated with 6-hydroxydopamine. *J. comp. Neurol.* **185**, 139–62.

——, ——, and Ary, M. (1979). Restoration of visual cortical plasticity by local microperfusion of norepinephrine. *J. comp. Neurol.* **185**, 163–82.

Kety, S. S. (1967). The central physiological and pharmacological effects of the biogenic amines and their correlations with behaviour. In *The neurosciences: a study program* (eds G. C. Quarton, T. Melnechuk, and F. O. Schmitt), pp. 444–51. The Rockefeller University Press, New York.

—— (1970) The biogenic amines in the central nervous system: their possible roles in arousal, emotion and learning. In *The neurosciences: second study program* (ed. F. O. Schmitt) pp. 324–36. Rockefeller University Press, New York.

—— (1972). The possible role of the adrenergic systems of the cortex in learning. *Res. Publs Ass. Res. nerv. ment. Dis.* **50**, 376–86.

Kruhlich, L., Hefco, E., and Read, C. B. (1974). The effects of acute stress on the secretion of LH, FSH, prolactin and GH in the normal rat, with comments on their statistical evaluation. *Neuroendocrinology* **16**, 293–311.

McCabe, B. J., Horn, G., and Bateson, P. P. G. (1979). Effects of rhythmic hyperstriatal stimulation on chicks' preferences for visual flicker. *Physiol. Behav.* **23**, 137–40.

Mason, S. T. (1984). *Catecholamines and behaviour.* Cambridge University Press, Cambridge.

Nottebohm, F. (1980). Brain pathways, for vocal learning in birds: a review of the first 10 years. *Progr. Psychobiol. physiol. Psychol.* **9**, 86–124.

—— (1981). A brain for all seasons: cyclical anatomical changes in song control nuclei in the canary brain. *Science* **214**, 1368–70.

——, Stokes, T. M., and Leonard, C. M. (1976). Central control of song in the canary, *Serinus canarius. J. comp. Neurol.* **165**, 457–86.

Pearson, R. (1972). *The avian brain.* Academic Press, New York.

Pröve, E. (1974). Der Einfluss von Kastration und Testosteronsubstitution auf das Sexualverhalten männlicher Zebrafinken (*Taeniopygia guttata castanotis* Gould). *J. Orn., Lpz.* **115**, 338–47.

Reader, T. A. (1978). The effects of dopamine, noradrenaline and serotonin in the visual cortex of the cat. *Experientia* **34**, 1586–7.

Rieke, G. K. (1980). Kianic acid lesions of pigeon paleostriatum: a model for study of movement disorders. *Physiol. Behav.* **24**, 683–87.

Ross, S. B. (1976). Long-term effects of *N*-2-chloroethyl-*N*-ethyl-2-bromobenzylamine hydrochloride on noradrenergic neurones in the rat brain and heart. *Br. J. Pharmac.* **58**, 521–7.

——, Johansson, J. G., Lindborg, B., and Dahlbom, R. (1973). Cyclizing compounds. I. Tertiary *N*-(2-bromobenzyl)-*N*-haloalkylamines with adrenergic blocking action. *Acta Pharm. suecica* **10**, 29–42.

Shallice, T. (1979). Neuropsychological research and the fractionation of memory systems. In *Perspectives on memory research* (ed. L.-G. Nilsson), pp. 257–277. Erebourn, Hillsdale, N.J.

Shaw, C. and Cynader, M. (1984). Disruption of cortical activity prevents ocular dominance changes in monocularly deprived kittens. *Nature, Lond.* **308**, 731–4.

Sillito, A. M. (1983). Plasticity in the visual cortex. *Nature, Lond.* **303**, 477–8.

Sporn, J. R., Wolfe, B. B., Harden, T. K., and Molinoff, P. B. (1977). Supersensitivity in rat cerebral cortex: pre- and postsynaptic effects of 6-hydroxydopamine at noradrenergic synapses. *Molec. Pharmac.* **13**, 1170–80.

Tanabe, Y., Nakamura, T., Fujioka, K., and Doi, O. (1979). Production and secretion of sex steroid hormones by the testes, the ovary, and the adrenal glands of embryonic and young chicken (*Gallus domesticus*). *Gen. comp. Endocrinal.* **39**, 26–33.

Teuber, H.-L. (1955). Physiological psychology. *A. Rev. Psychol.* **6**, 267–96.

Watabe, K., Nakai, K., and Kasamatsu, T. (1982). Visual afferents to norepinephrine-containing neurons in cat locus coeruleus. *Exp. Brain Res.* **48**, 66–80.

Wiesel, T. N. (1982). Postnatal development of the visual cortex and the influence of environment. *Nature, Lond.* **299**, 583–91.

—— and Hubel, D. H. (1963). Single cell response in striate cortex of kittens deprived of vision in one eye. *J. Neurophysiol.* **26**, 1003–17.

Yalow, R. S. (1980). Radioimmunoassay. *A. Rev. Biophys. Bioengng.* **9**, 327–45.

Young, J. Z. (1963). Some essentials of neural memory systems. Paired centres that regulate and address the signals of the results of action. *Nature, Lond.* **198**, 626–30.

# 10

# Physiological and morphological consequences of training

The first steps in the path that led to the IMHV were taken on the basis of experiments using precursors of protein and RNA. The reason for undertaking these experiments in the first place was that if memory involved cell growth then there is likely to be a change in protein and RNA synthesis in those brain regions where growth is occurring (p. 35). The experiments disclosed changes in the incorporation of the recursors into macromolecules as a consequence of imprinting. The changes in uracil incorporation could not be accounted for as some simple side-effect of the training procedure, but were found to be intimately related to the process of imprinting upon artificial objects. Autoradiographic studies implicated the IMHV in these changes. Bilateral destruction of this region impaired the ability of chicks to form a preference for such an object or to retain a previously acquired preference. These results and those of the studies which have been described in other chapters together demonstrate that the IMHV is critical for imprinting. The results suggest that the region is a crucial component of the recognition memory system. Further, a simple hypothesis that accounts for the experimental findings is that the left IMHV may itself be a store for the neural representation of certain objects toward which a young chick directs its filial behaviour. To be sure, the left IMHV cannot be the only store in intact chicks; but that it may function as a store is strongly suggested by the evidence (Section 7.1). If this suggestion is cautiously accepted, then it becomes possible to examine the assumption on which the first biochemical studies were based: that information storage involves morphological changes in neurones. The assumption may of course be wrong. The changes in RNA metabolism which were found, particularly in the IMHV, need not be associated with a change in cell morphology. They may reflect some more subtle aspect of neuronal function, such as a change in the rate of synthesis of messenger RNA coding for a neuropeptide. Having said this, the question still remains, are there morphological and, indeed, physiological changes in the IMHV associated with imprinting? The evidence for physiological changes is more conveniently considered first.

## 10.1 Physiological consequences of training.

Neurones in the IMHV of anaesthetized chicks discharge spontaneously, in the absence of deliberate sensory stimulation (Brown and Horn 1979). As a first step in analysing the physiological changes in the IMHV associated with imprinting we recorded this discharge after chicks had been exposed to a training stimulus (Payne and Horn 1982, 1984). As a control procedure recordings were also made from the hyperstriatum accessorium.

Chicks were primed for half an hour when they were approximately 21 hours old. Thirty-six chicks were exposed to the rotating flashing red box and eighteen chicks were exposed to the rotating stuffed jungle-fowl for a total of 2 hours. The chicks were then returned to the dark incubator until the following day. When they were approximately 46 hours old they were exposed to the same training stimulus, but on this occasion for 1 hour only. Each chick was in a running wheel during the 3 hours of training. The number of rotations made by the wheel was recorded and used as a measure of approach activity ('approach counts'). Approximately 1 hour after the end of training each chick was anaesthetized. Two microelectrodes were introduced into the left hemisphere of the brain. One microelectrode penetrated vertically into the hyperstriatum accessorium, the other penetrated vertically through the IMHV. The electrode was advanced in steps of 250 micrometres. At the end of each step the spontaneous discharge of units was recorded for 1 minute. At least three such recordings were made in a penetration. After these penetrations had been completed, no further penetrations into the brain were made. The mean firing rate of units in each penetration was calculated. At the time of recording, the prior history of the chick was not known to the experimenters. When recording was complete small lesions were made to mark the penetrations. The track of each electrode was reconstructed from drawings of stained sections of the brain.

For the thirty-six chicks which had been exposed to the red box there was a significant correlation between the total number of approach counts made during the 3 hour training period and the mean spontaneous firing rate of neurones in the IMHV. The correlation was negative; that is, the more chicks ran towards the box the lower was the mean firing rate of neurones in the IMHV (Fig. 10. 1(a)).

A different result was found for recordings made in the hyperstriatum accessorium of the same chicks. There was not a significant correlation between spontaneous impulse activity and total approach counts (Fig. 10.1(b)). This correlation coefficient was significantly different from the corresponding correlation coefficient in respect of the IMHV. Thus the relationships between neuronal activity and approach counts during training were regionally specific.

The correlation coefficients between mean firing rate in each region and approach counts made in the first hour of training were also investigated.

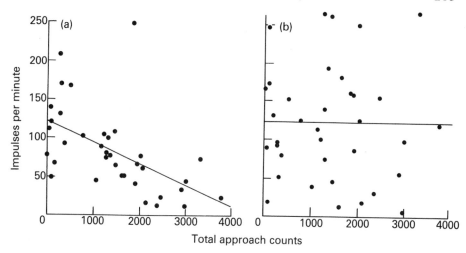

**Fig. 10.1.** Relationship between neuronal firing rate and approach activity during training for chicks exposed to the red box. Mean spontaneous firing rates are plotted against total approach activity during the 3 h training period. The lines were fitted by the method of least squares. The recording electrodes simultaneously penetrated through the IMHV and the hyperstriatum accessorium in each of the thirty-six chicks. (a) The IMHV. The correlation coefficient was significant ($r=-0.54$, d.f. 34, $P<0.01$). (b) Hyperstriatum accessorium. There was not a significant correlation between the two variables ($r=-0.02$, d.f. 34). The two correlation coefficients are significantly different ($P<0.05$). (After Payne and Horn 1984.)

When neuronal activity in the IMHV was a variable the correlation coefficient remained significant ($r=-0.50$, d.f. 34, $P<0.01$). When neuronal activity in the hyperstriatum accessorium was a variable the correlation coefficient remained non-significant ($r=-0.004$, d.f. 34).

For the chicks which had been exposed to the jungle-fowl there was not a significant relationship between the mean firing rate of neurones in the IMHV and (i) approach counts in the first hour of training or (ii) total approach counts (Fig. 10.2(a)). However, the two correlation coefficients ($r=-0.07$ in each case) had the same negative direction as, and were not significantly different from the corresponding correlation coefficients for the 36 box-trained birds. Accordingly, a weak effect of exposing the smaller sample of 18 chicks to the jungle-fowl cannot be excluded. The mean firing rate of neurones in the hyperstriatum accessorium was not correlated with total approach counts (Fig. 10.2(b)) or with approach counts in the first hour of training.

The apparent stimulus-specificity of the relationship between the impulse activity in the IMHV and approach counts might arise if the chicks which had been exposed to the jungle-fowl were less active during training than the chicks which had been exposed to the red box. There was no evidence that this was so. The mean number of approach counts in the first hour of

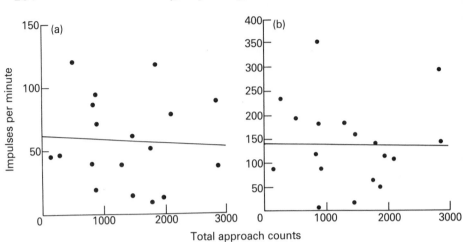

**Fig. 10.2.** Relationship between neuronal firing rate and approach activity during training for chicks exposed to the jungle-fowl. Conventions are the same as those for Fig. 10.1. The correlation between total approach counts and impulse activity in (a) the IMHV and (b) the hyperstriatum accessorium were not statistically significant. (After Payne and Horn 1984.)

training as well as the total number of approach counts in the 3 hour period of training did not differ significantly between box-trained and fowl-trained birds.

The differential effect of the imprinting stimulus on the correlation between approach counts and neuronal discharges in the IMHV is yet another example of the different consequences of exposing chicks to the stuffed jungle-fowl or to the red box (see Chapters 8 and 9). The electrophysiological analysis of events in the IMHV gives further support for a role for this structure in the imprinting process when the red box is used as the training object.

The interpretation of the electrophysiological results is a matter of speculation until more is known about the effects of the observed changes in impulse activity on the way in which information is processed in the IMHV. One possibility is that a lower discharge rate implies a higher level of inhibitory activity impinging on the recorded neurones. If such an inhibitory effect were selective, it could serve to exclude from the IMHV activity evoked by novel objects whilst allowing access for activity evoked by the the training object.

## 10.2 Morphological consequences of training

Changes in neural connections have often been postulated to underlie information storage in the brain (Tanzi 1893; Cajal 1911; Konorski 1948; Hebb

1949). For this reason attention was focussed on the synapse in studies which sought to investigate the morphological consequences of training. At the time the first of these studies of the IMHV was undertaken (Bradley, Horn, and Bateson 1979, 1981) no evidence had come to light to suggest a hemispheric asymmetry in the functions of the region. Nor was it then known that some of the neural systems engaged by artificial objects might be different from those engaged by the jungle-fowl. Fortunately in these studies, samples were taken from both the right and left hemispheres and an artificial object was used as the imprinting stimulus.

Dark-reared chicks were primed for half an hour when they were approximately 21 hours old. After priming the chicks were exposed to an imprinting stimulus. This was similar to the one used in the autoradiographic study (p. 73) except that the upward moving slit was red rather than yellow. The slit subtended a visual angle of approximately 2 degrees by 15 degrees at the eye. After priming, both groups of chicks were exposed to the training stimulus for 20 minutes and their approach activity was monitored. On the basis of this activity the birds were matched in pairs and the inactive chicks discarded (see p. 72). In each pair, one chick received no further training ('undertrained') and was returned to the dark. The other member ('overtrained') was exposed to the stimulus for a further 120 minutes in three sessions each of 40 minutes interspersed with intervals of 40 minutes spent in the dark incubator. After the final period of exposure the overtrained chicks were returned to the dark. All chicks were given a code number and, as usual, all subsequent procedures were performed 'blind'. About 6.5 hours after the beginning of training, when the chicks were approximately 30 hours old, they were anaesthetized. At this time the undertrained birds had been in the dark incubator for approximately 4.5 hours since the end of training; the corresponding time for the overtrained chicks was approximately 3 hours. The chicks were perfused with fixative to preserve the histological structure of the brain. A transverse section, approximately 1 millimetre thick, was then removed from the forebrain. The section contained a part of the IMHV. A small sample, or 'block' approximately 1 millimetre square, of the IMHV was then removed and ultrathin sections of it were cut. In order to measure a representative sample of synapses in the block, every tenth section, approximately, was examined using an electron microscope. Photomicrographs were taken of each section in a systematic way. There were twenty-five micrographs from each block of the IMHV. These micrographs, printed at a final magnification of $22\,200\times$ were used for quantitative analysis. A synapse was identified as a chemical synapse by the presence of synaptic vesicles, a thickening in the postsynaptic membrane and a cleft which separated the pre- and postsynaptic membranes (Fig. 10.3). Sampling techniques (Weibel and Bolender 1973; Mayhew 1979) were used to estimate the percentage area of micrograph occupied by cell bodies, presynaptic knobs (synaptic boutons), and den-

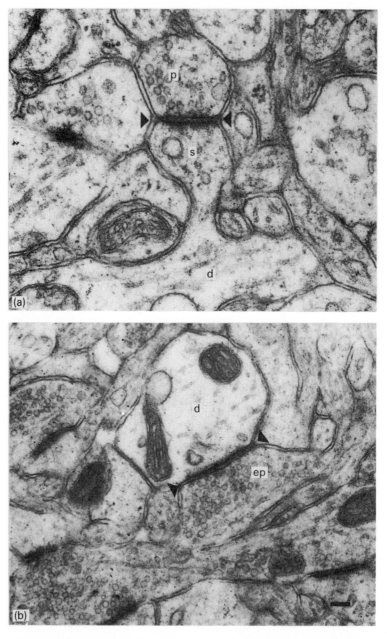

**Fig. 10.3.** Electron micrographs of some features of chemical synapses in the IMHV. The presynaptic elements contain vesicles. The region between the black arrows contains a zone in which the apposed membranes are thickened, the synaptic apposition zone. The thickening in the postsynaptic membrane is the postsynaptic density. It is separated from the presynaptic membrane by a narrow cleft. (a) Synapse between an axon terminal (presynaptic knob, or bouton, p) and a dendritic spine (s). (b) Synapse between an axon ('*en passage*', ep) and the shaft of a dendrite (d). Scale bar 100 nm. (After Bradley *et al.* 1981.)

dritic spines (Gray 1959). The ratio of the number of synapses present on the spines to those present on dendritic shafts was also calculated. A characteristic feature of the postsynaptic membrane is the presence of dense material on its cytoplasmic aspect (Fig. 10.3(a)). This material is referred to as the postsynaptic density (Peters *et al.* 1976). The length of the postsynaptic membrane containing this density was estimated. A total of 3711 synapses were examined from seven undertrained and seven overtrained birds. The data were obtained from the right and left IMHV of each chick. The twenty-five micrographs from each side of the brain of an overtrained bird together with those from the undertrained controls were shuffled at least twice. All measurements from these micrographs were made without knowledge of either the brain hemisphere or the behavioural experience of the chick. For each measure (for example the percentage area of micrograph occupied by synaptic boutons) each chick contributed two mean values, one for the left IMHV and one for the right. These mean values were used for statistical analysis.

There were no hemipsheric differences in and no significant effects of further training on the mean area occupied by synaptic boutons and dendritic spines (Table 10.1); the ratio of the number of dendritic spines to dendritic shaft synapses was also unaffected by the additional training. There was, however, a hemispheric asymmetry in the length of the post-synaptic density in the undertrained birds (Fig. 10.4(a)). In these chicks the mean length of the postsynaptic density in the right hemisphere significantly exceeded that in the left by $35 \pm 11.4$ nanometres. There was no significant hemispheric asymmetry in the overtrained chicks (Fig. 10.4(b)). Direct

**Table 10.1** *Estimates of areas occupied by synaptic boutons and dendritic spines in the IMHV (after Bradley et al. 1981)*

|  | Undertrained | | Overtrained | |
|---|---|---|---|---|
|  | Left hemisphere | Right hemisphere | Left hemisphere | Right hemisphere |
| Percentage of micrograph area per synaptic bouton ($\times 10^3$) | 470.43 ± 36.17 | 503.00 ± 45.01 | 472.43 ± 34.37 | 484.29 ± 27.92 |
| Percentage of micrograph area per dendritic spine ($\times 10^3$) | 250.29 ± 9.20 | 246.86 ± 15.39 | 265.14 ± 15.84 | 248.57 ± 13.85 |

Means ±s.e.m. are given according to treatment and hemisphere. Each micrograph represents an area of 80 μm².

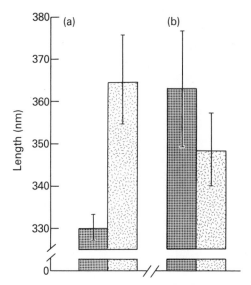

**Fig. 10.4.** Length of the postsynaptic density of synaptic apposition zones in the IMHV. Data for spine synapses and for shaft synapses were combined. Means ± s.e.m. plotted according to treatment and hemisphere (filled-square bars, left hemisphere; dashed bars, right hemisphere). (a) Undertrained birds. The mean length of the postsynaptic density in the right hemisphere exceeded that in the left by 10.6 per cent ($P < 0.025$). (b) Overtrained birds. Although the mean value for the right hemisphere was smaller by $15 \pm 16.4$ nm than the left, a relation opposite in direction to that found in the undertrained birds, the difference was not statistically significant. (After Bradley *et al.* 1981.)

comparison of the data from the left hemispheres of the overtrained and undertrained chicks showed that further training led to a mean increase of $33 \pm 14.6$ nanometres in the length of this zone; that is, to an increase in length of approximately 10 per cent ($P < 0.05$).

Overtraining eliminated the hemispheric asymmetry which was present in undertrained birds. Stewart and his colleagues (1984) also found an asymmetry in controls which was eliminated by training. In these experiments chicks were given passive avoidance training (see p. 123). Chicks which served as controls pecked a small bead which had been dipped in water; experimental chicks pecked a bead which had been dipped in methylanthranilate, which provoke an aversive response in the young birds. When shown a dry bead 24 hours after training, controls tended to peck it whereas trained chicks tended to avoid it. Stewart and his colleagues measured various aspects of synapse structure in part of the hyperstriatum ventrale. The area which they studied appears to lie within the anterior boundary of the IMHV. There was an asymmetry in the length of the postsynaptic thickening in control chicks. The mean length on the left side was shorter than that of the right. There was no such asymmetry in trained chicks. The elimination of the asymmetry appeared to have been achieved by a decrease in the length of the postsynaptic thickening on the right side and a small increase on the left.

In the imprinting situation the elimination of hemispheric asymmetry was achieved, in part at least, by an increase in the length of the postsynaptic density of synapses in the left hemisphere. We were not, however, able to exclude the possibility that training affected the IMHV region of both sides of the brain. For example, changes might have occurred very rapidly in the right hemisphere then, as a result of further training, the left hemisphere 'caught up'. In order to investigate this possibility and to gain further insight into the synaptic changes the study was extended by (i) adding a group of ten chicks which were dark-reared until they were killed 30 hours after hatching; (ii) increasing the number of chicks in the undertrained group by the addition of a further nine chicks to this group; and (iii) subdividing the synapses into those which ended on dendritic spines and those which ended on dendritic shafts (see example in Fig. 10.3). Because the additional chicks came from a different batch it was necessary, in order to combine the results of the two experiments, to standardize the data. Both studies contained a group of undertrained chicks. The data were therefore standardized against these groups of chicks. For convenience the effects of training on a given measurement were related to the value of that measurement in the dark-reared controls. Since the first study (Bradley *et al.* 1981) had failed to implicate in imprinting the areas of micrograph occupied respectively by presynaptic boutons and dendritic spines, these features of the micrographs were not studied in the larger sample of chicks (Horn, Bradley, and McCabe 1985).

There were no significant effects of training on the number of synapses per unit volume of tissue (numerical density) for spine or shaft synapses. Training was also without effect on the length of the postsynaptic density of shaft synapses. There was, however, an effect of training on the overall mean length ($\overline{Sp_L}$) of the postsynaptic density of spine synapses. The effect varied according to hemisphere. The value of $\overline{Sp_L}$ for the left IMHV of dark-reared birds was 286 ± 12.2 nanometres. This value was significantly exceeded,by 49.2 ± 17.8 nanometres, in chicks which had been trained for 140 minutes (Fig. 10.5). Training for only 20 minutes did not significantly effect $\overline{Sp_L}$ relative to its value in the dark-reared chicks. In contrast to the effects observed in the left IMHV, training was without significant effect on $\overline{Sp_L}$ in the right IMHV (Fig. 10.6).

These results extend the findings of the earlier investigation (Bradley *et al.* 1979, 1981) by demonstrating that (i) 20 minutes of training was not associated with a significant change in any measure of synapse morphology, (ii) a significant effect of the further period of training was only detected in

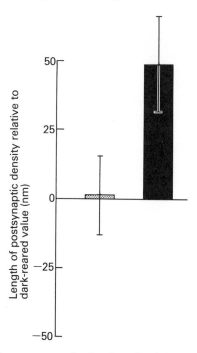

**Fig. 10.5.** Length of the postsynaptic density of spine synapses in the left IMHV. Data were standardized and expressed relative to the length of the postsynaptic density of spine synapses for dark-reared controls shown as 0. The mean difference between this value and those for undertrained (stippled bar) and overtrained chicks (black bar) respectively are shown. The bar associated with each mean is the standard error of the difference between that mean and 0. The differences between the mean of the overtrained chicks and those of the two other groups, respectively, were significant ($P < 0.01$). (After Horn *et al.* 1985.)

the left IMHV, and (iii) of all the measurements that were made, only the length of the postsynaptic density of spine synapses was affected by training. Relative to dark-reared controls, this mean increase in length represented a change of 17.2 per cent. If the postsynaptic density is, to an approximation, circular, then its diameter is a simple function of the estimated length (Weibel and Bolender 1973). Accordingly the increase in length of 17.2 per cent corresponds to an increase in area of approximately 37 per cent.

The chicks in the experiments described above were not given a preference test, though such a test had been given in an earlier study using the same stimulus (Bateson 1979). Chicks exposed to the stimulus for 21 minutes did not prefer it to a novel object. It is reasonable to suppose, therefore, that the undertrained chicks had not formed a preference for the training object. There were no changes in any measure of synapse mor-

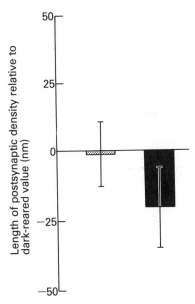

**Fig. 10.6.** Length of the postsynaptic density of spine synapses in the right IMHV. Data were standardized and are expressed as in Fig. 10.5. The mean length of the postsynaptic density of the dark-reared chicks was 294±7.2 nm. The smaller mean values of the trained chicks (undertrained, stippled bar; overtrained, black bar) were not significantly different from this value. (After Horn *et al.* 1985.)

phology in the right or left IMHV of these birds compared with their dark-reared controls. In contrast, chicks exposed to the training stimulus for 81 minutes showed a clear preference for it over a novel stimulus (Bateson 1979). The overtrained chicks were exposed to their training stimulus for well in excess of this time, so it may be inferred that they had formed a preference for it. The associated morphological change was selective both for hemisphere and synapse type.

The evidence of a hemispheric asymmetry in the response of the IMHV to training provided the initial impetus for the investigation, through brain lesions, of the roles of the right and left IMHV in imprinting. These studies provided evidence of a functional asymmetry in the roles of these two brain regions in memory (see Chapter 7).

The evidence for a change in synapse structure provided a possible link with the electrophysiological changes which are described in Section 10.1. The link was rather tenuous though, because different training regimes and different training objects had been used in the two sets of experiments. We therefore decided to enquire whether morphological changes were associated with training in chicks which had been exposed to the rotating flashing red box (Horn, Bradley, and McCabe 1985).

The training regime was the same as that described in Section 10.1. Briefly, when the chicks were approximately 21 hours old they were placed singly in running wheels and exposed to the red box for a total of 2 hours. The chicks were exposed to the box again the following day for a further hour. The number of wheel revolutions made by the chicks during training was recorded and provided a measure of approach activity. After the training the chicks were returned to the dark incubator. They were not given a preference test, though it may reasonably be inferred that they had developed a strong preference for the red box (see Table 8.1). The chicks remained in the incubator for 3 hours, and when they were approximately 46 hours old they were anaesthetized and perfused. The procedures which followed were similar to those described above with the addition that blocks of tissue were also removed from the hyperstriatum accessorium in the plane at which the electrophysiological recordings had been made (see Section 10.1). Blocks from both sides of the brain were removed for analysis. The numerical density of spine and shaft synapses and the length of the postsynaptic density of these synapses were estimated.

Only one mean value was significantly affected by training. The postsynaptic density of spine synapses in the left IMHV of trained chicks was significantly longer than that in the dark-reared chicks (Fig. 10.7). The magnitude of the increase was not significantly different from that found in the overtrained chicks of the previous study. Thus the same synapse type, den-

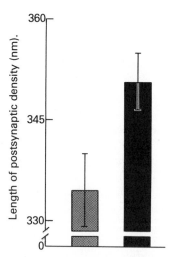

**Fig. 10.7.** Length of the postsynaptic density of spine synapses in the left IMHV. The effects of exposing chicks for a total of 3 h to the rotating red box. The bars represents the mean (±s.e.m.) length of the postsynaptic density for dark-reared (stippled bar) and trained chicks (black bar). The mean difference of 16±6.97 nm was significant ($P < 0.03$). (After Horn *et al.* 1985.)

dritic spines, and the same brain side, the left IMHV, were influenced by training on artificial objects even though the objects, the training regimes and the ages of the chicks when they were perfused were different in the two studies.

In the electrophysiological experiments the spontaneous firing rate of cells in the IMHV was found to be related to the chicks' approach activity during training (Fig. 10.1(a)). Was there a correlation between approach activity and the length of the postsynaptic density of spine synapses, $\overline{Sp_L}$ in the left IMHV? The number of approach counts made during the first hour of training was plotted against $\overline{Sp_L}$. There was a positive correlation between these approach counts and $\overline{Sp_L}$ in the left IMHV ($r=0.52$, d.f. 13, $P<0.05$). The correlation was not significant when approach counts during the second and third hours of training were used as variables ($r=0.12$ and $r=0.23$ respectively). Does this weakening of the correlation coefficient have any functional significance? Although 20 minutes of exposure to the red box is inadequate to establish a preference for this object (Bateson 1979), a high preference score may be achieved after 1 hour of exposure to it (see Fig. 9.5). This score is not much less than that achieved by control chicks trained for 80 minutes (see Fig. 9.7) or for 150 minutes (see Table 8.1; McCabe *et al.* 1981) using this imprinting stimulus. These data suggest, therefore, that the amount learned, and, by implication, the associated neural change are greater during the first hour of training than in the second and third hours (see Section 3.2 and Fig. 3.4).

None of the correlations between approach activity and individual values of $\overline{Sp_L}$ for the right IMHV or for the hyperstriatum accessorium was significant.

## 10.3 Comment and speculation

### 10.3.1 Specific or non-specific consequences of training?

The changes in length of the postsynaptic density may have little to do with memory. They may, however, be a consequence of some other aspect of the training procedure. For example, the morphological differences could reflect differences in the amount of visual experience or of locomotor activity between the various groups of chicks. These possibilities may be considered in two ways, one intrinsic and the other extrinsic to the data. So far as intrinsic considerations are concerned, some general effects on synaptic structure of visual experience or locomotor activity, or both, can be ruled out because training did not significantly affect any measure in the hyperstriatum accessorium or in the right IMHV. The development of synapses in the dark-reared chicks might have been retarded. If so, the retardation was highly selective in its effects since it was regionally specific, side-specific, and synapse-specific. Locomotor activity *per se* is unlikely to be the critical factor. One reason is that the only approach activity during the first hour of training was correlated with the length of spine synaptic junctions. The corresponding correlations using approach counts during the second and third hours of training fell far short of statistical significance. Approach in the first hour of training was, if anything, less than in the other two hours (Horn *et al.* 1985). Nevertheless, the general argument would be difficult to refute if the reason for implicating the IMHV in the learning process rested solely on the synaptic changes found there after training. This is not the case. Evidence extrinsic to the morphological data, evidence which has been reviewed in earlier chapter, implicates the left IMHV in memory processes.

### 10.3.2 Correlations

The postsynaptic density can be isolated from homogenates of the brain (Matus and Walters 1975). There is good evidence that receptors for neuro-transmitters are present in this density (Matus *et al.* 1981), so that in this sense it resembles the postsynaptic membrane of the neuromuscular junction (Jacob and Lentz 1979; Cohen 1980; Fambrough 1981). These considerations suggest that the increase in length of the density is associated with an increase in the number of receptors in the postsynaptic membrane.

Is it possible that the correlation between approach counts and $\overline{Sp}_L$ on the one hand and between approach counts and spontaneous impulse activity in the IMHV on the other are related in some way? The great majority of afferent fibres from the lateral geniculate body to the visual cortex of the cat end on dendritic spines (Colonnier and Rossignol 1969; Garey and Powell 1971; Horning and Garey 1981), and it has been suggested that spine synapses are excitatory (Gray 1959; Eccles 1964). In the Japanese quail (*Coturnix coturnix japonica*) the majority of long afferent fibres to the visual Wulst end on dendritic spines (Watanabe *et al.* 1983). The hypothesis that spine synapses are excitatory is also, therefore, a plausible one for some neurones in the avian brain. If this hypothesis is assumed for synapses in the IMHV, it is possible to postulate a relatively simple explanation for the correlation between approach activity and the morphological and physiological events in this brain region. The more chicks ran toward the training stimulus the longer was the postsynaptic density of spine synapses. Suppose that the afferent fibres ending on spine synapses contribute to the generation of spontaneous impulse activity in the postsynaptic cells. The longer the postsynaptic density the greater will be the influence of any spontaneous discharges in the presynaptic fibre on the discharge of the postsynaptic cell. Hence, even if the activity of the presynaptic fibre is held constant, the longer the spine junction the more efficiently would its activity be transmitted to the postsynaptic neurone. Accordingly if approach activity is positively correlated with $\overline{Sp}_L$, approach should also be positively correlated with the mean spontaneous firing rate. However, approach activity was negatively correlated with spontaneous firing rate (Fig. 10.1(a)). Thus the more strongly chicks approached the training object the longer was $\overline{Sp}_L$, but the lower was the mean firing rate of neurones. This reversal in sign of the correlation could be achieved if the cell with the modifiable synapse is inhibitory to the recorded cell.

### 10.3.3 Functions of dendritic spines

Much interest has centred on dendritic spines and on the modifiability of these structures. When mice are reared in darkness for 20 days there is a reduction in the number of spines per unit length of dendrite of certain cells in the visual cortex (Valverde 1967). When dark-reared mice are exposed to light, spine frequency increases with the duration of light exposure: after 4 days of exposure spine frequency reached a level which was not significantly different from that of light-reared controls (Valverde 1971). Fifkova and Van Harreveld (1977) found that the volume of dendritic spines on cells in the hippocampal region of rats increased when the afferent fibres to these cells were stimulated electrically. The physiological consequences of such changes may be considerable (Rall and Rinzell 1973; Rall 1978). The stem of some spine synapses is narrower than the distal spine head, which contains the synaptic membrane (see Fig. 10.3(a). When the synapse is depolarized current flows down its stem and along the shaft of the dendrite. Changes in the diameter of the spine stem would exert an influence on the functional 'weight' or efficacy of a synapse by affecting the spread of current into the dendritic shaft (Chang 1952; Rall 1974; Rall and Rinzel 1973; Koch and Poggio 1983). A consequence of this change in current flow would be to affect the probability of a spike discharge in the neurone, or to affect the magnitude of local synaptic interactions (for example dendro-dendritic; see Shepherd 1979). The changes in spine volume described by Fifkova and Van Harreveld (1977) are consistent with, but are not direct evidence for, an effect on the diameter of the spine stem. We did not find any significant change in spine volume, though small changes in stem diameter could have occurred but gone undetected (Bradley *et al.* 1981).

Most theoretical studies of dendritic spines have assumed that the membrane of the spine is passive in the sense that it does not generate action potentials. If this assumption is correct then the efficacy of a spine synapse can be shown never to exceed, and may be less than, that of a shaft synapse (for a review see Miller and Jacobs 1984). However, if the spine membrane is active rather than passive, the spine, by enhancing an excitatory postsynaptic potential (EPSP) may serve as a high-gain synaptic amplifier (Jack *et al.* 1975; Miller *et al.* 1984). It has been suggested, on the basis of computer simulation studies, that a spine with an active membrane delivers to the dendrite a larger charge than a spine with a passive membrane or a shaft synapse (Miller *et al.* 1984). Hence spines with active membranes may well exert a greater control than shaft synapses on the probability of discharge of the neurone. These considerations suggest that small changes in the length of the postsynaptic density provide a more effective way for the presynaptic cell to control the firing of the postsynaptic cell, or to control local synaptic interactions, than that provided by a change in the length of a shaft synapse.

The control that a synapse exerts on the postsynaptic cell may in part be a function of the distance of the synapse from the zone at which the potential is triggered. In cells for which this is the case the more effective control of the spike trigger zone would be achieved, other things being equal, by modifying synapses near to the zone than by modifying synapses remote from it. Clearly there is much room for manoeuvre.

### 10.3.4 Constraints on synaptic modification

Are the changes in spine synapses restricted to those synapses which were activated by the presynaptic fibre, or does the change occur in a non-restrictive sense, so that all synapses on the postsynaptic cell are changed? This question is one which raises a number of important issues. Suppose, to illustrate the point (see Fig. 10.8) presynaptic fibre A is one of a number which is activated by a stimulus, say the red box. Fibre B is not activated by this stimulus. Fibre A and B are presynaptic to cells 2 and 3, and 1 and 2 respectively. An impulse in fibre A evokes an impulse in cell 2, but not in cell 3 which, for the purposes of this argument, is inhibited. If activity in fibre A brings about a change in the length of the postsynaptic density, is the change likely to be restricted to junction A/2 or is the change also likely to affect B/2 which was not activated by the stimulus? A further possibility is that all synapses made by fibre A, including A/3, are modified as a consequence of activity in fibre A. The issue of synaptic specificity is not trivial.

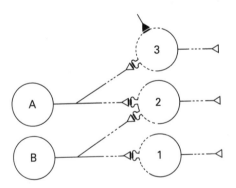

**Fig. 10.8.** Specificity of synaptic change. A stimulus excites fibre A but does not excite fibre B, which is silent. Fibre A is assumed to evoke a discharge in cell 2. Cell 3 is not excited to the point of generating an impulse because, for example, it is inhibited by some other input. If a condition for increase in length of the postsynaptic density is the conjoint firing of pre- and postsynaptic elements then only the synapse A/2 will be modified. Open triangles represent excitatory synapses and the closed triangle an inhibitory synapse. The broken lines indicate a scale change. The diameter of the spine head is likely to be rather less than 0.5 μm; the diameter of the soma may be some 50 times greater. For further discussion see text.

A single neurone in the visual cortex of the cat may receive up to 60 000 synaptic terminals (Cragg 1967); and a single afferent fibre may influence the activity of some 5000 neurones distributed around its terminal branches (Sholl 1956). If activity alone were sufficient to induce synaptic changes, then activity in such an afferent fibre would lead to a modification of its synaptic connections with all 5000 cells. And if some of these were activated and were excitatory to other cells, synapses throughout much of the brain would be strengthened as a result of the discharge of a single neurone. Alternatively, if activity in the postsynaptic cell led to a strengthening of all the synapses impinging on it, then there would be a severe limitation on the capacity of that cell to form part of a specific neuronal network.

A way of preserving synaptic specificity is to require that morphological changes will only occur at synapses at which there is a discharge in *both* pre- and postsynaptic elements. The logical issues which arise out of these considerations were clear enough to James (1890). He wrote, 'When two elementary brain-processes have been active together or in immediate succession, one of them, on reoccurring, tends to propagate its excitement into the other' (James 1890, Vol. 1, p. 566). Hebb (1949, p. 62) adopted a similar view. He wrote, 'When an axon of cell A is near enough to excite a cell B and repeatedly or persistently takes part in firing it, some growth process or metabolic change takes place in one or both cells such that A's efficiency as one of the cells firing B, is increased'. In other words, a solution to the problem of specificity is achieved if synaptic modification only occurs when there is conjoint firing of pre- and postsynaptic elements. Thus, if fibre A fires only cell 2, then only synapse A/2 is strengthened (Fig. 10.8). Synapse B/2 is not. Nor for that matter is synapse A/3, since the discharge in fibre A was not associated with a discharge in cell 3 (see also Section 10.3.6).

The requirement that the pre- and postsynaptic elements fire together *repeatedly* has a number of advantages. For example, it is possible that both pre- and postsynaptic neurones may discharge spontaneously, and the discharges may by chance occur together. The requirement of repeated conjoint firing reduces the likelihood that synaptic modifications will result from such chance events. Furthermore, if fibre A evokes a spike in cell 2 then this discharge will occasionally coincide with a spontaneous impulse in fibre B. The discharge in cell 2 may happen even though the spike in fibre B is subthreshold to cell 2. Provided that the discharge in fibre B does not consistently occur with a spike in fibre A, then synapse B/2 will not be strengthened. This is because the occurrence of a spike in fibre B does not repeatedly coincide with a spike in cell 2. Clearly the meaning of 'repeated' is important: how often the pre- and postsynaptic elements must fire together, and for how long, will depend on the physiological properties of the system.

The conjoint firing rule confers anatomical specificity to synaptic changes. Conjoint firing may therefore be a necessary condition for these changes to occur. It may even be that at some synapses conjoint firing is a sufficient condition: when the two cells discharge together a sufficient number of times the junction between them is modified (Baranyi and Feher 1981). At synapses that are involved in learning it is likely that something more is required (see Section 6.4). At such synapses an additional 'enabling' factor such as noradrenaline may be necessary (see Section 9.3). Indeed it is possible that different neural networks have different requirements for enabling substances: noradrenaline may be only one of a very large population of signalling molecules having enabling functions.

### 10.3.5 Cellular mechanisms

The change in length of the postsynaptic density could occur through the addition of new membranes to, or the modification/replacement of non-synaptic membranes in, the spine head. If the first process were involved the increase in surface area would be expected to lead to an increase in the volume of the spine. Such an increase did not occur (Table 10.1). It follows that the increased length of the postsynaptic density was not accomplished solely be inserting new membrane into the spine head. If there had been such an insertion it must have been accompanied by the retrieval of a corresponding area of membrane beyond the boundary of the synaptic junction. Alternatively, membrane beyond the boundary of the junction may have been transformed and recruited into the density.

At chemical synapses neurotransmitters act by binding to receptor proteins in the postsynaptic membrane. A molecule which interacts with a protein molecule is known as a ligand. At some synapses the transmitter binds to and changes the conformation of ion channels in the membrane. These 'ligand-gated' ion channels may then open and the resulting flow of ions across the membrane leads to a change in the membrane potential. At other synapses, including those which bind noradrenaline, the transmitter may exert its effect on the postsynaptic cell, not by opening ligand-gated ion channels, but through the agency of a 'second messenger' (for reviews see Kehoe and Marty 1980; Hartzell 1981). At these synapses the neurotransmitter, the 'first messenger', binds to a receptor in the membrane and so initiates a sequence of events inside the cell. The precise nature of the sequence depends on the receptor. For example, when noradrenaline binds to $\beta_1$-adrenergic receptors the enzyme adenylate cyclase is activated and the concentration of adenosine cyclic monophosphate (cyclic AMP), a second messenger, increases. Cyclic AMP governs many processes in the cell by activating a protein kinase. In contrast, if noradrenaline binds to $\alpha_1$-adrenergic receptors a sequence of events follows (see below) which may lead to an increase in the level of free calcium in the cytosol. Calcium may also function as a second messenger.

Calcium may exert its effects as a second messenger by altering the conformation of calcium-binding proteins (see Kretsinger 1981). One such protein, calmodulin, is present in all cells that have been examined. Like cyclic AMP, calmodulin regulates a wide variety of processes in the cell and may do so by interacting with many target proteins. In some cases both of these second messengers may control the response of the cell to a ligand and the two messengers may interact cooperatively or even antagonistically (see Rasmussen 1980). Recent work has demonstrated that calcium ions may enter the cell during the action potential (for reviews see Adams *et al.* 1980; Neering and McBurney 1984), passing through 'voltage-gated' channels. Llinás and his colleagues (Llinás and Sugimori 1980; Llinás and Yaron 1981) have provided good evidence that calcium enters the dendrites of certain mammalian central neurones. There is also evidence that several ligands besides noradrenaline can stimulate an increase in the intracellular level of calcium by mobilizing calcium from intracellular stores (Berridge 1982, 1984). Membranes of the smooth endoplasmic reticulum sequester calcium (see McGraw *et al.* 1980; Rasmussen and Barrett 1984). An extension of the smooth endoplasmic reticulum present in the cytoplasm of dendritic shafts has been observed to enter dendritic spines (Peters and Kaiserman-Abramof 1970). This tubular cisterna, which passes through the stalk into the head of the spine, becomes confluent with a system of membrane-bound sacs which form the spine apparatus (Gray 1959; Gray and Guillery 1963; Westrum *et al.* 1980). Although a typical spine apparatus is not invariabley present, simple sacs bounded by smooth membranes can usually be seen in dendritic spines (see Peters *et al.* 1976). For the purpose of the present model it is assumed that these membranes sequester calcium.

What sort of molecular scenario can be envisaged which leads to the observed changes in synapse morphology and which satisfies (i) the requirement of conjoint firing in pre- and postsynaptic cells and (ii) a requirement that the synaptic changes are contingent on the presence of an enabling substance? A possible scenario is one that envisages an influx of calcium ions which directly, or indirectly through calmodulin, affects processes which lead to a change in the structure of the postsynaptic density. The rule of conjoint firing is satisfied by the repeated occurrence of action potentials, closely spaced in time, in the presynaptic and postsynaptic neurones. Since the presynaptic fibre is assumed to excite the postsynaptic cell the synapse should be excitatory—an expectation that may be satisfied by the evidence that spine synapses in IMHV are modifiable (see Section 10.2 and 10.3.3). When an impulse invades the axon terminals a transmitter substance is released. This substance binds with receptor molecules presumed to lie within the postsynaptic density. Ligand-gated ion channels are opened, current flows across the membrane, and is recorded as an EPSP. If the EPSP is small the postsynaptic cell membrane rapidly returns to its resting state. If the EPSP is large enough an action potential may be generated in the postsynaptic cell, and be associated with a flow of current through the dendrites. Thus, if events are visualized from the postsynaptic side of the junction, an EPSP signifies a spike in the presynaptic fibre and an action potential signifies a spike in the postsynaptic neurone. These events therefore constitute the ingredients for 'recognizing' the conjoint discharge of pre- and postsynaptic elements. In the discussions which follow it is assumed that the membrane of the dendritic spine is passive (p. 215). The general arguments are also applicable if the spine membrane is active. This activity would be closely related to the EPSP; a spike in the axon would occur later, and hence comprise the necessary signal that the post-synaptic cell had fired.

The two 'signals' that represent the occurrence of a conjoint discharge could be used in a number of ways to trigger a sequence of events within the cell that could lead to a change in the postsynaptic density. One hypothetical sequence follows, though there is a good deal of speculation in it. The transmitter liberated by the presynaptic terminal is assumed to mobilize calcium from intracellular stores in the dendritic spine. If an action potential is generated in the postsynaptic cell by the EPSP a further influx of calcium through voltage-gated calcium channels might further elevate the local concentration of this ion in the vicinity of the postsynaptic density in the spine head. It is assumed that this concentration of calcium is achieved only if the ligand-activated and voltage-gated calcium movements occur in close temporal proximity, and that the two sets of events occur repeatedly (p. 217). This level of calcium concentration may be sufficient to activate calmodulin in synapses in which structural modification requires only that the rule of conjoint firing is satisfied. At synapses at which enabling substances are also required this concentration of calcium, whilst necessary, may not be sufficient to activate the calcium-binding protein. Calmodulin has four calcium binding sites. At least two calcium ions must bind before the molecule is activated. If noradrenaline is present and binds to adrenergic receptors, there would be a further mobilization of calcium. The local concentration of this ion may then be sufficient to alter the conformation of calmodulin, which then activates an enzyme which in turn may mediate the phosphory-lation of receptors in the synaptic membrane (Smilowitz *et al.* 1981). It is of some interest that a calmodulin-dependent protein kinase (Grab *et al.* 1981; Kennedy *et al.* 1983; Kelly *et al.* 1984), as well as calmodulin (Grab *et al* 1980), have been found in the postsynaptic density. The action of calcium may be highly localized because free calcium in the cytosol is rapidly taken up by internal membranes (Blaustein *et al.* 1980).

While certain levels of noradrenaline may be necessary for imprinting, noradrenaline may not be the only enabling substance involved. The strength of imprinting may be affected by locomotor activity, alertness, and attention, and these processes may be mediated by different neural systems which produce different enabling substances. It is possible, for example, that the influence of a more rapidly acting 'arousal' system adds to that assumed to be provided by the noradrenergic system. The medial septal nucleus in mammals has been thought to mediate an 'alerting' response (Green and Arduini 19954). The medial septal nucleus in the chick projects to the IMHV and is probably cholinergic (Davies and Horn 1983). Muscarinic binding sites for acetylcholine are present in the IMHV (Bradley and Horn 1981). Such sites, when they bind transmitter, have been shown to hydrolyse inositol phospholipids, which are present in cell membranes (see Berridge 1982; Downes 1982; Berridge and Irvine 1984). This hydrolysis leads to an increase of free calcium within the cell and may do so by mobilizing the ion from intracellular stores. These considerations suggest that numerous factors may interact cooperatively to influence the levels of free calcium in the cytosol and so regulate the extent to which calmodulin is activated. In this way an element of flexibility is brought to the control of the molecular machinery which neurones may deploy to modify their structure (see Berridge 1984). Such interactions would make it possible for highly non-linear increases to occur in, for example, the activation of calmodulin. Non-linear interactions could generate an 'all or none' response in this second messenger and so provide a 'print now' signal. This signal could rapidly convert transient electrical impulse activity into a morphological change and so create a more stable base for memory.

Since it is likely that receptors are constantly being replaced it follows that they are constantly being supplied from the cell body (Fambrough 1981), presumably by transport within the dendrites. In the IMHV, imprinting is associated with an increase in the mean length of the postsynaptic density and hence in the area of the spine membrane which it occupies. If the supply of receptor protein is increased to meet this demand, there is likely to be a surge in protein and RNA synthesis. It may have been this surge that was detected in the biochemical studies of imprinting (see Chapters 2 and 3). After training the number of receptors in the density would probably be greater than before, so that the steady supply of receptor protein in the cell body would have to be stepped up. This increased supply would involve only a small increase in protein synthesis if the rate of receptor turnover in the postsynaptic density were relatively slow, as appears to be the case in the neuromuscular junction (see Changeux and Mikoshiba 1978; Fambrough 1981). These considerations may throw some light on the observations that the incorporation of radioactive uracil into RNA, measured a day after training, was not significantly affected by the duration of the training period (Fig. 3.6(b)).

### 10.3.6 Presynaptic and postsynaptic changes

In this discussion interest has focussed on the postsynaptic part of the synaptic junction. The reasons for doing so were strictly empirical. The opposed membranes at a synapse both contain electron-dense material. At some synapses the density is asymmetrically arranged, being more pronounced on the postsynaptic side of the junction. At other synapses the density is symmetrically arranged (Gray 1959; Colonnier 1968). Because the postsynaptic membrane most consistently contains the more prominent density it had been the target of measurement in the studies of the IMHV and the hyperstriatum accessorium (Bradley *et al.* 1981; Horn *et al.* 1985).

There has in the past been some speculation as to which side of the synapse might be the site of plastic change. Hebb (1949, p.62) wrote, 'The most obvious and I believe much the most probable suggestion concerning the way in which one cell could become more capable of firing another is that synaptic knobs develop and increase the area of contact between afferent axon and efferent soma.' Griffith (1966, 1967, 1968) adopted a somewhat similar view and went on to suggest a mechanism for the change which satisfied the conjoint firing rule. Synaptic specificity could be achieved, he suggested, by the release from the postsynaptic side of a substance which exerts a retrograde influence on the presynaptic terminal. There is indeed some experimental evidence that *presynaptic* mechanisms modulate the plastic changes associated with the classical conditioning of a defensive withdrawal reflex, in which the siphon contracts, in the marine mollusc *Aplysia*. The evidence is based on a study in which a sensory neurone was impaled with a microelectrode through which a stimulating current could be passed (Hawkins *et al.* 1983). Action potentials in this neurone were temporally paired with an unconditioned stimulus, a series of shocks to the tail nerve. A neurone which supplies the muscles of the siphon was also impaled with a microelectrode. This motor neurone receives an input from the impaled sensory neurone. When spike activity in the sensory neurone preceded the unconditioned stimulus, the sensory input to the motor neurone was facilitated. The facilitation appeared to be presynaptic (see also Walters and Byrne 1983).

Surprisingly the facilitation did not appear to follow the Hebb rule (see Section 10.3.4) of conjoint firing in pre- and postsynaptic elements. Thus Carew and his collaborators (1984), using a similar procedure to that described above (Hawkins *et al.* 1983), found that activity in the motor neurone was neither necessary nor sufficient for facilitation. They excited the sensory neurone and the postsynaptic motor neurone by direct electrical stimulation, arranging for the sensory neurone to fire immediately before the motor neurone discharged. This procedure did not lead to a facilitation of transmission at the sensory neurone to motor neurone junction. Such a result is not, however, unexpected of synapses which may be involved a learning. Griffith (1966, 1967 page 34) pointed out that changes in the strength of transmission at Hebb synapses may occur only if some additional factor consequent on reinforcement is present (see also Section 6.4 and 9.3); that is, the conjoint activity of pre- and post synaptic elements is not a sufficient condition for synaptic modification. In order to determine whether such activity is necessary for synaptic facilitation, Carew and his collaborators (1984) hyperpolarized the motor neurone so that it did not fire action potentials during the 'training' procedure. This consisted of electrically exciting the impaled sensory neurone and then delivering the unconditioned stimulus. Transmission at the sensory neurone to motor neurone junction was facilitated, suggesting the involvement of some 'reinforcing' factor (Griffith, above) in this facilitation. The result also implied that the conjoint discharge of pre- and postsynaptic elements was not necessary for synaptic facilitation.

What are the implications of these results and do they unequivocally exclude a Hebb-type of mechanism? The unconditioned stimulus is believed to operate through a group of neurones which are widely connected to the terminals of sensory neurones (Hawkins *et al.* 1983; Walters and Byrne 1983). If this is so, and if the facilitation is indeed presynaptic, then all terminals of the sensory neurone should be facilitated. If these terminals are restricted to the motor neurones supplying the siphon, the facilitation would be functionally specific. But if the sensory neurone also innervates motor neurones supplying muscles not involved in the withdrawal reflex then it is difficult to see how either synaptic specificity or behavioural specificity could be preserved (Section 10.3.4). It is, however, possible that the facilitation observed by Carew and his colleagues followed a modified Hebb rule. The motor neurone which was impaled is one of a number innervating the muscles of the siphon (Kupfermann *et al.* 1974). These neurone, or a small population of them, may form a functional group such that when a sensory neurone fires, all motor neurones in the group are excited and may fire. Accordingly the inactivation of one motor neurone by hyperpolarization, would not preclude a discharge in the others. If the occurrence of this discharge is signalled to the modifiable synapse, this would receive information that an output of the functional group of motor neurones had occurred. During training there would be a conjunction of input, output, and reinforcing signals of the general kind proposed by Hebb and Griffith. The idea that a 'pool' of motor neurones may function as a group is well established from studies of the mammalian spinal cord; and the output is signalled back to the cord through small interneurones known as Renshaw cells (see Eccles 1957).

The possibility of the critical change at modifiable synapses occurring on the *postsynaptic* side of the junction was discussed by the author:

'One such change would be a growth in size of the synaptic knobs which, when active, would depolarize a larger area of membrane and be more likely to generate a spike in the post-synaptic neuron. So far as the author has been able to find out, however, no such growth changes have ever been observed. An alternative site for the hypothetical changes by which neurons may be functionally associated is the post-synaptic membrane. It is quite conceivable that changes on this side of the synapse may affect transmission if some quite plausible assumptions are made. If the number of molecules of transmitter substance liberated by synaptic knobs exceeds the number of reactive groups with which the molecules combine at the post-synaptic membrane, an increase in the number of reactive groups would lead to increased efficiency of synaptic transmission. Since the receptor molecule is probably a protein or lipoprotein, its synthesis is likely to be controlled by ribonucleic acid (RNA) in the cell cytoplasm' (Horn 1962, p. 276).

Since this was written other authors have suggested a postsynaptic locus for certain changes in synaptic function (Stent 1973; Heidmann and Changeux 1982) and Lynch and his colleagues have shown that a long-lasting facilitation of transmission in the hippocampus depends on an increased number of receptors in the postsynaptic neurones (Lynch *et al.* 1982; Lynch and Baudry 1984). The studies of the IMHV also implicate a postsynaptic structure. Furthermore, recent experiments have failed to detect a change in the concentration of two presynaptic marker proteins (Bradley *et al.* 1985). These findings do not, however, exclude changes in some presynaptic structures. Indeed, there is no intrinsic reason why only one side of the synapse should be modifiable. Kosower (1972) suggested that the primary change was in the presynaptic side of the junction. He postulated an increase in the area of the presynaptic membrane at which vesicles containing transmitter substance are released. Kosower suggested that the increased quantity of transmitter liberated by the synaptic bouton would be expected to '. . . lead to an augmentation in the number of receptor sites and an expansion of the postsynaptic receptor region . . .' (Kosower 1972, p. 3295). In short, a change on one side of the synapse may have repercussions on the other side. If, as the evidence suggests, the initial change is postsynaptic, then the associated molecular cascade, which may be triggered by the binding of a ligand to a receptor in the postsynaptic membrane, could lead to the production of a local hormone which might act back on the presynaptic terminal. For example, when the neurotransmitter acetylcholine binds to a membrane receptor, an inisitol lipid is hydrolysed to inositol trisphosphate and diacylglycerol. Diacylglycerol, a second messenger, may influence the synthesis of a hormone, prostaglandin, through an effect on arachidonic acid (see Irvine 1982; Berridge and Irvine 1984; Nishizuka 1984).

The expected consequence of a change in synaptic strength, particularly of spine synapses, is an increased probability that a spike in the presynaptic cell will evoke a spike in the postsynaptic cell, or modify synaptic interactions of the postsynaptic cell with adjacent neurones. Neurones in which synapses have been strengthened in this way are more likely to fire together after the synaptic changes, that is after training, than before. Training thus leaves a 'trace' in the central nervous system. If the trace occurs between neurones in an assembly initially activated by the presentation of an object, that assembly would form a neuronal representation of the object (Hebb 1949; Milner 1957). The stable, facilitated transmission occurring within this assembly would thus provide a basis of a memory for the object; the contextual richness of the memory may be achieved by linking this assembly to other assemblies formed by concurrent experiences and 'tagged' with a time label. But whether the trace functions in this way, whether it functions as a neural analogue of a hologram (Pribram 1966; Longuet-Higgins 1968), or whether it functions in some quite different way is not known (for discussion see Kohonen (1984).

### 10.3.7 Functional validation

Chicks may develop a preference for the jungle-fowl even in the absence of any visual experience. The preference emerges with the passage of time provided that the chicks are subjected to certain experiences (Section 8.2). It was suggested that the neural circuits that support this emerging preference may be functionally dependent on circulating levels of testosterone. The evidence for this view is indirect, but the hypothesis raises the question of how testosterone might act on such a system (Section 9.6). One possibility is that the synapses between neurones in the putative system are non-functional at the time of hatching and during the following few hours. Under appropriate circumstances a preference for the jungle-fowl emerges during this time. It may be supposed that, under these circumstances, synaptic transmission is established in the system through an action of testosterone. Testosterone, a steroid hormone, is not thought to exert its effect on its target cell in the same way that, say, noradrenaline does. The steroid hormone binds to a receptor in the cytosol. The activated receptor then binds to chromatin, initiating the sequence of events which leads to the production of specific proteins (see Yamamoto and Alberts 1976). There are many regions of the brain in which neurones selectively take up steroid hormones (see Goy and McEwen 1980). A particularly interesting example is found in the lower part of the rat spinal cord. Some neurones in this part of the cord form part of the circuit for controlling penile reflexes. The neurones accumulate testosterone. Arnold (1981) suggested that the androgens act on these motor neurones and so influence the circuits involved in copulatory behaviour. Precisely how the hormone effects these cells is not known. It may do so by a primary action on chromatin as discussed above. However, a more direct effect of the hormone on the neurones cannot be excluded since the hormone may influence the electrical activity of these cells within minutes or even seconds (see Andrew 1983).

## 10.4 Summary

When chicks were trained by exposing them to the rotating red box changes could be detected in the activity of neurones in the IMHV. The spontaneous discharge of neurones was negatively correlated with approach activity during training: the more chicks ran towards the box during training the lower was the neuronal firing rate. The effect was regionally specific since it was not found in the hyperstriatum accessorium. The effect was also stimulus-specific because no significant correlation was found in chicks which had been exposed to the jungle-fowl. Changes in the structure of synapses in the IMHV were studied in chicks trained by exposing them to the red box or to a horizontal bar rotating upwards, and flashing. Synaptic structures were modified by training whichever of these stimuli were used. In both cases training was associated with an increase in length of the post-synaptic density of synapses on dendritic spines. Synapses in the left IMHV were affected; no significant changes in the right IMHV were observed for any measure of synapse structure. The length of the postsynaptic density of spine synapses in the left IMHV was correlated with approach activity during training. Possible cellular mechanisms responsible for the changes in synaptic structure are considered. The significance of the changes in dendritic spines are discussed in relation to the possible functions of these structures (i) in controlling neuronal activity and (ii) in memory processes.

# References

Adams, D. J., Smith, S. J., and Thomson, S. H. (1980). Ionic currents in molluscan soma. *A. Rev Neurosci.* **3**, 141–67.

Andrew, R. J. (1983). Specific short-term latency effects of oestradiol and testoster-one on distractability and memory formation in the young domestic chick. In *Hormones and behaviour in higher vertebrates* (eds J. Balthazart, E. Prove, and R. Gilles), pp. 461–73. Springer, Berlin.

Arnold, A. P. (1981). Logical levels of steroid hormone action in the control of vertebrate behavior. *Am. Zool.* **21**, 233–42.

Baranyi, A. and Feher, O. (1981). Synaptic facilitation requires paired activation of convergent pathways in the neocortex. *Nature, Lond.* **290**, 413–15.

Bateson, P. (1979). Brief exposure to a novel stimulus during imprinting in chicks and its influence on subsequent preferences. *Anim. Learn. Behav.* **7**, 259–62.

Berridge, M. J. (1982). Regulation of cell secretion: the integrated action of cyclic AMP and calcium. In *Handbook of experimental pharmacology* (eds J. W. Kebabian and J. A. Nathanson), Vol. 58/II, pp. 227–70. Springer, Berlin.

—— (1984). Inositol triphosphate and diacylglycerol as second messengers. *Biochem. J.* **220**, 345–60.

—— and Irvine, R. F. (1984). Inositol triphosphate, a novel second messenger in cellular signal transduction. *Nature, Lond.* **312**, 315–21.

Blaustein, M. P., Ratzlaff, R. W., and Schweitzer, E. S. (1980). Control of intra-cellular calcium in presynaptic nerve terminals. *Fedn Proc. Fedn Am. Socs exp. Biol.* **39**, 2790–5.

Bradley, P. and Horn, G. (1981. Imprinting: a study of cholinergic receptor sites in parts of the chick brain. *Exp. Brain Res.* **41**, 121–3.

——, ——, and Bateson, P. P. G. (1979). Morphological correlates of imprinting in the chick brain. *Neurosci. Lett.* Suppl. 3, S84.

——, ——, and Bateson, P. (1981). Imprinting: an electron microscopic study of chick hyperstriatum ventrale. *Exp. Brain Res.* **41**, 115–20.

——, Davies, D. C., Horn, G., and Jorgensen, O. S. (1985). Imprinting and synaptic protein levels in the chick telencephalon. *Neurosci. Lett.* (in press).

Brown, M. W. and Horn, G. (1979). Neuronal plasticity in the chick brain: electro-physiological effects of visual experience on hyperstriatal neurones. *Brain Res.* **162**, 142–7.

Cajal, S. R. (1911). *Histologie du système nerveux de l'homme et des vertébrés*, Vol. 2, pp. 886–90. Maloine, Paris. [Republished 1955, *Histologie du système nerveux.* Instituto Ramón y Cajal, Madrid.]

Carew, T. J., Hawkins, R. D., Abrams, T. W., and Kandel, E. R. (1984). A test of Hebb's postulate at identified synapses which mediate classical conditioning in *Aplysia. J. Neurosci.* **4**, 1217–24.

Chang, H. T. (1952). Cortical neurons with particular reference to the apical dendrites. *Cold Spring Harb. Symp. quant. Biol.* **17**, 189–202.

Changeux, J.-P. and Mikoshiba, K. (1978). Genetic and 'epidgenetic' factors regu-lating synapse formation in vertebrate cerebellum and neuromuscular junction. *Progs. Brain Res.* **48**, 43–64.

Cohen, M. W. (1980). Development of an amphibian neuromuscular junction *in vivo* and in culture. *J. exp. Biol.* **89**, 43–56.

Colonnier, M. (1968). Synaptic patterns on different cell types in the different laminae of the cat visual cortex. An electron microscope study. *Brain Res.* **9**, 268–87.

—— and Rossignol, S. (1969). Heterogeneity of the cerebral cortex. In *Basic mechanisms of the epilepsies* (eds H. H. Jasper, A. A. Ward, and A. Pope), pp. 29–40. Little, Brown, Boston.

Cragg, B. G. (1967). The density of synapses and neurones in the motor and visual areas of the cerebral cortex. *J. Anat.* **101**, 639–54.

Davies, D. C. and Horn, G. (1983). Putative cholinergic afferents of the chick hyper-striatum ventrale: a combined acetylcholinesterase and retrograde fluorescence labelling study. *Neurosci. Lett.* **38**, 103–7.

Downes, C. P. (1982). Receptor-stimulated inositol phospholipid metabolism in the central nervous system. *Cell Calcium* **3**, 413–28.

Eccles, J. C. (1957). *The physiology of nerve cells.* The Johns Hopkins Press, Baltimore.

—— (1964). *The physiology of synapses.* Springer, Berlin.

Fambrough, D. M. (1981). Biosynthesis and turnover of nicotinic acetylcholin receptors. In *Drug-receptors and their effectors* (ed. N. J. M. Birdsall), pp. 155–63. Macmillan, London.

Fifkova, E. and Van Harreveld, E. (1977). Long-lasting morphological changes in dendritic spines of dentate granular cells following stimulation of the entorhinal area. *J. Neurocytol.* **6**, 211–30.

Garey, L. J. and Powell, T. P. S. (1971). An experimental study of the termination of the lateral geniculo-cortical pathway in the cat and monkey. *Proc. R. Soc. B* **179**, 41–63.

Goy, R. W. and McEwen, B. S. (1980). *Sexual differentiation of the brain.* MIT Press, Cambridge, Mass.

Grab, D. J., Carlin, R. K., and Siekevitz, P. (1980). The presence and functions of calmodulin in the postsynaptic density. *Ann. N.Y. Acad. Sci.* **356**, 55–72.

——, ——, and —— (1981). Function of calmodulin in postsynaptic densities. II. Presence of a calmodulin-activatable protein kinase activity. *J. Cell Biol.* **89**, 440–8.

Gray, E. G. (1959). Axo-somatic and axo-dendritic synapses of the cerebral cortex: an electron microscopic study. *J. Anat.* **93**, 420–33.

—— and Guillery, R. W. (1963). A note on the dendritic spine apparatus. *J. Anat.* **97**, 389–92.

Green, J. D. and Arduini, A. (1954). Hippocampal electrical activity in arousal. *J. Neurophysiol.* **17**, 533–57.

Griffith, J. S. (1966). A theory of the nature of memory. *Nature, Lond.* **211**, 1160–3.

—— (1967). *A view of the brain.* Clarendon Press, Oxford.

—— (1968). Memory and cellular control processes. In *Quantitative Biology of Metabolism* (ed. A. Locker), pp. 234–44. Springer, Berlin.

Hartzell, H. C. (1981). Mechanisms of slow postsynaptic potentials. *Nature, Lond.* **291**, 539–44.

Hawkins, R. D., Abrams, T. W., Carew, T. J., and Kandel, E. R. (1983). A cellular mechanism of classical conditioning in *Aplysia*: activity-dependent amplification of presynaptic facilitation. *Science* **219**, 400–5.

Hebb, D. O. (1949). *The organization of behavior.* John Wiley, New York.

Heidmann, T. and Changeaux, J.-P. (1982). Un modele moleculaire de regulation d'efficacite au niveau postsyanptique d'une synapse chimique. *C. r. Acad. Sci. Paris* **295**, 665–70.

Horn, G. (1962). Some neural correlates of perception. In *Viewpoints in biology* (eds J. D. Carthy and C. L. Duddington), Vol. 1, pp. 242–85. Butterworth, London.

——, Bradley, P., and McCabe, B. J. (1985). Changes in the structure of synapses associated with learning. *J. Neurosci.* (in press).

Horning, J. P. and Garey, L. J. (1981). The thalamic projection to cat visual cortex: ultrastructure of neurones identified by Golgi impregnation or retrograde horse-radish peroxidase transport. *Neuroscience* **6**, 1053–68.

Irvine, R. F. (1982). How is the level of free arachidonic acid controlled in mammalian cells? *Biochem. J.* **204**, 3–16.

Jack, J. J. B., Noble, D., and Tsien, R. W. (1975). *Electrical current flow in excitable cells.* Clarendon Press, Oxford.

Jacob, M. and Lentz, T. L. (1979). Localization of acetylcholine receptors by means of horse-radish peroxidase-α-bungarotoxin during formation and development of the neuromuscular junction in the chick embryo. *J. Cell Biol.* **82**, 195–211.

James, W. (1890). *The principles of psychology,* Henry Holt, New York. [Reprinted (1950) Dover Publications, New York.]

Kehoe, J. and Marty, A. (1980). Certain slow synaptic responses; their properties and possible underlying mechanisms. *A. Rev. Biophys. Bioengng* **9**, 437–65.

Kelly, P. T., McGuinness, T. L., and Greengard, P. (1984). Evidence that the major postsynaptic density protein is a component of a $Ca^{2+}$/calmodulin-dependent protein kinase. *Proc. natn. Acad. Sci. U.S.A.* **81**, 945–9.

Kennedy, M. B., Bennett, M. K., and Erondu, N. E. (1983). Biochemical and immunochemical evidence that the 'major postsynaptic density protein' is a subunit of a calmodulin-dependent protein kinase. *Proc. natn. Acad. Sci. U.S.A.* **80**, 7357–61.

Koch, C. and Poggio, T. (1983). A theoretical analysis of electrical properties of dendritic spines. *Proc. R. Soc. B* **218**, 455–77.

Kohonen, T. (1984). *Associative memory: a system-theoretical approach.* Springer, Berlin.

Konorski, J. (1948). *Conditioned reflexes and neuron organisation.* Cambridge University Press, London.

Kosower, E. M. (1972). A molecular basis for learning and memory. *Proc. natn Acad. Sci. U.S.A.* **69**, 3292–6.

Kretsinger, R. H. (ed.). (1981). Mechanisms of selective signalling by calcium. *Neurosci. Res. Program Bull.* **19**, 213–328.

Kupfermann, I., Carew, T. J., and Kandel, E. R. (1974). Local, reflex and central commands controlling gill and siphon movements in *Aplysia. J. Neurophysiol.* **37**, 996–1019.

Longuet-Higgins, H. C. (1968). Holographic model of temporal recall. *Nature, Lond.* **217**, 104.

Llinás, R. and Sugimori, M. (1980). Electrophysiological properties of *in vitro* Purkinje cell dendrites in mammalian cerebellar slices. *J. Physiol., Lond.* **305**, 197–213.

—— and Yarom, Y. (1981). Properties and distribution of ionic conductances generating electroresponsiveness of mammalian inferior olivary neurones *in vitro*. *J. Physiol., Lond.* **315**, 569–84.

Lynch, G. and Baudry, M. (1984). The biochemistry of memory: a new and specific hypothesis. *Science* **224**, 1057–63.

——, Halpain, S., and Baudry, M. (1982). Effects of high frequency synaptic stimulation on glutamate binding studied with a modified *in vitro* hippocampal slice preparation. *Brain Res.* **244**, 101–11.

McCabe, B. J., Horn, G., and Bateson, P. P. G. (1981). Effects of restricted lesions of the chick forebrain on the acquisition of filial preferences during imprinting. *Brain Res.* **205**, 29–37.

McGraw, C. F., Somlyo, A. V., and Blaustein, M. P. (1980). Probing for calcium at presynaptic nerve terminals. *Fedn Proc. Fedn Am. Socs exp. Biol.* **39**, 2796–801.

Matus, A. I. and Walters, B. B. (1975). Ultrastructure of the synaptic junctional lattice isolated from mammalian brain. *J. Neurocytol.* **4**, 369–75.

——, Pehling, G., and Wilkinson, D. A. (1981). α-Aminobutyric acid receptors in brain postsynaptic densities. *J. Neurobiol.* **12**, 67–73.

Mayhew, T. M. (1979). Basic stereological relationships for quantitative microscopical anatomy—a simple systematic approach. *J. Anat.* **129**, 95–105.

Miller, J. P. and Jacobs, G. A. (1984). Relationships between neuronal structure and function. In *Mechanisms of integration in the nervous system, J. exp. Biol.* **112**, 129–45.

Milner, P. M. (1957). The cell assembly: Mark II. *Physiol. Rev.* **64**, 242–52.

Neering, I. R. and McBurney, R. N. (1984). Role for microsomal Ca storage in mammalian neurones? *Nature, Lond.* **309**, 158–60.

Nishizuka, Y. (1984). The role of protein kinase C in cell surface signal transduction and tumour promotion. *Nature, Lond.* **308**, 693–8.

Payne, J. K. and Horn, G. (1982). Differential effects of exposure to an imprinting stimulus on 'spontaneous' neuronal activity in two regions of the chick brain. *Brain Res.* **232**, 191–3.

—— and Horn, G. (1984). Long-term consequences of exposure to an imprinting stimulus on spontaneous impulse activity in the chick brain. *Behav. Brain Res.* **13**, 155–62.

Peters, A. and Kaiserman-Abramof, I. R. (1970). The small pyramidal neuron of the rat-cerebral cortex. The perikaryon, dendrites and spines. *Am. J. Anat.* **127**, 321–56.

——, Palay, S. L., and Webster, H. de F. (1976). *The fine structure of the nervous system: the neurons and supporting cells.* Saunders, Philadelphia.

Pribram, K. H. (1966). Some dimensions of remembering: steps towards a neurophysiological model of memory. In *Macromolecules and behavior* (ed. J. Gaito), pp. 165–87. Appleton–Century–Crofts, New York.

Rall, W. (1974). Dendritic spines, synaptic potency and neuronal plasticity. In *Cellular mechanisms subserving changes in neuronal activity* (eds C. D. Woody, K. A. Brown, T. J. Crow, and J. D. Knispel), pp. 13–21. Brain Information Service, University of California, Los Angeles.

—— (1978). Dendritic spines and synaptic potency. In *Studies in neurophysiology* (ed. R. Porter), pp. 203–9. Cambridge University Press, Cambridge.

—— and Rinzel, J. (1973). Branch input resistance and steady attenuation for input to one branch of a dendritic neuron model. *Biophys. J.* **13**, 648–88.

Rasmussen, H. (1980). Calcium and cAMP in stimulus–response coupling. *Ann. N.Y. Acad. Sci.* **356**, 346–53.

Rasmussen, H. and Barrett, P. Q. (1984). Calcium messenger system: an integrated view. *Physiol. Rev.* **64**, 938–84.

Shepherd, G. M. (1979). *The synaptic organization of the brain* (2nd edn). Oxford University Press, New York.

Sholl, D. A. (1956). *The organization of the cerebral cortex*. Methuen, London.

Smilowitz, H., Hajian, R. A., Dwyer, J., and Feinstein, M. B. (1981). Regulation of acetylcholine receptor phosphorylation by calcium and calmodulin. *Proc. natn Acad. Sci. U.S.A.* **78**, 4708–12.

Stent, G. S. (1973). A physiological mechanism for Hebb's postulate of learning. *Proc. natn Acad. Sci. U.S.A.* **70**, 997–1001.

Stewart, M. G., Rose, S. P. R., King, T. S., Gabbott, P. L. A., and Bourne, R. (1984). Hemispheric asymmetry of synapses in chick medial hyperstriatum ventrale following passive avoidance training: a stereological investigation. *Devl Brain Res.* **12**, 261–9.

Tanzi, E. (1893). I fatti e le induzioni nell'odierna istologia del sistema nervosa. *Riv. sper. Freniat. Med. leg Alien. ment* **19**, 419–72.

Valverde, F. (1967). Apical dendritic spines of the visual cortex and light deprivation in the mouse. *Exp. Brain Res.* **3**, 337–52.

—— (1971). Rate of extent of recovery from dark rearing in the visual cortex of the mouse. *Brain Res.* **33**, 1–11.

Walters, E. T. and Bryne, J. H. (1983). Associative conditioning of single sensory neurons suggests a cellular mechanism for learning. *Science* **219**, 405–8.

Watanabe, M., Ito, H., and Masai, H. (1983). Cytoarchitecture and visual receptive neurons in the Wulst of the Japanese quail (*Coturnix coturnix-japonica*). *J. comp. Neurol.* **213**, 188–98.

Weibel, E. R. and Bolender, R. P. (1973). Stereological techniques for electron microscopic morphometry. In *Principles and techniques of electron microscopy* (ed. M. A. Hayat), Vol. 3, *Biological applications,* pp. 237–96. Van Nostrand Reinhold, London.

Westrum, L. E., Jones, D. H., Gray, E. G., and Barron, J. (1980). Microtubules, dendritic spines and spine apparatuses. *Cell Tissue Res.* **208**, 171–81.

Yamamoto, K. R. and Alberts, B. M. (1976). Steroid receptors: elements for modulation of eukaryotic transcription. *A. Rev. Biochem.* **45**, 721–46.

# 11

# A structure for memory?

As the analysis of cerebral function in imprinting progressed the search for mechanisms shifted from three large chunks of brain (Fig. 2.5(a)) to one small region, the IMHV. Whilst interest in this part began to wax, interest in the whole brain seemed to wane. However, the IMHV does not function in a vacuum. In order to understand the role of this region in the imprinting process it is necessary to have a deep knowledge of its organization, of the kinds of information to which it has access, and of the influences which it exerts on other parts of the brain. The purpose of this chapter is to discuss the little that is known of these subjects.

## 11.1 The connections of the IMHV

There are a variety of methods available for tracing pathways within the central nervous system. One method is to place a lesion in a particular site and to trace the resulting pattern of degenerating nerve fibres or terminals. Another is to stimulate neurones by passing a small electric current through electrodes and to search for short-latency evoked responses in other parts of the brain. Other methods, more recently introduced, take advantage of the fact that there is a two-way movement of materials along the processes of neurones, towards the axon terminals (anterograde), and away from the terminals towards the perikarya (retrograde). We employed these tracer techniques to analyse the connections of the IMHV in young chicks (Bradley, Davies, and Horn 1985).

Retrograde neuronal tracer techniques were first introduced by Kristensson and Olsson (1971). These workers injected a solution containing the enzyme horseradish peroxidase (HRP) close to axon terminals and found that the enzyme accumulated in the cell bodies of these axons. Kristensson and Olsson's work was done on peripheral nervous tissue, but the method was soon applied to the central nervous system (LaVail and LaVail 1972). The technique involves injecting a small volume of HRP solution into the brain of an anaesthetized animal. The interval between injection and the time the brain is fixed depends on the distance the enzyme must be transported within the cells and on the rate of transport. After fixation, the tissue is frozen, sections cut, and these sections incubated with an appropriate substrate. The sections may subsequently be counterstained. The HRP reaction product appears as dark granules within the cell body. HRP is not the only retrograde neuronal tracer that is available. Others such as the fluorescent dyes nuclear yellow and fast blue have the advantage that they label different structures in the perikarya. Fast blue, for example, labels the neuronal cytoplasm whereas nuclear yellow is concentrated in the nucleus (Bentivoglio *et al.* 1980). Cell bodies which contain one or both of these markers fluoresce when viewed under ultraviolet light.

There are a number of limitations to the use of these tracer techniques. The tracer may diffuse away from the region of injection and so be transported to perikarya which do not project to the region of interest. Fibres which pass through the injection site (fibres '*en passage*') may be damaged by the pipette used for delivering the tracer. The cell bodies of these fibres may subsequently be labelled even though their terminals do not end in the injection site. Fluorescent retrograde tracers may diffuse out of the perikarya and so spuriously label nearby cell bodies. These difficulties can largely be overcome by giving control injections into sites adjacent to the region of interest, by using more than one line of penetration to deliver the tracer, by using several intervals from injection to the time of fixation, and by using several tracers.

The sites to which neurones in a brain region project can be studied using anterograde neuronal tracer techiques. Neurones synthesize proteins which are transported from the perikarya outward along their cytoplasmic processes. If amino acides are injected in the vicinity of cell bodies the amino acids are taken up by the perikarya and incorporated into proteins which are transported within the cytoplasm. Under the conditions in which anterograde techniques are used, the injected amino acid is incorporated into protein only in the cell bodies, not in the axons or in the synapses located at or near the site of injection. The technique involves several steps: (i) injecting a radioactive amino acid into a region of the brain; (ii) waiting for a variable length of time for the labelled precursor to be incorporated and transported to the terminal field of axons arising from cells in the region; (iii) fixing and sectioning the brain; and (iv) using an autoradiographic method to visualize the pattern of silver grains (see p. 70). The pattern of grains is then related to the histology of the brain.

Some of the problems associated with the use of anterograde tracer techniques are similar to those associated with the use of retrograde tracer techniques, including diffusion of label from the injection site and the uptake and transport of unincorporated amino acid entering the cell through damaged axons. In addition there is a possibility that a radioactive precursor, having reached the axon terminals, will cross the synapse and pass into and label the perikarya of the postsynaptic cells. These and several other difficulties can be met, at least in part, by using some of the control procedures described in connection with retrograde tracers.

Retrograde or anterograde tracers were injected into the IMHV of light-reared day-old chicks to determine the sources of afferent fibres to this region and the areas to which it projects (Bradley *et al.* 1985). This study was necessary since, in the chick, relatively little was known of the connections of the hyperstriatum ventrale in general and of the IMHV in particular.

### 11.1.1  Connections with sensory systems and the brainstem core

There are four routes by which *visual* signals may reach the IMHV. The first of these routes includes the Wulst (Fig. 11.1(a)). Adamo (1967) placed

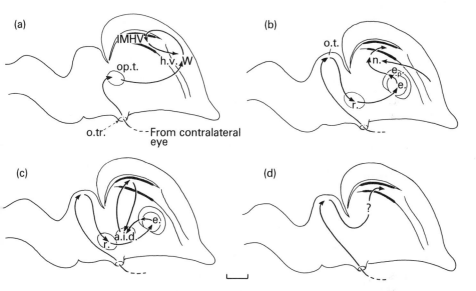

**Fig. 11.1.** Possible routes of visual input to the IMHV. (a) Neurones with cell bodies in all three layers of the visual Wulst (W) project to the IMHV. There are reciprocal connections between the IMHV and the hyperstriatum accessorium. Although the Wulst receives binocular input, only the pathways from the contralateral eye are shown. (b) The region of neostriatum (n.) which sends afferent fibres to the IMHV receives a projection from the hyperstriatum accessorium and the periectostriatal belt ($e_p$.). The periectostriatal belt is part of the tectofugal component of the visual system (see Appendix, Section A.3.1). (c) The periectostriatal belt also projects to the dorsal part of the archistriatum intermedium (a.i.d.). This structure is reciprocally connected to the IMHV. (d) Cell bodies in the optic tectum (o.t.) contain retrograde tracers which have been injected into the IMHV. There is some uncertainty about this pathway (see text). The outline brain sections illustrated in this and other figures in this chapter are diagrammatic; they may contain regions that would not be seen together in a single thin histological section. Other abbreviations: e., ectostriatum; h.v., hyperstriatum ventrale, the IMHV component of which is indicated by heavy lines; op.t., principal optic nucleus of the thalamus; o.tr., optic tract; r., nucleus rotundus. Scale bar in this, and in other figures in this chapter, refer to the brain outline and represent 2 mm, except where stated otherwise.

lesions in the Wulst of chickens and found degenerating terminals in the medial part of the hyperstriatal ventrale. It is not possible to determine from Adamo's data whether or not the region receiving the projection extends sufficiently far posteriorly to include the IMHV. Evidence for such a projection was obtained through the use of a retrograde tracer injected into the IMHV. Labelled cell bodies were seen in all layers of the Wulst: the hyperstriatum accessorium, the hyperstriatum intercalatus, and the hyperstriatum dorsale. After retrograde tracer has been injected into the hyperstriatum accessorium, labelled cell bodies were found in the IMHV. Thus this region is reciprocally connected to the hyperstriatum accessorium. Since the Wulst is a composite visual projection area (Appendix, Figure A.5(b)) and contains neurones which respond to visual stimuli (see Section A.3.1), it is highly probable that the projection from the Wulst to the IMHV carries visual signals.

A second route which may transmit visual information to the IMHV passes through the neostriatum. Parker and Delius (1972) detected cell discharges and large evoked potentials in response to light flashes whilst recording from the posterior part of the neostriatum of pigeons. Similar responses were obtained in this area in the Landes goose, *Anser anser* (Félix *et al.* 1983). There are at least two possible routes for visual signals to reach the neostriatum (Fig. 11.1(b)). The hyperstriatum accessorium projects to the neostriatum in the chicken (Adamo 1967) and in the burrowing owl, *Speotyto cunicularia* (Karten *et al.* 1973). Ritchie and Cohen (1977) found that the periectostriatal belt projects to the lateral part of the intermediate neostriatum in the pigeon. Nerve cell bodies in the intermediate and caudal parts of the neostriatum project to the IMHV (Bradley *et al.* 1985).

A third multisynaptic route which might transmit visual evoked activity to the IMHV is shown in Fig. 11.1(c). Ritchie and Cohen (1977) found that the periectostriatal belt also projects to the dorsal part of the archistriatum intermedium. This region has reciprocal connections with the IMHV.

A more direct visual input to the IMHV appears to arise from nerve cell bodies lying in a deep layer of the optic tectum (Fig. 11.1(d)). When HRP was injected into the IMHV, cells within the optic tectum were labelled. This result suggested that the two structures are connected together by a pathway which does not synapse in the thalamus. Although there is good evidence that auditory (Delius *et al.* 1979), cutaneous (Wallenberg 1903), and olfactory (Rieke and Winzel 1978) signals reach the telencephalon without synapsing in the thalamus, such a direct visual pathway has not previously been described in any vertebrate. For this reason, the experiments were repeated using fluorescent dyes as the retrograde tracers. When injected into the IMHV these tracers were also transported to perikayra in the optic tectum. The effect was quite specific. Retrograde tracers injected into structures adjacent to the IMHV could not be detected in the optic tectum. In an effort to obtain further information about the pathway an anterograde tracer was injected into the optic tectum. Labelling was seen over the known targets of tectal neurones, but no terminal labelling was seen in the IMHV. Thus the results obtained using retrograde and anterograde tracers were not consistent. The discrepancy would be resolved if the projection from the tectum to the IMHV proved to be a diffuse one and involved relatively few neurones, with widely spaced terminal arborizations. Such a distribution of terminals would not easily be detected using the anterograde tracer technique.

If all the pathways illustrated in Fig. 11.1 do indeed carry visual inputs to the IMHV then these inputs are likely to have diverse properties. What these may be can only be guessed at. Sensory messages are usually modified in their passage through synaptic junctions; the more synapses traversed, the greater the modification. For example, ganglion cells in the cats retina respond to diffuse light flashes. The axons of these cells synapse in the lateral geniculate body, the cells of which respond less briskly to diffuse flashes of light than do the retinal ganglion cells. The lateral geniculate body projects to the visual cortex. Cells in the visual cortex respond weakly, if at all, to bright flashes of light; these neurones have very specific stimulus requirements. For example, such a neurone may respond to a line located in its receptive field. The magnitude of the response may depend critically on the width and orientation of the line, its length, its direction, and the speed of movement (for a review see Hubel 1982). By analogy with the visual system of the cat, the transformation of input that occur in the multisynaptic pathways illustrated in Fig. 11.1(a), (b), and (c) are likely to be greater than those in the oligosynaptic pathway illustrated in Fig. 11.1(d).

The convergance of multisynaptic and oligosynaptic pathways in one structure is not unique and may indeed have important consequences for the processing of sensory information reaching that structure. Evidence for such consequences derives from studies of the inferior temporal cortex of the rhesus monkey, though it is not suggested that the IMHV is homologous with this region. The inferior temporal cortex is fed by an array of visual inputs (Fig. 11.2) which is similar in some ways to the array which projects to the IMHV. The route that passes through the visual cortex is likely to involve a minimum of five synapses, at least two within the retina, before reaching the inferior temporal cortex. This number is roughly similar to that in the pathways to the IMHV illustrated in Fig. 11.1(a), (b), and (c). A more direct route to the inferior temporal cortex passes through the optic tectum (superior colliculus, Fig. 11.2). Neurones in this structure do not project to the inferior temporal cortex directly: at least one synapse in the thalamus intervenes. This route resembles that shown in Fig. 11.1(d), although in this pathway there is no thalamic synapse. In the monkey, the multisynaptic route appears to exert different influences on the receptive field properties of neurones in the inferior temporal cortex from those exerted by the oligosynaptic route which passes through the optic tectum and pulvinar of

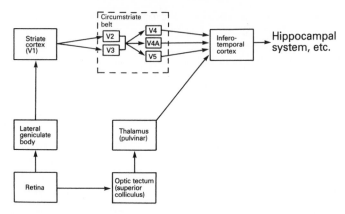

**Fig. 11.2.** Some visual pathways to the inferior temporal cortex of the rhesus monkey (*Macaca mulatta*). V1 is the striate, or primary visual cortex. V2, V3, V4, V4A, and V5 are subdivisions of the circumstriate belt. At least one synapse intervenes between input and output neurones in each region shown. Not all of the known visual pathways to and from the inferior temporal cortex are shown. (After Gross *et al.* 1974.)

the thalamus. When the pluvinar was destroyed, virtually none of the neurones in the inferior temporal cortex continued to have discrete receptive fields; when the striate cortex was destroyed the response properties of the receptive fields changed (Gross *et al.* 1974). These workers concluded that the spatial extent of the receptive fields was dependent on the input from the pulvinar (the oligosynaptic route), whereas the response properties of the neurones, their 'trigger' features, were dependent on the cortico-cortical (multisynaptic) input.

Although the inferior temporal cortex of the rhesus monkey is similar to the IMHV of the chick in receiving multisynaptic and oligosynaptic inputs, the analogy between the two systems should not be pushed too far. Bilateral removal of the inferior temporal cortex results in a marked impairment in visual discrimination learning. This deficit occurs with a great variety of discriminada, such as stimuli differing in pattern, size, shape, and colour, and with a wide variety of training methods (Gross 1973). In contrast, many forms of visually guided behaviour are unimpaired by lesions of the IMHV (see p. 88, Chapter 6, and Section 8.4.1).

No comparable studies of the interaction between multisynaptic and oligosynaptic visual pathways to the IMHV have yet been undertaken. Indeed, very few studies have been made of the visual response properties of neurones in the larger hyperstriatum ventrale. Morenkov and Khun (1977) recorded from neurones in the medial part of the hyperstriatum ventrale of the grey crow (*Corvus corone*). Neurones within a region which appears to correspond anatomically to the IMHV, had receptive fields that were relatively large, reaching diameters of 30–50 degrees of visual angle. These neurones responded preferentially to stimuli moving in a particular direction, that is, the neurones were directionally selective. Guselnikov, Morenkov, and Khun (1976) recorded from the hyperstriatum ventrale of adult pigeons. The responses of units in this region were not described in any detail although it is clear from the text figures that directionally selective units with localized receptive fields were recorded in the anterior part of the hyperstriatum ventrale. No electrode penetrations were made through the region corresponding anatomically to the IMHV. In contrast to these positive results, Wilson (1980) failed to detect any visually evoked activity in the hyperstriatum ventrale of 5-week-old domestic chicks. Wilson's stimuli were stationary or moving spots of light or moving edges or bars. The part of the hyperstriatum ventrale explored by Wilson lay deep to the hyperstriatum accessorium and therefore did not include the IMHV. However, Milne, Horn, and McCabe (unpublished observations) have recorded from the IMHV of 2-day-old dark-reared chicks and from visually experienced chicks up to 2 weeks of age. No visual responses were detected using similar stimuli to those used by Wilson, although a small number of units which responded weakly to diffuse flashes of light have been recorded in the IMHV (Brown and Horn 1979).

These diverse results are puzzling, but for a number of reasons they are not surprising and the discrepancies may be more apparent than real. The two studies in which unit responses to discrete visual stimuli were observed used, respectively, adult pigeons and crows as subjects whereas the negative results were found in the domestic chick. There may be species and age differences in the responsiveness of the IMHV to visual stimulation. Another difference is that Morenkov and his colleagues used unanaesthetized birds whereas the chicks were anaesthetized. This difference may be of some importance. Neuronal responses to sensory stimulation are not difficult to detect in the major sensory pathways of anaesthetized animals, especially if the recorded region is only a few synapses distant from the sensory receptors. In contrast, anaesthetic agents often have a profound depressant effect on transmission in multisynaptic pathways (see Clutton-Brock 1961; Brazier 1961; Brown and Horn 1977). This effect of anaesthetics is one reason why these agents tend not to be used when recording from regions that are synaptically remote from the sense organs. However, there is another reason why it is sometimes necessary to abandon anaesthetics when recording from structures in the brain. These agents abolish virtually all interesting aspects of behaviour such as attention, learning, and motor acts of a complex, or even quite simple, kind. It is reasonable to infer therefore that anaesthetics affect those brain regions that integrate the neuronal events on which these functions depend. It is not surprising that recent electrophysiological studies of brain regions that may be involved in these functions were conducted on unanaesthetized, behaving animals (see, for example, Wurtz and Goldberg 1971; Horn and Wiesenfeld 1974; Mountcastle 1976; Mora *et al.* 1976; Brown and Horn 1978; Wurtz *et al.* 1980).

Although units with visual receptive fields have not been recorded from the IMHV of anaesthetized chicks, it is worth emphasizing that the spontaneous discharge of neurones, as well as the structure of synapses in the region, are affected by training upon a visual imprinting stimulus (see Chapter 10).

The major *auditory* receiving area of the telencephalon is field L which lies in the caudal part of the neostriatum (see Section A.3.2 and Fig. A.6). In the chick field L lies adjacent to the medial part of hyperstriatum ventrale, being separated from this region by the lamina hyperstriatica (Scheich 1983). Field L overlaps part of the IMHV and extends caudally beyond its limits. The approximate relationships are indicated in Fig. 11.3. The auditory projection area lies medial to the visual projection area of the neostriatum which Parker and Delius (1972) described. Scheich (1983) divided field L into three regions in the rostro-caudal axis. He showed that the anterior and intermediate parts, one or both of which probably overlap with the IMHV, receive inputs from the cochlea of each side. Such an arrangement suggests that neurones in these regions are concerned with the localization of sound. They may also process species-specific calls (Scheich 1983; Scheich *et al.* 1979*b*). Whether or not this is so, the evidence available suggests that neurones in the anterior and intermediate parts of field L are capable of analysing complex auditory signals. In the chick, field L

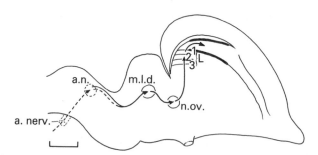

**Fig. 11.3.** Auditory pathways to the IMHV. Axons in the auditory division of the eighth cranial nerve terminate in the auditory nuclei of the brainstem. The subsequent pathways contain both crossed and uncrossed components. The primary auditory receiving area in the telencephalon is field L in the caudal neostriatum. The anterior part of this field overlaps the IMHV, but field L extends caudally, beyond the most posterior part of the IMHV. Field L is subdivided dorsoventrally into three regions with $L_1$ superficial and $L_3$ deep to $L_2$. Field L projects to the IMHV. Abbreviations: a.nerv., auditory division of the eighth cranial nerve; a.n., auditory nuclei in the medulla; m.l.d., nucleus mesencephalicus lateralis dorsalis; n.ov., nucleus ovoidalis; L, field L in neostriatum. Broken lines indicate structures on the contralateral side of the brain, continuous lines represent ipsilateral structures. For further details see Section A.3.2.

projects into the IMHV. When retrograde tracers were injected into the IMHV, labelled cell bodies were found in the adjacent neostriatum in the region corresponding to field L (Bradley *et al.* 1985). In the guinea-fowl, field L and the adjacent hyperstriatum ventrale are reciprocally connected (Bonke *et al.* 1979).

Neurones in the medial hyperstriatum ventrale of the domestic chick may not be activated by simple auditory stimuli. Scheich (1983) delivered 'sliding' (frequency-modulated) tones to chicks and assessed neural activity by measuring the uptake of radioactive 2-deoxyglucose (see Section 4.2). Whilst frequency-modulated stimulation was associated with strong labelling in field L, there was no evidence from the published figures that this stimulation was associated with labelling in the hyperstriatum ventrale (Scheich 1983). When tonal stimuli were delivered to guinea-fowls, there was strong labelling in field L, but relatively poor uptake of 2-deoxyglucose in the hyperstriatum ventrale (Scheich *et al.* 1979a). However, when species-specific calls were delivered to these birds, clear bands of 2-deoxyglucose labelling were visible in the hyperstriatum ventrale (Scheich *et al.* 1983). It is particularly interesting that this region is strongly activated by complex auditory stimuli, which include species-specific calls. Gottlieb (1971) showed that a following response is more likely to be elicited in mallard ducklings when a complex sound emanates from a mallard decoy than when the decoy is presented without the sound. Furthermore, many of the experiments on domestic chicks which have been described in other chapters (see, for example, Horn *et al.* 1979; Davies *et al.* 1985) have used audio-visual combinations during the training period. This procedure has been found to enhance the effectiveness of imprinting on a visual object. One explanation for the greater effectiveness of the compound stimulus is that the sound serves to direct the bird's attention to the visual object (Gottlieb and Klopfer 1962). Another possibility is that a complex auditory stimulus when combined with a visual stimulus exerts a more powerful influence on neurones in the IMHV than either stimulus alone. A microelectrode analysis, in behaving chicks, of the response properties of neurones in this region is critical if these issues are to be resolved.

*Somatic sensory* responses, evoked by lightly touching the beak, mechanically displacing feathers or gently disturbing them by air puffs, can be recorded from a caudal part of the neostriatum in the pigeon (Fig. 11.4). The projection is mainly contralateral (Erulkar 1955; Delius and Bennetto 1972). Both studies agree that the somatic sensory area is anterior and dorsal to the auditory projection area. Responses to somatic sensory stimulation have also been recorded in the neostriatum caudale of the Landes goose (Félix *et al.* 1983). In the chick, this area projects to the hyperstriatum ventrale including the IMHV (Bradley *et al.* 1985). In Erulkar's study, some of the points from which evoked responses were recorded lay within the medial hyperstriatum ventrale (Erulkar 1955).

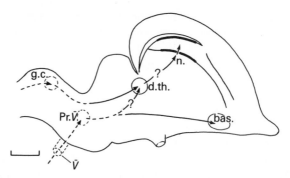

**Fig. 11.4.** Somatic sensory routes to the IMHV. Sensory input to the spinal cord reaches the dorsal thalmic nuclei (d.th.) by several routes. One route proceeds via a synapse in the gracile and cuneate nuclei (g.c.). The fifth ($V$) cranial nerve carries cutaneous input from the face and beak to the brainstem, and terminates in the principal sensory nucleus (Pr.$V$). The quintofrontal tract arises in this nucleus, and after partial decussation terminates in the nucleus basalis (bas.). Delius and Bennetto (1972) suggest that a limb of the tract terminates in the dorsal thalamus. This nucleus is thought by these workers to provide input to the somatic sensory region of the neostriatum. Cell bodies in this region project to the IMHV. Nerves, tracts and nuclei in broken outline are contralateral whereas continuous lines indicate ipsilateral structures. Question marks on tracts indicate routes suggested by electrophysiological evidence. (Modified after Delius and Bennetto 1972.)

The *olfactory system* is connected to the hyperstriatum ventrale by a route which does not involve the neostriatum (Fig. 11.5). In the pigeon lesions to the olfactory bulbs result in terminal degeneration in the ipsilateral hyperstriatum ventrale including the part corresponding to the IMHV (Rieke and Wenzel 1978). Responses can be evoked bilaterally in this structure following stimulation of an olfactory nerve (Macader *et al.* 1980). The results together suggest that the uncrossed input is a direct one, passing

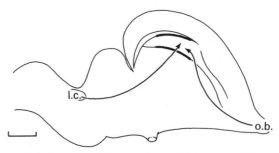

**Fig. 11.5.** Olfactory and coeruleal innervation of the hyperstriatum ventrale. In the pigeon, neurones in the olfactory bulb (o.b.) project to the hyperstriatum ventrale, including the region corresponding to the IMHV. Nerve fibres probably containing noradrenaline are present in the IMHV and it is likely that they arise from neurones in and adjacent to the locus coeruleus (l.c.) (see also Fig. A.7).

from the olfactory bulb to the hyperstriatum ventrale without an intervening synapse. In the crossed pathway, at least one synapse must intervene between the two structures.

The picture that emerges from these studies is that the IMHV in the domestic chick, or the region that corresponds to it in some other birds, receives inputs from virtually every sensory modality. The obvious exception is taste, though little is known about the telencephalic connections of the pathways mediating this sensation (Gentle 1975), and the same is true of the central connections of the vestibular system. The evidence for the projection to the IMHV of other sensory pathways is mainly, though not exclusively, anatomical, so that the precise nature of the input needs to be determined using electrophysiological techniques.

In addition to the connections from the sensory pathways, nuclei in the *brainstem core* almost certainly contribute ascending projections to the IMHV (Fig. 11.5). The pathway probably arises from perikarya in the locus coeruleus and adjacent nuclei of the brainstem, and contain catecholamines (see Section A.4 and Fig. A.7).

### 11.1.2 Connections with descending control systems

A major route by which the forebrain hemispheres may exercise control over more caudal parts of the brain arises in the archistriatum (Zeier and Karten 1971; for a review see Pearson 1972). A relatively massive bundle of nerve fibres arises from perikarya lying within certain nuclei in this structure (Fig. 11.6). The bundle is known as the occipitomesencephalic tract. The tract contains both crossed and uncrossed fibres and its axons terminate in the thalamus, in many nuclei in the brainstem and in the upper part of the spinal cord. The pathway affords a route for the direct control of movement through synapses in the spinal cord and also for the indirect control of movement through intervening structures. The occipitomesencephalic tract is connected to a layer of neurones in the optic tectum from which arise many of the outlet fibres of this structure. Although the optic tectum is a major visual area, it projects to many structures which do not have a visual function, including the spinal cord. The archistriatum also sends axons to the reticular formation of the midbrain and hindbrain. The reticular formation in turn projects to the spinal cord. Some axons in the occipitomesencephalic tract terminate in the locus coeruleus. Neurones in this nucleus project not only to the forebrain, but also to the spinal cord and cerebellum (Dubé and Parent 1981; Shiosaka *et al.* 1981). The cerebellum is, of course, involved in the control of posture and movement.

The dorsal part of archistriatum intermedium (Fig. 11.6, a.i.d.) is connected to the IMHV in the chick (Bradley *et al.* 1985) and probably also in the guinea-fowl (Bonke *et al.* 1979). In the chick the connections are reciprocal. Zeier and Karten (1971) found that, in the pigeon, even slight surgical damage to this part of the archistriatum resulted in prominent

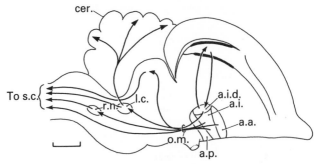

**Fig. 11.6.** Archistriatal connections with the IMHV over which influences on motor activities may be exerted. In this diagram are drawn four of the five major nuclei into which the archistriatum of the pigeon has been subdivided by Zeier and Karten (1971). Three nuclei contribute to the long descending pathway, the occipitomesencephalic tract (o.m.). One of these nuclei, the dorsal part of the intermediate nucleus (a.i.d.) is reciprocally connected to the IMHV. Only four of the many sites of termination of the tract are shown. These include the following: (i) The deeper layers of the optic tectum. The optic tectum may influence motor activity through the tectospinal pathway and also through its connections (not shown) with the reticular formation. (ii) The locus ceoruleus (l.c.). Two of the targets of this nucleus are the cerebellum (cer.) and spinal cord (s.c.). (iii) Reticular nuclei (r.n.) in the hindbrain, including the pons and medulla. These nuclei are probably the source of reticulospinal pathways. (iv) The upper, cervical part of the spinal cord. The descending projections of the archistriatum are both crossed and uncrossed. Other abbreviations: a.a., archistriatum anterior; a.i., archistriatum intermedium; a.p., archistriatum posterior.

degeneration in the occipitomesencephalic tract. Ritchie and Cohen (1977) found a projection from the periectostriatal belt to the dorsal archistriatum (Fig. 11.1(c)), a finding which implies that this is a visual receiving area. These two observations suggest that this part of the archistriatum may be concerned with the control of visually guided behaviour. The connections of the archistriatum with the optic tectum also point to a similar conclusion. The optic tectum of many vertebrates has been shown to be involved in visual tracking, whether this requires body, head or eye movements, or a combination of these movements, to follow the target (see Ingle and Sprague 1975; Wurtz *et al.* 1980).

The IMHV may also be connected to the archistriatum intermedium through an indirect route. When radioactive leucine was injected into the IMHV, a region of terminal labelling was seen over the lateral cerebral area (see Fig. 11.8). Other connections of this region have not been studied specifically in the chick. However, the lateral cerebral area lies close by the dorsal archistriate tract to which it may contribute axons. This tract projects to the archistriatum intermedium, which makes a major contribution to the occipitomesencephalic tract.

The connections with the intermediate parts of the archistriatum are not the only routes by which motor activity may be influenced by the IMHV. This structure has connections with the paleostriatum augmentatum (Fig. 11.8). In the chick these connections are reciprocal. As in the case of the dorsal archistriatum, there is a paucity of experimental evidence on the functions of the paleostriatum augmentatum although the evidence from comparative anatomy is suggestive of one function. Similarities in embryonic derivation and in histochemistry suggest that paleostriatum augmentatum is comparable to parts of the basal ganglia of mammals (see Reiner *et al.* 1984 and p. 294). Early clues to one of the functions of the basal ganglia came from clinical observations on human patients. A wide range of movement disorders are associated with lesions of these structures and it has been suggested that they have a major function in controlling slow voluntary movements (DeLong 1974; Kornhuber 1974). In pigeons chemical lesions of the paleostriatal complex, of which paleostriatum augmentatum is a major component, are followed by rapid rotations toward the side of the lesion, involuntary movements, and postural disturbances (Rieke 1980). The paleostriatal complex of pigeons may also be involved in learning (Mitchell and Hall 1984) and the possible involvement of this region in S′ has been referred to earlier (p. 143).

### 11.1.3 Connections with systems involved in agonistic behaviour and the expression of emotions

Not all of the long axons arising in the archistriatum pass into the occipito-mesencephalic tract. Lesions to the medial or posterior nuclei of the archistriatum of pigeons do not result in degeneration within this tract. These two nuclei project to the hypothalamus (Zeier and Karten 1971). The medial part of the hypothalamus in the pigeon has, as two of its targets, the lateral septal nucleus and the dorsomedial nucleus of the thalamus (Berk and Butler 1981). In the chick these nuclei both project to the IMHV (Fig. 11.7(a)). The IMHV in turn projects to the posterior part of the archistriatum and this connection appears to complete a circuit. The hippocampus (Fig. 11.7(b)) feeds into the circuit, indirectly through its connection to the septal nuclei (Krayniak and Siegel 1978*a*) and the hypothalamus, and through its direct connections to the IMHV (Bradley *et al.* 1985). The parahippocampal area, which lies adjacent to the hippocampus and to which it is connected, sends a bundle of axons to the posteromedial aspect of the archistriatum (Krayniak and Siegel 1978*a*).

The linking together of these various brain regions suggests that this system is concerned with visceral and endocrine functions and with the expression of emotions. In birds, as in many vertebrates, the hypothalamus is implicated in a multiplicity of control functions influencing sexual behaviour and other diverse endocrine-mediated responses to environmental change (see Hutchison 1978). Both the septal area and hippocampus exert

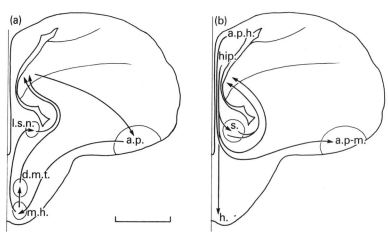

**Fig. 11.7.** Hippocampal and hypothalamic connections of the IMHV. (a) The structures which are connected may form a circuit controlling various viscero-endocrine functions. (b) The hippocampus (hip.) feeds into this circuit through its projections to the lateral (as well as to the medial) septal nucleus, to the hypothalamus (h.) and to the IMHV. For the purposes of illustration only the left forebrain is drawn. Other abbreviations: a.p., archistriatum posterior; a.p.h., area parahippocampalis; a.p-m., posteromedial aspect of archistriatum; d.m.t., dorsomedial thalamic nucleus; m.h., medial hypothalamus; l.s.n., lateral septal nucleus; s., medial and lateral septal nuclei.

an inhibitory effect on plasma corticosteroid concentrations in the pigeon, and so may mediate endocrine responses to stress (Bouillé and Baylé 1973, 1975). Parts of the system outlined in Fig. 11.7 are probably also implicated in the organization of attack and escape reactions (Vowles and Beazley 1974). Electrical stimulation of the medial nucleus of the archistriatum evokes attack responses in chickens (Phillips and Youngren 1971). Conversely lesions to the medial archistriatum have been found to reduce escape behaviour in wild mallard ducks (Phillips 1964). Attack and escape behaviour, when directed to conspecifics, are aspects of agonistic behaviour. Phillips and Youngren (1971) found that fear-like responses, expressions of emotional behaviour, could be elicited by stimulating the archistriatum or its output fibres. The anatomical distribution of the stimulus sites which evoked fear-like and attack responses overlapped, but were separate. Stimulating or destroying parts of the archistriatum had similar behavioural effects to those found in mammals when the amygdala is manipulated in these ways (see Kaada 1972). For this reason and because of their connection to the hypothalamus, the posterior and medial nuclei are considered to constitute the 'amygdaloid' part of the archistriatum (Zeier and Karten 1971).

The amygdaloid part of the archistriatum is not uniquely involved in the control of agonistic and emotional behaviour, any more than is the mammalian amygdala. These behavioural patterns may be modified by stimulating the hypothalamus, the septal nuclei, and the hippocampus (Macphail 1967; Cannon and Salzen 1971; Phillips and Youngren 1971; Vowles and Beazley 1974). The septal nuclei and the hippocampus are reciprocally connected in birds as they are in mammals. Damage to these structures in mammals affects exploratory behaviour, distractability, and learning (for a review see Gray and McNaughton 1983). Damage to the hippocampus and associated structures disturbs memory functions in ways that have been extensively described but which are as yet not fully understood (see Section 6.3).

The connections of the IMHV in the chick are summarized in Fig. 11.8. The region receives inputs from the thalamus and these are discussed below (Section 11.3). The projection of the IMHV to the lateral cerebral area, and the effects on imprinting and on passive avoidance learning of damaging

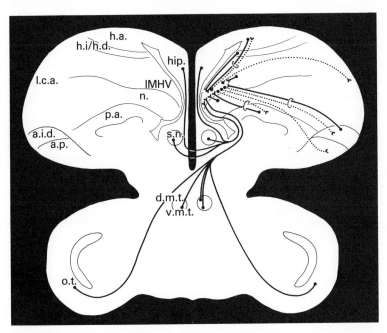

**Fig. 11.8.** Summary diagram of the connections of the IMHV. Afferent pathways are represented as continuous lines, efferent pathways as dotted lines. Many of the structures shown in the drawing do not lie in the same plane and the routes taken by the pathways do not all correspond to the actual route: the drawing is diagrammatic. Abbreviations: a.i.d., dorsal part of archistriatum intermedium; a.p., archistriatum posterior; d.m.t., dorsomedial thalamus; h.a., hyperstriatum accessorium; h.i./h.d., hyperstriatum intercalatus/hyperstriatum dorsale; hip., hippocampus; l.c.a., lateral cerebral area; n., neostriatum; o.t., optic tectum; p.a., paleostriatum augmentatum; s.n., septal nuclei; v.m.t., ventromedial thalamus.

this area in chicks have already been mentioned (Section 5.2 and (p. 125). Some effects on associative learning tasks of lesions to the lateral cerebral area in pigeons have recently been described. In one study the birds were required to discriminate between a red and a green light. Performance in this task was not impaired by the lesion (Mogensen and Divac 1982). In the other study the birds were trained on hue, intensity, and pattern discriminations. Performance on all tasks was impaired in lesioned birds (Delius *et al.* 1984). The different results of the two studies may be attributable to differences in the difficulty of the discrimination tasks, to differences in the time that elapsed between the surgical operation and training, or to some other factors as yet unknown.

The IMHV has diverse sensory inputs and most of these inputs will almost certainly have been subjected to substantial neural processing before reaching the structure. The IMHV is connected directly to the intermediate part of the archistriatum. This target of the IMHV is an important source of descending fibres from the cerebral hemispheres (Fig. 11.6). It is also possible that some at least of the connections of the IMHV to the hyperstriatum accessorium are to the non-visual part of this structure. The non-visual part of the hyperstriatum accessorium provides a major outflow from the forebrain hemispheres. These descending pathways almost certainly provide channels by which the cerebral hemispheres exercise control over motor activity (see Karten *et al.* 1973). A similar function may be served by the pathways linking the IMHV to the paleostriatum augmentatum (see p. 243). All of these connections strongly imply an involvement of the IMHV in the control of posture and locomotion. The region may also be implicated, through its connections with the posterior archistriatum and the septal system (Fig. 11.7), with affective and agonistic behaviour. Several of the connections that the IMHV makes with other structures are reciprocal, an arrangement which may confer functional precision through feedback control.

## 11.2  Chemical and cellular components of the IMHV

### 11.2.1  Neuroactive substances

The numerous inputs to the IMHV would be expected to secrete numerous neuroactive substances, that is, neurotransmitters and substances which regulate transmission and which are known as neuromodulators. Further diversity of neuroactive substances may arise from the secretions of neurones intrinsic to the IMHV.

Of four biogenic amines with transmitter properties, noradrenaline, dopamine, 5-hydroxytryptamine, and histamine, the first three are present in the IMHV (Davies *et al.* 1983; McCabe and Hunt 1983). The probable sources of some of these amine-containing fibres are cell groups located in the midbrain or hindbrain (see Section A.4 and Fig. A.7).

Acetylcholine is present in the pigeon telencephalon, though the regional distribution of the transmitter is not known. The distribution of acetylcholinesterase, an enzyme which hydrolyses acetylcholine, has been described for the forebrain of chicks which are 1–2 days old (Fig. 11.9). The distribution in 6-week-old chicks is similar to that of the younger birds. In addition to the areas which contain acetylcholinesterase, and which appear dark in Fig. 11.9, other areas, including the septal nuclei, also contain the enzyme. In the light of the discussion which follows (Section 11.3) it is interesting to note that in mammals too, the septal nuclei contain cells which stain for acetylcholinesterase (Lewis and Shute 1967). In chicks the enzyme is present in the hyperstriatum ventrale, including the IMHV. Within this region stained cell bodies are present. In addition the stain is present more diffusely, a finding which suggests that the enzyme is contained in nerve fibres and terminals. The possibility that acetylcholine is a transmitter substance in the IMHV is strengthened by the finding that muscarinic receptor sites, which bind acetylcholine, are present in a brain sample composed mainly of the IMHV (Bradley and Horn 1981). If acetylcholine is indeed a transmitter, it may be produced either by the terminals of long afferent fibres and/or by neurones intrinsic to the IMHV.

Davies and Horn (1983) investigated the possible source of the putative cholinergic afferents to the IMHV by combining retrograde fluorescent labelling with a technique for staining acetylcholinesterase histochemically. A fluorescent tracer was injected into the IMHV of day-old chicks. After an interval of 20 hours, to allow time for the tracer to be transported back to the cell bodies, the brains were removed and sections stained for acetylcholinesterase. By viewing the sections under tungsten bright-field

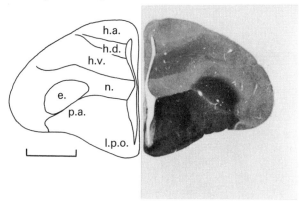

**Fig. 11.9.** Regional distribution of acetylcholinesterase in the chick telencephalon. The reaction product for acetylcholinesterase stains cell bodies and their processes and appears dark in the photomicrograph. The section shown is from the brain of a 2-day-old chick. Abbreviations: e., ectostriatum; h.a., hyperstriatum accessorium; h.d., hyperstriatum dorsale; h.v., hyperstriatum ventrale; l.p.o., lobus paraolfactorius; n., neostriatum; p.a., paleostriatum augmentatum. (After McCabe *et al.* 1982).

illumination, cell bodies containing the acetylcholinesterase reaction product could be identified. By switching to an ultraviolet light source it was
possible to decide whether the cell bodies also fluoresced. In some
telencephalic regions the fluorescent label and the brown acetylcholinesterase reaction product were seen in the same perikarya. Such neurones
therefore are likely to project to the IMHV; their distribution is shown in
Fig. 11.10. The septal nuclei and hippocampus are two major sources of
such fibres and the inputs are bilateral. The ipsilateral neostriatum also projects acetylcholinesterase-containing fibres to the IMHV, as do neurones in
the caudal part of the hyperstriatum ventrale. Since the activity of the
enzyme acetylcholinesterase has been found to increase transiently following the exposure of chicks to a visually conspicuous object (Haywood *et al.*
1975), it is possible that these afferents play a role in the imprinting
process.

Other neuroactive substances have been found in the IMHV. Thus
methionine-enkephalin is present in cell bodies and cholecystokinin is present in nerve fibres (McCabe and Hunt 1983). These peptides are
pharmacologically highly active and may excite, or inhibit, or exert a combination of these effects when applied directly to neurones. There is no
evidence as to whether or not γ-aminobutyric acid, a transmitter which is
contained in many inhibitory neurones, is present in the IMHV.

It will be apparent from this discussion that knowledge of the neuroactive
substances present in the IMHV is fragmentary. Since imprinting involves
changes in synapse structure (see Section 10.2) it is essential to know much
more about these substances. In particular it is important to know the
sources of the nerve fibres which contain the substances, the targets of these
fibres, and their synaptic organization within the IMHV.

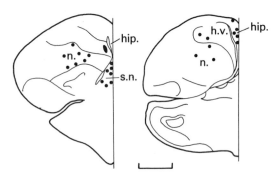

**Fig. 11.10.** Location of acetylcholinesterase-containing perikarya which project to
the IMHV. The site within the IMHV into which fluorescent tracer was injected is
indicated by the solid black area. The locations of double-labelled neuronal perikarya are indicated by filled circles. Outline diagram on the left is rostral to that on
the right. Abbreviations: hip., hippocampus; h.v., hyperstriatum ventrale; n., neostriatum; s.n., septal nuclei. Scale 2 mm. (After Davies and Horn 1983.)

## 11.2.2 Cellular organization

Little is known of the internal architecture of the IMHV. Using a histological technique (Golgi) which involves impregnating the tissue with silver nitrate, the images of neurones and some of their processes stand out with extraordinary clarity. Bradley and Horn (1982) found that nerve cell bodies in the IMHV are not arranged in laminae, unlike the arrangement of cells in the optic tectum or in the mammalian cortex. The cells in the IMHV were classified according to the size and shape of the perikarya. Four classes of cells could be identified by these criteria. Examples of three of the classes are shown in Fig. 11.11. The axon of the cells with pyramidally shaped bodies (Fig. 11.11(c)) commonly bifurcated before leaving the IMHV. These cells are, almost certainly, projection neurones. Whether other cells also project out of the region is not clear since their axons could not often be traced beyond the boundaries of the IMHV. Approximately a quarter of the cells had small pyramidal or stellate cell bodies and these are not illustrated in Fig. 11.11. These cells and their processes probably lie wholly within the IMHV. By comparison with neurones of similar shape and size in the mam-

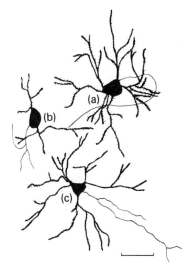

**Fig. 11.11.** Camera lucida drawings of neurones in the IMHV. A total of 140 cells were Golgi-impregnated and came from day-old light-reared chicks. Dendrites may be identified on the drawings by the presence of spines: axons are shown as smooth lines. (a) Fifty-six neurones (40 per cent) were large, with multiple origins of the primary dendrites. The course of the axons was highly variable. (b) Twenty-one neurones (15 per cent) had large ovoid bodies. The axons of these cells divided into a number of branches soon after leaving the cell body. (c) Twenty-seven neurones (20 per cent) had large pyramid-shaped bodies. The axons of these cells commonly left IMHV, often dividing into two branches in doing so. Scale 50 μm. (After Bradley and Horn 1982.)

malian spinal cord, it is probable that some at least of these cells have an inhibitory function.

What is needed now is to relate the cytoarchitecture of the IMHV, as revealed by light microscopy, to the ultrastructure and to the transmitter chemistry of the region. With this knowledge, with quantitative information about the arrangement and spacing of synapses, and with knowledge of the microelectrophysiology of the IMHV, it will be possible to gain more insight into the way in which this piece of neural machinery works.

### 11.3  Comment and speculation: cerebral circuits in birds and mammals

When the visual inputs to the IMHV were considered, reference was made to the inferior temporal cortex of monkeys because both brain regions receive visual inputs through multisynaptic and oligosynaptic pathways. Useful as this analogy may be, reasons were given for not pushing the analogy too far. Now that more details of the connections of the IMHV are known, however, it becomes reasonable to enquire whether any region of the primate brain corresponds in some functional or anatomical sense to the IMHV. The difficulty of making such comparisons is emphasized elsewhere (Section A.2). However, attention has already been drawn to the similarities that exist between the effects on memory of damage to the IMHV in the chick and of damage to certain structures in the brain of human and non-human primates (Sections 6.3 and 6.4). Are there grounds for supposing that the IMHV has anything more in common with these structures in the primate brain? In attempting to answer this question it is important to be clear how fragile is the basis of comparison. The central nervous system of mammals has been studied more intensively than has that of any other vertebrate class. Compared with what is known of the mammalian brain, knowledge of the avian bird is almost primitive. This discrepancy alone makes any comparison difficult, and the difficulty is compounded by the existence of large variation between species within each class. As a result, only relatively course-grained comparisons may be viable, if any are. These comparisons are based on similarities in embryological history, in connections, and in the physiology of the regions under consideration.

It is possible to be confident about the regions that the IMHV does not resemble. It does not resemble the primary sensory cortical areas of mammals. These areas, with rare exception, receive specific sensory inputs from sensory projection nuclei in the thalamus, a feature which does not characterize the inputs to the IMHV. Nor does the IMHV resemble the mammalian archicortex, which is composed mainly of the hippocampus and the dentate gyrus: the hippocampus is derived embryologically from the medial wall of the neural tube whereas the hyperstriatum ventrale is derived from the lateral wall (Fig. A.4B). The hippocampus projects to the IMHV and this connection provides an important clue. The field is narrowed further by the evidence that the IMHV receives a direct input from medial thalamic nuclei (Fig. 11.8). Two regions of the primate cerebral cortex receive inputs from medial thalamic nuclei and are strongly associated with the hippocampus. These regions are the prefrontal and the cingulate areas of the cortex (for a review of these areas see Brodal 1981).

The prefrontal cortex is the grey matter bounding the surface of the anterior part of the frontal lobe. The connections of the region will be considered in the same order as were the connections of the IMHV. Some of the connections of the prefrontal cortex are illustrated in Fig. 11.12. (1) The prefrontal cortex does not receive inputs from sensory relay nuclei in the thalamus. Nevertheless, sensory information reaches the prefrontal cortex from cortical regions adjoining the primary sensory fields; that is, this information reaches the prefrontal cortex from within the telencephalon. The IMHV has a similar arrangement for its sensory inputs: with the possible exception of one of several visual pathways, all sensory inputs to the IMHV arise in other regions of the telencephalon. (2) The prefrontal cortex does not appear to contribute directly to a major motor pathway from the cerebral cortex, the pyramidal tract. However, the region projects to the parietal lobe which makes an important contribution to this tract (Russell and DeMyer 1961). The prefrontal cortex also projects to parts of the thalamus,

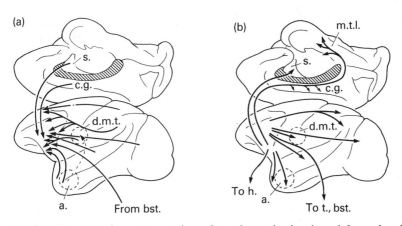

**Fig. 11.12.** Diagrammatic representation of a primate brain viewed from the side. The lower outlines in each pair of diagrams are lateral views. The anterior pole of the brain is to the left and the dorsal surface is uppermost. The upper outlines are inverted medial views of the brain. (a) Some of the main afferents to the prefrontal cortex are shown as solid lines ending in this region as arrow heads. Afferents come from other parts of the cortex, including the cortex of the cingulate gyrus (c.g.) and from some subcortical regions, including the ventral septum (s.), amygdala (a.), dorsomedial thalamic nucleus (d.m.t.), and brainstem nuclei (bst.). (b) Some of the main efferent connections are shown. Additional abbreviations: h., hypothalamus; m.t.l., medial temporal lobe; t., thalamus. (Based on Nauta 1971; Brodal 1981.)

to the reticular formation, and to the locus coeruleus. The IMHV does not send direct projections to regions outside the forebrain, but it connects with these regions indirectly via the dorsal and possibly the intermediate parts of the archistriatum. The prefrontal cortex projects to the basal ganglia; the IMHV projects to the paleostriatum augmentatum which has often been compared to that part of the basal ganglia which receives an input from the prefrontal cortex. (3) The amygdala, the hypothalamus, and the dorsomedial nucleus of the thalamus all project to the prefrontal cortex. If the posterior and medial parts of the archistriatum correspond to the amygdala, then these connections of the prefrontal cortex correspond closely with those of the IMHV which are illustrated in Fig. 11.7(a). (4) The prefrontal cortex is connected indirectly to the hippocampus. Neurones in this structure project to the septal nuclei which in turn project to the dorsomedial thalamic nucleus. Cells in this nucleus send their axons to the prefrontal cortex. In chicks the hippocampus projects directly to the IMHV as well as via the septal nuclei which lie in the dorsal part of the septum. This projection may be cholinergic (Davies and Horn 1983). The prefrontal cortex receives an input which may be cholinergic, from structures in the ventral part of the septum (Domesick 1976; Meibach and Siegel 1977). This system is found to be degenerated in human patients suffering from senile dementia of the Alzheimer type, a condition associated with severe amnesia (Davies and Maloney 1976; Whitehouse *et al.* 1982; Coyle *et al.* 1983; Mountjoy *et al.* 1984). (5) The prefrontal cortex is reciprocally connected to several of the regions from which it receives afferents. So too is the IMHV.

The similarities between the IMHV and the cingulate cortex, whilst less striking than those between the IMHV and the prefrontal cortex, are nevertheless worth describing. The IMHV receives input from the medially located dorsomedial and ventromedial thalamic nuclei. The cingulate cortex receives input from the medially located anteroventral and dorsomedial thalamic nuclei. In primates the lateral septal nucleus and a region of cortex, the subiculum, both project to the cingulate cortex. The subiculum may be comparable to the avian area parahippocampalis (Benowitz and Karten 1976; Krayniak and Siegel 1978*a*). Whilst this area does not project directly to the IMHV it may do so via its projections to the hippocampus and the septal nuclei (Krayniak and Siegel 1978*a*; Bradley *et al.* 1985). In primates the cingulate cortex sends fibres back to several of the structures from which it receives afferents, including the prefrontal cortex.

There are many differences in the connections of the IMHV in the chick, on the one hand, and those of the prefrontal and cingulate areas of the primate cerebral cortex, on the other; and even some of the similarities may be very loose indeed. For example, the dorsomedial thalamic nucleus of the pigeon and rat each receives projections from the ventral part of the septum (Krayniak and Siegel 1978*b*; Meibach and Siegel 1977); in contrast, whilst there is good evidence that in the pigeon this nucleus receives input from the hypothalamus (Berk and Butler 1981) the evidence for such a connection in mammals is not conclusive (Raisman 1966). Nonetheless, there is sufficient in common between the IMHV and the two areas of cerebral cortex to justify comparing their possible roles in memory.

In man, damage to the anterior and medial parts of the thalamus may result in severe amnesia (Brierley 1977). This part of the thalamus receives afferent fibres from many sources, but these include the amygdala and the septal nuclei. Through the septal nuclei, and nuclei in the hypothalamus, the anterior and medial parts of the thalamus receive the outputs of the hippocampus and the adjacent area of cortex, the subiculum. Damage to some or all of these regions is associated with amnesia. The prefrontal cortex and the cingulate cortex are direct or indirect targets for these structures. Warrington and Weiskrantz (1982) have suggested that the hippocampus may initiate storage in the frontal lobe, which includes the prefrontal cortex. Griffith (1966) had also suggested an interaction between the hippocampal region and the cortex. He suggested that the synaptic changes, considered by him to form the basis of memory, occur in the cerebral cortex, and that the synaptic changes are partly controlled by an input arising from neurones in the hippocampus. Squire and his colleagues (1984) and Milner (1985) adopted a modified form of this view. They suggested that structures in the medial temporal lobe, which includes the hippocampus, interact with structures in the neocortex. A consequence of this interaction is that the postulated neural changes in the neocortex are gradually consolidated over a relatively long period of time. Those memories which depend on this interaction cannot be established if the medial temoral lobe is damaged. Furthermore, those memories decay which at the time of the lesion were still in the process of being consolidated. As a result, there is a loss of memory in humans for events which occurred a few years before the lesion.

Whether or not this model is correct, there is good evidence that several brain areas in man and other mammals are interlocked in a system which is crucial for memory (see Weiskrantz 1982). Precisely what functions the different components have is uncertain, but that they have some function in memory is difficult to deny. In the chick, the IMHV, too, has such a function, through the memory functions of the left IMHV are different from those of the right (Chapter 7). There is a hint from the work of Krushinskaya (see Vinogradova 1978) that the avian hippocampus is also implicated in memory. Krushinskaya studied cedar birds (*Nucifraga caryocataces*) which hide nuts in stores. Following lesions of the hippocampus, the birds forget the location of the stores if separated from them for more than 3 hours. Sahgal (1984) investigated the effects of lesions to the hippocampus of pigeons on their performance in a recognition task. The birds were shown a stimulus, and a few seconds later were shown either the same stimulus again or a different stimulus. The birds pecked one key if the first and second stimuli were the same, another key if they were different. The pigeons with lesions of the hippocampus were impaired in this task.

Although there are similarities in the organization of the brains of birds and mammals there are also important, major differences. And whilst the brains of these two classes of vertebrates arise in embryogenesis from neural tubes that look remarkably alike, the internal architecture of the mammalian cerebral hemispheres is very different from that of the avian counterpart. It may be, therefore, that the similarities which have been described above between the organization of certain structures in the avian brain and the mammalian brain are coincidental. Yet the similarities are striking, notwithstanding the great gulf of time that separates birds and mammals from a common ancestor. The process of evolution may have struck on and selected a neural arrangement which is particularly efficient for storing, analysing, and retrieving certain kinds of information. It is most unlikely, of course, that there would be no variations on the theme. The detailed differences of the circuits that have been described are hardly surprising.

## 11.4  Summary

Neurones in the IMHV, unlike those in the mammalian cerebral cortex, show no sign of being arranged in laminae. A variety of cell types are present in the IMHV. Some of the neurones are probably intrinsic to the region whilst others project their axons to other parts of the brain. A number of neuroactive substances have been identified in the IMHV and these may serve as neurotransmitters or neuromodulators. The IMHV receives connections from most sensory systems, and with one possible exception the information transmitted to the region will have been processed in other sensory areas of the telencephalon. The IMHV is connected, indirectly, to one or both of the major outlets of the telencephalon. Through these connections it may exert some control over posture, locomotion, and visually guided behaviour. The IMHV is also connected to a system which may be implicated in aspects of agonistic behaviour, for example attack, escape, and in viscero-endocrine functions. The connections of the IMHV resemble those of the prefrontal and cingulate areas of the primate cerebral cortex. The neural systems to which the IMHV and these areas of cortex belong also resemble each other in having memory functions.

## References

Adamo, N. J. (1967). Connections of efferent fibers from hyperstriatal areas in chicken, raven and African lovebird. *J. comp. Neurol.* **131**, 337–56.

Benowitz, L. I. and Karten, H. J. (1976). The tractus infundibuli and other afferents to the parahippocampal region of the pigeon. *Brain Res.* **102**, 174–80.

Bentivoglio, M., Kuypers, H. G. J. M., Catsman-Berrevoets, C. E., Loewe, H., and Dann, O. (1980). Two new fluorescent retrograde neuronal tracers which are transported over long distances. *Neurosci. Lett.* **18**, 25–30.

Berk, M. L. and Butler, A. B. (1981). Efferent projections of the medial preoptic nucleus and medial hypothalamus in the pigeon. *J. comp. Neurol.* **203**, 379–99.

Bonke, B. A., Bonke, D., and Scheich, H. (1979). Connectivity of the auditory forebrain nuclei in the Guinea fowl (*Numida meleagris*). *Cell Tissue Res.* **200**, 101–21.

Bouille, C. and Bayle, J. D. (1973). Effects of limbic stimulation or lesion on basal and stress-induced hypothalmic-pituitary-adrenocortical activity in the pigeon. *Neuroendocrinology* **13**, 264–77.

——, —— (1975). Influence of septal nuclei on basal pituitary adrenocortical function in birds. *Neuroendocrinology* **18**, 281–9.

Bradley, P. and Horn, G. (1981). Imprinting: a study of cholinergic receptor sites in parts of the chick brain. *Exp. Brain Res.* **41**, 121–3.

——, —— (1982). A Golgi analysis of the hyperstriatum ventrale in the chick. *J. Anat.* **134**, 599–600.

——, Davies, D. C., and Horn, G. (1985). Connections of the hyperstriatum ventrale of the domestic chick (*Gallus domesticus*). *J. Anat.* **140**, 577–89.

Brazier, M. A. B. (1961). Some effects of anaesthesia on the brain. *Br. J. Anaesth.* **33**, 194–204.

Brierley, J. B. (1977). Neuropathology of amnesic states. In *Amnesia* (eds C. W. M. Whitty and O. L. Zangwill), pp. 199–223. Butterworth, London.

Brodal, A. (1981). *Neurological anatomy in relation to clinical medicine.* Oxford University Press, New York.

Brown, M. W. and Horn, G. (1977). Responsiveness of neurones in the hippocampal region of anaesthetised and unanaesthetised cats to stimulation of sensory pathways. *Brain Res.* **123**, 241–59.

——, —— (1978). Context dependent neuronal responses recorded from hippocampal region of trained monkeys. *J. Physiol., Lond.* **282**, 15–16P.

——, —— (1979). Neuronal plasticity in the chick brain: electrophysiological effects of visual experience on hyperstriatal neurones. *Brain Res.* **162**, 142–7.

Cannon, R. E. and Salzen, E. A. (1971). Brain stimulation in newly-hatched chicks. *Anim. Behav.* **19**, 375–85.

Clutton-Brock, J. (1961). The importance of the central nervous effects of anaesthetic agents. *Br. J. Anaesth.* **33**, 214–18.

Coyle, J. T., Price, D. L., and DeLong, M. R. (1983). Alzheimer's disease: a disorder of cortical cholinergic innervation. *Science* **219**, 1184–90.

Davies, D. C. and Horn, G. (1983). Putative cholinergic afferents of the chick hyperstriatum ventrale: a combined acetylcholinesterase and retrograde fluorescence labelling study. *Neurosci. Lett.* **38**, 103–107.

——, ——, and McCabe, B. J. (1983). Changes in telencephalic catecholamine levels in the domestic chick. Effects of age and visual experience. *Devl Brain Res.* **10**, 251–5.

——, ——, —— (1985). Noradrenaline and learning: the effects of the neurotoxin DSP4 on imprinting in the domestic chick. *Behav. Neurosci.* **99** (in press).

Davies, P. and Maloney, A. J. F. (1976). Selective loss of central cholinergic neurons in Alzheimer's disease. *Lancet* **ii**, 1403.

Delius, J. D. and Bennetto, K. (1972). Cutaneous sensory projections to the avian forebrain. *Brain Res.* **37**, 205–21.

——, Runge, T. E., and Oeckinghaus, H. (1979). Short latency auditory projection to the frontal telencephalon of the pigeon. *Exp. Neurol.* **63**, 594–609.

——, Jäger, R. and Friesel, M. (1984). Lateral telencephalic lesions affect visual discrimination in pigeons. *Behav. Brain Res.* **11**, 249–58.

DeLong, M. R. (1974). Motor functions of the basal ganglia: single-unit activity during movement. In *The neurosciences third study program* (eds F. O. Schmitt and F. G. Worden), pp. 319–26. MIT Press, Cambridge, Mass.

Domesick, V. B. (1976). Projections of the nucleus of the diagonal band of Broca in the rat. *Anat. Rec.* **184**, 391–2.

Dubé, L. and Parent, A. (1981). The monoamine-containing neurons in the avian brain: 1. A study of the brain stem of the chick (*Gallus domesticus*) by means of fluorescence and acetylcholinesterase histochemistry. *J. comp. Neurol.* **196**, 695–708.

Erulkar, S. D. (1955). Tactile and auditory areas in the brain of the pigeon. *J. comp. Neurol.* **103**, 421–57.

Félix, B., Kesar, S., and Roesch, R. (1983). Central localisation of somatic evoked responses in Landes goose. *Exp. Brain Res.* **53**, 173–82.

Gentle, M. J. (1975). Gustatory behaviour of the chicken and other birds. In *Neural and endocrine aspects of behaviour in birds* (eds P. Wright, P. G. Caryl, and D. M. Vowles), pp. 305–18. Elsevier, Amsterdam.

Gottlieb, G. (1971). *Development of species identification in birds*. University Chicago Press, Chicago.

—— and Klopfer, P. H. (1962). The relation of developmental age to auditory and visual imprinting. *J. comp. physiol. Psychol.* **55**, 821–6.

Gray, J. A. and McNaughton, N. (1983). Comparison between the behavioural effects of septal and hippocampal lesions: a review. *Neurosci. Biobehav. Rev.* **7**, 119–88.

Griffith, J. S. (1966). A theory of the nature of memory. *Nature, Lond.* **211**, 1160–3.

Gross, C. G. (1973). Visual functions of inferotemporal cortex. In *Handbook of sensory physiology* (ed. R. Jung), VII, 3B, pp. 229–38. Springer, Berlin.

——, Bender, D. B., and Rocha-Miranda, C. E. (1974). Inferotemporal cortex: a single unit analysis. In *The neurosciences third study program* (eds F. O. Schmitt and F. G. Worden) pp. 229–38. MIT Press, Cambridge, Mass.

Guselnikov, V. I., Morenkov, E. D., and Khun, D. C. (1976). Responses and properties of receptive fields of neurons in the visual projection zone of the pigeon hyperstriatum. *Neirofiziologiya* **8**, 230–6.

Haywood, J., Hambley, J., and Rose, S. (1975). Effects of exposure to an imprinting stimulus on the activity of enzymes involved in acetylcholine metabolism in chick brain. *Brain Res.* **92**, 219–25.

Horn, G. and Wiesenfeld, Z. (1974). Attentive behaviour in the cat; electrophysiological studies. *Exp. Brain Res.*, **21**, 67–82.

——, McCabe, B. J., and Bateson, P. P. G. (1979). An autoradiographic study of the chick brain after imprinting. *Brain Res.* **168**, 361–73.

Hubel, D. H. (1982). Exploration of the primary visual cortex, 1955–78. *Nature, Lond.* **299**, 515–524.

Hutchison, J. B. (ed.) (1978). *Biological determinants of sexual behaviour*. John Wiley, Chichester.

Ingle, D. and Sprague, J. (eds) (1975). Sensorimotor function of the midbrain tectum. *Neurosci. Res. Program Bull.* **13**, 169–288.

Kaada, B. R. (1972). Stimulation and regional ablation of the amygdaloid complex with reference to functional representations. In *The neurobiology of the amygdala* (ed. B. E. Elftheriou), pp. 205–81. Plenum Press, New York.

Karten, H. J., Hodos, W., Nauta, W. J. H., and Revzin, A. M. (1973). Neural connections of the 'visual Wulst' of the avian telencephalon. Experimental studies in the pigeon (*Columba livia*) and owl (*Speotyto cunicularia*). *J. comp. Neurol.* **150,** 253–78.

Kornhuber, H. H. (1974). Cerebral cortex, cerebellum and basal ganglia: an introduction to their motor functions. In *The neurosciences third study program* (eds F. O. Schmitt and F. G. Worden), pp. 267–80. MIT Press, Cambridge, Mass.

Krayniak, P. F. and Siegel, A. (1978*a*). Efferent connections of the hippocampus and adjacent regions in the pigeon. *Brain Behav. Evol.* **15,** 372–88.

——, —— (1978*b*). Efferent connections of the septal area in the pigeon. *Brain Behav. Evol.* **15,** 389–404.

Kristensson, K. and Olsson, Y. (1971). Retrograde axonal transport of protein. *Brain Res.* **29,** 363–5.

LaVail, J. H. and LaVail, M. M. (1972). Retrograde axonal transport in the central nervous system. *Science* **176,** 1416–17.

Lewis, P. R. and Shute, C. C. D. (1967). The cholinergic limbic system: projections to hippocampal formation, medial cortex, nuclei of the ascending cholinergic reticular system and the subfornical organ and supra-optic crest. *Brain* **90,** 521–40.

Macadar, A. W., Rausch, L. J., Wenzel, B. M., and Hutchison, L. V. (1980). Electrophysiology of the olfactory pathway in the pigeon. *J. comp. Physiol.* **137,** 39–46.

McCabe, B. J., Horn, G., and McGrath, G. (1982). The distribution of acetylcholinesterase in the chick telencephalon. *J. Anat.* **134,** 600–1.

—— and Hunt, S. P. (1983). Peptides and biogenic amines in the telencephalon of the domestic chick. An immunocyto-chemical study. *Neurosci. Lett.* Suppl. 14, S242.

Macphail, E. M. (1967). Positive and negative reinforcement from intracranial stimulation in pigeons. *Nature, Lond.* **213,** 947–8.

Meibach, R. C. and Siegel, A. (1977). Efferent connections of the septal area in the rat: an analysis utilizing retrograde and anterograde transport methods. *Brain Res.* **119,** 1–20.

Milner, P. (1985). The hippocampus and learning: a theory. In *Forms of individually acquired behaviour and their central mechansisms* (ed. M. M. Khananashvili), Gagra Talks, Vol. 8 (in press).

Mitchell, J. A. and Hall, G. (1984). Paleostriatal lesions and instrumental learning in the pigeon. *Quart. J. exp. Psychol.* **36B,** 93–117.

Mogensen, J. and Divac, I. (1982). The prefrontal 'cortex' in the pigeon. Behavioral evidence. *Brain Behav. Evol.* **21,** 60–6.

Mora, R., Roll, E. T., and Burton, M. J. (1976). Modulation during learning of the responses of neurons in the hypothalamus to the sight of food. *Exp. Neurol.* **53,** 508–19.

Morenkov, E. D. and Khun, D. K. (1977). Neuronal responses to visual stimulation in the hyperstriatal area of the brain of the crow *Corvus corone. J. evol. Biochem. Physiol.* **13,** 51–5.

Mountcastle, V. B. (1976). The world around us: neural command functions for selective attention. *Neurosci. Res. Program Bull.* **14,** Supplement.

Mountjoy, C. Q., Rossor, M. N., Iversen, L. L., and Roth, M. (1984). Correlation of cortical cholinergic and GABA deficits with quantitative neuropathological findings in senile dementia. *Brain* **107,** 507–18.

Nauta, W. J. H. (1971). The problem of the frontal lobe: a reinterpretation. *J. Psychiat. Res.* **8,** 167–87.

Parker, D. M. and Delius, J. D. (1972). Visual evoked potentials in the forebrain region of the pigeon. *Exp. Brain Res.* **14,** 198–209.

Pearson, R. (1972). *The avian brain.* Academic Press, London.

Phillips, R. E. (1964). 'Wildness' in the Mallard duck: effects of brain lesions and stimulation on 'escape behavior'. *J. comp. Neurol.* **122**, 139–55.

—— and Youngren, O. M. (1971). Brain stimulation and species-typical behavior: activities evoked by electrical stimulation of the brains of chicken (*Gallus gallus*). *Anim. Behav.* **19**, 757–79.

Raisman, G. (1966). Neural connections of the hypothalamus. *Br. med. Bull.* **22**, 197–201.

Reiner, A., Brauth, S. E., and Karten, H. J. (1984). Evolution of the basal ganglia. *Trends Neurosci.* **7**, 320–5.

Rieke, G. K. (1980). Kainic acid lesions of pigeon paleostriatum: a model for study of movement disorders. *Physiol. Behav.* **24**, 683–7.

—— and Wenzel, B. M. (1978). Forebrain projections of the pigeon olfactory bulb. *J. Morph.* **158**, 41–56.

Ritchie, T. C. and Cohen, D. H. (1977). The avian tectofugal visual pathway: projections of its telencephalic target, the ectostriatal complex. *Proc. Soc. Neurosci.* **3**, 94.

Russell, J. R. and DeMeyer, W. (1961). The quantitative cortical origin of pyramidal axons of *Macaca rhesus*. *Neurology* **11**, 96–108.

Sahgal, A. (1984). Hippocampal lesions disrupt recognition memory in pigeons. *Behav. Brain Res.* **11**, 47–58.

Scheich, H. (1983). Two columnar systems in the auditory neostriatum of the chick: evidence from 2-deoxyglucose. *Exp. Brain Res.* **51**, 199–205.

——, Bonke, B. A., and Langner, G. (1979*a*). Functional organisation of some auditory nuclei in the Guinea fowl demonstrated by the 2-deoxyglucose technique. *Cell Tissue Res.* **204**, 17–27.

——, Langer, G., and Bonke, D. (1979*b*). Responsiveness of units in the auditory neostriatum of the Guinea fowl (*Numida meleagris*) to species-specific calls and synthetic stimuli. II: discrimination of iambus-like calls. *J. comp. Physiol.* A **132**, 257–76.

——, Bock, W., Bonke, D., Langner, G., and Maier, V. (1983). Acoustic communication in the Guinea fowl (*Numida meleagris*). In *Advances in neuroethology* (eds J.-P. Ewert, R. R. Capranica, and D. J. Ingle), pp. 731–82. Plenum Press, New York.

Shiosaka, S., Takatsuki, K., Inagaki, S., Sakanaka, M., Takagi, H., Senba, E., Matsuzaki, T. and Tohyama, M. (1981). Topographic atlas of somatostatin-containing neuron system in the avian brain in relation to catecholamine-containing neuron system. II. Mesencephalon, rhombencephalon, and spinal cord. *J. comp. Neurol.* **202**, 115–24.

Squire, L. R., Cohen, N. J., and Nadel, L. (1984). The medial temporal region and memory consolidation: a new hypothesis. In *Memory consolidation* (eds M. Weingartner and E. Parker), pp. 185–210. Erlbaum, Hillsdale, N.J.

Vinogradova, O. S. (1978). Discussion. In *Functions of the septohippocampal system*, Ciba Foundation Symposium, Vol. 58, pp. 343–9. Excerpta Medica, Amsterdam.

Vowles, D. M. and Beazley, L. D. (1974). The neural substrate of emotional behavior in birds. In *Birds, brain and behavior* (eds I. J. Goodman and M. W. Schein), pp. 221–58. Academic Press, New York.

Wallenberg, A. (1903). Der Ursprung des Tractus isthmo-striatus (oder bulbostriatus) der Taube. *Neurol. Zentbl.* **22**, 98–101.

Warrington, E. K. and Weiskrantz, L. (1982). Amnesia: a disconnection syndrome? *Neuropsychologia* **20**, 233–48.

Weiskrantz, L. (1982). Comparative aspects of studies of amnesia. *Phil. Trans. R. Soc.* B **298**, 97–109.

Whitehouse, P. J., Price, D. L., Struble, R. G., Clark, A. W., Coyle, J. T., and DeLong,

M. R. (1982). Alzheimer's disease and senile dementia: loss of neurons in the basal forebrain. *Science* **215**, 1237–9.

Wilson, P. (1980). The organisation of the visual hyperstriatum in the domestic chick. I. Topology and topography of the visual projection. *Brain Res.* **188**, 319–32.

Wurtz, R. H. and Goldberg, M. E. (1971). Superior colliculus cell responses related to eye movements in awake monkeys. *Science* **171**, 82–4.

——, ——, and Robinson, D. L. (1980). Behavioral modulation of visual response in the monkey: stimulus selection for attention and movement. *Progr. Psychobiol. physiol. Psychol.* **9**, 44–83.

Zeier, H. and Karten, H. J. (1971). The archistriatum of the pigeon: organization of afferent and efferent connections. *Brain Res.* **31**, 313–26.

# 12

# Towards a synthesis

In reviewing the work that has been described in earlier chapters it is useful to ask two questions. In what way has the work advanced the understanding of memory and in what way has it advanced the understanding of imprinting?

## 12.1 Memory

### 12.1.1 Neuropsychological and neuroethological perspectives

In considering memory it may be useful to start by referring again to James' view that the retention of a past event is '. . . a morphological feature, the presence of these "paths", namely, in the finest recesses of the brain's tissue' (James 1890, Vol. I, p. 655). In fact James had a good deal more to say about memory than this. He made the point that to identify an 'image' as corresponding to some past event, rather than to a current event, it is necessary to relate that image '. . . with a lot of contiguous associates' (James 1890, Vol. I, p. 650). He illustrates the point with a scheme in which he allows *n* to be a past event, *o* its context (for example, concomitant events), and *m* some fact which becomes the occasion for the recall of the past event. The 'nerve centres' active in the thought of *m, n,* and *o* are represented as M, N, and O respectively (Fig. 12.1). Event *n* will be recalled, together with the context in which it occurred, if M excites N and O. James'

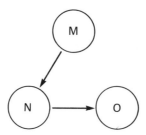

**Fig. 12.1.** William James' scheme '. . . to make the whole cause of memory plain'. Circled areas M, N, and O are 'nerve-centres'. N represents some past event, O represents the context in which the event occurred, and M represents a 'fact' which leads to the recall of the past event (James 1890, Vol. I, p. 655).

ideas about recall can easily be extended to recognition if *n* and *m* are one and the same object, differing only in that *n* was presented first.

James' model serves a useful purpose when considering the kinds of dissociation of memory that are brought about by lesions of the brain, particularly if the model is extended to include some of his ideas on habit. James visualized a habit as an act, often repeated, which is an expression of discharges in neural pathways which have been facilitated by use. Like Maudsley (1876) he considered that actions of habit required little or no intervention from the 'upper regions' of the brain. Certain kinds of associative learning tasks have some of the properties of a habit; and these properties may be accounted for as a strengthening of the links in those pathways excited by the stimulus and those controlling the response. An example of a possible pathway is shown in Fig. 6.6(b).

Changing the functional efficiency of the connections between the neurones activated by a particular stimulus and those controlling a particular response means that some neural representation of that stimulus has been formed which was not present prior to training. In this sense, there is in the nervous system some trace or simple memory of the stimulus. This memory is locked into the local circuit. Some simple forms of habituation may also be thought of in a similar way. Habituation is the process by which an unlearned response such as the orienting response to a novel stimulus or the withdrawal response of a part of the body to a cutaneous stimulus, gradually becomes extinguished as the stimulus is repeated. As the response wanes, transmission in the pathways linking the stimulus to the response becomes less efficient (see Section 1.1). Associative learning and habituation differ in many ways, but functionally they have at least one thing in common; training leads to a change in the capacity of the stimulus to influence behaviour. One aspect of associative learning is that a particular stimulus–response relationship becomes strengthened; one aspect of habituation is that the corresponding relationship becomes weakened. Certain forms of associative learning and habituation can occur when only parts of the central nervous system are intact (see Horn 1970). Just how much of the nervous system has to be intact is not clear, though the minimum requirements are obvious: enough of the sensory apparatus as is necessary for the discrimination to be possible, as much of the motor system as is required to control and execute the response, and in the case of some forms of associative learning as much as is required for the incentive system to operate (Sections 6.4, 9.1, and 9.3).

Simple habits may continue to be acquired by chicks with lesions of the IMHV, and by humans and monkeys with lesions of the medial temoral lobe or of the diencephalon. In the case of primates much thought has been given to seeking continuities between the amnesias found in humans and monkeys (see, for example, Weiskrantz 1966, 1982; Iversen 1976, 1983). One approach has been to distinguish between (*i*) the memory necessary to perform skills, or procedures, and (*ii*) the memory necessary to retain the outcomes of engaging those skills (see Ryle 1949) as well as for storing information which is not skill-like in character, as in object recognition. The former memory has been referred to as 'procedural', the latter as 'declarative' (Cohen and Squire 1980; Zola-Morgan and Squire 1984). Procedural memory is largely spared in amnesia whereas declarative memory is impaired. The expression 'procedural memory', faults and all (Weiskrantz 1985), lends itself to easy transfer from human to animal studies whereas declarative memory, with its implication of making explicit statements, does not. Perhaps the simpler terms 'reflexive' and 'reflective' (L. Weiskrantz, personal communication) more effectively capture the essential differences between the two kinds of memory dissociated by lesions of the medial temporal lobe, although the term 'reflective' has connotations which may not find universal acceptance amongst those who study animal learning.

In their assessment of human amnesia Warrington and Weiskrantz (1982) proposed that the amnesia appears when there is a disconnection between two memory systems. In one of these, the mediational memory system, memoranda can be '. . . manipulated, inter-related and stored in a continually changing record of events. It may be by recourse to this mediational memory system that normal subjects recall or recognize events as having the attribute of "memories" . . .' (Warrington and Weiskrantz 1982, p. 242). This system, in which items rich in contextual associates are stored, and which is impaired in the human amnesic syndrome, has some of the properties of the N and O systems postulated by James (Fig. 12.1). The second memory system stores relatively invariant facts about the world and thus to provide a stable knowledge base. This system is known as semantic memory (Tulving 1972). This memory is largely unimpaired in the human amnesic syndrome. It is possible that some facts about the world are acquired through associative learning (for example, 'Stop at a red traffic light'). The neural basis of such memories need be little different from those postulated to underlie habit memory or the memory for certain skills (see p. 261). However, the term 'semantic', with its implicit reference to words or symbols, whilst appropriate for describing some aspects of human memory, is not self-evidently appropriate for describing memory in animals. Until a satisfactory term is invented which is suitable for human and animal studies, perhaps the second memory system should be referred to as non-mediational memory. Mediational memory is defined both by its operations (Warrington and Weiskrantz 1982, p. 242) and by its vulnerability to certain brain lesions, especially damage to the medial temporal lobe, in humans and macaque monkeys; non-mediational memory functions are those which are invulnerable to such lesions.

The (non-mediational) memory for a habit may have its neuronal basis in the strengthening of a stimulus–response link, as suggested above. However, the outcome of a habit may be used, or serve to mediate in the acquisition of a new habit. When this happens it is also necessary to infer the formation of some internal representation of the outcome of the first habit in order to account for the use to which this outcome is put in other learning situations (see Dickinson 1980; Mackintosh 1985). Both non-mediational and mediational forms of memory may also be established during the course of habituation. Consider for example habituation of the abdominal skin reflex in humans. The abdominal muscles of a human subject contract if a light cutaneous stimulus is applied to the overlying skin. This response gradually wanes if the stimulus is repeatedly applied (Hagbarth and Kugelberg (1958). The memory not to respond may be represented by a block in transmission between the sensory neurones responding to the cutaneous stimulus and the muscles controlling the response (Section 1.1). Such a memory could appropriately be designated non-mediational. The subject may, however, remember that the stimulus had been applied repeatedly, and that the stimulus had gradually ceased to evoke a contraction of the abdominal muscles. Such a memory might appropriately be regarded as 'mediational'. Evidence that procedures which lead to habituation in animals other than humans, also generate two different neural representations or memories has been referred to earlier (Section 1.1.5; see also Mackintosh 1985).

The acquisition of some skills by macaque monkeys is unaffected by sectioning the fornix, whereas the acquisition of other skills is impaired by this lesion (Gaffan *et al.* 1984). The tasks that are unaffected by the lesion are relatively simple. In one such task, object A was presented with a reward and then object B was presented without a reward. The two objects were then presented together. In one experiment the monkey had to push the previously rewarded object (A) to one side to obtain half a peanut. Monkeys with fornix lesions performed just as well as controls. Tasks which were impaired by the fornix lesion involved responses that were the reverse of the animal's 'spontaneous tendency' (pp. 123–4). For example, monkeys were trained in the way described above, but were required to push aside the previously unrewarded object B. The successful performance of this task may involve the re-ordering, or 'manipulation' of responses and so require access to the postulated mediational memory system. Access may be impaired following a lesion of the fornix.

Warrington and Weiskrantz (1982) suggested that some crucial components of the mediational memory system are subserved by structures in the frontal lobes. They suggested that the amnesic syndrome occurs after severing the connections which link this memory system to semantic (non-mediational) memory systems; that is, whilst some skills may still be acquired after the lesion has been placed, the outcome of these skills cannot be stored in mediational memory. If Warrington and Weiskrantz's ideas are correct, then damage to the frontal lobes should be associated with a loss of memory. Indeed, the amnesic syndrome has been reported to follow damage to some connections of the frontal lobe (Mabille and Pitres 1913). Furthermore, memory deficits are not infrequently found in patients suffering from tumours of the frontal lobes (Hécaen 1964). There is, however, some controversy as to whether the deficits are specific to the frontal lobe damage, or are secondary to a more global interference with brain function occasioned, for example, by a rise in intracranial pressure (Walsh 1978; De Renzi 1982).

Some light may be thrown on this controversy by certain other observations. Aggleton and Mishkin (1983*b*) studied the memory impairments which followed lesions placed in the diencephalon of macaque monkeys. One of the lesions damaged a major part of the dorsomedial thalamic nucleus; the other lesion damaged mainly the anteroventral thalamic nucleus. Both lesions were associated with a moderate impairment of object recognition memory. Combined damage to both regions was necessary to produce a full-blown amnesia (Aggleton and Mishkin 1983*a*). In primates the prefrontal cortex is the major target of the dorsomedial thalamic nucleus whereas the cingulate cortex is the major target for the anteroventral thalamic nucleus (Section 11.3). If damage to the target cortical areas of these thalamic nuclei results in amnesia, Aggleton and Mishkin's results suggest that both areas of cortex must be damaged to achieve a maximum effect. A lesion in only one would, their results imply, not be associated with a full amnesia. It is therefore of interest that Whitty and Lishman (1966), in their review of brain lesions and memory in human patients, remarked that losses of memory had been reported to follow removal of the anterior part of the cingulate cortex. The losses were less consistent and less clearly defined than those of a full-blown amnesia, precisely the result that would be predicted on the basis of Aggleton and Mishkin's observations.

These considerations raise the possibility that mediational memory may be subserved by the cortical targets of the medial temporal lobe, channelled there in part through the medial thalamic nuclei. The major cortical targets are the cingulate and prefrontal areas. These areas are quite separate in primates (Fig. 11.12), but not in all mammals. In the rat, for example, the cortical projection of the two thalamic nuclei are closely interwoven (Divac *et al.* 1978). These findings suggest that the functions of the two areas are also closely interwoven. Although in primates the regions are separate, they are extensively interconnected.

Attention was drawn in Section 11.3 to the similarities between the connections of the IMHV in the chick and the connections of the prefrontal and cingulate areas of cortex in primates. No doubt it appears strange to compare the structures and functions of neural circuits in animals so different in kind as birds and primates. However, the experimental investigation of cerebral function in object recognition memory and in visual discrimination learning in non-human primates is a surprisingly recent development. So much so that in the first paragraph of the discussion section of their paper, Aggleton and Mishkin (1983*a*) wrote, 'The present experiments demonstrate, for the first time in the monkey, that a limited lesion of the medial thalamic region (MT) may produce a striking impairment in a test of visual object recognition and thus reproduce one of the core symptoms of "diencephalic amnesia".' This region of the thalamus projects to the prefrontal and cingulate areas of cortex. And damage to the IMHV, which has some anatomical similarities to these areas, also impairs visual object recognition without impairing some forms of associative learning (Chapter 6).

The evidence available suggests that the left IMHV may itself be a site for storing information. The changes in neural organization that have been found there after training have been described in Chapter 10 and will not be discussed here. The evidence does not exclude the possiblity that other regions, besides the IMHV, are involved in memory (see below); but the results suggest that some aspects of the storage necessary for recognition memory are subserved by a local area of brain. The IMHV appears to correspond to those regions of the primate brain which are part of the system involved in, and have been suggested to subserve mediational memory. The further study of the IMHV, and perhaps of the hyperstriatum ventrale in general, may thus throw more light on the way neural representations of events are formed, and on the way in which stored information is processed in a mediational memory system.

In chicks, the left IMHV system is not the only one to be involved in recognition memory. Another system, referred to as S′, is almost certainly involved as well (Chapter 7 and Section 8.5). It is inherently implausible that the two systems have the same function in memory; but there is as yet no experimental evidence to indicate what differences, if any, there are between them. Both the memory necessary for recognition and the memory necessary for storing the outcome of certain behavioural responses are impaired by lesions of the medial temporal lobe in humans and macaque monkeys (Zola-Morgan and Squire 1984). But the two kinds of memory may require quite different kinds of processing. Even object recognition memory may not involve a single process. Information about an object may be stored along with many or few contiguous associates (James 1890—see also Fig. 12.1; Huppert and Piercy 1978; Brown *et al.* 1982, 1983) and be updated and modified by subsequent experiences, subjected that is to many mediational interventions. Direct experimental evidence of diversity within mediational memory is lacking, possibly because neuropsychological insights into the different kinds of memory have only relatively recently been gained. Perhaps the further study of the left IMHV and S′ may help to refine these insights by bringing together the methods of neuropsychology and neuroethology.

## 12.1.2 Neurophysiological aspects

When information about an event is stored it it likely that the event is tagged in some way with a time label. This need was intuitively obvious to

James (1890), who suggested that the context in which an event occurred included the temporal context. Human amnesic subjects are severely impaired in the performance of tasks that depend on the temporal ordering of their experiences (Huppert and Piercy 1978). Time-tagging almost certainly occurs in many other animals as well. For example, if an animal forages for a renewable food source, such as nectar (see, for example, Kamil 1978) it is important not only to keep track of the occurrence of a past visit, but also the time of that visit. In this way the second visit may be timed to coincide with the renewed availability of food. What might be the physiological basis of the time-labelling? Are there neurones in the central nervous system which have clock-like properties?

Strumwasser (1973) has recorded from neurones in the isolated parieto-visceral ganglion of *Aplysia*. The isolated ganglion may be maintained in culture for several weeks. Many cells exhibit rhythmic discharges of spikes. The rhythms have a periodicity of approximately 24 hours, though the period varies from cell to cell (see Jacklet 1981). Neurones having rather precise times of discharge have also been recorded in the central nervous system of the rabbit (Vinogradova 1970) and cat (Horn 1962). For example, when recording from the visual cortex of unanaesthetized, unrestrained cats a small number of cells were encountered which discharged slowly with remarkable regularity. The distribution of the interval between successive impulses for each of five cells is shown in Fig. 12.2. These cells were all recorded from one animal. Each cell discharged a single spike whenever it fired, and each spike was followed by a long silent period lasting many seconds. The intervals between spikes were, for a given cell, distributed over a very narrow range. Occasionally prolonged periods of silence occurred between action potentials, but always these gaps were, to a close approximation, a multiple of the most commonly occurring interval (see Fig. 12.2, cells 2, 3, and 4). The rate of discharge of the regularly firing cells was quite unaffected by visual or other sensory stimuli. These neurones contrasted with others, simultaneously recorded, which were affected by one of these stimuli.

The mechanism of activation of the regularly firing cells was considered in the light of two simple hypotheses. On the one hand the cells might be part of a very long chain of cells showing reverberating activity. However, with the exception of cells 2 and 5 (Fig. 12.2), which came from the right and left hemispheres respectively, the mean value of the intervals of each cell differed significantly from that of all the other cells ($P<0.001$). Since all these units came from the same animal, it is necessary to suppose that there were at least four such chains showing reverberating activity, each firing independantly of the other. On the other hand, the pattern of discharge could have been an expression of some synapse-independent chemical excitatory process operating within each of the five cells. Strumwasser (1973) indeed demonstrated in *Aplysia* that the rhythmical discharges of the

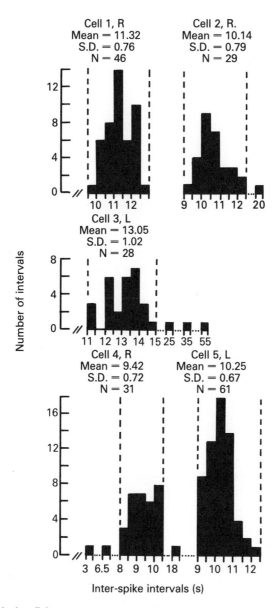

**Fig. 12.2.** Regularly firing neurones recorded from the visual cortex of an unanesthetized, unrestrained cat. The histograms represent the distribution of intervals between successive action potentials. The hemisphere in which each cell was found is indicated by L (left) and R (right). The mean and standard deviation (S.D.) given in seconds for each cell, refer to the intervals (*N* in number) enclosed by the broken lines. (After Horn 1962.)

recorded neurones continued when synaptic inputs to the cell were blocked with a pharmacological agent.

The evidence that regularly firing neurones exist gives no clue as to how they may be used to label a neuronal representation of an event, if indeed they are put to such use. This problem is clearly one that must be addressed in any physiological attempt to analyse the mechanisms of information storage in the brain.

The time of occurrence of an event is not the only item of contextual information that is stored with the event. It is also important to commit to memory the presence or absence of other objects or events, their spatial distribution, the sequence in which the events occurred, and so on. If there are neurones in the central nervous system whose responses depend on acquired contextual information, the hippocampal region within the medial temporal lobe is an obvious place to look for them. In experiments designed to search for and to investigate neurones of this kind rhesus monkeys were presented first with one stimulus, S1, and then with another, S2 (Brown and Horn 1978; Brown 1982). The stimuli were large or small circles or squares. The monkeys worked for a reward of fruit juice. They were trained to press a panel on the right if S1 and S2 were both of the same shape and size. They were trained to press a panel on the left if S1 and S2 were the same shape, but differed in size. For example if, in a given trial, S1 and S2 were both large squares, the correct response was to press the right panel; but if S1 was a small square and S2 a large square the correct response was to press the left panel (Fig. 12.3). During training and recording sessions the animal sat in a chair facing the panels and an oscilloscope screen on which the stimuli were displayed. For some units it was found that the response to a given stimulus differed according to whether it was presented as S1 or S2. For example the firing rate of one unit increased markedly when S2 was a small square if S1 had been a large square (Fig. 12.3(d)). The increase was significantly less if S1 had also been a small square (Fig. 12.3(c)) or if both S1 and S2 were large squares (Fig. 12.3(a). There was no marked increase in firing rate for any of the other possible stimulus configurations (Fig. 12.3(b), (e)–(h)). Hence for this unit the response was not determined solely by the immediately applied stimulus (S2) nor by the direction of movement of the monkey (right or left) but was dependent on the context in which the small square was presented.

When context is held constant, and an object is salient, that object may be recognized as familiar when it is presented a second time. Rolls and his colleagues (1982) have described units which may play a part in this recognition process. Unit activity was recorded from the anterior border of the thalmus of unanaesthetized, behaving rhesus monkeys. In these experiments an object was shown twice to a monkey. When first presented, the object was novel. Under these circumstances the monkey had to withhold licking a tube positioned immediately in front of his mouth to avoid obtain-

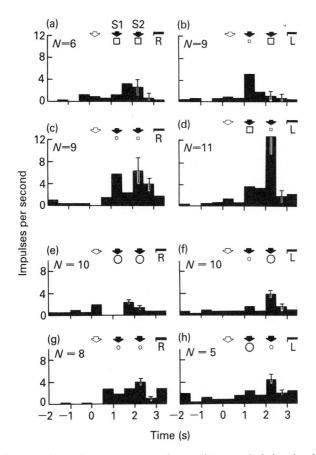

**Fig. 12.3.** Context-dependent response of a unit recorded in the hippocampal region of a rhesus monkey. Histograms of activity of the unit are summed for correct trials. Mean firing rates are shown. Error bars are standard errors. Eight different conditions are shown for the second stimulus (S2): stimulus large or small, circle or square. Response, press right (R) or press left (L) follows S2. *Open arrow,* cueing flash (0–0.5 s duration). *Closed arrows,* first stimulus S1 (1.0–1.5 s) and second stimulus S2 (2.0–2.5 s). For a correct trial, the press was made 3–6 s after the onset of the cueing flash. $N$ is the number of trials contributing data to the histogram. The neuronal activity associated with the presentation of S2 was compared between the eight conditions. The activity varied significantly between these conditions ($P < 0.001$). Note the marked increase in activity when S2 was a small square followed by a left press (histogram (d)). This activity was significantly ($P < 0.05$) higher than when S2 was a small square followed by a right press, and very significantly ($P < 0.01$) higher than when S2 was any other stimulus followed by either a left or right press. Thus, this unit's response was dependent not merely on the currently applied stimulus (S2=small square), nor solely on the motor response (left press), but on the context within which the stimulus was presented. (After Brown 1982.)

ing aversive saline. After the object had first been presented it was followed by the presentation of other visual stimuli. If the object was presented a second time, and in this sense was familiar, the monkey could lick the tube to obtain a reward of fruit juice. A population of neurones was found which responded to stimuli only when they were familiar. Furthermore, in a different, visual discrimination, task a number of these neurones was found to respond both to a familiar rewarded stimulus and to a familiar aversive stimulus. This result showed that, in a reward association task, the neurones responded on the basis of familiarity. The result is consistent with the work described in Section 12.1.1, of a dissociation of recognition and associative memory.

Clearly these are early days in the physiological investigation of neuronal activity in memory. But the microelectrode will continue to be a valuable tool in analysing this activity, provided that the right questions are asked of the animal and of the neurones whose responses are being investigated.

## 12.2 Imprinting

### *12.2.1 Sensitive periods in imprinting and in the development of the visual cortex.*

There are clear similarities between the procedures which in chicks lead to the development of social preferences and which in kittens influence the development of the visual cortex (Horn *et al.* 1973; Bischoff 1983). In each case the young animal is exposed to a stimulus during a sensitive period, and as a consequence of that exposure, changes can be detected in the nervous system and in behaviour. Since there are similarities in the procedures, and in the timing of these procedures, are there similarities in their consequences?

Consider first the effects on neurones of exposing the young animals to a stimulus in the sensitive period. In kittens, unilateral occlusion of an eye during the early weeks of life results in a functional disconnection of that eye from cells in the visual cortex (Wiesel and Hubel 1963; Hubel and Wiesel 1970). This effect is not observed in adult cats. An implication of the experiments of Wiesel and Hubel is that for a period, which reaches a peak toward the end of the first month of life, neurones in the visual cortex of kittens are highly plastic (see Section 9.1). During this period, the response properties of neurones in the kitten visual cortex can be manipulated, often in dramatic ways, by manipulating the visual input. Hirsch and Spinelli (1970) used specifically designed goggles, which were worn by young kittens, to restrict the visual input to lines of specific orientation. They found that when the visual input to one eye comprised only vertical lines, cells in the visual cortex could be activated from that eye only by vertical lines. Horizontal lines presented to that eye failed to excite cells in the visual cortex, though this stimulus would be expected to drive many cells in the cortex of a kitten reared in a 'normal' environment (Hubel and Wiesel 1962). The orientation preferences of cells in the visual cortex were also skewed towards the vertical in kittens which had been exposed to a visually restricted environment composed of vertical stripes (Blakemore and Cooper 1970).

It has been suggested that the visual Wulst of the avian brain is comparable to the mammalian visual cortex (Nauta and Karten 1970). This view has received some support from a study of the response properties of neurones in the visual Wulst of the barn owl (Pettigrew and Konishi 1976*a*). Neurones in this region have receptive fields which are similar in many ways to those of the adult cat; and, as in the cat, many neurones may be activated through both eyes. Such binocularly-activated neurones are lacking in the owl Wulst, as they are in the kitten visual cortex, following unilateral eye occlusion early in life (Pettigrew and Konishi 1976*b*).

Are the receptive fields of neurones in the visual Wulst of chicks modified by exposing them to an imprinting stimulus in the way that the receptive fields of neurones in the kitten visual cortex are modified by restricting the visual environment? Unfortunately there is no clear answer to this question. Wilson (1980) has described the receptive field properties of neurones in the visual Wulst of chicks between 5 and 6 weeks old. Milne, McCabe, and Horn (unpublished observations) have also recorded from this region and found units which responded to diffuse retinal illumination (see also Payne *et al.* 1984). But units with localized receptive fields were encountered only occassionally before the third week of life, even in visually experienced chicks which had been exposed to an artificial imprinting object. The apparent absence of an effect of imprinting on the receptive field properties of Wulst neurones must be treated with caution. It is possible that the anaesthetics used in these experiments depressed the responses of Wulst neurones in young chicks, but did not do so in older birds. However, units with localized receptive fields were recorded in the optic tectum of 2-day-old chicks, so if the anaesthetic does depress neuronal responsiveness, it does so selectively.

In the IMHV, the structure of neurones is modified by training (Section 10.2) and so is the spontaneous activity of units in the region even though this activity is recorded in anaesthetized chicks (Section 10.1). Little success has so far been achieved in detecting in the IMHV units with localized receptive fields (see pp. 236–7). There is as yet no evidence, therefore, that the dramatic changes in the organization of receptive fields which occur in the visual cortex of kittens as the result of rearing them in a visually restricted environment also occur in the visual Wulst or in the IMHV of chicks as a result of imprinting.

At the level of behaviour, a chick which has been trained on one object prefers it to other objects; that is, the chick's social behaviour changes. In contrast, no evidence has yet been given that kittens, after having been exposed to a visually restricted environment composed of, say, vertical stripes, form a social attachment to that environment. The general visual abilities of chicks do not appear to be impaired after imprinting, since the chicks avoid novel objects and peck accurately. Kittens, however, were originally thought to be virtually blind for contours perpendicular to the orientation that they had experienced (Blakemore and Cooper 1970). More recent reports have failed to confirm such a severe impairment of vision (Freeman and Marg 1975), though some aspects of visual performance are affected by rearing kittens in a visually restricted environment (Blasdel *et al.* 1977; Kratz and Lehmkuhle 1983). Evidently, then, the behavioural consequences of the exposure procedures are different in chicks and kittens.

The effects of monocular occlusion on neurones in the kitten visual cortex may be reversed by opening the previously occluded eye, and closing the previously exposed eye. The procedure does not reverse ocular dominance if it is conducted outside the sensitive period (Blakemore and van Sluyters 1974). This result contrasts with the continuing ability of chicks to learn through exposure after the sensitive period for imprinting is over (see below).

The above results, when considered together, do not exclude the possibility that the neuronal plasticity which underlies imprinting in chicks is similar to that found in the visual cortex of young kittens. However, there are no grounds for assuming that all forms of plasticity serve a similar functional role in the economy of the nervous system. The point can be made explicit by considering the developing central nervous system. The system is never more plastic than during embryogenesis; but it would be more than a little naive to suppose that the magnitude of the plastic changes provides a measure of the amount that is being leraned by the embryo. Whilst learning and memory are testaments of the plasticity of nervous tissue, not all forms of plasticity are testaments of learning and memory.

When imprinted chicks avoid novel objects the opportunity to learn about these objects is reduced. Imprinting may thus come to an end as a result of its own action, a view that was suggested some years ago by Sluckin and Salzen (1961). However, the avoidance response of chicks to novel objects can be weakened, or habituated, by continually exposing the chicks to these objects. Under these conditions the initial imprinting preference can be reversed. Thus Salzen and Meyer (1968) exposed one group of chicks individually to a blue ball during the first 3 days after hatching. The blue ball was suspended in the chick's cage. When given a simultaneous choice test the chicks preferred the familiar blue ball to a green ball. Each chick was then returned to its cage, but the blue ball had been replaced by a green ball. After 3 days of exposure to the green ball the chicks preferred it to the original blue ball. The chicks were then returned for 3 days to their cages from which both objects had been removed. When tested at the end of this time the chicks preferred the second object; that is, not only was the original preference reversed, but the reversal persisted. Had the chicks forgotten the original object? Evidently not, because the original preference could be restored under appropriate testing conditions (Cherfas and Scott 1981). This result, together with the finding that the preference for the second object persisted for some days, suggests that neural representations of both objects were present and that they were stable, at least for the period of the experiments. The reversal of a preference for an object does not therefore imply the erasure of the memory for that object. These experiments demonstrate that chicks can learn about objects by being exposed to them, and imply that the system subserving recognition memory has not lost its capacity to store information, after the sensitive period had passed. Neuronal circuits within the store which represents a particular object may not of course retain their full plasticity. If they were to do so, presumably memory for that object would be lost or degraded. But these circuits may retain some plasticity. In doing so, newly acquired information may become linked to and be used to update information already in store.

Since chicks continue to learn outside the sensitive period, what is it about the period that is 'sensitive'? May the sensitive period relate to the link formed between the neural representation of the mother, and the system controlling approach behaviour, the link rapidly reaching its full capacity for being strenghened? As a result of the link being strengthened in this way the chick would quickly, and with increasing vigour approach its mother. The chick will also avoid novel objects (see Fig. 7.11(c)). By being near to its mother, the chick can gradually learn about her and about other features of the world, secure from the attacks of predators and of hostile conspecifics. An additional advantage relates to Hinde's (1962, 1982) suggestion that the need for learning processes in filial imprinting arises because of the immature recognition mechanisms of the young bird. He points out that while adult animals can respond similarly to a given object no matter, within limits, what its distance or their angle of regard, the ability to do so depends on experience. Since a particular parent bird would present varied stimulus configurations to a young chick, which presumably does not have these 'perceptual constancies', any recognition mechanism that did not depend on experience would have to be very complex. The occurrence of the sensitive period would confer the advantage of ensuring that the chick is attached to a safe base whilst these perceptual constancies develop. Later, as the chick becomes familiar with the world, the attachment to its mother weakens. This weakening could be achieved, at the physiological level, by a process of habituation, perhaps synaptic depression, or even by the regresssion of synapses in the link between the approach system and the neural representation of the maternal object (see Fig. 7.11(b)). Long, close contact with this object, whether it is the natural mother or an artificial stimulus, may, through incremental synaptic changes (see Section 10.2), ensure that this representation is firmly established in the young bird's nervous system. It is also possible that the strength of this representation is the greater because the response of an uninscribed store to the first input may be greater than to subsequent inputs. In such ways may the animal's earliest experience contribute to the shaping of its later behaviour, including its choice of mate (see Lorenz 1935, 1937; Bambridge 1962; Guiton 1962, 1966; Schutz 1965; Salzen 1966; Bateson 1980).

## 12.2.2 Predispositions and acquisitions

Many animals have dispositions to respond, or to respond more strongly to some things than to others, and young precocial birds are no exception (see Seligman and Hager 1972; Hinde and Stevenson-Hinde 1973). The neural bases of these dispositions have been little studied. The differential effects of lesions to the IMHV on chicks' preferences for the rotating red box and the jungle-fowl provided a starting point for such a study, though even in this case the study is far from complete.

Using the sensitive simultaneous choice test, a preference for the jungle-fowl over the red box was found to develop quickly if the chicks were simply exposed to a complex visual pattern. A preference for the jungle-fowl also developed, but rather more slowly after chicks had been exposed for a few hours to diffuse overhead light, or allowed an opportunity to move about relatively freely in the dark for a similar length of time. The preferences did not appear in the absence of such experiences. The neural system underlying this emerging preference behaved *as if* it required to be validated in some way in order to become functional. Adequate locomotor activity or simple visual experience or both, serve to initiate the validation process (Section 8.2.2). The IMHV is not necessary for this emerging preference which, it was suggested, is supported by a special-purpose system of neurones whose activity may be influenced by testosterone (Sections 8.4.1 and 9.6). In this context, Lorenz's (1953, 1937) view of imprinting is of particular interest. He considered imprinting to be a '. . . very peculiar acquiring process . . .' which guides reactions '. . . directed to fellow-members of the species in general, but not to the object as an individual . . .'. This behaviour may be controlled by the postulated special-purpose system, although it should be emphasized that, in the domestic chick, the special-purpose system is not so finely tuned as to be a species-recognition system (Section 8.3). Lorenz's view is perhaps too restrictive to be a definition of imprinting, for the domestic chick at least, since there are continuities between predispositions and the consequences of experience. In the natural situation young chicks, once exposed to the visual complexity of their natural environment, would quickly develop a preference for certain features or stimulus elements of their conspecifics. Learning processes may then restrict this preference to particular individual animals. Thus the initial preference of the chick would guide it to an appropriate object, most probably its natural mother. Learning processes would then be engaged which would enable the chick to recognize her. Interactions between predispositions and learning processes also occur in song learning in certain birds (see Marler 1985), though these interactions are very common indeed (see Hinde 1982).

What neural mechanisms might have the properties of the postulated special-purpose system? It has recently become clear that some neurones in the temporal cortex of monkeys have quite remarkable response properties (Bruce *et al.* 1981; Perrett *et al.* 1982). Perrett and his collaborators found that about 10 per cent of cells in a restricted part of the temporal cortex of rhesus monkeys respond strongly to faces. The responses, to human or rhesus monkey faces, real or projected, were between two and ten times as large as those to grating, simple geometrical stimuli, or complex three-dimensional objects. The magnitude of the response of some cells was relatively unaffected by inverting the face of by changing its colour or size. By masking out or presenting parts of the face in isolation it was found that different cells responded to different features or subsets or features. Futhermore, for a number of cells, responses to the normal organization of cut-out or line-drawn facial features were larger than to jumbled control drawings. Perret and his colleagues considered that the neurones are part of a system specialized to code for faces or features present in faces. There was no evidence, however, that these neurones code for the faces of particular individuals. The neurones do not appear to be widely distributed in the brain. Nothing is known of the developmental history of these cells, nor is it known whether or not they are present in the temporal lobe of newborn monkeys. It is, however, of interest that, as judged by certain physiological criteria, young, human neonates prefer a schematic human face to a 'scrambled' face (Goren *et al.* 1975) and are more attentive to a real, motionless face than to schematic or scrambled faces (Stechler 1965).

It is attractive to suppose that the putative system of neurones outside the IMHV which supports the emerging preference for the jungle-fowl has properties akin to the 'face neurones' in the primate brain. In the chick, such a system would not be expected to be functional at the time of hatching (Section 8.2.2). The synapses within the system would, however, be expected to become functional, and the system validated, soon after the chicks begin to run about, the effect possibly begin mediated by testosterone (see Section 10.3.7). Neurones in this feature-detecting system might then be activated by particular elements of a complex visual environment, and even more effectively activated by the natural mother who may posses a near-optimum combination of the required trigger features. It has yet to be determined experimentally what these features are, though they need consist of little more than the eye and face together, or perhaps two circles and a few lines arranged in a particular configuration. Once the system has been validated, it may control approach behaviour in ways that have yet to be investigated experimentally.

The call for further experimental investigations is, perhaps, the right note on which to end. The note has been sounded repeatedly throughout this work and has served to emphasize the experimental and the exploratory nature of the enterprise. Opening the box containing the brain had consequences that were surprising. Hemispheric asymmetry, multiple stores, varied physiological constraints, and many other findings provided, and continue to provide, puzzles to be solved. Opening the box gave access to the cerebral machinery which subserves the acquisition, storage, and retrieval of information, pattern recognition, approach and avoidance activity, attention, and motivation. The study of how these and other processes interact to produce that remarkable and seemingly simple pattern of behaviour which testifies that filial imprinting has occurred, is only at its beginning.

## 12.3 Summary

Material presented in earlier chapters is reviewed. Consideration is given to the memory defects which follow lesions of the brain, particularly the medial temporal lobe and parts of the diencephalon of human subjects and macaque monkeys. The defects are compared with those of chicks with lesions of the IMHV. The memory necessary to perform skills is distinguished from recognition memory. The importance of context is emphasized and the properties of neurones whose responses are context-dependent and of neurones which respond to familiar objects are described. The relationship between imprinting and plasticity in the visual cortex of kittens is explored. The possible neural mechanisms underlying predispositions, and the way in which predispositions may interact with learning processes are considered in the context of species and individual recognition.

## References

Aggleton, J. P. and Mishkin, M. (1983*a*). Visual recognition impairment following medial thalamic lesions in monkeys. *Neuropsychologia* **21**, 189–97.
——, —— (1983*b*). Memory impairments following restricted medial thalmic lesions in monkeys. *Exp. Brain Res.* **52**, 199–209.
Bambridge, R. (1962). Early experience and sexual behavior in the domestic chicken. *Science* **136**, 259–60.
Bateson, P. (1980). Optimal outbreeding and the development of sexual preferences in Japanese Quail. *Z. Tierpsychol* **53**, 231–44.
Bischoff, H.-J. (1983). Imprinting and corticol plasticity: a comparative review. *Neurosci. Biobehav. Rev.* **7**, 213–25.
Blakemore, C., and Cooper, G. F. (1970). Development of the brain depends on the visual environment. *Nature, Lond.* **228**, 477–8.
—— and van Sluyters, R. C. (1974). Reversal of the physiological effects of monocu-

lar deprivation in kittens: further evidence for a sensitive period. *J. Physiol. Lond.* **237**, 195–216.

Blasdel, G. G., Mitchell, D. E., Muir, D. W., and Pettigrew, J. D. (1977). A physiological and behavioural study in cats of the effect of early visual experience with contours of a single orientation. *J. Physiol., Lond.* **265**, 615–36.

Brown, J., Lewis, V., Brown, M., Horn, G., and Bowes, J. B. (1982). A comparison between transient amnesias induced by two drugs (diazepam and lorazepam) and amnesia of organic origin. *Neuropsycholgia* **20**, 55–70.

——, Brown, M. W., and Bowes, J. B. (1983). Effects of lorazepam on rate of forgetting, on retrieval from semantic memory and on manual dexterity. *Neuropsychologia* **21**, 501–12.

Brown, M. W. (1982). The effect of context on the response of single units recorded from the hippocampal region of behaviourally trained monkeys. In *Neuronal plasticity and memory function* (eds. C. Ajmone Marson and H. Matthies), pp. 557–73. Raven Press, New York.

—— and Horn, G. (1978). Context dependent neuronal responses recorded from hippocampal region of trained monkeys. *J. Physiol., Lond.* **282**, 15–16P.

Bruce, C., Desimone, R., and Gross, C. G. (1981). Visual properties of neurons in a polysensory area in superior temporal sulcus of the macaque. *J. Neurophysiol.* **46**, 369–84.

Cherfas, J. J., and Scott, A. (1981). Impermanent reversal of filial imprinting. *Anim. Behav.* **29**, 301.

Cohen, N. J. and Squire, L. R. (1980). Preserved learning and retention of pattern analyzing skill in amnesia: dissociation of knowing how and knowing that. *Science* **210**, 207–9.

De Renzi, E. (1982). Memory disorders following focal neocortical damage. *Phil. Trans. R. Soc. B* **298**, 73–83.

Dickinson, A. (1980). *Contemporary animal learning theory.* Cambridge University Press, Cambridge.

Divac, I., Kosmal, A., Björklund, A., and Lindvall, O. (1978). Subcortical projections to the prefrontal cortex in the rat as revealed by the horseradish peroxidase technique. *Neuroscience* **3**, 785–96.

Freeman, D. N. and Marg, E. (1975). Visual acuity development coincides with the sensitive period in kittens. *Nature, Lond.* **254**, 614–15.

Gaffan, D., Saunders, R. C., Gaffan, E. A., Harrison, S., Shields, C., and Owen, M. J. (1984). Effects of fornix transections upon associative memory in monkeys: role of the hippocampus in learned action. *Quart. J. exp. Psychol.* **36B**, 173–221.

Goren, C. C., Sarty, M., and Wu, P. Y. K. (1975). Visual following and pattern discrimination of face-like stimuli by newborn infants. *Pediatrics, Springfield* **56**, 544–9.

Guiton, P. (1962). The development of sexual responses in the domestic fowl, in relation to the concept of imprinting. *Symp. zool. Soc. Lond.* **8**, 227–34.

—— (1966). Early experience and sexual object-choice in the Brown Leghorn. *Anim. Behav.* **14**, 534–8.

Hagbarth, K. E. and Kugelberg, E. (1958). Plasticity of the human abdominal skin reflex. *Brain* **81**, 305–18.

Hécaen, H. (1964). Mental symptoms associated with tumours of the frontal lobe. In *The frontal granular cortex and behavior* (eds J. M. Warren and K. Akert), pp. 335–52. McGraw-Hill, New York.

Hinde, R. A. (1962). Some aspects of the imprinting problem. *Symp. zool. Soc. Lond.* **8**, 129–38.

—— (1982). *Ethology: its nature and relations with other sciences.* Fontana, London.

—— and Stevenson-Hinde, J. (ed) (1973). *Constraints on learning.* Academic Press, London.

Hirsch, H. V. B. and Spinelli, D. N. (1970). Visual experience modifies distribution of horizontally and vertically oriented receptive fields in cats. *Science* **168**, 869–71.

Horn, G. (1962). Regular impulse activity of single units in the cat striate cortex. *Nature, Lond.* **194**, 1084–5.

—— (1970). Changes in neuronal activity and their relationship to behaviour. In *Short-term changes in neural activity and behaviour.* (eds G. Horn and R. A. Hinde), pp. 567–606. Cambridge University Press, Cambridge.

——, Rose, S. P. R., and Bateson, P. P. G. (1973). Experience and plasticity in the central nervous system. *Science* **181**, 506–14.

Hubel, D. H. and Wiesel, T. N. (1962). Receptive fields, binocular interaction and functional architecture in the cat's visual cortex. *J. Physiol., Lond.* **160**, 106–54.

—— and Wiesel, T. N. (1970). The period of susceptibility to the physiological effects of unilateral eye closure in kittens. *J. Physiol., Lond.* **206**, 419–36.

Huppert, F. A. and Piercy, M. (1978). The role of trace strength in recency and frequency judgements by amnesics and control subjects. *Quart. J. exp. Psychol.* **30**, 346–54.

Iversen, S. D. (1976). Do hippocampal lesions produce amnesia in animals? *Int. Rev. Neurobiol.* **19**, 1–49.

—— (1983). Brain lesions and memory in animals: a reappraisal. In *The physiological basis of memory* (ed. J. A. Deutsch), pp. 139–98. Academic Press, New York.

Jacklet, J. W. (1981). Circadian timing by endogenous oscillators in the nervous system: toward cellular mechanisms. *Biol. Bull.* **160**, 199–227.

James, W. J. (1890). *The principles of psychology.* Henry Holt, New York. [Reprinted (1950) Dover Publications, New York.]

Kamil, A. C. (1978). Systematic foraging by a Nectar-feeding bird, the Amakihi (*Loxops virens*). *J. comp. physiol. Psychol.* **92**, 388–96.

Kratz, K. E. and Lehmkuhle, S. (1983). Spatial contrast sensitivity in monocularly deprived cats after removal of the non-deprived eye. *Behav. Brain Res.* **7**, 261–6.

Lorenz, K. (1935). Der Kumpan in der Umwelt des Vogels. *J. Orn., Lpz.* **83**, 137–213, 289–413.

—— (1937). The companion in the bird's world. *Auk* **54**, 245–73.

Mabille, E. and Pitres, A. (1913). Sur un cas d'amnésie de fixation post-apoplectique ayant persité vingt-trois ans. *Revue Méd.* **33**. 257–79.

Mackintosh, N. J. (1985). Varieties of conditioning. In *Second conference on the neurobiology of learning and memory* (eds G. Lynch, J. L. McGaugh, and N. M. Weinberger). Guilford Press, New York (in press).

Maudsley, H. I. (1876). *Physiology of mind.* London.

Marler, P. (1985). Song learning: innate species differences in the learning process. In *The biology of learning* (eds P. Marler and H. S. Terrace), Dahlem Konferenzen. Springer, Berlin (in press).

Nauta, W. J. H. and Karten, H. J. (1970). A general profile of the vertebrate brain, with sidelights on the ancestry of cerebral cortex. In *The neurosciences, second study program* (ed. F. O. Schmitt), pp. 7–26. The Rockefeller University Press, New York.

Payne, J. K., Horn, G., and Brown, M. W. (1984). Modifiability of responsiveness in a visual projection area of the chick brian: visual experience is only one of several factors involved. *Behav. Brain Res.* **13**, 163–72.

Perrett, D. I., Rolls, E. T., and Caan, W. (1982). Visual neurones responsive to faces in the monkey temporal cortex. *Exp. Brain Res.* **47**, 229–38.

Pettigrew, J. D., and Konishi, M. (1976*a*). Neurons selective for orientation and binocular disparity in the visual Wulst of the barn owl (*Tyto alba*). *Science* **193**, 675–8.

——, —— (1976*b*). Effect of monocular deprivation on binocular neurones in the owl's visual Wulst. *Nature, Lond.* **264**, 753–4.

Rolls, E. T., Perret, D. I., Caan, A. W., and Wilson, F. A. W. (1982). Neuronal responses related to visual recognition. *Brain* **105**, 611–46.

Ryle, G. (1949). *The concept of mind.* Hutchinson, London.

Salzen, E. A. (1966). The interaction of experience, stimulus characteristics and exogenous androgen in the behaviour of domestic chicks. *Behaviour* **26**, 286–322.

Salzen, E. A. and Meyer, C. (1968). Reversibility of imprinting. *J. comp. physiol. Psychol.* **66**, 269–75.

Schutz, F. (1965). Sexuelle Pragung bei Anatiden. *Z. Tierpsychol.* **22**, 50–103.

Seligman, M. E. P. and Hager, J. L. (1972). *Biological boundaries of learning.* Appleton–Century–Crofts, New York.

Sluckin, W. and Salzen, E. A. (1961). Imprinting and perceptural learning. *Quart. J. exp. Psychol.* **13**, 65–77.

Stechler, G. (1965). The effect of medication during labor on newborn attention. *Science* **144**, 315–17.

Strumwasser, F. (1973). Neural and humoral factors in the temporal organization of behavior. *The Physiologist* **16**, 9–42.

Tulving, E. (1972). Episodic and semantic memory. In *Organization of memory* (eds E. Tulving and W. Donaldson), pp. 382–403. Academic Press, New York.

Vinogradova, O. (1970). Registration of information and the limbic system. In *Short-term changes in neural activity and behaviour* (eds G. Horn and R. A. Hinde), pp. 95–140. Cambridge University Press, Cambridge.

Walsh, K. W. (1978). *Neuropsychology: a clinical approach.* Churchill Livingstone, Edinburgh.

Warrington, E. K. and Weiskrantz, L. (1982). Amnesia: a disconnection syndrome? *Neuropsychologia* **20**, 233–48.

Weiskrantz, L. (1966). Experimental studies of amnesia. In *Amnesia* (eds C. W. M. Whitty and O. L. Zangwill), pp. 1–35. Butterworth, London.

—— (1982). Comparative aspects of studies of amnesia. *Phil. Trans. R. Soc. B* **298**, 97–109.

—— (1985). On issues and theories of the human amnesic syndrome. In *Second conference on the neurobiology of learning and memory* (eds G. Lynch, J. L. McGaugh, and N. M. Weinberger). Guilford Press, New York (in press).

Whitty, C. W. M. and Lishman, W. A. (1966). Amnesia in cerebral disease. In *Amnesia* (eds C. W. M. Whitty and O. L. Zangwill), pp. 36–76. Butterworth, London.

Wiesel, T. N. and Hubel, D. H. (1963). Single cell responses in striate cortex of kittens deprived of vision in one eye. *J. Neurophysiol.* **26**, 1003–17.

Wilson, P. (1980). The organisation of the visual hyperstriatum in the domestic chicks. II. Receptive field properties of single units. *Brain Res.* **188**, 333–45.

Zola-Morgan, S. and Squire, L. R. (1984). Preserved learning in monkeys with medial temporal lesions: sparing of motor and cognitive skills. *J. Neurosci.* **4**, 1072–85.

# Appendix: A sketch of the avian brain with particular reference to the domestic chick

This account of the avian brain is intended to provide a background to the experimental studies which are described in this book. For this reason the account is biased: more prominence is given to the visual pathways, to the projections of the brainstem core, and to comparisons of the avian and mammalian brains than would be justified in a more conventional treatment of the subject. Furthermore, the sketch is a vignette; a full portrait is not necessary for these purposes and in any case several excellent ones already exist (Kappers *et al.* 1936; Perason 1972; Cohen and Karten 1974; Macphail 1982).

To understand the neural mechanisms of a particular kind of behaviour, it is necessary to have some understanding of the machine which controls the behaviour. The machine in question is the brain of the domestic chick. What does this brain look like, what are its major subdivisions and how is it wired up?

## A.1 General form of the chick brain

The brain of a 2-day-old chick displaces just over 1 millilitre of water; it is approximately 20 millimetres long and 14 millimetres across at its widest. The brain (Fig. A.1) looks at first glance like the brain of many other vertebrates. The cerebral hemispheres, the cerebellum, and the brainstem are all present; and like the brain of other vertebrates the macroscopic organization of the chick brain is easy enough to understand if reference is made to its embryological development.

The central nervous system develops as a hollow cylinder of tissue, the neural tube (Fig. A.2(a)). The central cavity of the front end of the tube gives rise to the ventricular system of the adult brain and its substance is formed from the walls of the tube. Neurones and the 'supporting' glial cells are derived from the epithelium lining the tube. The neurones migrate outwards, thickening the walls of the presumptive brain, forming clumps which protrude as hillocks, or forming sheets which cover the surfaces of the tube.

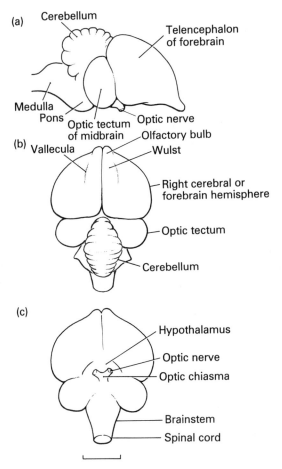

**Fig. A.1.** The brain of a 2-day-old chick viewed from the side (a), from above (b), and from below (c). Scale bar 5 mm.

At a very early stage of development three enlargements may be seen at the front end of the tube (Fig. A.2(b)). These will form the major division of the brain. The posterior vesicle will form the hindbrain, the most anterior one will form the forebrain, and the intermediate vesicle will form the midbrain. The forebrain will be composed of two major divisions, the diencephalon and the telencephalon. The most prominent features of the telencephalon will be the cerebral hemispheres. These are commonly referred to as the forebrain or the telencephalic hemispheres. They arise as evaginations of the anterior vesicle of the neural tube (Fig. A.2(c)). The walls of these evaginations will form the substance of the cerebral hemispheres and the cavities will become the lateral ventricles. The developing

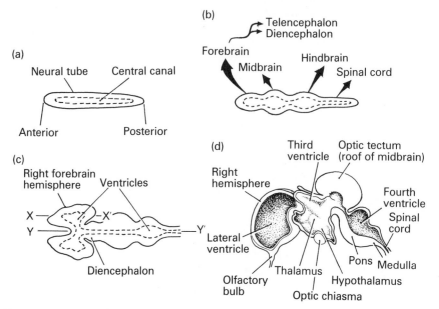

**Fig. A.2. (a)–(c)** Diagrammatic representations of stages in the development of the vertebrate brain. The brain is viewed from above. In (b) the outward-pointing arrows indicate the major adult structures that a vesicle will form. (d) Drawing of a dissection to show the right side of the brain of an 8-day-old chick embryo (After Lillie 1908). In this dissection the brainstem was cut in the median plane *Y–Y′* (c); the right forebrain hemisphere was cut in a paramedian plane X–X′ (c) to show the cavity, or lateral ventricle of the hemisphere.

brain buckles and this buckling further distorts the simple form of the original neural tube. These events have all occurred or are still occurring in the chick embryo at an incubation age of 8 days (see Fig. A.2(d)).

The cerebellum first appears as a bilateral proliferation of cells in the dorsal part of the posterior vesicle. The two masses of cells fuse in the midline to form a single, bilobed structure, the cerebellum. A similar proliferation of cells occurs in the intermediate vesicle which becomes the midbrain. The two masses so formed do not fuse. They eventually develop into part of the roof or tectum of the midbrain. Because of its association with the visual system, this part of the midbrain is known as the optic tectum (Fig. A.1).

The cavity of the neural tube just caudal to the developing telencephalon will form the third ventricle. This ventricle, together with the structure in its walls, will comprise the diencephalon (Fig. A.2(c)). These structures will include masses of cells arranged in discreet clumps or nuclei. Two major grouping of these nuclei will form respectively the thalamus and the hypothalmus (Fig. A.2(d)).

## A.2 Internal structure of the telencephalon

At the macroscopic level the avian brain bears a general resemblance to those mammalian brains in which the cerebral hemispheres are smooth. The internal structure of the forebrain hemispheres of the two classes of animals is, however, strikingly different. In transverse or coronal section the outer layer of the mammalian forebrain hemisphere is formed by the cerebral cortex. In unstained sections the cerebral cortex, which is composed of sheets of neurones, has a grey appearance. Deep to the cortex are millions of axons, many of which are myelinated; in this region the cell bodies or perikarya of neurones are absent. The great abundance of myelinated axons gives the unstained subcortical matter a glistening, white appearance. In the avian brain the grey and white matter are not so sharply demarcated. Indeed when sections of the chick forebrain are treated with dyes that stain perikarya, these cell bodies seem to be everywhere in the forebrain except in the ventricles. Nothing appears to resemble the cerebral cortex of mammals.

The chick forebrain is largely composed of plates of cells, the plates varying in length from side to side and from front to back (Fig. A.3). Here and there the sheets sweep round clusters of cells, such as the ectostriatum (Fig. A.3)b)). The three most superficial layers, in the anterior half of each cerebral hemisphere, form an elevation beside the midline. This relatively long, pillow-like elevation is known as the Wulst (Fig. A.1(b)). The Wulst comprises the hyperstriatum accessorium, the hyperstriatum dorsale, and sandwiched between the two, the intercalated nucleus, or the hyperstriatum intercalatus. Below the hyperstriatum dorsale in the anterior part of the brain, but immediately deep to the lateral ventricle posteriorly, is the hyperstriatum ventrale (Fig. A.3(e)). This structure lies over much the largest plate of cells in the forebrain, the neostriatum. The ectostriatum and archistriatum are roughly spherical accumulations of cells which are, to a variable extent, surrounded by cells of the neostriatum. The paleostriatum augmentatum, in the base of the forebrain, appears in cross-sections to form a cap over the paleostriatum primitivum (Fig. A.3(c), (d)). Medial to the ventricle are found the hippocampus and the septal nuclei.

Attention has already been drawn to the marked structural differences between the brains of birds and mammals. Are there any grounds for supposing that a given region of the avian brian is homologous with some region of the mammalian brain? One approach to this question has been to assume that if a region in adult mammalian and avian brains have similar embryological origins, then these regions are homologous (see, for example, Kuhlenbeck 1938; Källén 1962; Benowitz 1980). Soon after the cerebral vesicles have formed, a groove appears on the inner surface of their lateral walls. The groove extends a variable distance from front to back, dividing each vesicle into dorsal and ventral components (Fig. A.4(a)). The ultimate

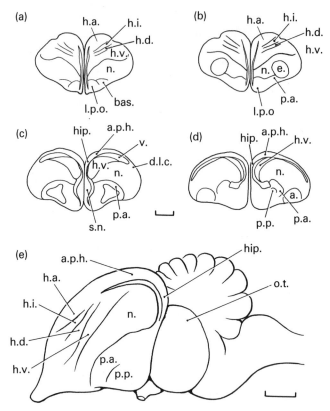

**Fig. A.3.** Outline diagrams of sections of the forebrain of a 2-day-old chick. The upper four outlines are of coronal sections of the brain. Diagrams (a) and (b) represent sections cut through the anterior one third of the forebrain (section (a) being anterior to section (b)). Diagram (c) represents a section cut through the intermediate third, and diagram (d) a section cut through the caudal third of the forebrain. (e) is a drawing of a longitudinal section of the brain cut just lateral to the midline. Abbreviations: a., archistriatum; a.p.h., area parahippocamalis; bas., nucleus basalis; d.l.c., dorsolateral corticoid area; e., ectostriatum; h.a., hyperstriatum accessorium; h.d., hyperstriatum dorsale; h.i., hyperstriatum intercalatus; hip., hippocampus; h.v., hyperstriatum ventrale; l.p.o., lobus paraolfactorius; n., neostriatum; o.t., optic tectum; p.a., paleostriatum augmentatum; p.p., paleostriatum primitivum; s.n., septal nuclei; v., ventricle. Scale bars 2 mm.

developmental fate of various regions of the cerebral vesicles is indicated, for the chick, in Fig. A.4(b)). In mammals the ventral component of the lateral wall of the vesicles give rise to a complex of structures known as the corpus striatum. The dorsal component is the pallium which will form the cerebral cortex. The medial part of this dorsal component will form the cortex of the hippocampus.

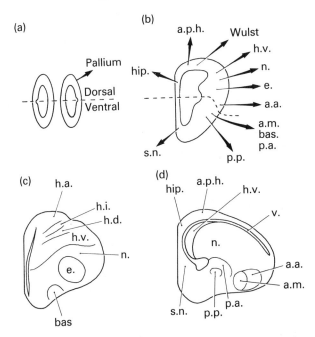

**Fig. A.4.** Diagrammatic representation of stages in the development of the telence-phalic hemispheres of the chick brain. Diagram (a) represents the two cerebral vesicles in an embryo of approximately 4 days incubation age. The broken line indicates the boundary between dorsal and ventral parts of the vesicles. (b) The right cerebral hemisphere. By the seventh day of incubation cells in the lateral wall have proliferated to form a bulge into the ventricle. The definitive structures into which the primordia are thought to develop are indicated ((c) and (d)). These diagrams represent cross-sections of the anterior (c) and caudal (d) parts of the brain of a 2-day-old chick. Abbreviations: a.a., archistriatum anterior (the intermediate and dorsal components of the archistriatum may also arise from the dorsal part of the cerebral vesicle); a.m., archistriatum mediale (the posterior nucleus of the archistriatum may also be derived from the ventral part of the cerebral vesicle); a.p.h., area parahippocampalis; bas., nucleus basalis; e., ectostriatum; hip., hippocampus; h.a., hyperstriatum accessorium; h.d., hyperstriatum dorsale; h.i., hyperstriatum inter-calatus; h.v., hyperstriatum ventrale; n., neostriatum; p.a., paleostriatum augmentatum; p.p., paleostriatum primitivum; s.n., septal nuclei; v., ventricle. This figure is based on the work of Kuhlenbeck (1938), Källén (1962), Karten (1969), Nauta and Karten (1970), and Benowitz (1980).

If the developmental history of the brain is used as a guide, then several brain regions of birds and mammals may be homologous. In particular, the mammalian neocortex appears to be homologous with several components of the hyperstriatal complex (including the hyperstriatum dorsale and the hyperstriatum ventrale) the neostriatum, and the ectostriatum collectively. The hippocampus and parahippocampal areas in the avian and mammaliam brains may also be homologous. The list of such comparisons is not exhaustive (see Källén 1962; Benowitz 1980), but the functional significance of these comparisons is not clear. If, by a variety of embryological criteria two structures appear to be homologous, it does not necessarily follow that they have similar functions. However, if the function of the structure is known in one animal it is certainly worth enquiring whether its counterpart in an animal of another class has a similar function.

## A.3 Sensory systems

Some of the signals generated in the nervous system by changes in the external environment reach the telencephalon. The routes by which the signals pass have been the subject of intensive study. Modern knowledge is based on the painstaking and often beautiful experiments performed by neuroanatomists towards the end of the last century and in the early part of the present century. This work has been extended greatly by the application of recently developed anatomical and physiological techniques to the study of sensory systems. The pigeon (*Columba livia*) is commonly used in these studies. The basic organization of the brain of this species appears to be similar to that of other species of bird that have been investigated (see Pearson 1972). It should be borne in mind, though, that there is considerable variation in the detailed cytoarchitecture of the brain between different avian orders and even between different genera in the same order (see, for example, Stingelin 1958; Cobb 1960*a,b*). The differences may be reflected in the fine structure and physiological properties of various brain regions and tracts. Where this note of caution has been disregarded in the following account it is because detailed statements about species differences would make the text even more laborious to read than it already is, especially for those whose primary interest lies in understanding the neural mechanisms of learning, rather than in understanding the comparative physiology of the avian brain.

### A.3.1 The visual system

In the pigeon fibres in the optic nerve cross completely in the optic chiasma (see Cowan *et al.* 1961). As a consequence, signals from the left retina pass to structures in or associated with the right side of the brainstem. The two main targets of axons in the optic nerve are the optic tectum and the thalamus (Cowan *et al.* 1961). The route which proceeds via the optic tectum is known as the tectofugal pathway; the other route is referred to as the thalamofugal pathway.

Fibres of the tectofugal pathway leave the optic tectum and project to the nucleus rotundus (Fig. A.5(a)). After synapsing, the pathway terminates in the central core of the ectostriatum (Karten and Hodos 1970). The ecto-

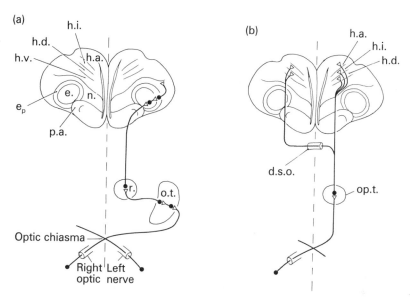

**Fig. A.5.** Diagrams of main ascending connections of the visual system. (a) Tecto-fugal pathway in which the retina projects to the contralateral hemisphere only. The connecting lines represent individual neurones in the fibre tracts. (b) The thalamo-fugal pathway. The lines connecting the principle optic nucleus of the thalamus (op.t.) represent tracts, not a single neurone. Other abbreviations: d.s.o., dorsal supraoptic commissure; e., ectostriatum; e$_p$., periectostriatal belt; h.a., hyperstriatum accessorium; h.d., hyperstriatum dorsale, h.i., hyperstriatum intercalatus; h.v., hyperstriatum ventrale; n., neostriatum; o.t., optic tectum, p.a., paleostriatum augmentatum, r., nucleus rotundus. The diagrams are not drawn to scale. (Modified from Karten 1969.)

striatum in turn projects to a belt of cells which partially surrounds it, the periectostriatal belt.

The thalamofugal system also carries information to the telencephalon (Fig. A.5(a)). In this pathway, fibres in the optic nerve terminate in a multi-nucleate complex in the thalamus. The complex is known as the principle optic nucleus of the thalamus. Axons of cell bodies in this nucleus project either to the ipsilateral or to the contralateral forebrain hemisphere. The ipsilateral projection terminates in all three components of the visual Wulst. The contralateral projection ascends through the dorsal supraoptic commissure (Hunt and Webster 1972; Karten *et al.* 1973). In the barn owl (*Tyto alba*) the majority of cells in the visual Wulst respond to stimulation of the two eyes (Pettigrew and Konishi 1976) though only a minority do so in the young chick (Brown and Horn 1979; Wilson 1980). The anatomical route by which binocular convergence in the hyperstriatum accessorium is achieved is not known. However, the deeper layers of the Wulst receive input from both sides. These layers project to the hyperstriatum accessor-ium (Bradley *et al.* 1985), and so could provide the necessary input. Whatever the route, the thalamofugal system ensures that information from both right and left eyes reaches the Wulst of each hemisphere in a highly organized manner. The tectofugal system by contrast is thought to convey information to a forebrain hemisphere from the contralateral eye only.

A small uncrossed visual pathway in young domestic chicks has recently been described (O'Leary *et al.* 1983). Fibres originating in the retina project to the ipsilateral thalamus and midbrain. The functions of this system have not yet been explored.

Regions of the forebrain other than the Wulst also receive a visual input. Visual evoked responses have been recorded in the posterior part of the neostriatum of the pigeon (Parker and Delius 1972) and in the Landes goose, *Anser anser* (Félix *et al.* 1983). It is possible that the visual input to the region arises from neurones whose cell bodies lie in the periectostriatal belt (Fig. A.5). Neurones within this belt also project to a cell group in the dorsal part of the archistriatum (Ritchie and Cohen 1977).

A pathway that has recently been described may provide a direct link from the optic tectum to the hyperstriatum ventrale (Bradley and Horn 1978; Bradley *et al* 1985). This route, by which visual information may reach the forebrain, is discussed further in Section 11.1.1.

### A.3.2 The auditory system

The principle route by which auditory information is transmitted from one ear to the contralateral telencephalic hemisphere in the pigeon is shown in Fig. A.6. Signals from the cochlea of the inner ear are transmitted to two nuclei in the medulla (Boord and Rasmussen 1963). Cells in these nuclei contribute axons to a tract known as the lateral lemniscus, which ascends in the contralateral side of the brainstem. A majority of these fibres terminate in the dorsolateral nucleus of the midbrain (Fig. A.6, m.l.d.). The pathway then continues to the nucleus ovoidalis in the thalamus, and after synapsing there, projects to a region of the caudal neostriatum known as field L (Karten 1967, 1968; Bonke *et al.* 1979). This then is the direct route from the inner ear to the forebrain. In fact the subtelencephalic auditory path-ways are a good deal more complicated than illustrated in Fig. A.6. Although the two medullary nuclei shown in this figure receive input from only the ipsilateral ear (Erulkar 1955), other nuclei in the brainstem receive signals from both ears (Erulkar 1955, Boord 1968). In the barn owl, infor-mation from the right and left auditory fields converge on to single cells in a part of the dorsolateral nucleus of the midbrain. This information is used to construct a precise map of auditory space (see Konishi and Knusden 1983). The auditory pathways are also tonotopically organized so that particular cells respond to particular sound frequencies (see Stopp and Whitfield

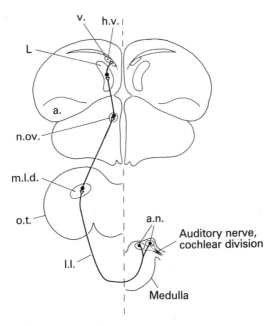

**Fig. A.6.** Diagram of main ascending connections of the auditory pathways. The primary afferent fibres in the cochlear (auditory) division of the auditory nerve terminate in two auditory nuclei (a.n.) in the medulla. Postsynaptic neurones project to other nuclei which includes one in the midbrain, passing there in the lateral lemniscus (l.l.). The midbrain nucleus, nucleus mesencephalicus lateralis dorsalis (m.l.d.) which lies deep to the optic tectum (o.t.), projects to the nucleus ovoidalis (n.ov.). After synapsing in this nucleus the pathway projects to field L and then on to the caudal part of the hyperstriatum ventrale (h.v.). Only the contralateral pathway is shown. Other abbreviations: a., archistriatum; n., neostriatum; v., ventricle. The diagrams are not drawn to scale. (Based on Karten 1968; Boord 1969; Bonke *et al.* 1979.)

1961; Zaretsky and Konishi 1976). The two functions of sound localization and sound frequency analysis appear to be kept anatomically separate (see Sachs and Sinnott 1978; Knusden and Konishi 1978).

Field L is tonotopically organized (Zaretsky and Konishi 1976; Scheich *et al.* 1979*a;* Scheich 1983). In the guinea-fowl, *Numida meleagris,* and in the starling, *Sturnus vulgaris,* single units in field L respond to complex sound patterns. Some neurones appear to be highly selective for particular components of species-specific sounds (Leppelsack and Vogt 1976; Scheich *et al.* 1979*b*). Field L projects to the caudal part of the hyperstriatum ventrale in the guinea-fowl (Bonke *et al.* 1979).

Evidence has been accumulating in recent years of an auditory pathway to the telencephalon which does not project to field L. Evoked responses to auditory stimuli have been found in the anterior part of the neostriatum in several species of birds, including the chicken (Harman and Phillips 1967) and pigeon (Ilyitchev _et al._ 1970; Delius _et al._ 1979). The pathway appears to project to a region of neostriatum close to the nucleus basalis (Fig. A.3(a)). It has been suggested (Karten 1968) that the evoked responses recorded in this region are artefactual, possibly arising from inadvertent stimulation of receptors for touch or vibration located in the beak. This explanation is unlikely to be correct since Delius and his colleagues (1979) have shown that bilateral destruction of the cochlea in the pigeon abolished the auditory evoked response. Furthermore, Kirsch and his collaborators (1980) recorded from single units in this region of the neostriatum in awake starlings and found units which responded to a variety of acoustic stimuli. These two sets of experiments strongly suggest that there is indeed an auditory area in the anterior part of the neostriatum. Although the anatomical pathway of this system is not known, it is a very fast conduction route to the telencephalon. So fast, in fact, that in all probability the pathway reaches the telencephalon without a synapse in the thalamus.

The general arrangement of the auditory pathways appears to be common to many species of bird. It would be surprising, however, if the detailed organization is invariant and that the auditory system of song birds, for example, is exactly the same as that of the other avian orders.

### A.3.3 The somatic sensory system

The pathways taken by signals arriving from the face region have been described in some detail, but relatively little is known of the route taken by the somatic sensory pathways in the spinal cord. Erulkar (1955) and Delius and Bennetto (1972) recorded somatic sensory evoked potentials from the telencephalon of pigeons. Responses were evoked by tactile stimuli delivered to the surface of the body as well as by stimulating the cutaneous nerves directly (Delius and Bennetto 1972). In both experiments responses to stimulation of the contralateral side of the body, including the head, were recorded in the caudal part of the neostriatum close to the midline. Similar results have been reported by Félix and his collaborators (1983) in their studies of the somatic sensory pathways in the Landes goose. The somatic sensory projection area in the neostriatum caudale of pigeons appears to lie in front of and above field L. Delius and Bennetto (1972) also recorded somatic sensory evoked responses in the anterior part of the Wulst, approximately in the region corresponding to the hyperstriatum intercalatus illustrated in Fig. A.3.(a).

One of the pathways carrying sensory information from the face was described many years ago by Wallenberg (1903). The primary afferent fibres innervating this region end in the brainstem. The postsynaptic neurones project directly to the telencephalon without relaying in the thalamus. The primary afferent fibres of the system are contained within the fifth cranial nerve. Wallenberg named the telencephalic projection, appropriately, the quintofrontal tract. This tract, which contains fibres from right and left sides, terminates in the nucleus basalis (Fig. A.3.(a)). In the pigeon and mallard duck, *Anas platyrhyncos,* units in this nucleus discharge in response to tactile stimulation of the beak, mouth, and tongue (Witovsky *et al.* 1973; Berkhoudt *et al.* 1981). The size of the nucleus basalis varies considerably from order to order and may reflect corresponding variations in the beak length and sensitivity. Zeir and Karten (1971) in their study of the pigeon archistriatum state that the nucleus basalis projects to the anterior nucleus of the archistriatum as well as to the overlying part of the neostriatum. The anterior nucleus of the archistriatum is derived from the dorsal part of the forebrain vesicle (Fig. A 4(b)). The nucleus is thought by Zeier and Karten (1971) to have a different function from the components of the archistriatum which are derived from the ventral part of the vesicle (see Sections 11.1.2 and 11.1.3.).

### *A.3.4 The olfactory system*

The primary afferent fibres of the olfactory system terminate in the olfactory bulb (Fig. A.1(a)). The size of this structure varies over a wide range. It is possible that much of the variation is attributable to the position occupied by the species in the macrosmatic–microsmatic range (see Cobb 1960*a,b*). Projections from the olfactory bulb reach the telencephalon without synapsing in the thalamus. In the pigeon, forebrain regions which receive afferent connections from the olfactory system include the paraolfactory lobe (Fig. A.3.(a),(b), l.p.o) and the hyperstriatum ventrale (Rieke and Wenzel 1978; Macadar *et al.* 1980).

## A.4 Projections of the brainstem core

The brainstem contains a variety of neural structures. These include long tracts of fibres which link together distant parts of the brain or connect structures in the brain with structures in the spinal cord. Short ascending and descending bundles of 'association' fibres link together nearby structures in the same side of the brain and 'commissural' fibres connect one side of the brainstem with the other. The brainstem also contains the motor and sensory nuclei of the cranial nerves. There are, however, other nuclei in the brainstem core whose existence has been known for many years, but whose functions are still subjects of much research even though some of these functions were glimpsed some years ago by Penfield (1938), G. Jefferson (1944), and M. Jefferson (1952) in their studies of human patients.

In man damage to a small amount of tissue in part of the brainstem core is associated with a loss of consciousness. A similar coma-like state is found in other mammals when the central regions of the brainstem are damaged (Lindsley *et al.* 1950; French *et al.* 1952). The early impression formed of the functions of the core system of the brainstem was the the system is implicated in more global aspects of neural function. The system was thought to modulate, amongst other things, the cycles of sleep and wakefulness, to control the levels of arousal and alertness, and to gate out unattended signals so that they do not impinge on 'higher' centres of the brain. Recent work lends support for some of these early impressions (see Hobson and Scheibel 1980).

In mammals several major systems arise from nuclei in the brainstem core and project forward to innervate seperately or together virtually all structures in the midbrain and forebrain. One system is known to be rich in the enzyme acetylcholinesterase and the other systems are known to be rich in the monoamines noradrenaline, dopamine, and 5-hydroxytryptamine respectively. Some of these systems of neurones are quite remarkable. Consider for example a system which contains noradrenaline and whose nerve cell bodies lie within a nucleus in the pons, the locus coeruleus. In the rat, axons from this small aggregate of cell bodies are distributed to virtually all major areas of the brain and spinal cord (Ungerstedt 1971). Whilst not all of the various subsystems are so extensively distributed, their fields of direct influence are generally much wider than are those of the specific sensory pathways.

There are comparable systems in the avian brain, though the evidence of a direct projection from the brainstem to the telencephalon is, in some instances, indirect. For this reason it is perhaps worth mentioning the techniques that are used to identify and trance the distribution in the brain of neurones which contain monoamines. Tissue sections are treated with formaldehyde vapour (Falck *et al.* 1962) or glyoxylic acid (Björklund *et al.* 1975). The monoamines react with these agents to form intensely fluorescent products; cells rich in monoamines may then be visualized microscopically by using an ultraviolet light source. Cells containing 5-hydroxytryptamine, or serotonin, exhibit a yellow fluorescence whereas cells containing the catecholamines dopamine and noradrenaline exhibit a green-yellow fluorescence. Special, usually pharmacological techniques are required to allow these two catecholamines to be distinguished.

Clumps of nerve cell bodies containing monoamines have been indentified in the brainstem of the pigeon (Fuxe and Ljunggren (1965), chicken (Ikeda and Gotoh 1971; Dubé and Parent 1981) and the warbling grass parakeet, *Melopsittacus undulatus* (Shioska *et al.* 1981). More specifically, catecholamine-containing neurones have been found in structures within the floor of the midbrain (the midbrain tegmentum). Such neurones have also been found more caudally in and around the region of the locus coeruleus as well as in the medulla (Fig. A.7). In mammals the midbrain tegmental clusters of cells contain dopamine whereas the more caudal clusters, especially in the locus coeruleus and associated areas, contain noradrenaline (see Lindvall and Bjökland 1978). The tegmental and coeru-

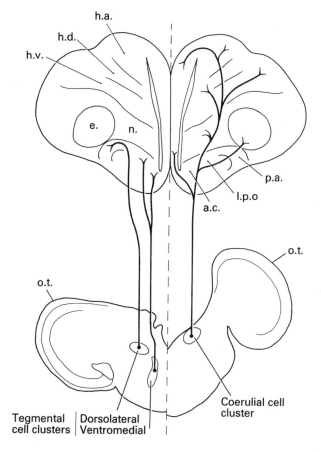

**Fig. A.7.** Possible forebrain projections of monoamine-containing neurones in the brainstem core. On the left are shown lateral and medial clusters of catecholamine-containing cell bodies in the midbrain tegmentum. The evidence available from work on chick, pigeon, parakeet, and zebra finch suggests that the axons of these cells project to the paleostriatum augmentatum (p.a.) to the lobus paraolfactorius (l.p.o.), and to the nucleus accumbens (a.c.). By analogy with the corresponding projections in the mammalian brain the catecholamine contained in the cell bodies is probably dopamine. On the right is shown the clusters of cells in and around the locus coeruleus. The region containing this nucleus lies caudal to that, shown on the left of the diagram, containing the tegmental cell clusters. In the parakeet, catecholamine axonal varicosities are distributed to all major telencephalic areas, may contain noradrenaline, and are probably the projections of the coerulial clusters of cell bodies. The forebrain distributions are based on studies of several species; the arrangement of catecholamine-containing neurones in the brainstem are based on studies of the chicken (Dubé and Parent 1981). The connecting lines in the diagram represent tracts not individual neurones. The diagram is not drawn to scale. Other abbreviations: e., ectostriatum; h.a., hyperstriatum accessorium; h.d., hyperstriatum dorsale; h.v., hyperstriatum ventrale; n., neostriatum; o.t., optic tectum; v., ventricle. For other references and further discussion see text.

leal catecholamine-containing cell clusters have different rostral targets both in mammals and in birds. In mammals, one group of dopamine-containing tegmental neurones (strictly speaking, cells within the substantia nigra) project to the caudate nucleus and the putaman (see Lindvall and Björkland 1978). These targets lie within the cerebral hemispheres and are part of a complex of nuclear masses which are involved in the control of movement. In birds one of the targets of the catecholamine-containing cells in the midbrain tegmentum is the paleostriatum augmentatum (Brauth *et al.* 1978; Kitt and Brauth 1981). It is therefore of considerable interest that the caudate nucleus and putaman on the one hand and the paleostriatum augmentatum on the other have similar embryological origins, both being derived from the ventral component of the primitive cerebral vesicle (Fig. A.4(a),(b)). Targets for another dopamine-containing tegmental cell cluster in mammals include the olfactory tubercle and the nucleus accumbens (Fig. A.7). In the zebra finch, *Poephila guttata*, a similarly localized group of tegmental cell bodies which contain catecholamines projects to the paraolfactory lobe and, probably, to the nucleus accumbens (Lewis *et al.* 1981). The evidence from comparative neuroanatomy therefore suggests that the catecholamine-containing neurones in the midbrain tegmentum in birds contains dopamine. This evidence is only suggestive; it is not conclusive. Even if the evidence were conclusive it is worth emphasizing that dopamine is not restricted to the basal forebrain structures shown in the left side of Fig. A.7. Davies and his collaborators (1983) have shown that dopamine is also present in the Wulst and in the hyperstriatum ventrale of the chick.

The coerulial system in mammals, as has been mentioned, is distributed widely in the forebrain. In the warbling grass parakeet nerve fibres or their terminals, containing catecholamines, have been observed in most major divisions of the telencephalon. Some, if not all of these neuronal processes probably arise in the locus coeruleus and adjacent nuclei (Tohyama *et al.* 1974; Takatsuki *et al.* 1981). Little is known of the projections of the catecholamine-containing neurone which have been found in the medulla.

Nerve cell bodies containing serotonin are present in the caudal part of the midbrain and in the medulla of the chick brain (Dubé and Parent 1981). The ascending projections of these cells remain to be elucidated.

Acetylcholine is present in the pigeon forebrain (Aprison and Takahashi 1965) though knowledge of its detailed distribution is indirect, and is based largely on studies of the distribution of the enzyme acetylcholinesterase. This enzyme can be identified histochemically. It is important, however, to bear in mind that the presence of acetylcholinesterase in neurones is not sufficient evidence that acetylcholine is used as a transmitter substance at the synapses which these neurones form with other nerve cells. Acetylcholinesterase is present in many forebrain areas in the young chick McCabe *et al.* 1982) and in the pigeon (Vischer *et al.* 1982). The micro-

scopic distribution of the stain for acetylcholinesterase in the chick telencephalon suggests that some of this enzyme may be contained within
nerve terminals (McCabe *et al.* 1982). Receptors which bind acetylcholine analogues are also present in the avian forebrain and vary in
concentration from region to region (Bradley and Horn 1981; Jerusalinsky
*et al.* 1981; Vischer *et al.* 1982). The presence of these receptors in a brain
region, together with the microscopic evidence that acetylcholinesterase
may be present in nerve terminals within that region, raises questions about
the source of these afferent fibres to the region. In the chick some of these
fibres are intrinsic to the forebrain: cell bodies localized in one region project to other regions (Davies and Horn 1983). Whether the majority of
putative cholinergic afferents to the forebrain are intrinsic to it, as they
appear to be in several mammals, is not known. In mammals the nucleus
basalis and the adjacent septal and diagonal band nuclei are major souces of
these afferents (Lewis and Shute 1967; Kimura *et al.* 1981; Mesulam *et al.*
1983). In the chick, acetylcholinesterase-containing cells in the septum project to the telencephalon (Davies and Horn 1983). The nucleus basalis (Fig.
A.3(a)) of the chick contains cell bodies which are rich in this enzyme
(McCabe *et al.* 1982), though the projections of these cells have not yet
been studied. However, there is no good evidence that the nucleus basalis of
the avian brain corresponds to that of the mammalian brain; and the difficulties of comparison are compounded by the existence of striking
interspecies differences in the anatomy of the nucleus (Gorry 1963). In
mammals some fibres containing acetylcholinesterase arise in the midbrain
tegmentum, and are considered to project to the neocortex of the cerebral
hemispheres (Shute and Lewis 1967). Evidence of a corresponding system
in birds is still lacking.

## A.5 Descending pathways from the cerebral hemispheres

Decerebrate birds in which the forebrain hemispheres have been removed
are relatively inactive. It has long been known, however, that decerebrate
chickens will walk when pushed and will fly when thrown into the air
(Flourens 1824, quoted by Liddell 1960). Decerebate mallard ducks exhibit
many seemingly normal movements and are able, for example, to preen,
head-scratch, wing-flap, and tail-wag (Phillips 1964). Thus the basic neural
mechanisims underlying these movements are organized at a subtelencephalic level. An analogous situation is found in the cat. In this animal the
neural mechanisms underlying the rhythmic movements of the hindlimbs in
walking are organized within the spinal cord (Shik and Orlovsky 1976). In
the normal cat these mechanisms are subject to control from higher levels of
the brain operating via long descending pathways to the brainstem and
spinal cord. Are there descending pathways from the forebrain of birds

which could also exercise control over neural circuits in the brainstem and spinal cord? Anatomical evidence demonstrates conclusively the existence of such pathways though their functions are poorly understood. One descending pathway originates in part of the archistriatum (Fig. A.3(d)). This is a complex structure composed of several nuclei (Zeier and Karten 1971). These nuclei fall into two major groups, according to their connections and possible embryological origins (Fig. A.4(b)). The posterior and medial components (the archistriatum posterior and archistriatum mediale) are connected to the hypothalamus and accordingly may be implicated in viscero-endocrine functions (see Zeier and Karten 1971). The anterior part of the archistriatum (archistriatum anterior and archistriatum intermedium together with its dorsal component) is associated with the somatic sensory-motor system. This component of the archistriatum is a source of long descending pathways from the cerebral hemispheres. The terminal fields of this pathway include the thalamus, optic tectum, and several nuclei in the middle and caudal parts of the brainstem, including nuclei in the brainstem core. The descending pathways also penetrate into the upper part of the spinal cord. These connections suggest that the pathways may influence subtelencephalic structures involved in the control of movement. The pathways could also control sensory inflow because a number of structures to which they are connected transmit sensory information, for example the optic tectum and somatic sensory nuclei in the medulla. In addition, the sensory-motor division of the archistriatum might affect more general aspects of behaviour since it has a relatively large terminal field in the region of the coerulial cell clusters of the brainstem core (see Section A.4).

The Wulst is also a source of fibres projecting out of the telencephalon. These projections have been studied in the domestic chick (Adamo 1967; Bradley *et al.* 1985), in the raven, *Corvus corax*, in the African lovebird, *Agapornis roseicollis* (Adamo 1967), and in the burrowing owl, *Speotyto cunicularia* (Karten *et al.* 1973). In the owl, where the Wulst is particularly well developed, there are two descending pathways. One pathway originates in the smaller anterior division of the Wulst and distributes fibres to nuclei in the brainstem, particularly to the red nucleus and the medial reticular formation of the hindbrain (Karten 1971). There is evidence that these nuclei, which are present in other vertebrate classes, project directly or indirectly to the spinal cord, exercising control over many aspects of locomotor activity (for reviews see Pearson and Pearson 1976; Brodal 1981). Some of the descending fibres from the anterior Wulst are also distributed to the spinal cord. It is of interest to recall that in the pigeon the anterior Wulst receives a somatic sensory input: evoked responses to direct electrical stimulation of sensory nerves can be recorded in this region (Delius and Benneto 1972). It is not known whether there is such a sensory field in the owl. If there is, then the organization of the anterior Wulst would be reminiscent of the motor cortex of some mammals: cells in the motor cortex may be activated by stimulation of the skin and deep tissues (see Brooks and Stoney 1971; Asanuma 1975).

The larger, posterior part of the Wulst has a visual function (Section A.3.1). This part of the Wulst is a source of fibres to several regions of the brain but mainly to synaptic stations in the visual pathways. Some of these stations lie within the telencephalon, for example the periectostriatal belt and the dorsal part of the archistriatum (see Section A.3.1); other stations lie below the telencephalon, for example the principal optic nucleus of the thalamus and the optic tectum. These projections, like corresponding projections from the sensory-motor part of the archistriatum, afford an opportunity to control the sensory input to the central nervous system. The control, in the case of the visual Wulst, appears mainly to be exercised within the visual system itself and in regions which may play a part in visuo-motor coordination.

### A.6 Summary

The avian forebrain contains a number of discrete sensory projection areas. In the visual, auditory, and somatic sensory pathways there are at least two discrete receiving areas for each system. Specific regions of the forebrain are sources of tracts through which control may be exercised over movement and sensory input. Cell groups in the brainstem core project directly to the forebrain and may exercise control of both local and global aspects of telencephalic function.

### References

Adamo, N. J. (1967). Connections of efferent fibers from hyperstriatal areas in chicken, raven and African lovebird. *J. comp. Neurol.* **131**, 337–56.

Aprison, M. H. and Takahashi, R. (1965). Biochemistry of the avian central nervous system. II. 5-Hydroxytryptamine, acetylcholine, 3,4-dihydroxyphenyl-ethylamine, and norepinephrine in several discrete areas of the pigeon brain. *J. Neurochem.* **12**, 221–30.

Asanuma, H. (1975). Recent developments in the study of the columnar arrangement of neurons within the motor cortex. *Physiol. Rev.* **55**, 143–56.

Benowitz, L. (1980). Functional organization of the avian telencephalon. In *Comparative neurology of the telencephalon* (ed. S. O. E. Ebbesson), pp. 389–421. Plenum Publishing, New York.

Berkhoudt, H., Dubbeldam, J. L., and Zeilstra, S. (1981). Studies on the somatotopy of the trigeminal system in the mallard, *Anas platyrhynchos* L. IV. Tactile representation in the nucleus basalis. *J. comp. Neurol.* **196**, 407–20.

Björklund, A., Falck, B., and Lindvall, O. (1975). Microspectrafluorometric analysis of cellular monoamines after formaldehyde or glyoxylic acid condensation. In *Methods in brain research* (ed. P. B. Bradley), pp. 249–94. Wiley, New York.

Bonke, B. A., Bonke, D. and Scheich, H. (1979). Connectivity of the auditory forebrain nuclei in the Guinea fowl (*Numida meleagris*). *Cell Tissue Res.* **200**, 101–21.

Boord, R. L. (1968). Ascending projections of the primary cochlear nuclei and nucleus laminaris in the pigeon. *J. comp. Neurol.* **133**, 523–41.

—— (1969). The anatomy of the avian auditory system. *Ann. N. Y. Acad. Sci.* **167**, 186–98.

—— and Rasmussen, G. L. (1963). Projection of the cochlear and lagenar nerves on the cochlear nuclei of the pigeon. *J. comp. Neurol.* **120**, 463–75.

Bradley, P. and Horn, G. (1978). Afferent connections of hyperstriatum ventrale in the chick brain. *J. Physiol., Lond.* **278**, 46P.

——, —— (1981). Imprinting. A study of cholinergic receptor sites in parts of the chick brain. *Exp. Brain Res.* **41**, 121–3.

——, Davies, D. C., and Horn, G. (1985). Connections of the hyperstriatum ventrale in the domestic chick (*Gallus domesticus*). *J. Anat.* **140**, 577–89.

Brauth, S. E., Ferguson, J. L., and Kitt, C. A. (1978). Prosencephalic pathways related to the paleostriatum of the pigeon (*Columba livia*). *Brain Res.* **147**, 205–21.

Brodal, A. (1981). *Neurological anatomy in relation to clinical medicine* (3rd edn). Oxford University Press, New York.

Brooks, V. B., and Stoney, S. D., Jr (1971). Motor mechanisms: the role of the pyramidal system in motor control. *A. Rev. Physiol.* **33**, 337–92.

Brown, M. W. and Horn, G. (1979). Neuronal plasticity in the chick brain: electro-physiological effects of visual experience on hyperstriatal neurones. *Brain Res.* **162**, 142–7.

Cobb, S. (1960*a*). A note on the size of the avian olfactory bulb. *Epilepsia* **1**, 394–402.

—— (1960*b*). Observations on the comparative anatomy of the avian brain. *Perspect. Biol. Med.* **3**, 383–408.

Cohen, D. H. and Karten, H. J. (1974). The structural organization of the avian brain: an overview. In *Birds, brain and behavior* (eds I. J. Goodman and M. W. Schein), pp. 29–73. Academic Press, New York.

Cowan, W. M., Adamson, L., and Powell, T. P. S. (1961). An experimental study of the avian visual system. *J. Anat.* **95**, 545–63.

Davies, D. C. and Horn, G. (1983). Putative cholinergic afferents of the chick hyperstriatum ventrale: a combined acetylcholinesterase and retrograde fluorescence labelling study. *Neurosci. Lett.* **38**, 103–7.

——, —— and McCabe, B. J. (1983). Changes in telencephalic catecholamine levels in the domestic chick. Effects of age and visual experience. *Dev. Brain Res.* **10**, 251–5.

Delius, J. D. and Bennetto, K. (1972). Cutaneous sensory projections to the avian forebrain. *Brain Res.* **37**, 205–21.

——, Runge, T. E., and Oeckinghaus, H. (1979). Short latency auditory projections to the frontal telencephalon of the pigeon. *Exp. Neurol.* **63**, 594–609.

Dubé, L. and Parent, A. (1981). The monoamine-containing neurons in the avian brain: 1. A study of the brain stem of the chicken (*Gallus domesticus*) by means of fluorescence and acetylcholinesterase histochemistry. *J. comp. Neurol.* **196**, 695–708.

Erulkar, S. D. (1955). Tactile and auditory areas in the brain of the pigeon. *J. comp. Neurol.* **103**, 421–57.

Félix, B., Kesar, S., and Roesch, T. (1983). Central localisation of somatic evoked responses in Landes goose. *Exp. Brain Res.* **53**, 173–82.

French, J. D., Amerongen, F. K. von, and Magoun, H. W. (1952). An activating system in the brain stem of monkey. *Archs Neurol. Psychiat., Chicago* **68**, 577–90.

Falck, B., Hillarp, N.-A., Thiene, G., and Torp, A. (1962). Fluorescence of catecholamines and related compounds condensed with formaldehyde. *J. Histochem. Cytochem.* **10**, 348–54.

Fuxe, K. and Ljunggren, L. (1965). Cellular localization of monoamines in the upper brain stem of the pigeon. *J. comp. Neurol.* **125**, 355–82.

Gorry, J. D. (1963). Studies on the comparative anatomy of the ganglion basale of Meynert. *Acta anat.* **55**, 51–104.

Harman, A. L. and Phillips, R. E. (1967). Responses in the avian midbrain, thalamus and forebrain evoked by click stimuli. *Exp. Neurol.* **18**, 276–86.

Hobson, J. A., and Scheibel, A. B. (1980). The brainstem core: sensorimotor integration and behavioral state control. *Neurosci. Res. Program Bull.* **18,** 1–173.

Hunt, S. P. and Webster, K. E. (1972). Thalamo-hyperstriate interrelations in the pigeon. *Brain Res.* **44**, 647–51.

Ikeda, H. and Gotoh, J. (1971). Distribution of monoamine-containing cells in the central nervous system of the chicken. *Jap. J. Pharmac.* **21**, 763–84.

Ilyitchev, V. D., Gurin, S. S., Temchin, A. N., and Voronezky, V. S. (1970). [Biological signal and functional characteristics of the auditory system in the pigeon.] *Zh. obsch. Biol.* **31**, 268–74 (in Russian).

Jefferson, G. (1944). The nature of consciousness *Br. med. J.* **1**, 1–15,

Jefferson, M. (1952). Altered consciousness associated with brainstem lesions. *Brain* **75**, 55–67.

Jerusalinsky, D., Aguilar, J. S., Brusco, A., and De Robertis, E. (1981). Ontogenesis of muscarinic receptors and acetylcholinesterase activity in various areas of chick brain. *J. Neurochem.* **37**, 1517–22.

Källén, B. (1962). Embryogenesis of brain nuclei in the chick telencephalon. *Ergebn. Anat. EntwGesch.* **36**, 62–82.

Kappers, C. V. A, Huber, G. C., and Crosby, E. C. (1936). *The comparative anatomy of the nervous system of vertebrates, including man.* MacMillan, New York.

Karten, H. J. (1967). The organisation of the ascending auditory pathway in the pigeon (*Columba livia*). I. Diencephalic projections of the inferior colliculus (nucleus mesencephali lateralis, pars dorsalis). *Brain Res.* **6**, 409–27.

—— (1968). The ascending auditory pathway in the pigeon (*Columba livia*). II. Telencephalic projections of the nucleus ovoidalis thalami. *Brain Res.* **11**, 134–53.

—— (1969). The organization of the avian telencephalon and some speculations on the phylogeny of the amniotic telencephalon. *Ann. N.Y. Acad. Sci.* **167**, 164–79.

—— (1971). Efferent projections of the Wulst of the owl. *Anat. Rec.* **169**, 353.

—— and Hodos, W. (1970). Telencephalic projections of the nucleus rotundus in the pigeon (*Columba livia*). *J. comp. Neurol.* **140**, 35–52.

——, ——, Nauta, W. J. H., and Revzin, A. M. (1973). Neural connections of the 'visual Wulst' of the avian telencephalon. Experimental studies in the pigeon (*Columba livia*) and owl (*Speotyto cunicularia*). *J. comp. Neurol.* **150**, 253–78.

Kimura, H., McGeer, P. L., Peng, J. H., and McGeer, E. G. (1981). The central cholinergic system studied by choline acetyltransferase immunohistochemistry in the cat. *J. comp. Neurol.* **200**, 151–201.

Kirsch, M., Coles, R. B., and Leppelsack, H. J. (1980). Unit recording from a new auditory area in the frontal neostriatum of the awake starling (*Sturnus vulgaris*). *Exp. Brain. Res.* **38**, 375–80.

Kitt, C. A. and Brauth, S. E. (1981). Projections of the paleostriatum upon the midbrain tegmentatum in the pigeon. *Neuroscience* **6**, 1551–66.

Knusden, E. I. and Konishi, M. (1978). Space and frequency are separately represented in the auditory midbrain of the owl. *J. Neurophysiol.* **41**, 870–84.

Konishi, M. and Knudsen, E.I. (1983). A theory of neural auditory space: auditory representation in the owl and its significance. In *Multiple corticle areas* (ed. C.

Woolsey). Humann Press, Clifton, N.J.

Kuhlenbeck, H. (1938). The ontogenetic development and phylogenetic significance of the cortex telencephali in the chick. *J. comp. Neurol.* **69**, 273–301.

Leppelsack, H. J. and Vogt, M. (1976). Responses of auditory neurons in the forebrain of a song bird to stimulation with species-specific sounds. *J. comp. Physiol. A.* **107**, 263–74.

Lewis, J. W., Ryan, S.M., Arnold, A. P., and Butcher, L. L. (1981). Evidence for a catecholaminergic projection to area X in the Zebra finch. *J. comp. Neurol.* **196**, 347–54.

Lewis, P. R. and Shute, C. C. D. (1967). The cholinergic limbic system: projections to hippocampal formation, medial cortex, nuclei of the ascending reticular system and the subfornical organ and supra-optic crest. *Brain* **90**, 521–40.

Liddell, E. G. T. (1960). *The discovery of reflexes.* Clarendon Press, Oxford.

Lillie, F. R. (1980). *The development of the chick.* Henry Holt, New York.

Lindsley, D. B., Schreiner, L. H., Knowles, W. B., and Magoun, H. W. (1950). Behavioral and EEG changes following chronic brain stem lesions in the cat. *Electroenceph. clin. Neurophysiol.* **2**, 483–98.

Lindvall, O. and Björklund, A. (1978). Organization of catecholamine neurons in the rat central nervous system. In *Handbook of psychopharmacology* (eds L. L. Iversen, S. D. Iversen, and S. H. Snyder), Vol. 9. pp. 139–231. Plenum Publishing, New York.

Macadar, A. W., Rausch, L. J., Wenzel, B. M., and Hutchison, L. V. (1980). Electrophysiology of the olfactory pathway in the pigeon. *J. comp. Physiol. A.* **137**, 39–46.

McCabe, B. J., Horn, G., and McGrath, G. (1982). The distribution of acetylcholinesterase in the chick telencephalon. *J. Anat.* **134**, 600–1.

Macphail, E. M. (1982). *Brain and intelligence in vertebrates.* Clarendon Press, Oxford.

Mesulam, M. M., Elliot, J. F., Levey, A. I., and Wainer, B. H. (1983). Cholinergic innervation of cortex by the basal forebrain: cytochemistry and cortical connections of the septal area, diagonal hand nuclei, nucleus basalis (substantia innominata), and hypothalamus in the rhesus monkey. *J. comp. Neurol.* **214**, 170–97.

Nauta, W. J. H., and Karten, H. J. (1970). A general profile of the vertebrate brain, with sidelights on the ancestry of cerebral cortex. In *The neurosciences, second study program* (ed. F. O. Schmitt) pp. 7–26. The Rockefeller University Press, New York.

O'Leary, D. D. M., Gerfen, C. R., and Cowan, W. M. (1983). The development and restriction of the ipsilateral retinofugal projection in the chick. *Devl Brain Res.* **10**, 93–109.

Parker, D. M., and Delius, J. D. (1972). Visual evoked potentials in the forebrain region of the pigeon. *Exp. Brain Res.* **14**, 198–209.

Pearson, R. (1972). *The avian brain.* Academic Press, London.

—— and Pearson, L. (1976). *The vertebrate brain.* Academic Press, London.

Penfield, W. (1938). The cerebral cortex of man. I. The cerebral cortex and consciousness. *Archs Neurol. Psychiat., Chicago* **40**, 417–42.

Pettigrew, J. D., and Konishi, M. (1976). Neurons selective for orientation and binocular disparity in the visual Wulst of the barn owl (*Tyto alba*). *Science* **193**, 675–8.

Phillips, R. E. (1964). Wildness in the mallard duck: effects of brain lesions and stimulation on 'escape behavior' and reproduction. *J. comp. Neurol.* **122**, 139–55.

Rieke, G. K., and Wenzel, B. M. (1978). Forebrain projections of the pigeon olfactory bulb. *J. Morph.* **158**, 41–56.

Ritchie, T. C., and Cohen, D. H. (1977). The avian tectofugal visual pathway: projections of its telencephalic target, the ectostriatal complex. *Proc. Soc. Neurosci.* **3**, 94.

Sachs, M. B., and Sinnott, J. M. (1978). Responses to tones of single cells in the nucleus magnocellularis and nucleus angularis of Redwinged Blackbird (*Agelaius phoenicus*). *J. comp. Physiol. A* **126**, 347–61.

Scheich, H. (1983). Two columnar systems in the auditory neostriatum of the chick: evidence from 2-deoxyglucose. *Exp. Brain Res.* **51**, 199–205.

——, Bonke, B. A., and Langner, G. (1979*a*). Functional organisation of some auditory nuclei in the Guinea fowl demonstrated by the 2-deoxyglucose technique. *Cell Tissue Res.* **204**, 17–27.

——, Langner, G., and Bonke, D. (1979*b*). Responsiveness of units in the auditory neostriatum of the Guinea fowl (*Numida meleagris*) to species-specific calls and synthetic stimuli. II: discrimination of iambus-like calls. *J. comp. Physiol. A* **132**, 257–76.

Shik, M. L. and Orlovsky, G. N. (1976). Neurophysiology of locomotor automatism. *Physiol. Rev.* **56**, 465–501.

Shiosaka, S., Takatsuki, K., Inagaki, S., Sakanaka, M., Takagi, H., Senba, E., Matsuzaki, T., and Tohyama, M. (1981). Topographic atlas of somatostatin-containing neuron system in the avian brain in relation to catecholamine-containing neuron system. II. Mesencephalon, rhombencephalon, and spinal cord. *J. comp. Neurol.* **202**, 115–24.

Shute, C. C. and Lewis, P. R. (1967). The ascending cholinergic reticular system: neocortical, olfactory and subcortical projections. *Brain* **90**, 497–520.

Stingelin, W. (1958). *Verleichend morphologische untersuchungen am Vorderhirn der Vogel auf cytologischer und cytoarchitektonischer Grundlage.* Hebling and Lichtenhahn, Basle.

Stopp, P. E. and Whitfield, I. C. (1961). Unit responses from brain stem nuclei in the pigeon. *J. Physiol.,* **158**, 165–77.

Takatsuki, K., Shiosaka, S., Inagaki, S., Sakanaka, M., Tagaki, H., Senba, E., Matsuzaki, T. and Tohyama, M. (1981). Topographic atlas of somatostatin-containing neuron system in the avian brain in relation to catecholine-containing neuron system. I. Telencephalon and diencephalon. *J. comp. Neurol.* **202**, 103–13.

Tohyama, M., Maeda, T., Hashimoto, J., Shrestha, G. R. Tamura, O., and Shimizu, N. (1974). Comparative anatomy of the locus coeruleus. I. Organization and ascending projections of the catecholamine containing neurons in the posterior region of the bird, *Melopsittacus undulatus. J. Hirnforsch.* **15**, 319–30.

Ungerstedt, U. (1971). Stereotaxic mapping of the monoamine pathways in the rat brain. *Acta physiol. scand.* suppl. 367, 1–48.

Vischer, A., Cuénod, M., and Henke, H., (1982). Neurotransmitter receptor ligand binding and enzyme regional distribution in the pigeon visual system. *J. Neurochem.* **38**, 1372–82.

Wallenberg, A. (1903). Der Ursprung des Tractus isthmo-striatus (oder bulbostriatus) der Taube. *Neurol. Zent.* **22**, 98–101.

Wilson, P. (1980). The organisation of the visual hyperstriatum in the domestic chick. II. Receptive field properties of single units. *Brain Res.* **188**, 333–45.

Witkovsky, P., Zeigler, H. P., and Silver, R. A. (1973). A single unit analysis of the nucleus basalis in the pigeon. *J. comp. Neurol.* **147**, 119–28.

Zaretsky, M. D. and Konishi, M. (1976). Tonotopic organisation in the avian telencephalon. *Brain Res.* **111**, 167–71.

Zeier, H. and Karten, H. J. (1971). The archistriatum of the pigeon: organization of afferent and efferent connections. *Brain Res.* **31**, 313–26.

# Author Index

# Subject Index

abdominal skin reflex 263
acetylcholine 221, 224, 247–8, 294–5
acetylcholinesterase 247–8, 292, 294–5
acquisition vii, 83–8, 94–7, 99
activity of chicks
  controlling for 49, 54, 87–8, 93, 213–14
  imprinting and 162–3, 220, 274
  selection on basis of 72, 73, 84
  *see also* approach activity
adrenocorticotrophin (ACTH) 48, 179
affective behaviour 178, 243–6
African lovebird 296
age
  catecholamines and 181–3
  developmental 38, 39, 41
agonistic behaviour 243–6
alcoholics, chronic 116
alertness of chicks 64–5, 220, 221
altrical species 26
amino acids 35–6, 45, 232, *see also*
  lysine
amnesia 91–2, 116–18, 252, 253, 261–2,
  263–4, 266
  'diencephalic' 116, 265
amygdala, mammalian 244, 245, 252, 253
anaesthetic agents 237, 271
androgens 193, 225
*Aplysia* 13–14, 15, 17–18, 20, 222, 266
approach activity 62, 87, 202
  postsynaptic density and 213, 214–15
  [³H] uracil uptake and 62, 63, 65, 72
approach behaviour 99, 143–6, 188
archicortex 136–7, 250
archistriatum 74, 101, 283, 284, 296
  anterior 285, 291, 296
  behaviour and 243–5, 246
  IMHV and 241–3, 246
  intermedium 233, 234, 241–2, 245, 296
  medial nucleus 243, 244–5, 285, 296
  posterior nucleus 243, 244–5, 296
  sensory input 242, 288, 291, 296
artificial imprinting stimuli 27, 37, 38, 51, 73,
  175–6, 205
  duration of exposure to 55–60
  noradrenaline and 181, 187
  predispositions and 151–73
  as reinforcers 111, 114–15, 118, 119
  *see also* jungle-fowl; red box

associative learning 25, 107–26, 246, 261, 262
  IMHV and 107–115, 122–6, 148
  recognition memory and 115–18, 270
auditory pathways 238–9, 288–90
auditory stimulation
  habituation 7–8, 22
  imprinting and 27, 73, 77–80, 84, 186, 239
autoradiographic studies 69–81, 103, 232
avoidance behaviour 102, 118, 121, 144–6,
  272–3
avoidance task passive 99, 123, 124, 125, 143,
  208

basal ganglia 243, 252
behavioural state, tests of 87–8, 93–4; *see also*
  activity of chicks: motivation
birds
  brain of 280–97
  compared with mammals 250–4, 264–5,
  283–6, 295
'blind' sight 102
brainstem 11, 280, 281, 290, 296
  core 178, 241, 291–5
'buffer' storage in right IMHV 134–7, 143,
  146–7

calcium ions 17, 18, 20, 218–19, 220, 221
calmodulin 219, 220, 221
canary *(Serinus canarius)* 140, 193
catecholamines 241, 292–4; *see also*
  dopamine; noradrenaline
cats 214, 235, 266, 267, 295
  habituation 3, 4–5, 12, 23
  neuronal plasticity 180, 188, 270–1, 272
cedar birds *(Nucifraga caryocataces)* 253
cerebellum 241, 242, 280, 281, 282
cerebral cortex 283, 284
cerebral hemispheres 280, 281
  decerebration 99, 295
  descending pathways 246, 295–7
  division of 49–55, 78
  lateral part, *see* lateral cerebral area
  unilateral lesions 102, 129–48
chaffinchs *(Fringilla coelebs)* 24

311